Jörg Gertel, Katharina Grüneisl (eds.)
Inequality and Mobility

Social and Cultural Geography | 56

Jörg Gertel (Prof. Dr.) is a professor of Arabic Studies and Economic Geography at Leipzig University. His education took him to the universities of Damascus, Cairo and Khartoum. He also taught and conducted research at Freiburg University and several times in Seattle and Auckland. His research focuses on the wider Mediterranean region and tackles questions of food security, mobility, market dynamics, and the situation of young people.

Katharina Grüneisl (Dr.) is a postdoctoral research fellow in Geography at the University of Nottingham. Her current research examines gendered relations of work in Jordan's industrial zones for export-oriented garment manufacturing. She completed a PhD in Human Geography at Durham University in 2021 and has since held postdoctoral positions at Universität Leipzig and the École des Hautes Études en Sciences Sociales (EHESS) in Paris. Her dissertation project examines urban change through the lens of the used clothing economy in Tunisia's capital city.

Jörg Gertel, Katharina Grüneisl (eds.)
Inequality and Mobility
Capabilities and Aspirations in Post-Revolutionary Tunisia

[transcript]

GEFÖRDERT VOM

Bibliographic information published by the Deutsche Nationalbibliothek
The Deutsche Nationalbibliothek lists this publication in the Deutsche Nationalbibliografie; detailed bibliographic data are available in the Internet at https://dnb.dnb.de

This work is licensed under the Creative Commons License BY-SA 4.0. For the full license terms, please visit the URL https://creativecommons.org/licenses/by-sa/4.0/.
Creative Commons license terms for re-use do not apply to any content (such as graphs, figures, photos, excerpts, etc.) not original to the Open Access publication and further permission may be required from the rights holder. The obligation to research and clear permission lies solely with the party re-using the material.

2025 © Jörg Gertel, Katharina Grüneisl (eds.)

transcript Verlag | Hermannstraße 26 | D-33602 Bielefeld | live@transcript-verlag.de

Cover design: Jan Gerbach
Printing: Elanders Waiblingen GmbH, Waiblingen
https://doi.org/10.14361/9783839467459
Print-ISBN: 978-3-8376-6745-5 | PDF-ISBN: 978-3-8394-6745-9
ISSN of series: 2703-1640 | eISSN of series: 2703-1659

Printed on permanent acid-free text paper.

"From irregular migration to a precarious economy, from deferred dreams to the reality of forced flight, Inequality and Mobility offers a reflection of a society challenged by insecure livelihoods and the demand for dignity. This volume is not simply a Tunisian case study, but rather a contemporary anthropological reading of the post-revolutionary reality in the Maghreb: a space where besieged desires intertwine with the dynamics of hesitant change, and where hope for a dignified future continues to rise from the depths of marginalization."

HOUDA LAROUSSI, University of Carthage, Tunis; author of *Tunisia in Crises. Local Tensions and Conflicts in a Post-Revolutionary Context*

"This volume is a much-needed, innovative contribution on the interconnectedness of some of the most pressing challenges of our time as they dominate the larger Middle East. Focusing on the case of Tunisia, Inequality and Mobility provides rich empirical material and fresh insights into the struggles of daily life under continuous authoritarian rule after the failed Arab up-risings of a decade ago. It opens new perspectives for comparison across the region, from the Mediterranean to the Mashreq."

NADIA AL-BAGDADI, Central European University, Vienna; co-editor and co-director of *Striking from the Margins – State, Religion, and Devolution of Authority in the Middle East*

"Inequality and Mobility represents an invaluable collection of studies on the struggles and aspirations of the Tunisian people in the aftermath of the 2011 revolution. The essays conjoin economic and sociological analysis with fine-grained ethnographic accounts of the textures and vicissitudes of individual lives confronted with economic precarity, racial discrimination, and a political system that forcefully, if inconsistently, stifles and instrumentalizes mobility. This superb volume is a crucial resource for those seeking to understand the complex challenges faced by the peoples of North Africa in their search for a life of dignity, equality, and prosperity."

CHARLES HIRSCHKIND, University of California, Berkeley; author of *The Ethical Soundscape. Cassette Sermons and Islamic Counterpublics*

Contents

Preface 13

Imagining Futures
Capabilities and Aspirations – An Introduction
Jörg Gertel & Katharina Grüneisl 15

Inequalities.
Resource Struggles in Diverse Economies

Introduction
Myriam Amri 35

Asymmetric Economies and 'Informal' Work
Jörg Gertel & Enrica Audano 39

Tunisian Women in the Labour Market
Thouraya Garraoui 67

A Political Economy of Borderscapes
Myriam Amri 81

Fuel Smuggling From Libya via the Border Town of Ben Gardane
Fathi Shâfi'i 95

A 'Clean' President
Political Metaphors of Waste and Clean-Up
Jamie Furniss & Maha Bouhlel 107

Barbéchas – Waste Collectors
Margins of Society or Centre of a Circular Economy?
Hanen Chebbi 121

Self-Governance
Collective Resource Management in Jemna and Awlad Jaballah
André Weißenfels 137

Mobilities.
Aspirations for a Dignified Life

Introduction
Ann-Christin Zuntz 153

Shattered Trust
Aspirations for Emigration among Young Tunisians
David Kreuer & Jörg Gertel 157

Coping with Disparities
Urban Development in Tunisia
Hatem Kahloun & Johannes Frische 175

Daily Mobilities
Young People in the Urban Periphery
Souhir Bouzid 187

The Dream of Integration
Civic Participation of Sub-Saharan Migrants in Tunis
Olfa Ben Medien 197

Municipalities and Migration Governance
Ambiguous Surveillance and Assistance in Tunis
Hiba Sha'ath 209

'Too many Africans'
Racialising Urban Peripheries in the Face of Tunisia's Economic Precarity
Shreya Parikh 221

Working Lives
Syrian Refugee Women's Intimate Labour and Mobilities in Tunisia
Ann-Christin Zuntz, Asma Ben Hadj Hassen & Marwen Bouneb 233

The Trap of 'Voluntary Return'
Forced Returns of Tunisian Migrants
Wael Garnaoui 245

Epilogue: Mobility and Racism in Sfax and Beyond
Khaoula Matri & Ann-Christin Zuntz 257

Appendix

References 271

Acknowledgements 297

About the Authors 301

IMAGINE the existence of a German ministry,
– operating through an implementing organization –
that aims to establish and fund
an international academic exchange and research platform
in a postcolonial country in North Africa.
Next, imagine you might enquire within this frame
about the meaning of inequality and mobility.
What if, after the project starts a regulation pops up, entitled
'No Gain No Loss',
a regulation that translates into unequal pay for invited fellows:
each person is entitled only to the pay they would
receive in their home institution/country, no more, no less?
Let's also imagine
– that although all fellows reside and work together for months –
that this means that post-docs from German institutions
are paid up to 3,000 Euro/month,
while those from North African institutions receive about 600 Euro/month.
'Equal Pay for Equal Work',
however, is rejected.

Preface

This edited volume is the outcome of an intensive phase of academic collaboration between a group of Early Career Researchers from different social science disciplines in Tunisia starting in September 2021. The spark for this collaboration was provided by the Merian Centre for Advanced Studies in the Maghreb (MECAM), founded in Tunis as an initiative of the German Federal Ministry of Education and Research (BMBF) in cooperation with the University of Tunis in 2020. MECAM convened five Interdisciplinary Fellow Groups (IFG). In autumn 2021, Leipzig University was engaged to address and investigate *Inequality and Mobility* (IFG II) in contemporary Tunisia. Seven doctoral and post-doctoral fellows – with a shared interest in this topic – relocated to Tunis for three months to advance their individual research projects and to engage in an innovative format of collective learning and exchange. Bringing together researchers from North African, European and American institutions, and across the disciplines of anthropology, political science, sociology, geography and urbanism, the Fellow Group provided a laboratory for translation from the outset, both in a linguistic and in a more figurative sense. It was thus not only the frequent switching between the group's three working languages – English, French and Arabic – but also the transposition of methodological and conceptual approaches from one disciplinary tradition or body of scholarship to another that defined both the unique challenge and richness of this academic exchange and collaboration.

From the first meeting, this Fellow Group extended its invitation to Tunisian and foreign researchers based in Tunis, defining itself as the core of an evolving and open network of academic collaboration. Beyond the MECAM fellows, diverse Tunisian and Tunisia-based researchers joined the weekly seminars, thematic workshops and collaborative research excursions that opened spaces for collective reflection on *Inequality and Mobility* a decade after the 2011 revolution. The expectation was for each researcher to come with a new or on-going empirical research project, to share different iterations of it, and to advance and develop it over the course of the collaborative endeavor. Overcoming the often highly individualized nature of social science research – particularly at the doctoral stage, where single authorship is obligatory – the goal was to share not only the findings, but also the at times messy processes and practices of 'actually doing research'. For instance, a postdoctoral and doctoral researcher invited the group to their field sites in Siliana, a rural governorate in Tunisia's interior where questions of resource scarcity and water governance have become central challenges for local development. Others shared their on-going research on urban (im)mobility through research excursions with students from Tunisian institutions (University of Tunis, ISTEUB); seminars at different Tunisian universities (Université of Tunis, Sousse, and Sfax); or online associating Tunisian and foreign institutions and researchers; or through public events such as book discussions and film screenings (e.g. in cooperation with International Alert, or the Tunis art gallery Le Central). Such collaborative and experimental forms of 'doing research' in Tunisia favored urgent discussions about the politics of knowledge production on and in Tunisia, especially under the rapidly changing post-revolutionary conditions (Bendana 2017; Dakhlia 2023). Rather than assuming that a mere location change – in this case to Tunis – can guarantee a decentering of dominant modes of knowledge production, the Fellow Group became a space for critical reflection on the structural inequalities inherent to research practices that favor extraction and perpetuate the dominance of the Western academy (Sukkarieh/Tannok 2019).

This edited volume is but one of the diverse outputs from the experimental research collaboration in Tunisia. It offers a collection of original empirical research – ethnographic, qualitative and quantitative – conducted mainly between 2020 and 2023, including an intensive workshop in Nabeul in June 2022, and subsequently presented at the Insaniyyat Conference at Manouba University in Tunis in September 2022.

Katharina Grüneisl
Jörg Gertel

Imagining Futures
Capabilities and Aspirations – An Introduction

Jörg Gertel & Katharina Grüneisl

> Poverty is many things, all of them bad. It is material deprivation and desperation. It is lack of security and dignity. It is exposure to risk and high costs for thin comfort. It is inequality materialized.
>
> Appadurai (2004: 64)

After the 2011 revolution, Tunisia became a symbol of the struggle for dignity, freedom, and justice. It became a beacon of hope for an entire region, where other similar popular uprisings had descended into violence. Bringing to an end the authoritarian rule of Ben Ali, the popular uprisings made a multitude of new developments possible, paving the way for a process of institution-building, transitional justice, and democratic transition. Now, more than a decade later, the outlook has once again dramatically changed: newly won political freedoms that led to democratically elected but rapidly changing government coalitions, are now being curtailed yet again; the economy is in disarray, especially after the crisis induced by the Covid-19 pandemic, the rise in prices for essential goods, and the impacts of drought and poor water management on local agriculture. Socio-economic inequality has expanded rapidly over the past decade, as has increasing resentment and violence against 'others', feelings that were recently instrumentalised by Tunisia's president Kais Saied against a growing minority of Sub-Saharan African migrants in the country. Consequently, the desire to leave the country to build a future elsewhere has grown unabatedly, resulting both in an acceleration of the 'brain drain' that deprives Tunisia of its highly educated younger generation, and in the rise of illegal departures that cost many less privileged young Tunisians their lives. All of this occurs in the context of global dependencies, rendered acutely visible through the impacts of the Russia-Ukraine war on global wheat markets and unprecedented food insecurity in North Africa (Gertel 2023).

Situated in the decade or so of political and socio-economic turmoil following the 2011 revolution, this volume investigates the relations between *Inequality and Mobility* in contemporary Tunisia. Not only does this allow for the analysis of persisting disparities, it also reveals contestations and negotiations regarding alternative ways of imagining possible futures. Taken together, the contributions presented in this volume argue that the ability to act for a better future – the capabilities – depend not only on a sustained access to resources, but also on an environment that enables multiple forms of desires, imaginaries, and subjectivities – the aspirations. To explore the overarching theme of inequality and mobility from diverse conceptual and methodological angles, as well as empirical perspectives, the chapters in this volume are structured around three overarching questions: First, which forms of inequality have shaped Tunisia in the past and what new dimensions of inequality are determining its present? Next, what are the impacts of inequality on mobility and vice-versa? Finally, how will these interdependencies between inequality and mobility determine Tunisian futures, in terms of enabling new possibilities for dignified livelihoods?

Counter-Revolution and Socio-Economic Crisis

While much of the research presented in this volume was thought out, or began to be carried out, in the context of post-revolutionary societal opening-up in Tunisia, the work was discussed again and completed against the backdrop of an accelerating counter-revolution. On July 25 2021, the elected president of Tunisia, Kais Saied, dissolved the Ennahda-backed government of Hichem Mechichi, suspended parliament and lifted the immunity of its members. This presidential power grab occurred at a moment of political deadlock that had rendered the Tunisian parliament ineffective as a legislative organ, and at a time when widespread anger in Tunisia against the government's mismanagement of the Covid-19 pandemic, as well as ever-louder allegations of corruption came to the surface. While Kais Saied's decision was thus celebrated by a majority of Tunisians, and was considered by many a long-awaited step to dethrone the Islamists, others immediately warned against a return to authoritarianism, or rather, a new form of populist dictatorship (Khiari 2022).

The rallying cry of the 2011 Tunisian revolution was 'freedom, dignity and social justice' (*hurriya, karama, 'adala ijtima'iyya*). The process of transitional justice and political opening-up post-2011 allowed new possibilities for imagining and discussing alternative forms of economic and social order that could enable a life of dignity for all Tunisians: from a radically new agricultural system focused on food sovereignty (Ayeb/Bush 2019), to an economy structured around the goal of job creation for all (Kaboub 2012), or a decolonisation of monetary institutions and reform of central banking (Ben Rouine 2022). However, a decade later, the prospects for achieving such alternative visions to the prevalent neoliberal and 'extroverted' economic policies seem rather bleak. The unsustainable foreign debt spiral has accelerated further; the country remains highly vulnerable to world market shocks due to its strong import dependency and export-oriented industrial production and agriculture; while unemployment has grown further. In addition, the more recent dismantling of democratic institutions and reorganisation of local governance under Kais Saied has paralysed much of Tunisia's state administration, slowing down vital infrastructure projects and political reform processes. The socio-economic inequalities young Tunisians grapple with today – globally and within their own country – are perceived and articulated as injustices (Melliti et al. 2018). Yet as political claim-making has once again become risky under Kais Saied's authoritarian rule – and is often considered futile after the perceived 'failure' of 'the revolution' (*al-thawra*) – such systematic exposure to injustice without avenues for agency translates into exacerbated feelings of frustration and anger (Melliti 2022, 2023; Laroussi 2024).

The period of collaborative research and discussion (2021–2024) of which this edited volume is a product was thus marked by political turmoil and deepening socio-economic crisis in Tunisia[1]. Kais Saied and his government revoked much of what had been regarded as the key democratic achievements and institutions of the transition (Marzouki 2022): this ranges from the dissolution of Tunisia's 2014 constitution to the dismantling of post-2011 flagship institutions like the Truth and Dignity Commission (IDV) to the repeal of judicial independence. Simultaneously, Tunisia's socio-economic crisis became increasingly tangible for an ever-larger part of society in the wake of the COVID-19 pandemic (Mansour/Ben Salem 2020, Laroussi 2021). The exponential rise of Tunisia's public and external debt provoked an unprecedented financial crisis, leaving the state struggling to pay the high public sector wage bill as well as vital wheat and medicine imports (Rehbein 2021). In spring 2022, shortages in staple foods such as sugar, vegetable oil, rice, coffee, milk, and subsidised bread thus occurred for the first time since Tunisia's independence, and have since turned into a regular feature of everyday life (Tanchum 2021; Gertel 2024a). In addition to new difficulties for commercial and household provisioning due to such unpredictable shortages, rapid price inflation – accelerated by the reduction in fuel subsidies – has severely affected the purchasing power of even middle-class Tunisians (Amri 2023).

Rising unemployment and price hikes disproportionately affect the urban and rural poor, who remain concentrated in the structurally disadvantaged, interior regions of Tunisia's north-west, centre-west and south. The stark regional inequalities that first sparked the 2010 uprisings in Tunisia's interior regions (Allal 2016; Ayeb 2011) have only increased in the aftermath of the 2011 revolution, triggering a sense of profound injustice, but also of complete hopelessness that finds expression in public suicides, protest movements, and in the on-going exodus of youth from the rural hinterlands. The impacts of climate change and poor resource governance amplify already-existing injustices. Water scarcity is particularly affecting population groups in the inland regions, is forcing farmers to abandon previously irrigable land, and more and more households are having to rely on the infrequent public drinking water supply (Mzalouat 2019). In addition, the long-term effects of environmental pollution – most prominently in the southern phosphate mining areas, and in the Gulf of Gabes and Sfax where toxic phosphorus has entered coastal waters – destroy livelihoods and living environments and push people to move (Robert 2021). In Tunisia's southern and western regions, youth unemployment remains extremely high, and often the only viable income-earning opportunities are in the informal border economies with Libya or Algeria (Meddeb 2016). For those who migrate to the rapidly growing, and largely illegally built, peripheries of Tunisia's wealth-

---

1   The World Bank writes about 'a decade of lost growth' after the 2011 revolution with average growth levels of 1.7% between 2011 and 2019, accompanied by rising unemployment (World Bank, 2024).

ier coastal cities, opportunities on the job market are scarce and salaries are low, making it impossible to repeat the social ascension that many rural-urban migrants of their parent generation managed (Miossec 1985). As unemployment also more greatly affects those with university diplomas, many highly-qualified find themselves unable to enter the job market. They remain blocked in a 'contained' state (Gertel 2018b) of prolonged 'waithood', unable to leave their parents' home and commence an autonomous adult life (Hmed 2016). This pushes young Tunisians to accept precarious or low-skilled employment despite having high qualifications, and it means they are unable to replicate the middle-class lifestyles of their parents for their newly founded families (Gertel 2024b). The rapid degradation of the public health and education system in Tunisia over the past years has moreover placed a new financial strain on families as they increasingly seek private services, adding to severe levels of private household debt (Salman 2023).

Enforced Immobility and Aspirations for Better Futures

Unprecedented constraints on opportunities for social mobility have been compounded by an increasingly stringent border regime that has negatively affected cross-border mobility for all Tunisian passport holders. European border externalisation policies have been stepped up in Tunisia post-2011, both through the securitisation of Tunisia's southern and western borders, and through security cooperation with Tunisia's coastguard, designed to curb the ever-greater influx of migrants from Tunisia's shores into Europe (both of Tunisian and foreign nationalities) (Breda et al. 2023). Such European policies of border closure were complemented with so-called 'soft measures' – prominently funded through instruments such as the EU Trust Fund and implemented through third parties such as think tanks and civil society organisations – with the goal of preventing Tunisia from turning into a major migration transit route (Zardo 2020). Simultaneously however, legal channels for the migration and travel of Tunisians to Europe were curtailed, with the exception of targeted recruitment programmes for highly qualified young Tunisians, such as trained doctors or engineers. Both the officially announced temporary visa limits and the unofficial quotas have led to a volatile and unpredictable visa regime that shifts the decision on the right to leave Tunisia into the hands of private service providers. Tunisians of all social classes, age and gender groups are exposed to long and costly bureaucratic procedures and profound uncertainty as they can be denied access to education, professional development, medical care or travel in Europe and North America (Terradot 2023). Such a restrictive visa regime affects, of course, young people the most, especially men from lower social classes, who have watched their legal options for European migration dwindle

This enforced immobility for ever-larger parts of Tunisian society has resulted in a surge of illegal and risky departures by boat towards Italy, resulting in mass death in Tunisia's Mediterranean waters (Zagaria 2019, 2020). In addition, the externalisation of European migration control to Tunisia has brought about grave human rights abuses and has caused environmental and social harm to diverse communities (Chemlali 2023). Mobilisation and conflict result – as was the case after a migrant boat capsized under unknown circumstances off the coast of Zarzis on September 18 2022, resulting in the death of 18 young men from the coastal town. The authorities' cover-up of the incident (known as 18/18), and the unidentified burial of some of the retrieved corpses. raised suspicion and caused indignation amongst local residents and families of the deceased, leading to protests and a violent state response (Bisiaux et al. 2023). Yet, European attempts to stop transit migration have remained largely unsuccessful. The related net increase in arrivals of Sub-Saharan Africans into Tunisia, mainly across the Algerian border, has put a considerable strain on local authorities with rapidly growing migrant communities, while simultaneously enabling news forms of economic exploitation (Cassarini 2020). The externalisation of Europe's racialised border regime has also conjured up new forms of xenophobic political discourses in Tunisia. In a speech held on February 21 2023, Tunisia's president Kais Saied mobilized the racist 'great replacement theory', warning against 'hordes of illegal migrants' as 'source of crime and danger', instrumentalising popular fears and resentment in a context of worsening socio-economic crisis. This unleashed an unprecedented wave of anti-black police violence and arrests, as well as racist attacks by ordinary Tunisians, targeting Sub-Saharan African migrants, as well as Tunisian nationals with black skin colour (Cassarini/Geisser 2023).

Enforced immobility through European border closure of Tunisians and migrants from elsewhere in Africa thus produces diverse forms of violence, and curtails young people's aspirations for travel, education abroad, or professional and personal futures in countries that offer greater opportunities than contemporary Tunisia. The 'harga', the Tunisian term used for irregular migration, is often considered the only way of 'escaping social death' by Tunisia's youth (Zagaria 2019), especially in light of the political deadlock and socio-economic pressure that characterise contemporary life in Tunisia. The feeling of 'being stuck' and condemned to stasis and 'waithood' has severe social and psychological impacts on young people, impeding both their personal and professional fulfilment (Garnaoui 2023).

Capabilities-Aspirations Framework

In order to investigate the complex relationships between inequalities and mobilities, we apply a modified approach, entitled the Capabilities-Aspirations Framework (Carling 2001; 2002; de Haas 2021). While both elements of this framework tackle highly connected fields of everyday life, they analytically open up two different fields of practices to a more analytical approach. The notion of capability captures the importance of resources and is crucial to explaining inequalities. In contrast, the notion of aspiration, emerging from processes of identity formation is key to understanding mobilities. However, these two axes of the approach are only separated on the analytical level; in everyday life, the access to resources and identity formation are inextricably linked and interrelated, shaping multiple forms of livelihoods. While Carling/Schewel (2018) and de Haas (2021) aim to develop new concepts of human mobility in order to expand classical approaches (e.g. leave behind simple push and pull models) and better comprehension of agency and non-movements (e.g. involuntary immobility) – our scope of study attempts a wider-reaching explanation, and requires different conceptual foundations than their earlier versions. We aim to apply the reworked Capabilities-Aspirations Framework (introduced by us in Gertel/Grüneisl 2024) to investigate the linkages between inequality and mobility in Tunisia.

Capability The concept emerges from two strands of discussions: One is about the access to resources and the ability to act, based on the classical approaches of Giddens and Bourdieu, while the second one is about the capabilities of freedom and/or dignity to live a fulfilling self-determined life, based on the approaches of Sen and Nussbaum.

The first perspective on capability is related to the Giddens ([1984] 1990a) understanding of resources and Bourdieu's ([1983] 1986) concept of capital. Both share the conviction that the access to resources (or to capital) is crucial to the ability to do things. Core to Giddens take on society (1990a) is social action and its properties. He underlines the precondition for action and the crucial role of resources: 'Agency refers not to the intentions people have in doing things but to their *capability* of doing those things in the first place' (ibid. 1990a: 9; emphasis added). Stressing capability refers to the importance of resources, because it is the access to and the control of these that creates the prerequisites for action. Subsequently, the structures of social systems are of central importance, as they are composed of 'rule-resources complexes': 'Analysing the structuration of social systems means studying the modes in which such systems, grounded in the knowledgeable activities of situated actors who draw upon rules and resources in the diversity of action contexts, are produced and reproduced in interaction' (ibid. 25). Giddens further differentiates between authoritative and allocative resources, with the first originating from the coordination of the actions of human beings and the latter from the control over material products or certain aspects of the material world. Hence, the interrelation between cognition and action in respect to resource availability and the capability to act becomes apparent (Gertel 2007).

Bourdieu (1986) places his argument alongside a critique of conventional economic theory, that, according to him, reduces the universe of exchanges to merely commodity exchange, allegedly driven by economic self-interest and the maximisation of profit. Economic theory as Bourdieu sees it thus defines all other forms of exchange as noneconomic and therefore as altruistic. Bourdieu instead reintroduces a new notion of capital, comprising of different forms. Capital exists as economic, social, and cultural capital. Economic capital is directly convertible into money and is explicitly suited to be institutionalised in the form of property rights. Cultural capital materialises as embodied, objectified, and institutionalised capital, such as titles. Lastly, social capital is made up of social obligations and is equated with resources based on group membership and social networks. Overall, he comprehends capital as accumulated labour, whether in its materialised or its incorporated form, but the accumulation of labour requires time. Bourdieu further stresses the embeddedness of economy within society and is able to trace articulations of power relations down to the human body, as the social position within society is determined by the quantity and structure of available capital (i.e. a concrete resource portfolio).

Combining Giddens' insights into rule-resource-complexes and Bourdieu's concept of capital reveals that the notion of resources comprises linkages to biopolitics (i.e. body of a person), labour (i.e. redistribution of risks in family-livelihoods), and property rights, (i.e. granted and negotiated by communities and state) and thus also to the discursive construction of rules. Based on these considerations, four forms of resources can be distinguished (Gertel 2007; 2010): (a) Incorporated resources which are bound to the body (e.g. nutritional and health status); (b) socially institutionalised resources, related to the subject (e.g. social obligations); (c) allocative resources, that are linked to property rights (e.g. fixed capital such as land); (d) monetary resources, also dependent on property rights, but easily exchangeable (e.g. money). This perspective offers several advantages. Using Giddens' notion of resources, the connection between individual actions and social structures is addressed, while Bourdieu's concept of capital permits a more comprehensive view of exchange processes. The resource concept further renders socio-economic processes accessible for empirical investigations. Processes such as the accumulation of resources (or capital), their mutual convertibility, and their use by third parties, have an impact on livelihood-security and ultimately shape human bodies. Given the limited reversibility of processes such as marginalisation, precarisation, and dispossession, human bodies are to be understood as the final instance of societal space. The distribution and access to resources are thus foundational to inequality (Gertel 2018a).

Following the argument above, we comprehend societal inequalities in Tunisia as the gap between 'what is' and 'what might have been' – in relation to the notion of structural violence in the sense of Galtung (1971) (Gertel/Grüneisl 2024: 41). There are two principal sets of explanations for this widening gap: classical resource-oriented approaches, corresponding to the political economic considerations of Giddens and Bourdieu on the one hand, and concepts of capabilities based on equitable opportunities and emotions such as fears or desires on the other.

Harvey's (2003) 'Accumulation by Dispossession' offers an entry point for discussing a political-economic explanation of social inequality. Two mechanisms drive the societal split, namely, the expansion of the capitalist system into areas that were not previously involved in market oriented profit-making, and the concentration of capital and power in the hands of a few actors. Instrumental in this are the processes of privatisation and financialisation, increasingly shifting profitmaking away from commodity production towards the use of financial capital (cf. Krippner 2011). Das (2017) criticises Harvey's concept and contrasts his considerations with his own approach of 'accumulation through exploitation', bringing the perspective of the Global South more into focus. In this approach, historical processes of colonial domination and the ongoing exploitation disenfranchising local livelihoods need to be addressed (cf. Tsing 2005; Li 2014). Complementing this, Milanovic's (2016) analysis of global inequality reveals the spatial shift of wealth away from Europe and the formation of new Asian middle and upper classes during the peak phase of globalisation (1988–2008). Although fundamental for the understanding of shifting resource access, these approaches remain largely capital-oriented, and are conceptualised from a materialistic perspective. Equal opportunities are not addressed, and the specificities of the MENA region are not considered.

The second set of explanations for the notion of capabilities explicitly goes beyond resource driven approaches, which are considered to be too narrow and exclusive of too many important aspects of everyday life. Reality, as authors like Sen and Nussbaum argue, is complicated and any evaluation of how well people are doing should seek to be as open-minded as possible. Their approach to capability entails two normative claims, namely that the freedom to achieve well-being is of primary moral importance, and that well-being should be understood in terms of people's capabilities and 'functionings'. In this way, the capability framework 'changes the focus from means (the resources people have and the public goods they can access) to ends (what they are able to do and be with those resources and goods)' (Robeyns/Byskov 2023: n.p.).

> For the capability approach, the ultimate ends of interpersonal comparisons are people's capabilities. [I]t asks whether people are able to be healthy, and whether the means or resources necessary for this capability, such as clean water, adequate sanitation, access to doctors, protection from infections and diseases, and basic knowledge on health issues, are present. It asks whether people are well-nourished, and whether the means or conditions for the realization of this capability, such as having sufficient food supplies and food entitlements, are being met. It asks whether people have access to a high-quality education system, to real political participation, and to community activities that support them, that enable them to cope with struggles in daily life, and that foster caring and warm friendships (ibid.).

The capability approach thus put the kind of lives people have reason to value at the centre of their argument (Nussbaum/Sen 1993). One position relates this to freedom (Sen 1979; 1985; 1989; 1999), while another one relates to human dignity (Nussbaum 2001; 2011).

In 'Equality of What?' Sen (1979) argues that in order to evaluate people's well-being we need to not only consider the resources they have, but also what they are able to do and who they can be with those resources. Key to Sen's argument are three assumptions. Sen is convinced that individuals differ in their ability to convert the same resources into valuable functionings (he also calls these 'beings' and 'doings'). Individuals are obviously not the same, and they have different aptitudes; these can also change over time, so the availability and the command over the same resources cannot be standardised. Moreover, people can internalise, to a certain extent, the harshness of their circumstances – so they no longer desire what they never expect to achieve. Sen captures this phenomenon as 'adaptive preferences'. Even adults, for example, might not be (fully) aware that they are overworked and sick. He further stresses that people do have valuable options between different actions, even in contexts of deprivation. Thus, there is an important difference between actual achievements ('functionings') and effective freedom ('capability'). For example, one might decide to fast during Ramadan, even in situations when he or she already suffers from malnutrition – that is their effective freedom (cf. Wells 2023). This comes back to Sen's notion of capability. The doings and beings (or functionings) vary from being well nourished, to having self-respect, or preserving human dignity. In this sense, a person's capability represents the effective freedom of an individual to choose between different combinations – between different kinds of life – that they have reason to value (Nussbaum/Sen 1993: 3).

After having been awarded the Nobel prize for economy in 1998 (in relation to his entitlement approach to explain hunger) Sen's work on capabilities has been employed extensively in the context of human development. Here, 'poverty' – such as in Tunisia – is understood as deprivation in the capability to live a good life, and 'development' is seen as capability expansion. Sen stresses (2004: 24):

It is important to keep the issue of equity constantly in view, because of its extensive reach. There is no basic tension—as is sometimes alleged—between freedom and equity. Indeed, equity can be seen in terms of equitable advancement of the freedoms of all people. […]. Seen in this way, it is possible to make consistent use of both the basic concepts of liberty and equity in assessing the demands of social inclusion and the contingent merits of cultural diversity.

While Sen formulates the concept of capabilities in order to identify ways to achieve equality (and freedom), for Nussbaum, human capabilities also form a precondition for meaningful human development, but she is more explicit about one's abilities to live a dignified human life. She defines dignity generally as the right of a person to be treated respectfully for their own sake (including other humans). Nussbaum presents a list of ten fundamental capabilities originating from the requirements for dignity that have a cross-cultural dimension (2011: 33–4):

- Life – being able to live a full normal human lifespan;
- Bodily health – being able to have good health, including adequate nutrition;
- Bodily integrity – being able to move freely from place to place and safe from violent assault;
- Imagination and thought – being able to use the senses, to imagine, think, and reason;
- Emotions – being able to have attachments to things and people outside ourselves;
- Reasoning – being able to engage in critical reflection about the planning of one's life;
- Affiliation – being able to live with and alongside others, including the social bases of self-respect and a life without humiliation;
- Other species – being able to care and relate to animals, plants, and the world of nature;
- Play – being able to laugh, play, and enjoy oneself;
- Control – being able to participate in political choices that govern one's life, including the protections of free speech; and also
- Rights – being able to have equal property rights as others.

Nussbaum is convinced that a life deprived of any of the above capabilities is not a dignified human life. Moreover, if someone lacks access to these capabilities, it is also a failure of society to respect human dignity.

People may be unequal in wealth, class, talent, strength, achievement, or moral character – but all are equal as bearers of an inalienable basic human dignity that cannot be lost or forfeited (Nussbaum 2012: 61).

It is thus crucial for human beings to have dignity, be perceived as equal to others, and have a 'communal life' which satisfies all human needs, and consequently guarantee a life 'in a morally virtuous world' (cf. Gluchman 2019: 1131). In order to implement these ideas in everyday life, Nussbaum suggests that her list should be debated, local specifics and thresholds identified, and then incorporated into national constitutional guarantees, international human rights legislation, and international development policy (cf. Wells 2023). According to Gluchman (2019: 1137) Nussbaum takes little interest however in individual self-development. She mainly focuses on the obligations and responsibilities of society, states, and governments for creating conditions for a 'full-value life', i.e. a life in accordance with human dignity. What has disappeared from her argument is the individual and their responsibility for the extent to which they can make the most of their capabilities, possibilities, and opportunities (ibid.).

In summary, the concept of capabilities originates from two bodies of discussions: One is about the access to resources and the ability to act, while the other is about freedom, equality, and the dignity of living a fulfilling self-determined life. They are not exclusive of one other, but they do have different entry points, shifting the focus from the means (e.g. access to resources) to the ends (e.g. ability and scope to utilise these resources). The normative goal is to live the kinds of life people have reason to value – a dignified human life.

Aspiration The second part of our Capability-Aspiration Framework addresses the notion of aspiration. In his understanding of migration, de Haas (2021) treats the notion of aspiration rather descriptively and relates it exclusively to migration. But aspirations are also contained in lifeworlds or lifestyles, as complex and dynamic as these are (Behrends 2024; Gertel 2024b). De Hass, however, emphasises the migration focus and starts by underlining that 'the concept of migration aspirations expands the notion of migration agency into the subjective realm' (ibid. 17; cf. Carling/Schewel 2018). He claims that aspirations are conceptually distinct, but not empirically independent from capabilities (ibid. 18). For example, he assumes that education in rural areas, or experience with consumerist urban lifestyles, changes people's notions of a good life, so they may begin to aspire to migrate. De Haas further distinguishes between intrinsic and instrumental dimensions of migration, following a similar vein to Sen's take on freedom, but fails to analyse the constitutive elements of aspirations. In this, he has similar shortcomings to Nussbaum, both having little interest in the formation of subjectivities. It is here where our argument begins.

In order to comprehensively analyse the notion of aspiration, we investigate three aspects in more detail: identity, as the continuous construction of self (Hall 1992); imagination, as a force of social formation and mobilisation (Appadurai 1997); and resonance, as a means of relationship with the world – formed by affect, emotion, and expectation of self-realisation – in which the subject and world are in contact and modify each other (Rosa 2019). Therefore, we understand the notion of aspiration as a composite, and assume that the capacity to aspire is unequally distributed in society. The insights from the works of Hall, Appadurai, and Rosa are crucial for tying our argument together.

A first aspect of aspiration is addressed with the question of identity. The social construction of identities has so far been considered and theorised mainly within the framework of cultural studies. Hall deals explicitly with the question of cultural identity under the conditions of modernity (1992). He argues that a 'crisis of identity' is changing the major structures and processes of modern societies, while also undermining those frames of action that anchor individuals in the social world (ibid. 275). More precisely, a particular type of structural change is transforming societies: namely, the increasing fragmentation of cultural landscapes of class, gender, sexuality, ethnicity, race, and nationality that have previously assigned us as social individuals to fixed places in society, according to Hall. These fragmentations alter personal identities and undermine our perceptions of ourselves as integrated subjects. The loss of the stable 'perception of self' is referred to as the 'de-location' or 'de-centring' of the subject (ibid. 275). This set of 'double displacements' – the decentring of individuals from their place in the social and cultural world and from themselves – triggers a 'crisis of identity' (ibid. 275). Hall (1992) ties the structural change causing this crisis back to late modernity and assigns the term globalisation to it (ibid. 277). Drawing on Giddens (1990a) and Harvey (1989), he highlights the speed and extent of structural transformations in modernity, the ongoing ruptures with previous conditions, and the shift and multiplication of social power centres as the main discontinuities that characterise globalisation. The connection between identity crises and the structural transformation of modern societies is not simply one of cause and effect; but rather, what is clear according to Hall's argument, is their increasing interconnectedness and the mutual feedback over the period of modernity alone. The centring of the subject (invention of the enlightened autonomous individual) and its decentring (fragmentation of the individual) has far-reaching consequences. Acting subjects of late modernity are understood by Hall (and partly understand themselves in this way) as no longer having a stable identity, but constitute themselves out of several, also contradictory and incomplete 'identities'. The processes of identification are thus open, variable, and ambivalent. At the same time, the illusion of the continuation of a unified self is continually being built. Actors draw on remembered experiences (anchored and structured by the unifying 'narrative of the self' (Hall 1992, 277)), transport them, selectively and context-dependent, via interactions outside the body, and continue to further develop their re-imagined self.

As emphasised elsewhere (Gertel 2024b: 4), we assume that personal experiences, particularly of violence and powerlessness, but also traumata experienced by loved ones, can shape the repertoire of memories (Nikro/Hegasy 2018 for Morocco; Lazali 2022 for Algeria). This can change individual life plans or even collective political commitment. Referring to the Egyptian revolution, Matthies-Boon (2023) argues that the multi-level traumatic status subordination (including imprisonment and torture) of the Cairene activists destroyed the potential of revolutionary collective becoming. Trauma is therefore not only personal, but also social. Matthies-Boon (2023: 1) refers to this as '*Breaking Intersubjectivity*'. According to this argument, ruptures in self-understanding and the lifeworlds of people, such as migrants or refugees, become accessible to empirical investigation (cf. Behrends 2024). In critical situations, 'belonging' forms – at least temporarily –a social anchor, a relationship between contested ontological security and social identity (Giddens 1990a: 60, 375). Behrends (2024), focusing on the borderlands between Chad and Sudan, emphasises that 'belonging is relational and co-constituted, particular in highly uncertain situations like war, displacement and large-scale humanitarian and development aid, and it is connected to the diverse knowledge and situational practices of actors' (ibid. 12). The execution of routines and the pursuit of belonging in situations of great uncertainty, in which it is hardly possible to plan ahead (Gertel 2018a), thus becomes a decisive challenge for the discursive formation and stabilising narrative of the (decentred) self.

Scott (1991) further elaborates on the meaning and construction of experience and explains the relationship between discourse and identity:

> Treating the emergence of a new identity as a discursive event is [...] to refuse a separation between 'experience' and language and to insist instead on the productive quality of discourse. Subjects are constituted discursively, but there are conflicts among discursive systems, contradictions within anyone of them, multiple meanings possible for the concepts they deploy. And subjects do have agency. They are not unified, autonomous individuals exercising free will, but rather subjects whose agency is created through situations and statuses conferred on them. Being a subject means being 'subject to definite conditions of existence, conditions of endowment of agents and conditions of exercise' (in: Adams/Minson 1978: 52). These conditions enable choices, although they are not unlimited (Scott 1991: 793).

According to Scott, three interlinked aspects are significant for the connection between identity construction and experience-making: (contradicting) discourses, the construction of subjects, and their agency. We will focus on the notion of discourse before we turn to the second aspect of aspiration, namely the question of imagination and its relation to agency.

Foucault ([1972] 1991) coined the concept of discourse. Discourses are heterogeneous linguistic acts that cannot be traced back to a single author. However, they are also not free-flowing constructions, but rather they are always embedded and often institutionally anchored in society with material counterparts. For our argument, their importance is in their ability to structure access to resources. For example, the question, 'What does agricultural production mean for the future of Tunisia?' involves problematising the conditions about who has 'the right to narrate' in answering this question (e.g. nomads, subsistence farmers, scientists, or bureaucrats; Spivak 1988), who speaks for whom (e.g. men for women, the literate for the illiterate), and who has the means to define terms and topics to represent particular slices of practices (e.g. through the institutionalisation of expertise). Last but not least, it is important to examine how the corresponding authority is codified linguistically and perpetuated in terms of content (e.g. through the materialisation via plans and the development of programmes, for example, to settle nomads or to subsidise agricultural inputs). Discourses therefore structure the access to resources.

Appadurai (1996) addresses the second aspect of aspiration. In the context of cultural globalisation, he emphasises that a new social practice emerges, namely that of imagination. He argues that imagination broke out of its special expressive realm of art, myths, and rites, and has since become a part of the daily mental exercise of common people (ibid. 5). In contrast to fantasy, which tends to emphasise the private and individual, imagination creates ideas, connotes project-orientation, and consequently becomes a basis for collective action (ibid. 7). From this he emphasises that imagination has become the property of collectives, which he calls 'community of sentiment' (ibid. 8): groups of individuals, who may have never meet face-to-face but who start to think of themselves as, for example, Indians or Malays. He stresses: 'The world we live in today is characterised by a new role for the imagination in social life' (ibid. 31). To grasp the new role of imagination, he discusses three ideas: the older idea of images, especially mechanically produced images, the idea of imagined communities in the sense of Anderson (1983), and the French idea of the imaginary (*imaginaire*) – as a constructed landscape of collective aspirations (ibid. 31). Subsequently, imagination is understood as a new social practice.

> Imagination has become an organised field of social practices, a form of work, [a]nd a form of negotiation between sites of agency (individuals) and globally defined fields of possibility. [T]he imagination is now central to all forms of agency, is itself a social fact, and is the key component of the new global order (Appadurai 1996: 31).

The repositioning of imagination as a force of social formation and mobilisation (Appadurai 1996), as well as in the preoccupation with individuals' relationship with the world, conceptualised as 'resonance' (Rosa 2017), are necessary for explaining the formation and capacity of aspirations. According to Appadurai, aspirations contain at least three properties: they have something to do with wants, preferences, choices, and calculations; they are never simply individual but rather formed during interaction; and that aspirations about having a good life filled with health and happiness exist in all societies (Appadurai 2004: 67). According to his understanding, the capacity to aspire is unevenly distributed in societies:

> [T]he better off you are in terms of power, dignity, and material resources, the more likely you are to be conscious of the links between the more and the less immediate objects of aspiration. Because the better off, by definition, have a more complex experience of their relation between a wide range of ends and means, because they have a bigger stock of available experiences of the relationship of aspirations and outcomes, because they are in a better position to explore and harvest diverse experiences of exploration and trial, because of their many opportunities to link material goods and immediate opportunities to more general and generic possibilities and options. [T]hey are more able to produce justifications, narratives, metaphors, and pathways through which bundles of goods and services are actually tied to the wider social scenes and contexts, and to still more abstract norms and beliefs (ibid. 68).

Although this reflects a rather resource oriented and utilitarian argument, Appadurai (2004) links the scope of experiences to the availability of resources (and to capability) and opens up the notion of aspiration. He terms the unequal capacity to aspire as 'navigation capacity' (ibid. 69). On account of different experiences, privileged members of society are more capable when navigating between norms, wants, and wishes. In relation to Sen's work, he emphasises, that 'the capacity to aspire provides an ethical horizon within which more concrete capabilities can be given meaning, substance, and sustainability' (ibid. 82). Imagination and the capacity to aspire are thus addressing the multifaceted relations between different groups in society and their positioning in the world.

The third aspect of aspiration is addressed with the notion of resonance. Understanding the relationships between subjects and world is Rosa's (2019) object of inquiry. The key mechanism in his project is the notion of resonance, a mode of responsive relation (ibid. 174). He starts his argument by claiming that one's position in the world can only be determined via analysing one's attitude toward and experience of the world.

> Whether or not a given subject manages to develop and maintain constitutive axes of resonance depends, on his or her (physical, biographical, emotional, psychological, and social) disposition; and on the (institutional, cultural, contextual, and physical) configuration of segments of the world in which he or she operates; and finally, on the relationship between these two factors (ibid. 16).

A premise of his argument is that modern societies are geared toward continuous progress by means of growth, acceleration, and innovation, creating a temporal and spatial tendency toward escalation. Since human beings, exposed to these conditions of modernity, are unable to develop any certainty about what a good life is, including happiness, 'they are all but forced to concentrate instead on their level of resources' (ibid. 22). Rosa, however, subscribes to the idea that resource endowment does not ensure a happy life per se. In this respect he also criticises Sen and Nussbaum (although to different extents) who, although seeking to avoid fixing determinations of quality of life to material prosperity, remain subject to a materialistic logic – as they suggest that the quality of life increases with one's abilities and opportunities (ibid. 22). Rosa however, is convinced that quality of life and its social conditions cannot be measured simply by access to resources, but requires examining subjects' relationships to the world. He views the access to resources as a prerequisite for a successful life, but insufficient to shape it (ibid. 26). He argues that social conditions 'form, shape and otherwise influence not only the cognitive or conceptual but all aspects of human beings' relationship to the world', including their corporeal, existential, intentional, and evaluative aspects (ibid. 37).

Therefore, we understand the notion of aspiration as a composite, constituted by the interrelation of three elements. These relationships are neither linear nor are they based on mono-causal concatenations, but instead they represent changing fields of possibility, in which – depending on resource access – the capacity of aspirations is formed by three dynamics: (a) The aspirations and ambitions of subjects are rooted in the identity formation and the continuous construction of the self, while the identity of subjects is embedded in discourses and based on agency and capabilities. (b) Imagination embodies both a site for forming aspirations and is simultaneously a force of social formation and mobilisation. While some ideas and wishes formed in our imagination are not (yet) expressible in words, our intentions represent verbal expressions and a linkage to the world (Searle 1983). It is from here where (c) resonance becomes crucial in shaping the subjective disposition for aspiration. Resonance as a form of relationship with the world is formed by affect, emotion, interest, and expectation of self-realisation, in which subject and world are in contact and modify each other. Aspiration, in this sense, shapes decisions.

Figure 1: Capabilities-Aspirations Framework

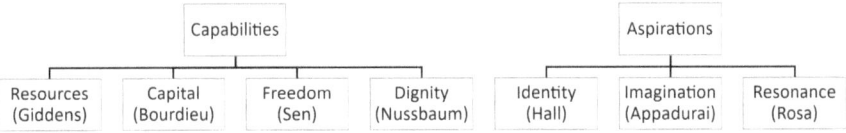

As we have discussed, the Capability-Aspiration Framework encompasses a field of ideas. On the one hand the ability to act – as experienced through inequalities and mobilities – depends on access to resources, which is determined by rules, and on the other hand on dispositions and aspirations that emerge from processes of identity formation, given that the capacity to aspire is unequally distributed in society.

Figure 1 provides an overview of the terms and analytical categories of which our Capabilities-Aspirations Framework is composed. It does not show the interrelation between the concepts as they cannot be described in a simplified and unambiguous way. The idea of capabilities builds on the insights of inequality caused by the varying access to different forms of resources (or 'capital') and complements these with Sen's and Nussbaum's notions of freedom and dignity. This shifts the focus in the description of inequality from the means to the ends. On the other hand, aspirations are constituted by the interrelation of identity (Hall), imagination (Appadurai), and resonance (Rosa), which represent different approaches to conceptualising the subjective constructions of the self in relation to communities and the world.

About the Book

This volume is structured into two parts that raise overlapping questions on the multiple linkages between inequality and mobility. The first part focuses on economies and resource struggles. Economies are here approached intentionally in the plural, as emphasis lies on exploring the multiple spheres of resource governance and livelihood-making that co-exist in contemporary Tunisia, beyond official delimitations of 'the economy' (Mitchell 2008). Illicit border economies, or informal work in urban commerce or waste economies in fact provide an essential life-line to innumerable Tunisians today, but remain often conceptualised purely in the negative, as a problem space that escapes regulation and measurement. Here, in contrast, these sites of economic agency become a starting point for examining, first, how people negotiate access to resources, often through intricate strategies of mobility. Second, how they encounter the state, and how politics emerge, from negotiations and contestations over resources; or from their scarcity or insufficient management. Third and finally, resource struggles are located at multiple scales, bringing into focus local governance – and particularly the newly elected municipalities in post-2011 Tunisia – as a crucial site of citizen-state encounters and political contestation. While recent decisions by the authoritarian regime of Kais Saied have put a halt to a decade-long process of decentralisation reforms, several chapters in this volume explicitly document and discuss the possibilities for political change and alternative resource governance that emerged at the local level, both through formal and informal channels.

The second part centres on diverse forms of human (im)mobility that both shape people's experiences of inequality and injustice, and become avenues for articulating and realising aspirations for a dignified life. This book examines mobilities – or enforced immobility – at different scales and with multiple directionalities: from cross-border migration and flight towards, out of, and back to Tunisia; to everyday urban commutes in the capital city Tunis. Many of the chapters focus on individual trajectories and experiences of past mobility, or on aspirations for future mobility, foregrounding how people make sense of their own decisions or situations that either allow or force them to move, or that let them choose to remain or force immobility. Other chapters shift focus to the new forms of social order – and indeed, racial segregation and discrimination – that have resulted from cross-border mobility to contemporary Tunis, demonstrating how the presence of migrant communities poses new questions for urban governance and reshapes everyday realities of life in the city. As some of the research shows, inequality can be both a trigger and a cause of mobility, as international migration becomes the only 'way out' for marginalised Tunisians and migrant communities at the present conjuncture of intensifying violence and socio-economic crisis. Yet, at the same time inequality also impedes opportunities for mobility, exposing the socially and economically marginalised to situations of blockage or waiting – be it for the next bus or for an opportunity to leave the country. Such constraints on mobility, and indeed the stigmatisation and criminalisation of certain bodies on the move, are here prominently analysed as forms of structural and institutional violence that characterise the lives of many young Tunisians (cf. Gertel et al. 2024).

The chapters demonstrate how diverse forms of cross-border mobility – and aspirations framed around it – characterise people's lives in contemporary Tunisia, despite policies of enforced immobility. Some chapters directly tackle Sub-Saharan African migration to Tunisia, exploring the new challenges and forms of racialised discrimination – as well as opportunities for participation and community-building – that have emerged in local governance and through the urban co-existence of migrant and host communities in Tunisia's capital city Tunis (Ben Medien; Parikh; Sha'ath, this volume). Other chapters focus on the migration of young Tunisians to and from Europe, analysing both aspirations for out-migration (Kreuer/Gertel, this volume) and the impact of so-called 'voluntary return' programs for illegal Tunisian migrants in Europe (Garnaoui, this volume). Beyond the dominant narrative that links cross-border mobility in Tunisia to linear south-north migration towards Europe, the research presented in this volume highlights the diverse forms of exceptional and everyday mobility that reconfigure Tunisia's borders and socio-economic realities. To do so, some chapters offer close-up empirical insight into the diverse material circulations that turn borders not only into spaces of violence, but also into sites of economic opportunity and state encounters (Amri; Shâfi'i, this volume). Another chapter examines the gendered working lives of Syrian refugees who construct new livelihoods in contemporary Tunisia (Zuntz et al., this volume). All of these chapters place emphasis on people's aspirations and strategies for navigating constraints on mobility and inequality in access to resources in contemporary Tunisia. In doing so, they elucidate critical linkages between (im-)mobility and inequality, and go beyond a spectre of 'crisis' to excavate alternative stories, visions, and possibilities for better futures.

The contributions do so, first, by working at different scales: from the urban micro-scale – the district or neighbourhood – to the level of the municipality or greater metropolitan area; from the village – or single oasis settlement – to the level of the governorate or region; and across borders and bounded sites, by following the circulation of goods and people. This implies that the chapters pay attention to the ways in which space articulates inequalities. On the one hand, the analysis foregrounds tendencies of spatial segregation or isolation, both racialised and class-based (Parikh, this volume); on the other hand, belonging to a shared place or territory can also become the basis for devising alternative modes of resource governance or participation between diverse constituents (Weißenfels, this volume). Second, the qualitative and in part ethnographic research presented here foregrounds actors and agencies that often remain invisible or overlooked, as they operate illicitly or are socially stigmatised. From informal waste pickers (Chebbi, this volume), to urban commuters living in largely informally built-up neighbourhoods (Bouzid, this volume), to fuel smugglers (Shâfi'i, this volume); this edited volume gives centre stage to the everyday strategies and aspirations of marginalised communities in present-day Tunisia. Third, the contributions to this book unsettle simplistic understandings of the state as a single, coherent actor (Mitchell 1991), foregrounding instead the multiple registers of action, and diverse rationales that characterise how the state takes effect or is indeed encountered in contemporary Tunisia. Consequently, several of the chapters in this book trouble neat distinctions between formal and informal economy and work (Amri; Gertel/Audano, this volume) or formal and informal governance and space (Kahloun/Frische; Weißenfels, this volume). Moreover, the research in this volume advances an understanding of 'the political' that goes beyond a narrow view of state politics, focusing on political materialities – such as waste (Furniss/Bouhlel, this volume) – or perceptions of the state and its absence, for instance on the labour market (Garraoui, this volume). The epilogue ultimately reveals the spatial effects and social consequences of mobility aspirations when these are exposed to a politically led racist discourse (Matri/Zuntz, this volume).

Inequalities.
Resource Struggles in Diverse Economies

Introduction

Myriam Amri

Tunisia's Economies: Who knows the Economy?

In 2014, the World Bank issued a report on Tunisia entitled 'The Unfinished Revolution'. Shifting from its usual expert tone, the bank issued a puzzling *mea culpa*. It acknowledged that its previous reports had repeatedly misrepresented the country's economy as one of durable growth and had 'too easily overlook[ed] the fact that its engagement might perpetuate the kinds of economic systems that keep poor people poor' (World Bank Group 2014: 27). The bank called Tunisia a 'shiny facade' (ibid. 26) where representations of economic growth did not match the material realities of persistent dispossession. This premise, the gulf between representations and realities on the ground, informs our engagement with the political economy of present-day Tunisia.

Before the uprisings of 2011, there was an official narrative in Tunisia, posited by the state and reinforced by international institutions and Western lenders, of durable growth and economic stability (Hibou 2011a; Tsourapas 2013; Kaboub 2014; Zemni 2015). On world maps, Tunisia, small and tucked between two neighbouring oil economies Algeria and Libya, was singled out as an 'emerging economy', the advanced stage for developing countries (Meddeb 2010). Yet when the uprisings of 2011 began, that representation crumbled, revealing an economy held together by debt, and where growth numbers were inflated through creative accounting (Allal 2011; Hibou 2011b; Zemni/Ayeb 2015). The reality that became clear to actors in and outside the country was of a system broken for decades: unemployed graduates who were promised the education-to-job pipeline (Blavier 2016; Weipert-Fenner 2020); stark differences between coastal regions and the country's interior strategically forgotten by the state (Belhedi 1999; Bechir 2018); and elite co-optation fostering family monopolies and entrenching dispossession (Gherib 2012; Malik/Eibl 2019). Since the revolution, the rosy narrative of an emerging but mighty small country has been unsettled yet without any kind of resolution: moving from crony capitalism to neoliberal encroachment (Jouili 2023; Mullin 2023); from subsidies keeping prices low to decade-long inflation (Amri 2023); and from manipulated exchange rates to the fall of the Dinar (Tunisian Observatory of the Economy 2021).

Yet, if representations do not account for material realities, perhaps it is because they never do. As Mitchell, Callon and MacKenzie remind us 'the economy' is a construction that renders it a sphere outside of political life and only legible to experts (Mitchell 2002; Callon 2007; MacKenzie et al. 2007). As such, if what constitutes Tunisia's economy has unravelled, it is also because economic practices defy the measurements that attempt to contain them. Instead, as the chapters of this section will show, it is by investigating the complex realities on the ground, people surviving, accumulating, resisting, and imagining alternative futures in times of crisis, that we can perhaps begin to sketch a picture not of *the* economy but of a political economy attentive to the inextricability of the material and the representational (Keane 2003).

A Few Threads in Tunisia's Economies

A critical political economy of Tunisia foregrounds economic practices as plural phenomena constituted through the sociopolitical. The chapters in this section highlight key features that rattle the sense of *an* economy.

Despite discourses representing Tunisia as urban and de facto modern, Tunisia remains a country where rural life is at the epicentre of socio-economic processes (Gana 2012). Weißenfels (this volume) in his chapter on alternative property rights in the Tunisian South reminds us that struggles over land are essential to understanding the relations between inequalities and resources. Centring agrarian life historicizes movements across the country, through the rural exodus of those who have become the working poor and whose labour sustains other sectors of the economy (Chabbi 1999). Moreover, the agrarian question foregrounds the struggles over land sovereignty (Elloumi 2013), food justice (Ayeb/Bush 2019), and the environment (Bouhlel/Furniss, this volume) that mark contemporary politics.

In state and international institutions' narratives, Tunisia is seen as a country whose key resource is its human capital. Yet this perspective erases the stark differences of class, gender, and location that inform the experiences of educated youth, as Garraoui's chapter in this volume highlights. Education as the path towards a better middle-class life became the ideological cornerstone of the authoritarian state since Tunisia's independence. Both the Bourguiba and Ben Ali regimes constructed their base by selling a middle-class ethos, of an educated population, with access to credit and aspirations to modernity, yet perceived as apolitical (Hibou 2011b). We can understand the middle-class illusion through the Framework of Capabilities-Aspirations, as Gertel/Grüneisl highlight in the book's introduction, meaning 'as the gap between "what is" and "what might have been"' (page 19). The gap between people's material lives, the promises made by the system, and their aspirations help us contend with the cycle of 'revolution and its disenchantments' (Bardawil 2020) marking life since 2011. In recent years, the middle-class as an aspirational project, as a de facto social class, and as an institutional discourse has crumbled. Class divisions have grown, especially between elites and the working-class while increasing indebtedness has kept people in cycles of dependency. Indebtedness as it trickles from individuals to social groups to the state's sovereign debt is a generative lens into local (Salman 2023), national (Djerbi 2023), and transnational politics (Alami 2021). Tunisia's debt regime, emerging from a predatory banking sector aided by the state constitutes a mirror of capitalist processes across North Africa and the Middle East.

Informality and the State

When asking what constitutes the economy of Tunisia, we grapple with the dizzying information reiterated by mainstream media and state institutions, that 30 to 50 per cent of the Tunisian economy is supposedly informal. This so-called informal economy spans multiple sectors, modes of accumulation, and regimes of labour across Tunisia, from contraband trafficking which alters the fabric of border towns (Amri; Shâfi'i, this volume) to the myriad of modalities of undeclared work that includes both skilled and unskilled labourers in the 'course a la *khobza* (Meddeb 2011)', (literally 'the race for bread', i.e., the daily struggle or hustle to get by) that organizes labour in space and time. These examples highlight how the informal is a catchall word that flattens the different combinations that articulate accumulation, regulation, and governance. The work of lumping these activities as informal and then positing them as the radical opposite of the formal, operates as a mode of governmentality (Foucault 1991), meaning a way to control, contain, and discipline using knowledge production, here of the economy. It puts anything that occurs beyond the state as informal, imbuing it with amoral qualities that relieve the state of responsibility towards fair compensation, economic rights, or social security. Instead, and as Chebbi and other contributions to this volume showcase, what happens in the broad category of the informal is central to an everyday political economy that constructs alternative futures beyond institutional constraints. As Gertel/Audano (this volume) remind us, informal economies are plural, they reorganize space and open up questions about economic power while helping decipher what alternatives are being produced within the cracks. Informal practices also produce new geographies that decentre the sites of wealth accumulation to consider what happens between regions, in working-class neighbourhoods, or at borders (Malik/Gallien 2020; Meddeb 2021). Through a focus on informality, we move beyond methodological nationalism to instead locate the transnational flows that reorganize margins and centres alike. For example, as Amri shows in this volume, the informal organizes borders away from their representations as exceptional geographies, marginal spaces, or lawless lands to instead locates borders as key sites for exchange and circulation across North Africa.

Finally, we are left with the state as a concept and as the site of power that is inextricable from our understanding of Tunisia's political economy. This book tracks the relationship between the economy and the state, meaning how the state becomes a site, a tool, or a node for a plethora of economic practices (Mitchell 1991; Ferguson 1994; Goswami 2004; Appel 2019). The notion of the state has been central to recent works on Tunisia, as a node for capture (Capasso 2021), a site of surveillance regimes (Pluta 2020), and the main interlocutor in social movements (Allal/Bennafla 2011). This scholarship and this edition do not assume a coherence of the state but locate how power invests the state. The chapters here follow the state through an ethnographic lens, meaning they examine daily strategies to resist the state (Weißenfels, this volume), demand the state (Furniss/Bouhlel, this volume), or operate in lieu of it (Amri; Chebbi; Shâfi'i, all this volume). Instead of the state per se, we are concerned here with actions, discourses, sites, and power effects that reimagine the state in a myriad of ways.

Overall, this volume resists looking at Tunisia as a site of exceptional processes, against tendencies often layered with orientalism that see the country and the Arab region more broadly as a space of difference. This book ultimately argues that it is instead through a critical political economy attentive to practices, politics, and social processes that we can better grasp Tunisia, North Africa, and even global capitalism today.

Asymmetric Economies and 'Informal' Work

Jörg Gertel & Enrica Audano

IMAD: 'I work as a fishmonger, which is sometimes exhausting. I have to wake up early enough in the morning to make sure I can buy and sell fish. The problem is that I cannot work every day because of the weather. When it's too rainy or windy the fishermen do not go fishing. But thank God the business is still profitable. I get up at 3 am every morning and go to the port. There, all the work depends on the boats and fishing vessels, and, of course, also on the porters who carry the boxes of fish from the fishing vessels. From the port I go inside the fish market and inspect the fish and the other goods. I call my customers, such as smaller fishmongers, restaurant owners and the like, and ask them what goods they require that day and what quantity they need. I give them detailed information about types of fish available and their prices. Then we negotiate and discuss the price. Of course, I for sure make a profit. There is no doubt about it. Whether the fish is sold per kilo or per box, I take my share. Then, I add four percent, the cost of the ice and other expenses. I don't currently pay taxes, but you can if you want to. But every day the prices are different, they change on an hourly basis'.

Imad from Nabeul, single, 43 years old

SABA: 'I work as an accountant in an export company for olive oil. It takes a journey to get to work, but I've gotten used to it and it's still better than being unemployed. Unemployment makes me nervous, it's complicated and leads to loneliness. My job is to keep track of the invoices for olive oil handled inside or purchased outside the company on a daily basis. I have to track everything that has been bought and is related to the company. If the boss is not there, I have to tell him about everything we buy. The work is easy, but sometimes tiring, and sometimes I have to work online after working hours, especially when I have to reconcile and check the accounts. Saturdays are public holidays, but when a customer comes to the company to collect goods, I have to be there to receive the cheque and assess it in the office, because we don't trust the other workers.
The work requires a lot of concentration and you are responsible for every mistake. Sometimes many customers come in at the same time and you have to know how to deal with them without losing customers, because it's about money and contracts on

behalf of the owner. The boss looks at you as 'capital' before he looks at you as a person. And when there's a lot of money involved, he 'doesn't know' you, he doesn't respect working hours: I have to keep working until the sales contract is signed. But not every day is stressful, only the period during the olive season from December to March. The boss has his own olive groves, but he also buys other quantities, stores them and sells them after the season'.

Saba, 31 years old, accountant in a private company in Tunis, has a written contract

These two interviews are part of a larger study on employability (see below) conducted during the first winter of the Covid pandemic in 2020/21 which hit Tunisia comparatively hard. They exemplify different working situations embedded in globally integrated production and exchange systems. The first person, a self-employed fishmonger, represents the unskilled workforce with earlier working experience, in his case as an agricultural labourer. The second person, a female accountant, represents a university graduate who has a written employment contract. Both are trading agricultural commodities (fish or olive oil) and emphasise the seasonality of their work. While the fish trader does not pay taxes and works for the national Tunisian market, the contracted accountant works for a foreign (French) company that is expected to be formally registered. Whether, or how much the company actually pays taxes and counts as 'formal' remains an open question.

In this chapter we address the performance and the boundary making of what is termed 'the economy' in Tunisia, in order to better comprehend remunerated work, particularly the kind of work labelled as 'informal', as it allegedly constitutes one of the economy's key components. Conceptually we consider the economy to be a composite entity that consists of varied production, exchange, consumption and reproduction processes. Work is often only attributed to the sphere of production, which, of course, neglects unpaid work (Bennholdt-Thomsen 1984; Wong 1984), other forms of bodily engagement (Sadawi 1969; Mernissi 1975), and ultimately the sphere of reproduction itself (Gibson-Graham 2008; Bhattacharya 2017; Djerbi 2024). Offering an alternative reading to simple dualistic distinctions, such as between state and economy or between formal and informal labour, is a challenge, which we capture with the term 'asymmetric economies'. Asymmetric exchange processes are not based on an equilibrium, but rather produce winners and losers and enable the accumulation of capital, while simultaneously producing livelihood crises. We therefore analyse the meaning of 'work' under conditions of insecurity and uncertainty. The empirical investigation furthers the Capability-Aspiration Framework (Gertel/Grüneisl, this volume) and captures individual entry conditions to remunerated labour (e.g. required skills), its everyday features and properties (e.g. vulnerabilities and dependencies), and its outcomes (e.g. satisfaction with work and its decency). By doing so, we aim to reposition the understanding of 'informal' work and to unveil its articulations with local and globally interconnected production and exchange processes in an age of technoliberalism – i.e. the interaction of neoliberalism, technology and knowledge production (Gertel 2023).

Conceptualising 'Work': Insecurity and Uncertainty

In mainstream economic science 'the economy' is conceptualised as separate from society, opposed to the state, and demarcated from the supposedly non-economic. 'Non-economic' on the one hand refers to subsistence production, including the household, since at first glance, no money circulates and no measurable value creation takes place in either case (Wong 1984; Wallace 2002; Gonáles de la Rocha 2007). On the other hand, everything classified as informal (including irregular, illegal or prohibited activities) – that allegedly oppose a (western) concept of state – is also classified as non-economic; often because it evades (western) metrics, is difficult to measure, and thus often escapes central administration, taxation and governance. In contrast, and according to Mitchell (2007: 247), these (constructed) borders to the non-economic are better represented not as a thin line, but rather envisioned as a broad terrain, a border region that can encompass the entire area of what is called capitalism. This region is the arena of political struggles in which new moral claims, arguments about justice and forms of aspirations are negotiated (cf. Gertel/Grüneisl, this volume). In postcolonial countries, such as Tunisia, this 'border terrain', the sphere of capitalism – comprehended not as context, but as a project (Appel 2019: 2) – might cover the entire national territory, and even extend beyond it (cf. Amri, this volume), is always 'in the making'.

At the same time, the concept of the state remains ambivalent, especially in terms of its relationship with 'the economy' – as being either detached from it or intrinsically part of it. One perspective sees the state as standing outside the economy: the closest it can come as an external entity is as the source of regulatory measures that structure the economy. In this situation it should define and regulate economic actors' relationships, while also controlling and guaranteeing compliance with the law. From another perspective, the economy cannot exist without the state. State power is seen as part of the economy and its institutions as enmeshed with it; institutions guarantee property rights, and assume the right to enforce laws, violently if necessary (Blomley 2003). So where are the boundaries of the economy, particularly if we focus on work as a constitutive part of it? To further investigate this question, we will discuss the impact of unequal development from a recent historical perspective, tackling the different phases of development, including globalisation and financialisation in the context of technoliberalism.

Since the late 1970s, the global economy has become increasingly neoliberal, fuelled by economic recessions and neoconservative economic ideas (Harvey 2005), shaping a 'new international division of labour' (Fröbel et al. 1977). For the Global South in particular, it often marked the end of welfare state policies, changing the relations between state and market in the post Second World War development era (Escobar 1995). After the 'international debt crisis' in the mid-1980s, economic restructuring further accelerated globally, and also in Tunisia (Hibou 2009). Deregulation led to a reduction in state influence and at the same time to a strengthening of market forces. It included, among other things, the dissolution and privatisation of state-owned enterprises with mass redundancies, the weakening of trade unions, the reduction of state subsidies, and also opened new opportunities for foreign direct investment. Globalisation became omnipresent (Milanovic 2016). In the Global North, this implied the end of 'normal working conditions', the further flexibilisation of work, and precarisation that started to affect the middle-class (Dörre 2019). In the Global South, including North Africa, the effects of structural adjustment measures have caused an increase in poverty, a further polarisation of society and an expansion of insecurity and uncertainty undermining livelihood conditions (Gertel/Hexel 2018). Labour and mobility have been interlocking in new ways, including rural-urban migration, labour migration abroad and within the larger Mediterranean area increasingly driven by displacement and flight (Zapata-Barrero/Awad 2024; Zuntz 2024). In the wake of financialisation dynamics, investments in labour often earn significantly less than investments in the capital market (Krippner 2012; MacKenzie 2021; Harrington 2024). This has led to increased inequalities, also in the labour market and has resulted in asymmetrical pay and growing insecurity (Mayer-Ahuja 2023; Pettit 2024). More recently, platform- and crowd-work started to grow without trade unions having a say in shaping labour conditions. With the Covid pandemic the relation between digitisation and labour has compounded this development by expanding work from home-office constellations, facilitating the blurring of working hours, further undermining labour-based solidarity. Adding to these forms of dispossession (Gertel et al. 2024a) and blended with accelerated data transmission and rapidly decreasing transparency are the expected negative consequences of artificial intelligence on labour markets.

In the vein of these developments – neoliberal expansion, flexibilization of work, and devaluation of labour through the dynamics of financialisation – there are two conceptual framings to comprehend the notion of work: top-down and bottom-up approaches, which have different starting points and scopes. To begin with, we address mechanisms of asymmetrical economic integration, applying Santos's classical approach on 'Shared Space' (1979). Then we focus, bottom-up, on the interplay of insecurity and uncertainty, inscribed in unequal local livelihoods, shaping remunerated work, by discussing Gibson-Graham's concept of 'Diverse Economies' (2008). In both cases the spaces of the 'border terrain' between the non-economic and economic are contested as Sarah Wright underlines when she claims 'the geographies of our economic lives are at once deeply saturated with capitalist relations and full of values and practices that go beyond and beneath capitalist exchange' (Wright 2010: 298).

Top-down: How is the integration of economic spheres conceptualised from a developmental take? From an early perspective of economic geography, referring to postcolonial countries (termed Third World at the time), processes of superimposition are crucial. Quijano (1974) and Santos (1979) argue that after World War Two new, external economic forces superimpose local, traditional economic activities. They consider this to be the root cause of societal polarisation. How do processes of superimposition roll out? On the one hand, the processes of capital-intensive, spatially concentrated industrialisation and agricultural modernisation are pushing traditional economic activities (e.g. subsistence production) further and further back, without them disappearing completely. On the other hand, they combine, while retaining their hegemony, with the older 'sectors' that have been degraded to the 'marginal pole' (Quijano 1974: 300–302) or the 'lower economic circuit' (Santos 1979). As a consequence, the relative importance of the older sectors in the overall system decreases and they gradually lose control over production, resources, and markets. Simultaneously, the close interlinking of the economies implies a permanent transfer of capital from the lower to the upper circuits of the peripheral economies and from there to the metropolitan centres of the global economy. The permanent outflow of capital makes the overall structure increasingly heterogeneous and contradictory.

In 'The Shared Space', Santos (1979) observes this polarisation dynamic in urban economies of the Third World. He argues that, due to technical modernisation in industry and agriculture, employment rates are falling, with the result that the majority of the population is dependent on the lowest incomes and casual jobs, and only a minority of the population can earn higher incomes (ibid. 17). Thus, extreme income disparities characterise the urban population, which therefore participates in the urban economy with different purchasing power potential and unequal access to consumer goods. The resulting quantitative and qualitative differences in the consumption process reproduce the lower and upper economic circuits of the urban economy. This leads to a permanent withdrawal of capital from the locally limited economic activities of the lower circuit and results in social deformations, assuming ever-greater proportions in the course of the polarisation processes. The mechanisms of asymmetrical exchange processes and the integration of even the smallest local areas and units of reproduction (e.g. households) into the system of international division of labour thus manifest themselves in a polarisation of spatial and social structures and perpetuate poverty even in the most dynamic centres of growth.

More recently, Likic-Brboric/Schierup (2012) have addressed the integration of peripheral economies during asymmetric globalisation processes, while not only the deep-rooted exchange entanglements but also both, the limitation of labour rights (Hertel 2009; Blanton/Blanton 2016), and the re-commodification of labour (Papadopoulos 2005; Rosewarne 2012) are expanding (for Tunisia cf. Hibou 2009; Weißenfels 2024). The superimposition of modern circuits, empowered by commodification and neoliberal globalisation thus transforms the boundaries of the (local) economy. The latter approaches shift the focus away from structural effects of economic dynamics to address the state and its responsibility for guaranteeing equal labour rights as both incontrovertible and indispensable. This reference to the state will be further scrutinised in the following.

Bottom-up: For decades, the framing of informal economic activities has been used to comprehend the different role of the state in postcolonial societies, particularly, if contrasted, for example, to OECD countries. From a Eurocentric perspective, formality is represented as the norm and informality as the deviant (McFarlane/Waibel 2012), while, for example, in African economies – in the vein of the same logic – most economic activities are not registered with government bodies, nor are they seen as contributing to the formal economy, for example, as they do not pay taxes, such as Imad, the fishmonger from the opening quote. However, the analytical picture is more complicated. If we continue to (wrongly) assume that there are only two distinct economic spheres, formal and informal, we can see that their relationships are dynamic, interrelated, asymmetric and, at times, contradicting. Such conceptual binaries, however, primarily classify a Western view of postcolonial societies (Bryceson et al. 2009). To undo this image the diverse economies approach opens up new possibilities to capture the notion of work in more than one dimension (Gibson-Graham/Dombroski 2020).

In the mid-1990s Gibson-Graham wrote against the prevailing public opinion that liberalism in terms of capitalism (and democracy) remained the one and only reliable exchange system after the collapse of the Soviet Union. In 'The End of Capitalism (As We Knew It) – A Feminist Critique of Political Economy' ([1996] 2006a) they unexpectedly proclaimed the rather provocative 'End of Capitalism'. Gibson-Graham argue in favour of a new economy from a feminist perspective and promote its implementation through theory formation and scholarly activism. After years of engagement, they characterise their approach in 'Diverse Economies' (Gibson-Graham 2008); opposing economic liberalism, the economy should rather be thought of as socially more comprehensive than Western-style capitalism, opening up an imaginative space for economic alternatives. This shift also includes non-market transactions, such as unpaid household work and other forms of underestimated economic practices. Gibson-Graham state:

> What is intriguing, however, is that 'marginal' economic practices and forms of enterprise are actually more prevalent, and account for more hours worked and/or more value produced, than the capitalist sector. Most of them are globally extensive, and potentially have more impact on social wellbeing than capitalism does (ibid. 617).

They thus concentrate on forms of often ignored exchange mechanisms and actors, building (implicitly) on insights from early development studies about the role of women, reproductive work, and household economies (cf. Smith et al. 1984). In their second book 'A Postcapitalist Politics' Gibson-Graham (2006b) apply an iceberg metaphor to illustrate the asymmetrical relations between a capitalist economy, containing a visible form (above the waterline) namely that of wage labour, and a multiplicity of so far rather invisible activities (below the water line) of Diverse Economies (ibid. 70). The term invisible contains two meanings: one in the sense of not being registered or even accepted, approved or taxed by the state; and second as not (yet) represented in conventional scientific thinking. They, therefore, demand to include a plurality of property relations as constitutive for economies in our thinking (Gibson-Graham 2008: 616). The diverse economies approach relies on community projects and empowers bottom-up grass-root movements. Scholarly activism, originating in particular from their academic home, namely, from poststructuralist economic geography, is crucial; it is based on enactment and on performativity for creating new economic worlds, opening up new possibilities for engaging, by using 'weak theories' that are not confirming what we already know, but rather provide a space of freedom and possibility, welcoming surprise and tolerating coexistence (ibid. 619) with more-than-human entities. The two authors conclude that this cannot be successfully implemented without active identity work and performativity. They are convinced that understanding the world is necessary to change it, and to change our own understanding 'is to change the world' (ibid. 615).

How are these approaches able to capture the more recent dramatic expansion of both insecurity (i.e. problems with access to resources) and uncertainty (i.e. limitations in securing the future) that affect and shape local livelihood conditions in North Africa (Gertel 2018a; Gertel et al. 2024a)? Concerning the conceptual notion of work Thieme (2018) observes that young people in Nairobi are engaging in an everyday struggle, they navigate precarious situations to advance their own, and sometimes shared interests against the odds (ibid. 529; see Hecking 2021 for Algiers; Grüneisl 2021 for Tunis). She labels this as a hustle economy:

> 'The hustle' is advanced as a collective condition of individual insecurity [...] navigating uncertainty in irregular employment. (ibid. 530). [It] infers a constant pragmatic search for alternative structures of opportunity outside formal education, employment, and service provision. It assumes a continuous management of risk associated with living and working beyond formal institutional norms (Thieme 2018: 537).

These activities are not considered as unfolding outside the capitalist economy. On the contrary, non-economic and economic activities are comprehended as articulated, building a formative part of capitalist exchange, value adding and accumulation processes. In their recent edited volume 'Beyond the Wage: Ordinary Work in Diverse Economies' Monteith et al. (2021) set the stage by claiming:

> Many of the concepts that we have to describe work – informal, precarious, decent – are constructed against the ideal type: work in industrial capitalism. Yet this model of work is a historical and geographical exception (ibid. 1).

Narrowing down the framing of the plurality of work into a single notion, namely in that of 'paid labour' repeats and rectifies the story that promised the 'proper job' as norm and telos of 'development' (Ferguson and Li 2018: 1).

> That this promise has so often ended up a broken one does not diminish its attraction, as is clear in the rhetorical appeals of politicians the world over: Jobs, jobs, jobs! The limited ability to think beyond the promised-land of jobs for all afflicts not only politicians, but scholars as well (ibid. 1).

Understanding and capturing 'the economy' from a conventional position is, therefore, not opening up our understanding, but rather fixing an out-dated image of 'power-geometries' (Massey 1993); this becomes manifest in the simplistic classification of formal and informal. To mark the difference, we, following Gibson-Graham (2008), instead use the notion of 'economies'. Their imbalance, enforced by unbridled capital accumulation, leads to an asymmetry that excludes the majority of society from equal opportunities for a fulfilling life (cf. Gertel/Grüneisl 2024). We thus address the importance of 'work' under conditions of insecure and uncertain livelihoods, revealing individual entry conditions to remunerated work, its features, properties and its consequences. We are moreover convinced that the plurality and multiplicity of economic processes determining 'work' are not based on an equal footing, but are embedded in different local conditions. Local, in this respect does not necessarily relate to a territorial proximity, but also relates to intertwined social and economic interactions that are stretched over place and time.

Representing 'the Economy' in and for Tunisia

The International Labour Office (ILO) furthers the conventional representation of the economy as a dichotomous grid of informal and formal spheres, including that of work. This is not only reifying the key role of nation states in guaranteeing and maintaining a neoliberal economy, it also prevents a high-resolution empirical view into the manifold practices of diverse economies, as is evident in the working lives of Tunisians like Saba and Imad, displaying the multifaceted articulations of legal and unregistered activities. However, the term 'informal economy' has been used and referred to in ILO publications for decades and has become a catch-all category that represents the informal economy as the world's number one employer. About 2 billion people, equivalent to more than 60 percent of world's employed population, are accordingly working in informal economies (ILO 2018). Particularly in Africa, related economic activities would, in line with this metric, comprise more than three quarters (87%) of all economic units (ibid. 17). ILO stresses that the rate of informality decreases, with an increasing level of education. With particular reference to Tunisia, ILO (2022) records 'high rates of unemployment (15% unemployment as a share of the labour force, 27% for higher education graduates in 2019), [and] regional inequality between the coast and the interior regions' (ibid. 17). Another key issue ILO emphasises is the high rate of youth not in education, employment or training (NEET) in both rural areas (33% for men, 50% for women) but also in urban areas (20% for men, 32% for women). Moreover, Tunisia is experiencing the so-called MENA paradox: while the education gender gap has disappeared, only 25 percent of working-age women, compared to 70 percent of working-age men, are employed in the so-called formal sector (ETF 2011). Theis simple, yet misleading, image of the economy is complemented by the categorisation of informal activities as predominantly small and therefore implicitly insignificant: About 88 percent of enterprises in Tunisia have no employees or, to broaden the picture, up to 97 percent are micro-enterprises with five or fewer employees, while the latter account for only 11 percent of the total value added in 2018 (UNDP 2020: 25). The majority of them, up to 65 percent, are operating in the informal sector (ILO 2022, 17). In the following we ask, how far this picture is reasonable and helpful, if we approach the conditions of livelihoods and work through the concept of asymmetric economies?

Methodology

The ACCESS program, the African Centre for Career Enhancement and Skills Support, a project collaboration between six African universities and Leipzig University, aims to further the understanding of employability. Together, we facilitated a collective research project in order to investigate the connections between university graduates and their involvement in informal economies. Over the period spanning October 2020 to January 2021, during the first year of the Covid-19 pandemic, fieldwork involving face-to-face interviews was carried out in six African countries, namely in Benin, Ghana, Kenya, Nigeria, Rwanda, and Tunisia. In each of these countries a team comprising three individuals, one of whom was a post-doctoral researcher, conducted a total of 240 interviews, resulting in 1,440 interviews across all six countries. The research team endeavoured to achieve an even distribution of interviews within each country, with the aim of recruiting 65 per cent of participants from the capital and urban regions, 25 percent from rural areas, and 10 percent from border regions. This distribution has been designed to capture the diverse range of activities within 'informal' economies, with a lesser degree of variation observed in rural settings and distinct activities prevalent in border regions.

Table 1: Structure of the Sample: Age Groups

	Share	Gender (Share: Male)	Education (Share: Univ.)	Has children (Share: Yes)
Young (<30 years)	26	75	27	8
Middle (30–39 years)	30	71	34	40
Old (40+ years)	43	72	2	73
All (n = 235)	100	72	19	46

Note: All numbers are given in percent.

In Tunisia, interviews were conducted in Arabic and some in French, with approximately 51 percent of interviews centred on the capital, Greater Tunis. We used the following introduction to identify people who were willing to participate in the interview:

> Often planners, politicians, but also social scientists seem to apply an understanding of labour markets that is largely restricted to conditions in the formal sector. Knowledge about job requirements, necessary qualifications and skills in different spheres of the everyday economies – particularly in the agricultural and 'informal' sectors – is rather limited. We, therefore, aim to interview ordinary people active in these economic fields about their personal working experiences.

Selected interviewees had to have worked for money during the last three months. This methodology thus emphasised the investigation of individuals and their occupational engagements in a specific social, spatial, and temporal frame. Following the reflections about 'situated knowledge' (Haraway 1988) the findings are not representative for the national context, but represent a wide scope of diverse economic practices in Tunisia.

About 72 percent of the 240 people interviewed in Tunisia were male and 28 percent were female. This corresponds to the official national labour force participation in Tunisia with 34 percent of female and 66 percent of male involvement (INS 2017). The average age of the interviewees is 43 years, with the youngest interviewee born in 2003 and the oldest in 1948. Of them, one fourth was younger than 30 years old, about one third was between 30 and 39 years old, while close to one half is 40 years and older (see Table 1 for further details).

The distribution of gender in these three groups is almost equal, ranging between 71 and 75 percent male. We distinguish four groups of educational attainment:[1] 'low' (no formal training to primary education) equalling 30 percent of the respondents; 'medium' (intermediate or secondary school) making up 33 percent; and 'high', comprising those

---

1 The spectrum of educational qualification stretches from 'none' to having obtained a PhD (none = 3%; read and write = 3%; primary school = 24%; secondary school = 33%; baccalaureate = 9%; technical diploma = 8%; university = 19%; and PhD = 1%).

with baccalaureate and technical diploma (18%); and lastly those holding a university degree (19%) (see Table 2 for further details).

The four groups are of different age: University graduates are the youngest (mean: 30 years), the groups with medium and high educational backgrounds are in the middle (both means: 37 years), while those from the less qualified group are the oldest among the interviewees (mean: 43 years). This corresponds to their living situation (see Table 3): The largest group lives with their own family (without parents) and amounts to 39 percent. They are predominately from the oldest cohort, less educated and almost all of them (93%) have children. The second largest group, with 31 percent, still lives with their parents, has a high educational or university qualification, and is predominantly young with almost no children. Two other groups are of equal size with ten percent each: one, where the respondents live together with their parents in one house, while having their own household (38% of them with children); the others are living alone, often for reasons of divorce or being widowed (here 42% have children). Finally, a small group of seven percent, often university graduates, lives in shared apartments, often together with friends. Correspondingly, the responsibility as carers (i.e. for children) is unequally distributed between these groups – characterising the oldest groups as most frequently in charge of the next generation. This comes along with an asymmetry in formal education.

Paid Work in Asymmetric Economies

Work under conditions of insecurity and uncertainty is discussed in five steps: the economic situation during the Covid pandemic; the economic structures of work and decent work; requirements, skills and formal qualifications for the job; the importance of earlier learning processes; and finally, life and work satisfaction. All this is done by juxtaposing university graduates with other workers in order to scrutinise differences in work and livelihood performances related to varied educational backgrounds. The spectrum of occupation and working engagement is large and ranges from farmer, construction worker, blacksmith, taxi driver, street food vendor, hawker, trader, waiter, driver, painter, plumber, butcher to restaurant owner, teacher, consultant, secretary, cleaner and hairdresser, and also includes, for example, the fishmonger and the accountant from the opening quotes, among many others. Numerically, the largest segment classifies itself as 'worker' with continuous employment, but no social insurance (41%),[2] this is followed by 'day labourers' (19%), self-employed persons with qualifications but no higher education (16%), and by those who are self-employed in the service sector (10%), while employees with continuous employment and social insurance (6%) and the self-employed with higher education (4%) follow. The remaining three percent are either self-employed in agriculture, are part of a family business with remunerated labourers or are public employees with permanent employment and social insurance.

---

2   For details concerning this employment profile that distinguishes ten different groups see Gertel (2018b)

Table 2: Economic Situation (2020/21) / Educational Background

	Low	Medium	High	University	All
Very good	0	0	0	5	1
Good	14	22	31	36	24
Bad	28	37	36	46	37
Very bad	58	41	33	14	39
	(71) 100	(78) 100	(42) 100	(44) 100	100

Note: All numbers are given in percent. Numbers in brackets represent individual cases (n= 238). 'Low' equals no formal to primary education; 'Medium' represents intermediate or secondary school); and 'High' comprises baccalaureate and technical diploma, while the last group are people with a university degree.

Table 3: Current Living Situation / Age Group

	Distribution (%)	Young	Middle	Old	Has children
Living with parents (same household)	31	56	36	13	1
Living together with parents in one house (own household)	10	8	14	9	38
Living with own family (without parents)	39	8	36	61	93
Living alone	10	8	4	15	42
Living in a shared apartment (e.g. with friends)	7	16	8	1	12
Other	3	5	3	2	14

Note: All numbers in percent. 'Young' = less than 30 years; 'Middle' = between 30 and 39; 'Old' = 40 years and older. The category 'Has children' (46% on average) refers to each group of the six different living situations; the column percentage is hence meaningless and is not adding up to 100 percent.

Life and work situations changed for most people during the Covid-19 pandemic, sometimes dramatically. The following statements from interviewees illustrate the spectrum of experience, ordered by the of severity of being affected by the pandemic:

Samir, 20 years old, completed primary school and lives with his parents in Sidi Bouzid. He sells petrol, smuggled from Algeria and describes his work and the effects of the pandemic:

> Although the boss makes a lot of money, workers like myself are not getting anything; we are gaining fatigue, dirt and the smell of gasoline and insults from the boss. I unload the goods coming from the borders through Kasserine. I bring the goods to the

garage and I fill up the gasoline for the customers. It is such dangerous work, especially in summer, because the gasoline is not secured and it can self-ignite at any moment. This happened in 2015, the garage burned down because of an ignition in the petrol containers. The Corona virus did not affect our work. We work day and night during summer and winter because our boss knows some officials.

Fatima from Nabeul is 64 years old and married. She has no formal education and has worked as a home-baker for 15 years:

> I bake barley and wheat bread (*tabuna*). It is exhausting work, especially during the hot summer days, but I do not have any other choice. During Covid, honestly, I continued working as usual, because I work at home, no one bothers me and I do not have contact with people. But for some days I did not work because the flour was not available in the shops and the quantity, I had was not sufficient, so I left it for my family.

Souhair, 33, is single, completed secondary school and works as a dental assistant. She lives together with her parents in Hawaria and emphasises:

> I like this job. I clean the clinic, sanitise the materials and prepare everything for the doctor. I organise the appointments for the doctor and I am responsible for the phone. During Covid, I continued working as usual. I got the same salary, but I had more working hours, because I had to sanitise the clinic and the reception room more intensely.

Mona, 40 years old, completed primary school and lives in Ariana in Greater Tunis. She is divorced with two children, and has worked as hairdresser for 20 years:

> Before the coronavirus, we did not stop working but since the pandemic women do not come as frequently to the salon as before. This is why we closed for a long period; it was also because of the shrinking number of weddings. Brides give me extra money in normal times to do them in stunning makeup and some women give me extra money to serve them before others, especially when they are busy or they have a private party. My work is so tiring, especially in summer: it is the season of weddings. We work all day. I am standing up and I go back home with swollen legs. Currently, we work, but it is different, we do not have brides, we have just normal clients, they are workers or housewives. The coronavirus affected us but we keep working, because women want to be beautiful and sometimes, they want to change their looks.

Saba, from the opening quote, holds a university degree. She also lives with her parents in Tunis and has a written contract for her work as accountant. She states:

> The virus has had effects on many people. During Covid only guards continued to work. Personally, I also continued to work from my house online, and I received my salary. But when people did not come to work the boss cut missing labour input from the salary. In general, the virus affected our business, the number of customers decreased, and we could not export olive oil during the quarantine period.

Salwa is 24 years old, single, is also a university graduate and just started her job as laboratory technician. She lives with her family in Ben Gardane at the Libyan border:

> I work in a medical laboratory, where I take blood tests. Covid is affecting my work so much. I live in fear from the moment I go out of my home until I go back. I wear a mask all day, I do not take it off – I am afraid of infection or infecting my mother. The workload has increased and people do more analysis: they hallucinate [...] but my salary is the same.

Imad, the fishmonger from Nabeul whom we also know from the opening quote, completed secondary school. He emphasises:

> During the Covid pandemic my work decreased about 90 percent. The coronavirus affected the work a lot: we lost money. Everything has changed. I didn't get paid – some of my customers have not paid to date. They could not find the money to pay me, even though I know they are honest and like to pay me. Of course, I also wasn't able to pay some people like the porters either, but it's not a huge amount. In our business, the people most affected by the pandemic are the middlemen [like me]. They are exposed. They are working, but they have not received any money during this time and have not been able to secure their livelihood. It is the same: they sell goods and get no money. They are, I think, the most affected. I can say that my work has decreased a lot. I used to work every day, but now I only work about 4 to 7 days a month.

Hussain 43 years old from Hammamet also completed secondary school and works as a taxi driver:

> I am married and I have two kids. It is acceptable work, but it is so tiring and the income is limited. Indeed, I am suffering. I work the whole day to earn 20 Dinar [about 6.5 Euro in 2020]. Covid affected our work negatively. My income decreased to half. Some taxi drivers even lost their work because some owners of the taxis decided to work themselves in this critical period because they needed the money and cannot pay drivers. We live in a crisis; there are no tourists, and just few customers who still work in the factories.

Muhammad, 37 years old, single, who lives together with his parents, completed primary school and works as a daily worker in construction, states:

> I work to live, no more no less. It is so exhausting. When I work I eat, when I don't work I don't eat. The coronavirus destroyed us, may God protect us... I am always in need of money and there is barely any work. I may work for a day and don't find work for a week.

Aside from emotional strain, the economic impact of the Covid-19 pandemic on those in employment was also quite unequal: Those engaging in strategic parts of the economy, such as baking bread, acting in the medical or pharmaceutical sector or doing business in food provisioning, were sometimes not affected at all. Others have been severely affected and had to stop working, while still another group could continue work, but suffered from income losses (c.f. Gertel/Kreuer 2021; Gertel et al. 2024c). The two graduates have had different experiences: Saba worked in a safe space at home on the internet during the pandemic, while Salwa was responsible for blood tests in a laboratory. She lived in fear of catching the virus or spreading it within the family.

In order to situate these personal statements in a larger social context we asked the interviewees to assess the recent economic situation of their families. Only one quarter consider it as 'good' or 'very good', while three quarters see it as 'bad' or even 'very bad' (Table 4), reflecting the problematic situation of work and life during the first year of the Covid-19-pandemic.

This contrasts with their assessment concerning the economic situation in the pre-pandemic era, a year earlier. Then, 58 percent considered their situation as good or very good, while only 42 percent classified it as bad or very bad. Relating the two moments in time, the category 'very bad' experienced, by far, the largest increase. Based on this dramatic shift, revealing the economic insecurity the interviewees faced during the first year of the Covid-19 pandemic, we differentiate three groups of vulnerability (Table 5): 'Resilient' are the ones whose economic situation has been good or very good in the past and did not change in Covid-19 times; 25 percent are in this group. From the interviewees quoted above only Souhair, the dental assistant, belongs in this group. 'Poor' are all those whose economic situation has been bad or very bad and also did not change during the pandemic – this is the case for Samir who sells smuggled petroleum and for Fatima who bakes bread for the community; this group accounts for 42 percent. 'Exposed', in contrast, are the ones whose economic situation changed during the pandemic into bad or very bad – affecting 33 percent of the sample population, including the two graduates Saba and Salwa. Imad, the fishmonger, also belongs to this group. Not a single person of the entire sample experienced a change to better economic conditions during the Covid-19 pandemic. In addition, there is a clear gendering of insecurity: the 'poor' are mostly male, and the 'exposed' are mostly female, although the resilient group has an almost balanced gender distribution (Table 5).

If the sample groups are compared in terms of their formal educational qualifications, it can be seen that university graduates have the largest proportion of resilient people (41%), only few are poor (23%) and about one-third is part of the exposed group (36%). The largest share of the poor is found among those with low formal education (66%), while the highest share of the exposed is among those with high educational background (48%) (Table 6).

Economic consequences from the Covid-19 pandemic are thus group specific and varied: During the first year of the pandemic the volume of work decreased for almost all workforces, projects became postponed, jobs were lost, and during shutdown and quarantine in spring and summer 2020 some even experienced a complete interruption of their work for months – while remote work, particularly for the more educated, started to become increasingly established (Gertel et al. 2024c).

Table 4: Economic Situation: Before and During Covid-19

	Before Covid-19 2019/20	During Covid-19 2020/21	Change
Very good	3	1	-2
Good	55	24	-31
Bad	35	36	+1
Very bad	7	39	+32
	100	100	

All numbers in percent (n= 240).

Table 5: Vulnerability – New Economic Situation with Covid-19 Pandemic

	All (%)	Gender: f/m (n = 66 / 174)
Resilient	25	29 / 24
Poor	42	26 / 48
Exposed	33	46 / 28
	100	100 / 100

Note: Vulnerability is not the same as poverty. Vulnerable groups are defined as follows: 'Resilient' = economic situation was and is good and very good, before and during Covid-19 pandemic; 'Poor' = economic situation was and is bad and very bad, and thus did not change. 'Exposed' = economic situation changed under the Covid-19 pandemic into bad and very bad.

Table 6: Vulnerability / Education

		Education			
	Share	Low	Medium	High	University
Exposed	32	20	33	48	36
Poor	42	66	45	21	23
Resilient	25	14	22	31	41
	100	100	100	100	100

All numbers in percent (n= 240).

Even in this exposed situation during the pandemic, although their work was insecure or uncertain, interviewees did not use the notion of informal economy to describe it. For them the idea of an informal economy remains a foreign, often unknown concept. Only so-called experts or academics apply it. While the notion of 'informality' is important for the state, it is very often of no meaning for people living in poverty or insecurity (for a different perception among graduate women, see Garraoui, this volume). Is this than an expression of a missing 'right to narrate' (Spivak 1988)? Things are not that easy. These people can express and explain their economic situation, but are they able to shape the discourse about (informal) economies, if the state is the main obligatory passage point (Callon 1986), that mediates and – to a specific extent – controls interactions and discourses? The absence of the concept of informal economies in people's navigation of their livelihoods combines, moreover, with the ambivalent representation of the 'informal economy' by the ILO: coined as an important sector, inevitable for growth on the one hand, while related businesses are portrayed on the other hand as small or insignificant. The performative power to put models into practice therefore lies more with scientists, 'development experts' or public administrators than with workers. The practices necessary to navigate between registered and unregistered, legal and illegal activities, for enterprises, such as laboratories (where Salwa works), or export companies (employing people like Saba), include employing workers with the necessary qualifications. But these navigational practices are invisible in dualistic concepts. How fully the latter produce 'new geographies that decentre the sites of wealth accumulation' (Amri, this volume, page 35) is an interesting question for further research. In asymmetric economies however, exploitation and accumulation are deeply enmeshed in a multitude of ways.

What kind of structural insecurities are thus inscribed in the working conditions that increase the risk of economic vulnerability? In order to approach this question, we inquired three aspects: the discontinuity of work (e.g. temporary work opportunities and times without paid work), variability of payment (e.g. income is not always paid for the work carried out), and fluctuating income stability (e.g. shifting amounts, depending on work and salary conditions). The empirical findings reveal two trends: on the one hand insecurity grows when discontinuity of work, variability of payment and income instability increase. On the other hand, the insecurity of working conditions also grows with a decreasing educational level, from university graduates to those with no or only primary education (cf. Table 7).

These conditions become manifest as uncertainty in everyday life, rendering the livelihoods of the most exposed groups even more insecure and making planned consumption extremely difficult. University graduates most frequently enjoy stable working conditions, while serious exposure is often inscribed into the lives of the less educated. For them the flexibility to adapt to changing conditions is no longer sufficient; it has reached its limit, as access to resources that make action possible in the first place is constrained by their lack of labour income. These uncertainties unfold independently, but sometimes of course also as a result of crises such as the pandemic.

In order to contextualise these conditions and to enable comparisons between different labour situations, we relate these assessments on asymmetric economies to the concept of decent work, as promoted by the International Labour Office (cf. ILO 2024). Respondents had to assess seven statements from the ILO repertoire on a scale from 1 ('I do not agree') to 5 ('I fully agree'), placing 3 as arithmetic mean with the wording of 'so-so', while 2 equals the expression 'I somewhat disagree' and 4 'I somewhat agree'. The average overall scores in the sample range between 1.7 and 3.3 points, depending on the statement (Table 8).

Table 7: Discontinuous and Variable Work / Education
'What kind of remunerated work are you doing now in your current job? Please check the three ticks: work continuity, income continuity and income stability'

	Low	Medium	High	University	All
Discontinuous work	59	32	33	14	37
Fluctuating payment	73	42	33	34	48
Variable income	85	71	57	34	66
Stable working conditions	**13**	**28**	**40**	**59**	**31**
Extremely exposed	63	45	40	33	50

Note: All figures are percentages and represent answers with 'Yes'. 'Stable working conditions' (displayed in bold) represent situation when none of three aspects of insecurity (work, payment, income) is discontinuous or variable, while 'Extremely exposed' stands for situations when all three aspects of insecurity apply; they are fluctuating, variable or discontinuous (n = 235).

Table 8: Decent Work / Educational Background

	Low	Medium	High	Uni	All
I feel that I am protected if I become unemployed (insurance, benefits, programmes, etc.).	1.7	1.5	1.9	1.7	1.7
I think I have opportunities to advance professionally (promotions, skills, etc.).	1.8	2.2	2.6	2.5	2.2
My work schedule – including working hours, obligations and required flexibility – allows me to manage my life well.	2.8	2.5	2.9	2.6	2.7
What I earn through my work allows me to live my life with dignity and independence.	2.7	2.8	3.3	2.7	2.8
My work is not exposing me to dangerous situations: I feel that my health and my safety are not threatened.	2.5	2.5	3.1	3.2	2.8
My work contributes to my personal and professional fulfilment.	2.5	2.7	3.1	2.8	2.8
I am free to think and express my opinions about my work.	3.1	3.3	3.5	3.3	3.3
n	(71)	(78)	(42)	(44)	(235)

All numbers represent averages resulting from a scale between one and five (1 = 'I do not agree': 5 = 'I fully agree'); Numbers in brackets represent the quantity of individual cases.

Obviously, statements with an average score below 3 points are positioned between the meaning 'I do not agree' and 'so-so'; thus, indicating a structural vulnerability of the work context. The totality of answers reveals the different importance of protection and exposure concerning labour conditions: The highest exposure starts with inadequate protection against unemployment (1.7), followed by missing opportunities to advance professionally (2.2) and a rather unsatisfactory work-life balance (2.7). This is followed by the still mediocre relation between income and a life of dignity and independence (2.8), and also relates to the exposure to dangerous conditions (2.8) and the contribution of work to personal and professional fulfilment (2.8). Being able to freely express personal opinions however, gets the highest score (3.3).

Juxtaposing university graduates to other groups of the sample it becomes clear that they do not always achieve the highest score and do not even reach the average standards for decent work in most categories. Their lowest score relates to the protection against unemployment (1.7) and equals the average of the sample. Four other scores range between 2.5 and 2.8 points, which means that in all cases they lag behind the group with the second-highest level of education concerning their assessment of professional advancement, their workload, their balance between income and a life in dignity, as well as the contribution of work to professional fulfilment. The answers to two other statements surpass the imagined arithmetic average of three points: University graduates achieve the highest score of the sample only for one statement, namely, concerning their non-exposure to dangerous situations (3.2). Still higher is their assessment of being able to express their personal opinions freely (3.3); however, even here they come second after those with baccalaureate or a technical diploma. If all seven statements are summarised (i.e. as average of means), the previous picture is confirmed: all four educational groups achieve only scores below the mean value of three points (low = 2.4, medium = 2.5, high = 2.9, and university graduates = 2.7 points; Table 9).

Decent work conditions are thus far from being achieved, and graduates only come in second place. From a gender perspective women assess their working conditions as better (3.1) than men (2.4) – which opens up new questions for further research.

After analysing the significance of the Covid-19 crisis for professional activity, discussing labour related insecurities and highlighting the aspects of decent work, we will address the required skills for different occupations. We opted to ask the interviewees to describe the necessary qualifications of a potential person who would replace them at their workplace. This approach was chosen to better understand the structure of skills, as well as to uncover hidden evaluations of the necessary competencies and the appreciation or frustration towards different aspects of their occupation. By the following descriptions, we aim to provide some insights into the abilities and strengths deemed essential for performing their job (see also Chebbi, investigating the disenfranchised working conditions of waste collectors in Tunis; Parikh for Sub-Saharan Africans in Greater Tunis, and Zuntz et al. for Syrians working in Tunisia, all this volume). The statements disclose both accounts of the required skills as well as challenging attributes of their own working profile. We will encounter some familiar and some new interviewees.

Table 9: Decent Work Index / Education

	Female	Male	All
Low	2.8	2.3	2.4
Medium	a 3.1	2.4	2.5
High	b 3.7	2.7	2.9
University	3.0	2.5	2.7
All	3.1	2.4	2.6

Note: The index is calculated by unifying the individual averages of the seven statements in Table 8 (n=235). (a) represents only 8 cases, (b) represents 11 cases, all other groups represent 20 and more cases.

Fatima from Nabeul, who bakes bread, is convinced:

> This work does not require any qualification. The only thing she [the imagined replacement, JG] should know is how to bake bread in the *Tabuna* and she has to bear the hot temperature coming from the *Tabuna*. Especially in summer, it is like baking in hell. Sometimes, I burn my hand. In this case she'll have to keep working. Personally, I got used to it – I no longer feel the pain when I burn my hands.

Knowing how to produce *Tabuna* needs, of course, a bundle of skills that were not identified or named by Fatima. To bear the hard-working conditions is another requirement – a challenge and a stressing factor. Hussain from Hammamet, who works as a taxi driver, assesses a possible replacement as follows:

> He should be an old man. I am talking seriously: he should be an old man who has no hope in this life and no engagements. This work means suffering. My wife also works, but she cannot help me because her salary is so low; but at least she has her pocket money. I think that a young man cannot work as a taxi driver. He should have some skills, but I believe that it will be unfair that a young man works as a taxi driver. He will harm himself – he should find another work with horizons, so he can satisfy his family. I do not advise any young man to work as taxi driver.

Also, Muhammad, the day labourer from Cap Bon, is sure:

> I cannot bring someone to work in my place because it is not stable work. This work requires someone who does not feel ashamed of work and who can bear fatigue.

Salwa from Ben Gardane, working as laboratory technician, emphasises:

> This work requires someone who is cheerful and patient [...]. Of course, the scientific degree is at the top of requirements, you cannot work in a lab without it. It is about people's lives: you should concentrate while you are doing your work.

Other interviewees complement the picture with their statements: Mona, secretary in a wood company in Madnine, emphasises, among other properties, the necessity of language skills:

> The person engaging in this job must be so patient, he must be quiet with customers and he must not show his feelings when he talks with them. It should be someone who is relaxed when he answers phone calls, and able to speak French. Also, mastery of computer skills is important in our work.

Hamadi from Tunis works as pharmacist and is convinced that hard training and the ability to pay attention are required key skills:

> I do not find the work difficult as I have had professional training for two years. The training was difficult because there are hundreds of names of treatments. It requires someone who has a good memory, who is focused and can read medical prescriptions. Most of the time the writing of doctors is not clear, but with practice I got used to it and I can understand it. It requires someone who pays attention and who can deal with customers: they are sick or elderly and they need special treatment. Also, he should be able to bear long working hours.

Said, who runs a mill for grinding spices and cattle feed in Sidi Bouzid, is very particular about an imagined replacement:

> This person should have work experience in a mill of two or three years. This work is a little bit risky. Anyhow, he should be hard working. And even if he has experience, I cannot leave him alone. When there is tough work that requires using the big machine, I have to work myself. I do not allow him to do it. The machine costs at least 4,500 TND [about 1,600 Euro], it was cheap at the time when I bought it, but now it is more expensive. Any mistake can damage the motor. Its handling does not require physical strength, but he should always read the parameters before turning the machine on. However, I am not educated, so how can I look for someone educated.

Yasser, an owner of a restaurant in Nabeul, is convinced:

> For a replacement: I cannot find a worker like me. It is impossible to find someone who works like the proprietor! But if I am obliged, I would look for someone who is clean and reliable; he should be cheerful, he should welcome clients with a smile, and he should provide good, quick service. Above all, he must be smart, this is more important than the food, both the worker and the food must be clean and neat. He should have a good appearance with a shaved beard and he must wear an apron; and, of course, he should have an idea about working in a restaurant.

The demands placed on people in their professional activities are varied and sometimes very specific, but in addition to individual requirements, they also have similar features. In order to better understand and characterise these features, we asked the workers about the special skills and general attitudes that are important and necessary to do their work (Table 10).

Table 10: Skills / Educational Background
'Which requirements are important for your job?'

	Low	Medium	High	Uni	All
Patience	8.6	8.3	8.4	8.9	8.5
Ability to concentrate	7.8	8.1	8.6	8.6	8.2
Moral commitment	7.2	8.4	8.2	8.8	8.1
Communicative abilities	7.2	8.1	8.3	9.0	8.0
Fast comprehension	6.9	7.8	8.0	8.6	7.7
Mental endurance	7.1	7.5	8.2	7.7	7.5
Physical endurance	8.6	8.0	7.1	5.6	7.5
Ability to solve problems	6.5	7.2	8.0	8.0	7.3
Strong faith	7.3	7.1	6.8	7.5	7.2
Physical strength	8.3	7.7	6.3	5.2	7.1
Calculative abilities	6.4	7.1	7.0	7.6	7.0
Able to obey orders	6.1	7.2	7.5	6.9	6.8
Well-groomed outfit	5.5	6.1	6.9	6.4	6.1
Read and write	3.9	5.3	6.7	8.9	5.8
Able to reflect on situations	4.5	5.6	6.1	6.4	5.5
Only men can do this job	6.3	6.6	4.7	2.7	5.3
Creativity	4.3	5.6	6.0	5.7	5.3
Pedagogical skills	2.8	4.6	5.8	7.8	4.9
Craftsmanship proficiency	5.2	5.3	5.5	3.0	4.8
Foreign languages	2.5	3.2	4.3	7.3	4.1
Imagination	3.1	3.7	4.6	4.9	3.9
IT skills	1.5	2.3	3.7	6.8	3.2
Being able to memorise information	2.8	2.3	2.9	5.6	3.2
Mechanical skills	2.7	3.3	2.7	1.9	2.7
Only women can do this job	3.1	2.4	1.9	2.3	2.5

Note: Numbers represent averages resulting from a scale between one and ten points (1 = 'Absolutely unimportant', 10 = 'Absolutely important').

From 25 aspects to be ranked between 1 ('absolutely unimportant') and 10 ('absolutely important') four skills stand out as being very important for all groups across their educational background: patience, the ability to concentrate, moral commitment, and communicative abilities – they achieve scores between 8.0 and 8.5 points. Among them patience is most important in the workplace. Seven other skills, ranging between 7.0 and 7.7 points, follow, namely: fast comprehension, mental and physical endurance, the ability to solve problems, strong faith, physical strength, and calculative abilities. Two further skills complement the first half of the 25 aspects: these are the ability to obey orders, and to wear a well-groomed outfit.

It is striking, however, that the four educational groups identify different skills as most important (Table 11).

For university graduates these are communicative abilities, while for the lowest educational group physical endurance ranks first, and for the two other groups moral commitment and the ability to concentrate stands out. Patience and also the ability to concentrate are shared by all groups and are among the top five required skills – sometimes, of course, taking different positions and with other scores. While communicative abilities are important for almost all, but is not rated by the lowest educational group, another friction between the four groups becomes visible when physical endurance, identified by the two lowest educational groups, is juxtaposed to moral commitment that is important for the two formally better educated groups – those with baccalaureate, technical diploma and university graduates. Cognitive, language and IT skills most frequently result from higher formal qualifications, while physical and mental endurance are associated with lower formal education and sometimes come along with the notion of masculinity (e.g. only men can do this work). Hard, sometimes dangerous work, and constant physical work combines with almost non-existent career prospects to make workers like taxi driver Hussain and day labourer Muhammad disappointed, hopeless and embittered.

From this point it is interesting to know, how prepared the interviewees had been for the demands and challenges of their jobs. We asked them about the situation, when they started with their recent work, whether the skills they had acquired in earlier times met the requirements and demands they were facing now.[3] While about one third of the university graduates (36%) were convinced that the skills they had acquired earlier did not match the requirements and demands of the recent job at all, this increases to 41 percent of the formally less educated and to 45 percent for the two other educational groups. Not the majority, but a fairly large group thus feel that they were not sufficiently qualified for the conditions and requirements of their new job. Subsequently, we investigated the strategies applied to acquire the missing skills (Table 12). To this end, employees most frequently asked experienced people and also stated that learning by doing is important to them – more than half of the entire sample pursued these strategies. Trailing far behind is online training, participation in workshops provided by associations, and reading books, while taking private lessons is only an option for a minority.

---

3   The full range of answer options (n = 235) is as follows: 1 = Not at all (42%); 2 = Very little (7%); 3 = Little (15%); 4 = So-so (7%); 5 = Much (10%); 6 = Very much (6%); 7 = Completely (15%).

Table 11: Five Key Skills / Educational Background

Low	Medium	High	Uni
Physical endurance (8.6)	Moral commitment (8.4)	Ability to concentrate (8.6)	Communicative skills (9.0)
Patience (8.6)	Patience (8.3)	Patience (8.4)	Patience (8.9)
Physical strength (8.3)	Communicative skills (8.1)	Communicative skills (8.3)	Moral commitment (8.8)
Ability to concentrate (7.8)	Ability to concentrate (8.1)	Mental endurance (8.2)	Fast comprehension (8.6)
Consolidated faith (7.3)	Physical endurance (8.0)	Moral commitment (8.2)	Ability to concentrate (8.6)

Note: Numbers represent averages resulting from a scale between one and ten points (1 = 'Absolutely unimportant', 10 = 'Absolutely important').

Table 12: Acquiring Missing Skills ('Yes') / Education

	Low	Medium	High	Uni	All
Asking experienced people	47	58	60	60	55
Learning by doing	44	55	60	55	52
Online training	3	10	17	21	11
Workshops by associations	4	5	14	21	9
Reading books	1	8	12	21	9
Taking private lessons	1	5	5	7	4

Note: All numbers in percent.

Even if the Tunisian state is the main obligatory passage point to reify the discourse about informality, these findings and the above statements reveal that the transfer of formal education, knowledge, and skills as preconditions for remunerated work are only to a very limited extent controlled by the state. Learning occurs directly, immediately and personally through learning by doing, from the advice of others and in changing face-to-face interactions. This is crucially important. But learning processes are increasingly also crossing and stretching beyond national boundaries: they are mobile and might be tied to migration experiences, encoded in travelling models of know-how, they also move in digital scapes and materialise as remote aspirations, shaping imagination, longing, resource access and become ultimately manifest in local livelihoods, including the chances of a decent life.

Finally, we thus asked the workers to assess their overall situation concerning life and work. A scale ranging from 1 (lowest satisfaction) to 10 (highest satisfaction) represents the answers to the question: 'How would you assess your own recent satisfaction with life?' Four observations are crucial: Generally speaking, satisfaction with life is very low, corresponding to the quite frequent negative experiences occurring during this first year of the pandemic. It scores only an average of 3.7 points in the sample (Table 13). Given that the arithmetic mean of the applied scale would be 5.5 points (1 point +10 points / 2), it is far below this average, ranging between the 'lowest satisfaction' (1 point) and 'So-so', as the textual representation of the arithmetic mean (5.5 points). Second, the better the economic self-assessment of the interviewees, the higher is the satisfaction with their own life. Gender differences are crucial however: Women rate their satisfaction with life higher than men – and also their economic situation. Thirdly, the comparison between one's own life and the outside world shows a more positive assessment of one's own situation. The societal picture becomes even more negative. The average for the sample is only 3.0 points for other people's life satisfaction. This difference between 3.7 and 3.0 points reveals that even in situations of misery, there might be a personal attitude of optimism – that means: others appear even worse off. Finally, the relation between educational background and life satisfaction shows a positive trend from those with a low educational background (up to primary school) to a high educational background (baccalaureate or a technical diploma). However, university graduates are slightly less satisfied with their lives than the group with a 'high' educational background. Again, there are gender differences to observe. While a clear trend can be seen among male employees, it is women who generally rate their satisfaction with their own lives higher than men, but at the same time their assessment reveals a large gap of satisfaction between those with a high level of education compared to university graduates.

From life satisfaction we finally come to the meaning of work (Table 14). The answers to the question 'Do you like this job?' reveal a changing trend. In comparison to life satisfaction, the assessment of work is far more positive; the difference makes up two score points. The majority of working people have rather positive associations with their work, despite or precisely because of the Covid-19 pandemic. About 37 percent say that they like their job either 'a lot', 'very much' or 'absolutely'. A further 26 percent position themselves in the middle range of the answer options, responding 'so-so'. So, almost two thirds are very satisfied or at least are not dissatisfied with their work.

A further insight indicates that job satisfaction varies with educational attainment. The degree of satisfaction towards one's own occupation grows slightly with increasing educational level – with the exception of the university graduates. Again, gender differences also matter. While male respondents have much the same appreciation of their work across different educational backgrounds, women's assessment is more pronounced, achieving the highest score again in the group with a 'high' formal education, which underlines the findings of Garraoui's work (this volume).

Table 13: Satisfaction with Life (Other People/Own) / Economic Situation (2020/21)

	Other people	Own	Cases
Very good	–	–	2
Good	3.3	5.0	58
Bad	3.1	3.6	87
Very bad	2.6	2.9	92
	3.0	3.7	239

Note: Numbers represent averages resulting from a scale between one and ten points (1 = 'Lowest satisfaction', 10 = 'Highest satisfaction'). The last column represents the number of individual cases (n = 239).

Table 14: Satisfaction with Job and Life / Education

	Job	Life	Job: f/m	Life: f/m
Low	(5.9) 4.1	3.1	(6.1)/(5.7)	3.3/3.1
Medium	(5.6) 3.9	3.5	(5.1)/(5.7)	4.3/3.5
High	(6.3) 4.4	4.3	(8.0)/(5.7)	5.6/3.8
University	(6.0) 4.2	4.1	(6.6)/(5.4)	4.1/4.1
All	(5.9) 4.1	3.7	(6.6)/(5.7)	4.1/3.5

Note: f = female, m = male. Two different scales are at work: for 'Job', the given numbers in brackets (means) are not original data; they have been adjusted. In order to be able to numerically compare the two spheres, satisfaction with job and life, the different answer options have been standardised. Answer options to the question 'Do you like this work' can range from 1 = 'Not at all' to 7 = 'Absolutely', while answers related to the satisfaction with life range from 1 = 'Lowest satisfaction' to 10 = 'Highest satisfaction'. To adjust the numerical means from seven to ten maximal points, these numbers for Jobs have been multiplied by the factor 1.429.

Conclusion

In this chapter on asymmetric economies, we offer an alternative reading to conventional economic studies in order to challenge simplistic analytical dichotomies, such as those between state and economy or between formal and informal labour. The ontological use of these dichotomies remains opaque: it oscillates between (theoretical) models and (everyday) practices. Conceptually, asymmetrical exchange processes are not based on an assumed equilibrium, but produce winners and losers – as, for example, the accumulation of financial capital and other resources by a very few (such as in split second billion-dollar transactions), while simultaneously producing persistent livelihood crises for large sections of society. Freedom, dignity and the safeguarding of basic needs, a central demand of the revolutions in North Africa, are therefore still to be achieved. Tunisia is a showcase for the emergence of asymmetric economies. The superimposition of local structures by the capitalist economy and the expansion of asymmetrical exchange processes, enforced during the colonial era, fostered – according to Santos (1979) argument – the integration of the smallest local areas and units of reproduction (such as households) into the global exchange system. This manifested itself over time in a polarisation of spatial and social structures and perpetuated poverty even in the most dynamic centres of growth.

Building on this starting point and using the concept of diverse economies as an empirically driven bottom-up perspective, we investigate the meaning of remunerated work, based on the considerations of situated knowledge (Haraway 1988), that all knowledge is influenced by the specific material, social, and cultural contexts in which it is produced. We juxtapose the understanding of the International Labour Office (ILO) with our fieldwork data in order to show that everyday local economic practices matter ontologically. This focus does not allow short-sighted classificatory assumptions, such as the notion of the 'informal economy' to be applied. The latter has rather become a catch-all category, using data of unclear quality, that is often presented as being without alternative, while also in the Tunisian case it is reifying the image of a national economy, based on well-defined boundaries. But neither the 'informal' sector nor the 'informal' economy translates from a concept or a proxy model easily into practices – where, for example, does the informal start and where does it stop? Does one work 'in' the informal sector? Economic activities never emerge in isolation; they are highly enmeshed with and result from social relations, they are driven by emotions (Zelizer 2005), and are articulated with actions and developments in and of institutions operating beyond the local. Capitalism shifts borders – constantly.

We therefore address the importance of work under conditions of insecure and uncertain livelihoods, revealing individual entry conditions to remunerated labour, its features, properties and consequences. The data underline that the Covid-19-pandemic have had a dramatic effect on income earners who engage in asymmetric economies – about three quarters assess their families' situation as bad or even very bad. This combines with structural insecurities of working conditions. They become manifest in the uncertainty of everyday life, rendering the livelihoods of the most exposed groups even more fragmented and making precautionary actions, and even basic tasks, such as obtaining enough to eat, extremely difficult. No longer is the flexibility to adapt to changing conditions enough, as low income means restrict access to sufficient resources. Educational backgrounds do make a difference: While university graduates most frequently enjoy stable working conditions, the less educated, and particularly those with no or a very low level of school qualifications, are seriously exposed to risks in their working lives, such as the discontinuity of work, variability of payment and fluctuating income stability. This fits with the overall picture of decent working conditions for any in the sample being far from achieved. These findings also relate to the skills acquired informally, but also delineate the human capital of workers. Capabilities and opportunities in life are asymmetrically distributed, even within this group of interviewed people engaging in asymmetric economies. Cognitive skills, language and IT knowledge are often the result of higher formal qualifications, they contrast with skills like physical and mental endurance, frequently associated with masculinity, and lower formal education. When the two areas of formal education and personal skills are negatively linked, for example, when low formal education is associated with hard, physical work, exposure to dangers and limited promotion opportunities, this fosters low aspirations, disappointment, hopelessness and bitterness. In line with these findings, life satisfaction is generally very low, particularly driven, of course, also by the Covid-19 pandemic. Work remains, despite everything, important for identity and positive self-narration – work is often highly regarded, and is seen as offering options for the future. In contrast, technocratic top-down narrations of economy with simple models and empty catchwords, forge a disastrously narrow picture of knowledge, that may lead to devasting political or economic decisions.

Acknowledgement

We are grateful to the ACCESS program, the African Centre for Career Enhancement and Skills Support (https://access-centre.org), organized by Leipzig University, that facilitated this study. It is financed by the EXCEED Programme of the German Academic Exchange Service (DAAD). The study covers six African countries, including Tunisia. It was initiated and coordinated by Jörg Gertel and Enrica Audano, but from the very beginning this was a co-productive project involving the cooperation of many people. In Leipzig, as well from the two authors, David Kreuer and Christel Eissner contributed to develop the questionnaire, while in Tunisia we would like to thank particularly Karim Mnasri, Sawsen Ben Moussa and Malek Houri for conducting the fieldwork and preparing the data. Without the organisational input of Hamadi Tizzaoui, our partner from Tunis University, this study would not have been possible

Tunisian Women in the Labour Market

Thouraya Garraoui

> HANAN: 'Did you know that the women we celebrate on Women's Day are in fact not the same as the women in the workforce'?
>
> Interview with Hanan in Tunis (October 2021)

HANAN'S statement reveals a key dilemma of identity construction for Tunisian women: On the one hand, the positive public image of 'the ideal woman' is that of an educated and employed (upper-class) woman, on the other hand the reality of everyday experiences in the recent context of labour market inequalities and insecurities belies this. This double meaning reflects the situation of Tunisian women in the labour market – it has long been subject to discussion. Since gaining independence from French colonisation in 1956, successive Tunisian governments have passed laws in support of women's rights. They helped form a brilliant picture of the Tunisian woman. She is seen as an ideal representation of free, educated, and successful women in the MENA region. This ideal woman is however a mere image – a made-up creation, a public face for the world. As a symbol for all Tunisian women, she – the constructed ideal type – is represented in the state' reports and publications, and used as a reference point to demonstrate Tunisia's participation in 'modern development'. However, this is only half of the story, because there is also another reality – the local livelihoods of women struggling to make ends meet in everyday life. In these cases, Tunisian women are facing various troubles; increasingly so as female job opportunities and participation in the labour market continue to be marginalised, underpaid, and misrepresented – especially after the events of the Arab Spring in Tunisia, 2011 (Assad et al. 2017). The often precarious situation of females active in the labour market in Tunisia mirrors the deteriorating socio-economic conditions following the revolution. A multidimensional crisis has caused a shortage of resources, impacting livelihoods, a rise in social tensions, and a lack of security and support, as indicated in the introduction of this book. The powerful members of society exert control over resources and mobilise their powers to dominate marginalised groups, including working women, leading to widening inequalities and compelling them to experience forced mobility or immobility, depending on their aspirations and abilities.

Based on the stories of five young women, all of working age, this chapter aims to display and analyse the everyday experiences, challenges, and sufferings of females in the Tunisian labour market. Their stories represent the situation of both single and married graduates, working in different segments of the economy. Occupation in the public economy – or in any organisation owned and operated by the government – is seen as a preferred choice for women due to its socio-economic security, while employment in the private economy is often considered less secure, but still ranked higher than engaging in the informal sector, which offers the least secure and sometimes illegal working conditions. But does this picture hold true in reality?

Tunisia's weak economic development since the revolution in 2011 reflects the deepening inequalities between genders and between females themselves. The classic labour theory often distinguishes only between unpaid (domestic) activities for women and paid work for men (cf. Darmangeot 2016), while Marxist inspired feminists use the sexual division of labour theory and the economic class-approaches to show how females are more disadvantaged than the males of any class. The intersection of gender based social networks with other social networks reveals however female exploitation by both their families and the capitalist regime (cf. Galerand/Kergoat 2014). I apply however a different approach. The 'Diverse Economies' (Gibson-Graham 2008) perspective allows me to capture the stratification of workforce in asymmetric economies (Gertel/Audano, this volume). Based on these reflections and through semi-structured interviews, this chapter analyses the experiences of the five women alongside their working biography.

I start my argument with a methodological introduction in order to identify and position the five women in the larger field of unemployed graduates in Tunisia. It is only by unveiling their social position that we are able to know for whom they speak. I will then address their identity construction as Tunisian women. This type of newly educated woman is expected to leave 'the family home' and start looking out for herself, using education as a tool for social upward mobility via inclusion in the labour market and aspiring to improved economic independence. Next, I will follow the women's paths from their graduation up until the moment of the interviews, in order to understand their struggles and continuous efforts for repositioning in the labour market. Finally, I will tackle the question of gender discrimination. In reconstructing the trajectory of their job seeking journeys and their working experiences, I will reveal the mechanism of marginalisation, of systematic exclusion, and the suffering of females in the labour market, regardless of the nature of their jobs. These women face various forms of inequality that hinder their ability to access resources and secure their livelihood. This, in turn, impacts their capabilities, aspirations, imaginations, and how they shape their identities.

A note on the methodology: This chapter is one outcome of my research as a doctoral student at the University of Leipzig (2020–2023), where I investigated the situation of unemployed graduates in Tunisia. The following findings are mainly based on qualitative methods. Five in-depth interviews were conducted in order to collect labour market experiences of women, representing university graduates from the middle and lower classes. This mini-sample is composed first of Fatima and Amna, who were my ex-roommates in Greater Tunis from October 2018 to June 2019. Between the 8th and 10th of June 2022, I conducted semi-structured virtual interviews with them through a Messenger App. The sample also includes Amira, Hanan, and Asmaa, who I met during a protest march organised by the Unemployed Graduates (*diplômés chômeurs*) in Tunisia. With them, I conducted semi-structured, face-to-face interviews in different public places in Tunis during October 2021. These interviews were recorded via smartphone. All interviews were held in Arabic, in the Tunisian dialect. The use of the local language made my interviewees feel more comfortable as all were able to express themselves fluently. To interpret the findings, I applied a content analysis. Each interview was at first separately scrutinised before I used a comparative analysis to identify similarities and differences. Then, the quotes were selected, organised, and contextualised according to the goals of the chapter. I also collected statistical data between September 2019 and June 2022 from the National Institute of Statistics website and library.

Official statistics can provide a meaningful foundation for situation-specific qualitative data. However, there are only a few indicators used in the reports released by Tunisia's National Institute of Statistics to help with identifying and characterising graduate women, who are active in the workforce. As a result, there is a void in the numerical representation of employed or unemployed female graduates by motherhood, marital, socioeconomic status, income or strata. For this reason, I use my own fieldwork data to classify and position the five women selected for this chapter within a statistical universe (Garraoui 2023). The quantitative part of my doctoral research was carried out in the summer of 2021. Between July and September, 360 university graduates living in Greater Tunis and aged between 24 and 44 years, including both women and men, were interviewed in 12 localities. This included 166 female graduates who comprise the reference to which I relate the five interviews. I chose to use their assessment of the economic position of the family in order to categorise women in the workforce. Accordingly, I divided the female interviewees into three economic categories (Table 1), showing that, on the one hand, most interviewed females see their families in a 'good' economic situation (53% for singles and 65% married). However, the notion of 'good' often means 'it barely works' – their livelihoods are exposed (Gertel 2018b). On the other hand, women originating from families with 'bad' economic situations constitute a minority in the sample, they amount to 19 percent for singles and 13 percent for married women. It is clear that this group lives in economic insecurity and often cannot plan ahead as uncertainty is omnipresent.

The position and status of the five interviewees are shown in Table 2 & 3. Three of them fall into the category of single females from families with a 'good' economic situation. A married woman from a 'good' economic household and a married woman from a poor background make up the remaining two interviewees.

At the time of writing, a considerable number of people in Tunisia assume that a woman's economic condition is based on the stability of her family or on her spouse's economic situation. This is reflected in the relative positions of the five women in society. Their economic situation is not solely dependent on their personal situation, but rather linked to their family's educational and financial resources (cf. Gertel 2018; Audano 2023). Two of the women interviewed do not have a job or a consistent source of income, but they assess their financial condition as okay and consider themselves to be in a rather good economic situation. Their reliance on the financial support of their family largely explains this. When compared to married women, single women who still live with their family of origin are less capable of contributing to the living costs. A female's responsibilities change in tandem with her marital status and the birth of children. Generally, her financial situation depends on the husbands' salaries, although women may contribute to the cost of living, often a result of her class position, revealing the mechanism of intersectionality (Braune 2018). Female's financial responsibilities grow especially after having children, depending, of course, on child-care obligations. Hanan's meagre wage as a salesperson in the private sector forces her to share household duties with her spouse. She, on the other hand, assesses her economic situation as poor and therefore implicitly her class position based on her husband's precarious financial status as well. Amna, a judge with a respectable salary, calculates the same way but with a different outcome. Amna reckons her financial state is neither good nor bad, but rather that it is quite good because of her husband's financial situation and her ability to utilise her own money for tasks after having had a child.

The five women's current professional situation is a result of their more or less successful transition from university to the workforce. They have all had different employment experiences that reflect the forced mobility from one job to another due to their hopes for a better future, their demanding jobs and their limited resources. These women are among numerous vulnerable social groups in Tunisia who face similar insecurities, including individuals involved in smuggling, irregular migrants, and workers in an unstable circular economy, as explored in subsequent chapters. How did the women begin their working lives? Fatima, for example, started working as a school teacher in 2016. However, she spent just one year using her academic qualifications as a secondary school teacher. She was sexually harassed by a parent and also by one of her secondary students, which paints a dramatic and unpleasant image of her work situation. Because of this, Fatima decided that she would always choose to work with young children as a teacher or as an animator. Amna first entered the workforce as a helper for an autistic student in a private primary school where she met Fatima. Before being recruited as a judge in the public sector, this work experience was regarded as a temporary job. Amira is a different case because she has not yet completed her transition from academics to the workforce. After 12 years of being unemployed (2011–2022), she is still without a job, she considers the lack of job offers, the expansion of corruption and the economic decline in Tunisia as the key reasons for her prolonged unemployment. Asmaa is a student at the Faculty of Human and Social Sciences of Tunis. During her summer vacation, she was employed as a photographer for a private business and currently, she is unemployed. Following graduation, Hanan finally worked repeatedly as a low-level labourer in factories and still works as a salesperson in different stores. Due to difficult working conditions, she has changed jobs many times and is still aspiring for a better job, which she hopes would be in the public sector. This job aspiration serves as her potential ticket to the upper class, where she imagines herself as the epitome of an ideal Tunisian woman, the same woman we celebrate on Women's Day.

Table 1: Marital Status and Families' Economic Situation of Females in Greater Tunis

Marital Status	Families' Economic Situation			
	Very Good	Good	Bad / Very Bad	All
Single	29	53	19	100
Married	22	65	13	100

Note: Answers in percentages. 'Bad' and 'Very Bad' are in the same category, as the latter consists only of two cases (n=166). Source: Garraoui (2023); Fieldwork 2021.

Table 2: Marital Status and Families' Economic Situation of the Interviewees

Economic Situation	Amna	Asmaa	Amira	Hanan	Fatima	All
Good => Single females	–	X	X	–	X	3
Good => Married females	X	–	–	–	–	1
Bad => Single females	–	–	–	–	–	0
Bad => Married females	–	–	–	X	–	1

Source: Fieldwork (2021–2022).

Table 3: Social Profile of Interviewees

Name	Age	Marital status	Class	Degree	Discipline	Graduation year	Employment situation	Economies
Amna	26	M	Mid	BA	Private law	2019	Judge	Public
Asmaa	24	S	Mid	BA	Geography	2019	Unemployed	–
Amira	37	S	Mid	BA	Private law	2011	Unemployed	–
Hanan	43	M	Low	Technician	Electricity	2002	Saleswoman	Private
Fatima	29	S	Mid	BA	History	2016	Teacher	Private

Source: Fieldwork 2021–2022. Note: The only two women with children are Amna and Hanan. Marital status: M=married, S=single. Class (Mid=middle, Low=lower) is based on self-assessment.

Identity Constructions of Women in the Labour Market

Hanan does not believe in a common identity for all Tunisian women and thus employs subjective criteria to construct a woman's identity. She distinguishes between different identities depending on women's perceptions of their economic class. According to her, a woman from an economically well-off class would always be working in good conditions and cannot be compared to a university graduate who is working in the private or informal sector. The portrayal of her perspective of 'the women we celebrate on Women's Day' is consistent with an ideal portrayal of a symbolic woman who has successfully graduated from university and is living a good life (i.e. originating from an upper class). This imagined person is, however, not the same one that, as an embodied human being, is participating in the labour market. This 'employed woman' may also be a university graduate, but she has to be considered as vulnerable and exposed to situations of unemployment and exploitation in the work place. Hanan sees herself as part of this often unrepresented category of women who work in the private economy and experience hard work conditions. This group of women suffers from a scarcity of resources that impacts their self-identification, especially when subjective elements are taken into account in shaping the identity of educated but poor women.

Fatima, contrary to her self-assessment of the economic situation of her family of origin, sees herself as a person that is suffering, exposed, and exploited. She distinguishes between exploited women who are working in the public sector and exploited women working in the private or informal sector, highlighting the exacerbated inequalities among active females depending on their employment circumstances. The marginalisation of women in the public sector might be expressed as obstacles or unjust treatment in her workplace, but she still considers this to be better than the alternative of being fired from work or disenfranchised in other kinds of ways. This displays how different levels of power – in terms of challenges and benefits – are unequally distributed between the females. Consequently, this reveals the social hierarchy where employed females working in the public economy are working under conditions of exploitation (Makinnon 1987), but are still in a better position when compared to the remainder of employed women, especially those working in the informal economy. Fatima frames this as: 'There is a difference between exploitation of a first kind, exploitation of a second kind, and exploitation of a third kind'. Notwithstanding the fact that existing laws support women's rights, women continue to face social obstacles and various aspects of discrimination in the labour market revealing their feelings of injustice, mistrust of laws, and rethinking the revolution goals from 2011 that led to unexpected contradictory results, as mentioned in the introduction of this volume. Since independence, Tunisian women are still expected to perform a great deal of unpaid work as maids in their families' homes and as married women in their households. A woman's main role is to become or be a housewife. The paid work is often still left to the men, who are considered to be the supreme authority in the family only because of their gender. For this reason, the importance of women is, depending on class and livelihood situation, often reduced to that of a housewife.

But a top-down transformation by the state has been underway for decades and the imagined 'ideal' woman was ascribed a key role to the modernisation of society. After political independence the most important innovation was the 'personal states code' which consists of a series of laws, proclaimed on the 13th of August, 1956 by order of Ali Bey of Tunis, which was then implemented on the 1st of January, 1957, with the aim to establish equality between men and women in several areas. As a result of this law Tunisian women have been given more freedom to work outside their household. They also benefitted from the abolishment of polygamy and raising of legal marriage age, and were able to better enhance their professional status thereafter. Taking care of household affairs had been replaced by educational achievement in some part. Consequently, females' illiteracy rates have decreased from 96 percent in 1965 to 26 percent in 2014 (INS 2014). Rising educational rates and new identity options increasingly helped Tunisian housewives transform into 'educated' housewives. These educated women simultaneously engaged in paid and unpaid activities. They also had to make sacrifices though: they had to organise the household and care for the husband and children, either by themselves or with the support of siblings and relatives, all while also working for money. This reveals the gap between political visions and juridical prescriptions on the one hand, and the complexities of the everyday reality on the other.

The theory on the sexual division of labour (Giguère et al. 2020) applies the terms 'capitalism', 'exploitation', and 'work conflicts' to explain male domination and asymmetrical power relations in work contexts. Too often the domestic work by women is not considered labour. Therefore, females are subjected to excessive exploitation, both at home and also in the work place. Amna, as mother and judge, is an expert in both law and family management and exemplifies this. She characterises employed Tunisian women as 'fighters' even if they work in the public economy: 'Being a woman in Tunisia means that you are a fighter between work, home, and child-rearing. Motherhood itself is a full-time job'. An opposite and rather male-dominated perspective is reflected in a Tunisian proverb that states 'A woman has only her house, whether she has been educated or not'. This reveals how a part of the Tunisian society still assesses and judges women, even after they have graduated. This perspective disparages educational achievements in comparison to the vision of being a housewife. Women with multiple roles are usually subject to misrepresentation and exploitation at the same time.

All five interviewees feel that, as college graduates, they have a responsibility to ensure the stability of the family's economic situation. This sense of obligation reflects temporarily expanded social reciprocity relationships. Their families have invested in their education because they consider a college degree as a promise for a secure future in the best case, and if nothing else, an investment to reduce uncertainty. Parents often save large portions of their money to fund the educational aspirations of their children's futures (Garraoui 2023). For example, Hanan is aware of the hard sacrifices her father, a poor farmer, made to enable her to go to university. He considered it the only way to improve his family's economic situation. However, the implementation of this idea dates back to before the 1990s, when the Tunisian state was still hiring university and secondary school graduates to work in the public sector. At that time, a university degree was considered the key to social advancement to a higher socioeconomic position. However, although the economic conditions have changed since then, Tunisian families still believe in this now out-dated social promise (ibid.). Women in particular, who continue to prefer permanent employment in the public sector, study hard to obtain a diploma, as they see this as a prerequisite for employment with the state and thus for realising a family dream. Amira expresses her sense of responsibility in supporting her family in saying:

> Even when I wanted to work in the private sector, it was not to earn my own income, but rather to support my father and mother who invested a lot of money for my education and I wanted to give them something back.

Similarly, Amna shares her experience before marriage: 'Yes, at that time my situation was not very bad, but I wanted to support myself and my family'. These female graduates are taking responsibilities and are ready for sacrifices in order to support their (extended) families, even at the expense of their wellbeing and livelihoods. This puts women under stress to become a 'super human-being' and that she has to accept sacrifices, 'more than she can handle', according to Fatima.

In conclusion, the stereotypical statements about women and their role in the labour market are hardly meaningful. The five Tunisian women reveal a spectrum of different identity positions. Despite individual socialisation, personal development, and different social careers, they experienced similar structures of exclusion and disregard that have shaped their experience and thinking, not to mention embodied imprints, such as from sexual harassment. Scott draws attention to this when she states that 'the social and the personal are imbricated in one another and that both are historically variable. The meanings of the categories of identity change and with them the possibilities for thinking the self' (Scott 1991: 795). Therefore, it is problematic to simplistically assume that social contexts, perspectives, and societal positions of women allow us to conceptualise a unified collective identity. The women portrayed may be united by the profile of former college graduates who face specific difficulties in the labour market due to their gender and economic class. Yet, despite similarities, they are also unequal. Some of them (temporarily) take on an identity of the suffering and exploited, while others, of the responsible and educated woman, may also have to make sacrifices.

Women's Discrimination in the Labour Market

The five women have different employment experiences to share. Based on her engagement in two different economic spheres, Amna reports on her lived inequalities. After a miserable experience in the informal economy, she got the opportunity to work in the public sector – and now believes that she is lucky, as she was able to upgrade her position. In her first job she worked as a caregiver of an autistic child, where she was hired by verbal agreement. The payment was low and the working conditions were not secured. She earned only 600 Dinars per month (about 178 Euro in November 2018) for six hours of work per day. She did not receive social insurance nor were vacation or employment rights granted to her. Now, she is working in the public sector as a judge and she receives a good salary, has legal work hours, and regulated vacation rights. But these benefits in the public sector do not compensate for the persisting fragility of working conditions. Amna expresses her feeling of being tired due to an ever-increasing workload, as the number of employees is not growing at the same pace as the number of expanding duties. She is entrusted with several tasks at the same time, which gives her the feeling that she cannot do justice to the tasks. As the stress increases and recovery time decreases, she begins to feel exploited.

Fatima and Hanan have also worked in different jobs. They describe their employment experiences similarly, even if there have been some differences. Both women keep changing jobs because they are subjected to bad employment conditions and suffer from a lack of financial resources. They share the experiences of working without contracts or social insurance and they were hired via oral contracts. To describe the position of an employee without a legal contract and social insurance Tunisians use the local term *taht hit* (under the wall). This term signifies that the employee is hidden, misrepresented, and working outside the boundaries of the legal workplace, thus lacking security. Both women have been exposed to exploitation and discrimination. However, Hanan was luckier than Fatima because she could quit her job when she felt insecure. Fatima, unfortunately, was, as we already know, subject of violence during her work as a secondary teacher in a private school. She has been sexually harassed many times just because of her gender. 'I also remember that I was physically and morally attacked when a woman tried to dig her nails into my eyes and used the worst kinds of profanity'. As we follow Fatima's daily experiences and delve into other cases presented in the following chapters, it becomes evident that mobility and workplace security pose significant challenges in Tunisia. These issues were particularly amplified during the post-revolutionary period, marked by heightened levels of violence, conflict, and social upheaval. Sadly, women were often on the receiving end of harassment and violence, highlighting the urgent need for change. Hanan refers to another issue: to the unequal choices women have in the labour market. She is convinced that the family's economic situation pre-defines female's inequalities in the labour market. She believes that women from low economic classes, who lack resources, are more exposed to exploitative working conditions in the informal economy. She illustrates her beliefs with this example:

> I know a woman, who has a master's degree, but she works as a cleaning lady in the commune. [...]. And she works for less than 200 Dinars (about 60 Euro in October 2021) a month. But why does she work? This woman continues working in the same job because she needs the money.

According to her understanding, women from well-off families would have options to look for alternatives, as they do not experience the same financial pressure. They can make choices, such as Asmaa, who preferred to continue her academic research after a miserable working experience in the informal economy. At the time when she had quit her despised job, her family was taking care of her study and life expenditures.

Women's inequalities in the labour market are also reflected in official unemployment statistics. The unemployment rates are unequally distributed between females according to the age groups: 74 percent of the female unemployment rate is 'produced' by women aged between 20 and 34 years (INS 2014, researcher's calculation). More precisely, the highest rate (33%) concerns women aged between 25 and 29 years, which represents a group of young adults in the transition period between education and a first job. Unemployment among these individuals mirrors the national trend of youth unemployment, highlighting a discrepancy between demographic changes and economic downturn. Ben Amor (2012) explains: 'This is linked in particular to non-integration or difficult integration rather than recruitment. Similarly, this unemployment is described as categorical, affecting graduates of higher education' (Ben Amor 2012: 6). When referring to the level of formal instruction, it is important to consider that female graduates are, indeed, the most affected by unemployment when compared to the rest of women who are of working age. In 2014, unemployed female graduates represented 44 percent of the total female labour force, which was the highest reported rate. Unemployment rates increase in parallel with the level of education. University female graduates are thus facing greater challenges in entering the labour market, which is more open towards non-qualified and often underpaid employees. This is particularly the case for female graduates in law, economy, and management, as they are the most affected by unemployment and gendered inequality. Their skills are not matched with the labour market requirements, which demand either non-qualified graduates for simple tasks like assembling and packaging, or graduates specialising in the usage of technologies and innovations.

Female university graduates spend long periods of time looking for jobs that match their qualifications (Observatoire National de l'Emploi et des Qualifications 2013).

> This situation shows the Tunisian paradox of graduate and non-graduate employment. Indeed, the relationship between the level of education and the unemployment rate has been transformed in favour of the non-graduates (Kthiri 2019: 9).

As a result, job seeking or unemployment periods are longer for female graduates, which subjects them to stressful psychological situations where they are the victims (cf. Bakari 2015). Fatima describes her situation with the following words: 'The most difficult experience of unemployment is the psychological damage and suffering that has made my whole life turbulent and unbalanced'. Moreover, female graduates often experience competition, envy, discrimination, and/or valorisation only because of their university degree. Their level of education becomes an indicator of the growing inequalities between women and men and between women themselves in the labour market. Hanan has been discriminated because of her university degree. She thinks that she was only fired from her job because her manager was envious that she was holding a higher educational degree. Fatima had the same impression when her female manager in the child-care school tried to devalue her efforts. Fatima reported that her non-graduate manager was envious of her educational level and that she assigned her cleaning tasks for that reason. The manager was also disparaging her work, blaming her, and systematically devaluing her results at the end of each month. Amna has also suffered from the behaviour of the school guard who was belittling her by using demeaning expressions. Moreover, her female colleagues were trying to degrade her efforts during the first period of the job. However, the treatment changed when they learned that she as a university graduate was waiting for a job as a judge.

> Their behaviour towards me changed only because they accidentally learned from one of my escort companions that I was waiting for my judgeship. The way they treated me

became the opposite and they started to flatter me, offering me help and even some services.

Amna's experience can be considered an exception on account of her university degree, and probably more so resulting from her employment perspective as a judge, which transformed her into an allegedly important person 'with influence'. This saved her from further discriminations.

In brief, this section highlights the unequally distributed structural inequalities between females in the labour market. The better positions are held by female graduates who come from well-off class positions and are working in the public economy, while females who have not graduated or come from lower classes often work in informal economies and are more likely to be exposed to marginalisation and discrimination from both male and female bosses as well as colleagues. These kinds of inequalities can be seen as partly responsible for the weakening of the female position in the work place.

Gender Inequalities in the Labour Market

Gender inequalities represent another aspect of labour market discrimination, as highlighted in the official statistics. Female labour participation is considered weak in comparison with the male rates. Both, the employed female population and the female activity rate in the labour market rose from 19 percent in 1975 to 28 percent in 2014. Simultaneously, the male rates decreased from 81 to 72 percent. This slight increase of the women's entry into paid labour is an outcome of the diversification of the economic fabric that offers more opportunities for female employment in different sectors. Bakari (2015) explains that the growth of female participation in the labour market is due to the expansion of the education, health, and service sectors. Changing mind-sets and the establishment of work codes have also contributed to this expansion. He further considers the demographic evolution during the 1990s as responsible for creating a stronger female labour demand.

Moreover, the on-going non-separation of entanglements between unpaid domestic activities and paid work has strengthened the male domination of labour (c.f. Giguère et al. 2020). Women accept unpaid work without sharing the responsibility with men equally. This has given a 'green light' that ultimately strengthened males' domination in economic activities and the related networks, which diminished female participation in the labour market as a result. On the one hand, unequal job creation privileges males (Observatoire National de l'Emploi et des Qualifications 2013). On the other hand, this is further compounded by the uneven regional distribution of job offers that are concentrated in urban and coastal areas; labour opportunities thus require spatial mobility. Because of social restrictions, females – predominately those from the lower classes and interior regions – are often hindered in moving to a city or to make a long commute to a workplace. This forced immobility makes women's integration into the labour market less likely to be achieved and they are exposed to unemployment or accept local jobs in the informal economy as a result (Asaad et al. 2017; Baccouche 2018).

According to Fatima's experiences, females are exposed to exploitation in the work place more often than males. They still face very bad working conditions sometimes, even with the establishment of the employment code. According to the public data, females are employed in different positions and economic sectors. Private employers often prefer to grant women a working opportunity only so as to facilitate easy and socially accepted mechanisms of exploitation. From the employer's perspective, recruiting a female means fewer costs. Low salaries, long working hours, and illegal working conditions are more frequently accepted by females than males. Fatima emphasises:

> These were difficult moments and I always wanted to overcome them. But I cannot receive the same conditions as men.

Speaking from personal experience, Asmaa addresses the question of the gender wage gap. She was working as a photographer in a private store in 2021. Next-door was a private library with four employees, one of whom was a woman. All the employees were responsible for receiving and organising materials. However, even though the female was doing the same sales operations as the men, she was paid less than them. Asmaa comments:

> She was in charge of selling things and worked like them. But they were getting 400 Dinars (about 140 Euro in August 2019), while she was only receiving 250 Dinars (about 75 Euro at the same period).

These examples reveal situations where employed women are exposed to gender discriminations. However, these inequalities in the labour market are not only affecting employed women, but they are also relevant for unemployed women. Official data confirm that more women than men are unemployed. Between 1975 and 2018 female unemployment rates increased from 11 to 23 percent (INS 2019), while male unemployment rates increased more slowly in roughly the same period, amounting to only 12 percent. This, once again, confirms the difficulties that women face in entering the labour market (cf. BIT 2015). There are also multiple periods of insecurity: Fatima as a university graduate has been jobless several times. She describes the impact:

> I experienced unemployment after graduation between May and September 2016. It was a bad experience when I remained for a period of time without work and income, especially in Tunis, due to pressures to pay rent, electricity, water, transport, food and all other related expenses. The psychological effects were very strong and depressing.

With these words, Fatima describes her experience of remaining unemployed for five months after graduating in 2016. She considers her periods of unemployment as the hardest times she ever faced. As a female living away from her family and trying to prove herself, she did not receive any support. But she faced the bad feelings bravely and managed a very stressful situation by herself.

Long-term unemployment (i.e. for more than three years) occurs more frequently for females (24%) when compared to males (18%) (INS 2014). This chiefly concerns unemployed female graduates. They stay unemployed for a long duration. According to the Observatoire National de l'Emploi et des Qualifications report (2013), about 39 percent of women are employed in sectors or activities that are completely outside of their specialties or training, in contrast with only 20 percent for men. Assad et al. highlight:

> Educated young women are therefore more likely to be 'trapped' by the opportunities available in their local labour markets. But it may not correspond to their educational qualifications (Asaad et al. 2017: 2).

When Fatima realised that she would not find employment in the public sector, she sought a permanent job in the private sector. However, most job opportunities in the private sector are in industry and agriculture and are more suitable for men or women without a university degree, as the working conditions are harsh and the work is poorly paid. Therefore, Fatima continued to look for work in education where her employment aspirations could be satisfied. This is why, she repeated many times, that the hardest challenge for her was the job-seeking journey: 'The difficulty here lies in the whole searching process'. Or: 'The most difficult thing is the journey to find work'. And: 'At the beginning of each year, the job seeking journey begins'. Females often look for employment opportunities that also correspond to their private situation. Their professional activities in these cases have to be complementary and should not interfere with the time reserved for domestic work. This can be achieved at the expense of the salary, time management, or other employment rights. This kind of complexity in everyday life is often not represented by labour theories or by official publications. This can be explained by the rigidity of capitalism and the lack of implementation of existing laws, combined with a public, male-dominated rhetoric that degrades and disciplines women in society in order to maintain traditional structures. So, are Tunisian women to be seen as victims or are they part of what is happening? Does the situation of women after the revolution reflect the general economic deterioration at the lowest end or was it the best that was possible under the given circumstances?

Conclusion

Since gaining its political independence, the Tunisian government has taken significant steps towards improving the status of women in the country and recognising their crucial role in building modern societies. These efforts have led to increased educational opportunities, greater participation in the workforce, and improved access to socio-economic and political rights for women. Despite these measures, women still face various forms of inequality, insecurity, sexism, patriarchal exploitation, and other deprivations in the labour market. These challenges are exacerbated by their disadvantaged socio-economic status, stemming from their limited access to resources and capabilities. The situation has further worsened during Tunisia's post-revolution phase. The country is grappling with economic decline, social conflicts, and political disturbances that disproportionately impact the society as a whole, but has a greater negative effect on women. The recent developments make it more challenging for women, particularly those from lower and middle-class backgrounds, to secure employment and access livelihood resources. They are particularly vulnerable to unemployment, discrimination, and exploitation, and often have to balance paid employment with domestic responsibilities, further adding to their already difficult circumstances. Under these conditions, women's aspirations develop into a demand for their basic rights as valuable, non-discriminatory participants in working life on an equal footing with men. To address this issue, the findings of the chapter, along with the sexual division of labour theory and employment theories, suggest a need to redefine the concept of work to encompass both paid work and household responsibilities, including care work. Additionally, it is crucial to restore the workforce as a source of innovation and productivity, regardless of gender. This requires revising employment regulations and norms in the labour market and workplaces to ensure gender equality and equal opportunities for women and men, as well as among women themselves. Moreover, it emphasises the significance of translating laws into practical actions and treating all women equally under the law, regardless of their backgrounds, particularly in the private and informal sectors. In these situations, work output and contributions should be the only criteria considered, rejecting any form of discrimination based on differences. To pave the way for a brighter future, I also recommend concentrating on improving the actual working and living conditions of women, rather than solely relying on the implementation of laws and policies on paper. By broadening the perception of free, educated, and empowered Tunisian women, we might seek to enhance opportunities for females across all backgrounds to achieve such status. This effort is aimed at empowering not only the privileged few but also marginalised Tunisian women in the workforce, with the goal of celebrating all Tunisian women as equals on Women's Day.

Acknowledgement

This work is based on the research supported by the ACCESS Network (African Centre for Career Enhancement and Skills Support; https://access-centre.org) and Leipzig University with the funding from DAAD and the Federal Ministry of Economic Development and Cooperation (BMZ).

A Political Economy of Borderscapes

Myriam Amri

A Triad to Set the Scene

First, a person. AICHA is seventy-two years old. She is short and walks upright despite a small hunch that has grown in the past few years. She recalls the border always as *qbal* (before). Before the border between Tunisia and Algeria closed for more than two years, from March 2020 to July 2022. Before the revolution of 2011. At other times 'before' refers to a period in the past few years when crossing and 'working the border' were easier. Aicha is a trafficker, though neither she nor anyone around her would refer to her as such. The term trafficker, or *knatri* (contraband trafficker) evokes a masculine figure that haunts imaginaries of crisis-ridden Tunisia today. No, instead, Aicha 'buys-and-sells' between Tunisia and Algeria. She does not use the infamous Isuzu semi-trucks that have become the trademark vehicles of contraband trafficking. Rather she organizes herself with other women from the region to pay a driver in a private car who takes them back and forth. Other women, whose purses are tighter, take public transportation to the *hadd*, the border, that they cross by foot until they arrive in Algeria and take a cab. Aicha buys-and-sells from the city of Tabarka in the Northwest of Tunisia to the city of El Kala in Algeria, a few kilometres away from the border. Sometimes she does not even make it to El Kala but stops at one of the stores on the way, which cater to Tunisian traders looking to buy cheap Algerian products. There she pays in Tunisian Dinars, which reassures her. Algerian currency is too hard to count and the money changers at the border are known to be scammers. From Algeria, Aicha brings different products; sometimes a whole wheel of Algerian red cheese known to be more delicious than its Tunisian counterpart, and at other times household cleaning supplies. She brought in air fresheners for a while because their small format and high prices would yield more profits than other commodities. She brings in small quantities to avoid getting them confiscated by customs agents or have to pay a bribe that would cost her more than she makes. The only period where she brought in more goods – like entire chickens she would sell in town – was when she became friends with one of the customs agents, a higher-ranked one, and would make him food in exchange for looking the other way.

Aicha is not an exceptional character. Instead, she is representative of the mundane border-work that escapes stereotypical imaginings of what constitutes a border. Profiles of traffickers call into question the allure of the border as a romanticized space of male bandits at the edges of the nation. Through Aicha, I want us to attune ourselves to the gender dynamics that make up the fabric of border economies. Rather than imagining that male traffickers are replaced by women – as if borders became sites of emancipation – it might be helpful to consider how different social actors deploy gender binaries in everyday transactions at borders.

Second, a commodity. 'Touch this one, it's as soft as silk'. I pass my fingers through a narrow opening in the plastic bag and touch a brown duvet. I close my eyes and sigh. 'It's very soft indeed'. I am in the town of Ben Gardane, one of the cities in the Southeast of Tunisia closest to the border with Libya. The market is quiet on a Sunday afternoon as all the *rahalat*, the bus trips filled with people coming from the entire country to go shopping in Ben Gardane, have left. Though I came here for research purposes I am now eyeing the soft brown duvet with an enamoured gaze while I picture myself wrapped in it during one of the cold humid days of Tunisian winters. The duvet cost 130 Dinars in Ben Gardane but almost 250 Dinars if I were to buy it instead in a market in Tunis. The price of the commodity increases the further away from the border it is. Indeed, it is easier to bring goods across the border than it is to move them from border towns to the rest of the country. Barricades of the National Guard – the police between towns – are strategically placed on routes all across Tunisia, stopping cars and asking for the one thing a commodity smuggled across countries does not have: a receipt. In order to evade law enforcement, traffickers have a few strategies: bribes, having people on the lookout, and using smaller national roads instead of highways. For this duvet, there is another scheme – using a logistics company that operates formally. These companies' trucks are known and therefore do not get stopped, and even if they did the company produces release certificates that legalizes the transport of merchandise across the territory. The duvet I am eyeing can hardly be called an (il)licit commodity. It has been bought in Turkey's large wholesale market, though it was made in China. It was then sent in a container ship to the port of Tripoli and driven through Libya until the Tunisian border. The duvet crossed the border in the truck of a trader in broad daylight and arrived at Ben Gardane. It was only in the crossing from Libya to Tunisia that the duvet became de facto contraband, no taxes paid on it, and no receipts produced.

The soft brown duvet illustrates the entanglements between formal and informal economies, where border crossing constitutes only a small part of the transnational circulation of commodities. The lifecycle of the duvet unsettles the marking of goods as (il)licit, illegal, coming from the informal economy or the black market. Rather commodities pass through circuits that exist beyond the imagined boundaries between 'the economy' versus the 'contraband economy', revealing how formal versus informal or licit, illicit, and illegal come together in transnational flows of exchange.

Third, an image. In the photograph, you can see a table. A crowded table. On it, cash organized by types of banknotes more or less piled on top of one another. There are packs and packs of ten and twenty Dinars, a few banknotes of fifty Dinars and small piles of Euros and Dollars. There is almost always cash and there is often something else next to the cash. Gold jewellery, pills, boxes of medicine, brown packs concealing weed, rifles, semi-automatic weapons … The photographs are released almost daily, with a caption that says 'official announcement from the national customs agency'. The captions share where the possessions were taken, border posts along Tunisia's Eastern and Western borders, and stash houses often in poor governorates like Sidi Bouzid that are in-between smuggling regions and larger cities. The photographs are released on the Tunisian customs' social media page, which takes and shares pictures of arrests and possessions taken, often through these spectacular arrangements where large tables are filled with cash, gold, drugs, and weapons. Some photographs even show the equipment used for smuggling; trucks and cars with zoomed-in images of concealed trunks and hidden safe boxes. At times they are even photographs of people arrested, positioned with their arms over their heads, their faces barely blurred. The captions of these photographs detail the times and locations of the arrests depicting 'traffic', 'illegal', 'schemes' and 'networks'. These photographs are shared widely by media outlets that often copy-paste directly from the police forces' press releases.

These images are only a small example of the work of producing borders as exceptional. This economy of photographs reinforces social discourses on borderscapes as sites of lawlessness that require policing. In doing so, a certain 'allure of the border' as a sensational space is produced. Border economies become akin to illegal and dangerous smuggling that hoards money and passes dangerous goods into the nation-state.

Introduction

I begin with this triad – person, object, and image – to attune us to the myriad of ethnographic possibilities that can be observed at borders. How can we apprehend processes of exchange and circulation ethnographically, meaning by attending to the mundane as multifarious but also as the basis for theory-making?

How do we theorize the circulation of goods like make-up brought by a female trader, cigarettes smuggled through desert routes at night, red coral fished from protected maritime sites in Algeria, sent to the Tunisian Northwest and hidden in ships headed to Southern Italy, medicine passing through Tunisian pharmacists to Libyan cities and a set of comforters with an infamous tiger on them, made in Central Anatolia, shipped to the port of Tripoli, brought without receipts to the border-post of Ras Gadir, carried by a transportation company to be sold in the market of Boumendil in downtown Tunis? What is the link between Aicha and her air fresheners from the North of Algeria, a soft duvet sold in Ben Gardane, and a photograph of contraband cash from an arrest by customs? What is the difference between the northwestern border of Tunisia and the Southeastern one? How does one attend to the specificity of borderspaces while also revealing how they bring together on national and transnational scales?

Goods, circulation routes, and individuals that work the border are so multiple and different that they require us to ask: What constitutes a border economy? Can we even speak of a single entity 'the border' and a linked phenomenon, 'the economy'? And finally, how do we study circulations across borders, not as exceptional, informal, or illegal but rather as core phenomena that produce the sense of an 'economy'?

In this chapter, I grapple with the contradiction that makes a border economy, as it places the border as a different, if not an exceptional site for economic exchange, as much as it is a space through which various modes of circulation, beyond the binary of formal versus informal, travel. The inherent instability of the border, as geography and as concept, is nonetheless generative. By beginning by a border, I highlight how processes of exchange and circulation use but are not restricted to borders. I foreground instead a *political economy of borderscapes* that attends to the social fabrics of exchange and circulation. Moreover, I show how it is in the constitutive tension between representations and ethnographic realities that border economies get produced as sites for economic livelihoods as much as for state control. Ultimately, I show how border economies are neither just about borders, nor they are just about the economy in the strictest sense.

To do so I keep the triad of person, object, and image as a running thread throughout the chapter. Though they are mutually constitutive, they help devise a political economy of borderscapes. First, entering through the account of people working the border offers a glimpse into the social structures that make borders, as they deploy individuals not as ideal types of traffickers, but instead as embedded in social networks and gendered performances. Second, by following what commodities move through borders, we attend to the heterogeneity of exchange and circulation processes that cannot be restrained to border spaces. Finally, investigating the slippage between state representations – in images or discourses – and the multiple lifeworlds that make border economies, pries open the 'power-effects' (Foucault 1991) of these representations, as they serve to criminalize what is imagined beyond the national economy. Through these ethnographic insights, this chapter ultimately argues that entering the economy through borders means investigating social processes stretching across geographies and scalar articulations working with or in friction with a sense of a national economy. By unsettling the notion of the border economy, this chapter shows that investigating economic practices at borderscapes in fact offers new insights into what the economy is in the first place.

Theory and Methodology

The notion of a border economy, which exists in state representations and social discourses, imagines a different economy happening at the nation's edges. At the same time, it is also a scholarly notion that merits further unpacking. I locate how a 'border economy' is first and foremost a key device in making of the economy as a bounded sphere, an object of intervention, knowledge, and rule.

Scholars of political economy have long shown how 'the economy' has been produced historically as the seminal object of modern power. Timothy Mitchell (1988) reveals how the nature of power has shifted through devices that 'enframe' and 'contain'. The notion of border economy contains, within a space, economic processes as if they were separated from others and limited to a scale of the border. Similarly, Callon (2006) highlights how economists have rendered practices that are heterogenous and multiple into an abstract and performative object called the 'economy'. In their seminal work on borders, Van Schendel and Abraham (2005) lament how social scientists, in over-determining the national scale, have reified borders and the economic processes occurring at borders, as exceptional. These works show the collusion between popular and academic representations as they concomitantly make the border into a contained site of knowledge and rule. Indeed, the production of knowledge on borders cannot be separated from the hegemonic representations that already circulate on borders. They are co-produced, meaning to interrogate borders theoretically is to acknowledge, refuse or be in conversation with the politics of border representations in the first place.

A conception of the economy as a bounded sphere cannot be separated from the scale through which this economy operates: the national scale. Historically, the making of the economy as a distinct sphere emerges from the production of a national space that becomes the naturalized scale of intervention (Goswami 2004; Mitchell 1998). The concept of border economy plays a central role here because it imagines a scale of the economy, not necessarily as transnational but rather overlaid onto the national economy. In other words, a border economy is an economy at the edges of the nation, thereby always centring the national scale first. In considering the frame of national economy today, anthropologist Hannah Appel (2017) highlights 'how national economies become both intelligible, possessing representational unity or naturalized authority, and compelling – the stuff of fantasy and desire, power and subjugation' (295). Her sense of the national economy as a space of 'as-if' mirrors the sense of a border economy possessing both 'power effects' (Foucault 1991) – as different modes of control and policing happen at the border – and representational power – the border is exceptional and dangerous to the nation-state. In other words, a border economy is the necessary mirror of a national economy. The border economy becomes a constitutive outside that threatens the notion of the economy as occurring naturally within the boundaries of a nation-state and therefore gets criminalized. The term 'border economy' reveals the ideological and political work of naturalizing the nation-state, criminalizing marginal regions, and producing hierarchies of what constitutes a sanctioned, good and moral economy.

To pry open the sense of a border economy, I consider instead what would it mean to look at economic practices at borders as enmeshed in larger socio-economic phenomena. I collapse together mundane economic practices that invest the border as a site of passage and accumulation with more sensational practices at the border like smuggling, trafficking, or contraband. Van Schendel/Abraham (2005) foreground the notion of the (il)licit as a moving spectrum of circulation of various goods that come in ever-changing interactions with regulatory authorities. However, even the notion of the (il)licit exceptionalises the border as a space where a specific kind of exchange occurs. As such, the (il)licit does not quite resolve yet the 'allure of the border' in scholarship that often centres the exceptional nature of the political economy of borders. For Malik and Gallien (2020: 740), border economies matter because they make the fabric of statecraft, as 'borderlands are spaces where markets and states are co-constituted'. This opens up the question of how to study borders by attending to the specificity of the scale they conjure without exceptionalising them? Is there even such a thing as a border economy, an economy at borders, or an economy of borders? What is the use of the scale of the border?

In the case of Tunisia, borders are often examined through smuggling or governance. Perhaps there are funding incentives that nudge research towards a security lens or perhaps there are actually security questions to be posed by border regimes. Yet, research on borders ought to be read next to state representations of chaos at its borders. In

Tunisia in recent years, the figure of the contraband trafficker, in particular, has crystallized passions and deviated conversations away from class struggles, capitalist extraction and the state's role as an agent of economic capture. Contraband traffickers themselves are not outside capitalist capture, but they have been cast as separate from the crony capitalism of bankers, state agents, and elites. Instead, the *knatri* is a danger like no other. As such, in this terrain of saturated representations, the role of scholarship in debunking these tales becomes ever more important.

Methodologically, studying borders remains a puzzle for ethnographers. In this chapter, the border implies the territorial demarcations of the nation-state. Yet that definition is already unstable as territorial borders are never fixed, their colonial constructions at times contested while we increasingly notice processes of externalisation of borders (cf. Garnaoui, this volume) or the production of racial borders inside national spaces (cf. Parikh, this volume). Rather than confining borders to the nation-state, I begin with territorial borders while acknowledging the capaciousness of the term 'border'. The oscillation of borderscapes as both invisible and hyper visible speaks to a methodological conundrum on how to study a space without containing it. How do we conduct research at borders without reifying them and reproducing the sense of borders 'as real'? The question requires us both to take borders seriously, while also unsettling their hold on collective imaginaries. To enter a border through its actors, has often meant a kind of hyper masculinist ethnography – smuggling with smugglers – which raises major ethical questions. Instead, I am attuned to the discomfort of border research, a gendered discomfort, but one that pushes the researcher to remain in a generative liminal in-between, not completely studying the border for itself and not completely discarding it either. The gendered discomfort comes from the fact that both representations and realities at borders reify gender binaries. The contraband traffickers, *knatria*, are represented as these hyper-masculine figures, as much as the large majority of them are indeed men. Border economies are not sites for female liberation, because though they might be perceived as threats to the nation, they *are* little threats to the patriarchal representations that make nation-states and borders alike. As such the research spaces I had to navigate were mainly masculine and even when – as with Aicha who begins this chapter – women were involved, they were also surrounded by men – sons and brothers, drivers, border agents, money changers. It is in the methodological tension of studying *with* men or hearing *from* men while attempting to be careful about the hyper-masculinist representations that might be reproduced that I began to feel discomfort. Discomfort, a bodily affect, becomes a way to foreground the liminal, the neither/nor that is essential to attend to border economies.

In my ethnographic inquiries with people 'working' or 'living' at the border, I often encountered comparisons across borders. If I began with a first border, it is because my research on the Tunisian-Algerian border brought me to the 'second border', between Tunisia and Libya. In the Northwest of Tunisia, the border with Libya gets often recalled as a point of comparison, both to contrast the openness and plenitude of the Libyan border and to point to a shared history of marginalization where border regions remain forgotten in state development projects. In these conjurings, the idea that 'the state does not like its borders' was often repeated. More than discursive comparisons, traders themselves often work across borders. In the South, smuggling routes pass through the Algerian or Libyan border depending on goods needed, oil prices, and the security regime at a given time. In the North, traders, especially before the revolution, often crossed the entire country to buy goods in Libya allowing comparisons across spaces. Finally, illegalized migration brings the Mediterranean seascape in relation to land borders as Europe externalizes its borders and migrants get stranded in North Africa or as dispossessed young people from the Northwest, who can no longer live off smuggling, take new routes to Europe from Algeria. Moreover, borders are part of geographies with varied economic structures. For example, agriculture and border trade often happen in similar vicinities, and workers shift from the former to the latter. These processes require us to understand these regions not only as border regions but rather as spaces of intense economic circulation not solely oriented around borders.

As such I unpack the concept of border economy without fully doing away with it. Instead, I show how through an idea like border economy, a sense of the economy as a bounded object comes to be strengthened. By saying this, I open up both a theoretical and methodological inquiry. What does it mean to unsettle a concept without replacing it with another? In doing so, I want to emphasize that borders exist, in the practices of states but also in the practices of people who labour on and across them. Borders exist for states and for all kinds of transnational and global institutions who choose to criminalize, participate or ignore economic processes at the border. The border is a strategic line for intervention and representation. Moreover, there are economic processes that take the border as a site for accumulation, exchange, and circulation. Yet by constituting these as border economies, we forget that the border is a site inextricable from transnational scales which overlap in various arrangements depending on the actors and commodities circulating.

Keeping the triad of person-commodity-discourse, I weave into the story two figures of border economies; Salah who works as a contraband trafficker at the border with Algeria, and Marouene who is a money changer in the town Ben Gardane near the border with Libya. The observations recounted by these two individuals tell us something of the political economy of borderscapes in Tunisia. The stories enmesh individuals, commodities and circulations with the modes of representation – of borders as sites of criminality and suspicion – they are caught in.

A Person is a Gendered Social Network

'There's no more border, no more smuggling, no more anything!' exclaims Salah. I grab my tea and drink a sip. I began to ask a question but the sound of exclamations at the next-door table stops me. We are sitting in a coffee shop in a small town in the Northwest of Tunisia. Today, most of the chairs are turned towards the screen on the opposite wall showing the crushing loss of the Esperance Sportive de Tunis, one of Tunis's main football teams. Salah glances at the TV as his face turns into a grin. I try again. 'What do you mean'? 'Is this because of your winter arrest'? I continue. Salah owns an Isuzu truck, a highly valued good in the border zone between Tunisia and Algeria. The Isuzu trucks have become seminal objects in the imagination of border contraband, as people routinely joke that to own an Isuzu is to be a trafficker. In the past few years, small trucks have no longer been allowed in the border posts between Algeria and Tunisia. In doing so, authorities have entrenched a separation between illegal smuggling which passes through routes other than border posts, and illicit trading using private cars and which strategically plays with the quantities of goods and the relations of bribery with customs agents.

Salah is from a mountain village nearby Algeria, another requirement in order to smuggle goods in and out of the border. Trafficking in the Northwest operates radically differently from the more known Southern contraband routes. Here, families from small villages closest to the *khatt*[1] (the line) have a monopoly on what passes or not. Indeed, most contraband has to go through intricate mountain routes that only the 'children of the area' know of. The kin relations do not end at the *khatt* but rather extend into villages located on the Algerian side where families – whose relatedness precedes colonialism – receive packages and give money. As Ghanem (2020) working on the Algerian side of the border has shown, most people have kin across the border and these relations have served as a departure point for smuggling since the demarcation of borders in the postcolonial era.

The lines between trafficker, worker, and law enforcement are often blurred as within the same family one often finds a customs agent, a trafficker, and a labourer too. Salah himself has a brother in the forestry administration, another one who illegally migrated to France before the revolution and the last one who is a coral diver working with smugglers in Algeria. Kinship relations at borders are conduits for cross-border circulation. They constitute part of extended social networks that rely on relations of trust, rather than legal enforcement, to maintain functioning economic activities.

Kinship relations are also deployed metaphorically against national identity. Kinship tropes of neighbouring countries as *khawa khawa*[2] or as 'cousins' often get mobilized to assert the relations of trust necessary for cross-border trade. In another setting, in the town of Medenine in the Tunisian south near the border with Libya, a trader listed to me last names from the South that he deemed originally 'Libyan' last names. These historical narratives of lineage produce fictive kin relations, that mobilize tribal identities that pre-date colonial times. Yet these discourses are often brought together with other tropes that reify belonging to the nation-state. Tunisian border traders joke that they are sly, in contrast to the perceived naivete of Libyans who 'do not know how to count' or the sternness of Algerians who are too stubborn for business. The co-existence of tropes of transborder belonging with national stereotypes draws attention to the necessity of overlapping scales that produce multiple identities mobilized in different ways at borders.

The gendered aspect of border trade – Aicha in contrast to Salah – bears recalling. It emerges in my own ethnographic inquiry, as a woman conducting research by borders. In bringing Salah's story – typically masculine – to the forefront, I highlight the importance of gender without pretending that it means an ethnography of women. Instead, it is precisely the gender essentialisms that render borderscapes generative sites from which to unpack gender. For example, it is because women are perceived by male customs agents as less threatening than men that they get mobilized as traffickers too.

---

1 The *khatt* (line) refers to a specific Tunisia-Libya border road but interestingly gets used as synonymous of "border" across Tunisian borderscapes.
2 'Brother-brother', a popular expression used between Algerians and Tunisians.

Yet borders produce new forms of gendered domination. At the Libyan border, women from the poorest governorates like Sidi Bouzid, unable to find work in agriculture, move to Ben Gardane and work as fuel smugglers. Often, they do not own cars and work as drivers under the supervision of men. This kind of exploitative labour mirrors that of female agricultural workers who have become a public symbol of gender exploitation in Tunisia in recent years (cf. Garraoui, this volume). Precisely because the border is still imagined as a specifically male space, these women are invisibilised. In contrast, Aicha, whose story opens the chapter, uses the border to her own advantage, playing with the price differences between Tunisia and Algeria to make an income. Her border labour is embedded in a kinship network where she is a matriarch and provider. Salah, too, exists at the border because of his familial relations that stretch across border lines. These stories, from Salah to Aicha, to the women in Ben Gardane, reveal how borders operate similarly to other spaces of circulation, playing representations against each other and using social networks as the basis of exchange.

Commodities Moving Through Border Regimes

Moving from Salah himself to Salah's work helps consider the many modalities of exchange, and circulation encompassed under the notion of border economy. Salah is not really solely a trafficker. He does everything, transportation, manual labour, a few businesses here and there, and the smuggling of red coral or electronics from Algeria. He used to at least. He swore off trafficking these days after his car was seized at the border last winter, making him run from one court to another and pay a large fine in order to get his beaten-up white Isuzu back. As Maxim Bolt (2012) has shown for the Zimbabwe-South Africa border, the entanglements between formal and informal labour are central to the making of borders, as 'unregulated business and law-bound waged employment constitute one another' (117). Indeed, most petty contraband traffickers deploy their activities across a spectrum that blurs the distinctions between formal, informal, and illegal.

As Salah once explained, every border village has its informal entryways controlled by village men that traffickers have to negotiate with. Trafficking worked differently before, when the border posts of Melloula in the North of Tunisia and Hammam Bourguiba near the town of Aïn Drahem were sites of open corruption, as traffickers always accounted for the *rashwa* (bribe) for Algerian and Tunisian officials. According to local tales, the high days of contraband were during the years of the revolution from 2010 to 2011 when police forces were terrified to even argue with young men crossing and the focus on other regions left the Northwest at peace. Today, things are very different. Most traffickers lament the progressive and growing criminalization of harmless border smuggling. They noticed how much more suspicious authorities have grown, banning trucks without a commercial patent, and restricting access to single men traveling alone. Then with the Covid-19 pandemic, the border shut completely which rendered smuggling through mountain routes even more dangerous as the military was deployed across both sides.

Border economies exist in entanglements with local, national, and global processes that have transformed economic dynamics at borders and elsewhere. The temporalities of border regimes are central to understanding the shifting processes of circulation. Key moments like the opening of the Tunisia-Libya border after 1987, mark material and ideological transformations in cross-border trade (Meddeb 2020). Border workers of all sorts often evoke that moment as the turning point for the transformation of southern border areas. The date does not mean cross-border trade was absent before but rather denotes the production of temporalities by social actors to make sense of their own trajectories at borders. In a similar vein, the time of the revolution not only marks national collective imaginaries but ones at borders too. The period of uncertainty that followed the events of December 2010 and January 2011 intensified smuggling as traders and traffickers took advantage of the reshuffling of the police state. At the same time, the period of the revolution gets romanticized and removed from the global processes of border surveillance that have increased not just in Tunisia but in the region in the past decade often under the cover of security. Finally, the pandemic of Covid-19 marked borders anew as states closed their frontiers altogether. The Tunisian-Algerian border which remained closed for more than two years is particularly illustrative as its closure coincided with what Algerians call 'a revenge for the *hirak*'[3] where the health situation became an excuse for state control.

Because of how dangerous smuggling became during the pandemic, only high-return goods circulated, mainly drugs, fuel, medicine, and red coral. Recently Salah's village became a hotspot of an investigation around the death of an Algerian man who was trafficking pills with young men from the Tunisian side. The rumours were that the Algerians came without the money hoping to rip off the Tunisians, who responded by throwing rocks at them. One of the rocks hit an Algerian, killing him instantly. The investigation was from the Algerian side but they quickly sent Tunisian police units to the village to find the perpetrator. 'They'll close in on us even more now', Salah says sighing. 'There's no work in *contra* and there's no future at this border'.

To see borders from the perspective of the state seldom attends to the layered processes that both make and break borders. Following Schendel and Abraham (2005), I locate the extent to which borders are sites of anxiety for the state. Through economic practices that take the border as a site of exchange and accumulation, we come to understand that it is perhaps too simplistic to imagine the state as anxious or all-empowering at its borders. Instead, economic arrangements deploy state agents as part and parcel of the *political economy of borderscapes*. Accepting bribes or looking away is not a Tunisian, authoritarian, or Arab state agent's particularity. The nature of borders themselves requires this incommensurable gap between representation and practice. A border is excessive in the sense that it is essential for representational power at the same time as a glance at this scale reveals layered and complex processes which escape representations. Borders, because they are excessive, also unsettle the imagined homogeneity and coherence of the state. State agents come into daily contradictions with state imperatives to police and control the border, showing how one should locate the state as a site of fragmented institutions organizing social actors with contradicting agendas.

The border, rather than a fixed category, changes temporally, spatially, and in relation to the governance of states and global regimes. The broader context of a border informs the political economy of circulation and exchange at borders.

---

3   Expression from a research interview. The *hirak* was a social movement in Algeria in 2019.

Against State Representations

'*Irhab* and *tahrib* are two different words for a reason' explains one of the panellists.

Next to me, Marouene's body moves closer to me as his fingers touch my bare arm. He pinches me. I jump in my seat, then look around the room alarmed to see if anyone saw my body rising from the chair and back. I turn towards him. He winks at me and whispers. 'It's what we were talking about this morning'. I sigh, smile, and cover with my hand my bare arm where the trace of the pinch has turned into a pink-red spot on my skin. Marouene owns a money-changing shop in the town of Ben Gardane, a mere twenty kilometres from the border with Libya, and the main hub for cross-border trade in Tunisia. The informal money-changing shops occupy the city centre and are open 24/7, serving Libyan families, all types of traders, and diasporic Tunisians from the south. The main street of Ben Gardane is filled all day with cars coming in and going to the nearby border post of Ras Gadir. Cars with Libyan plates often have families inside them, at times three generations packed into the same vehicle and at others young men cruising in their brand-new vehicles. The cars with Tunisian plates look different, old automobiles and broken pickups that do not have paperwork, some literally held together by ropes, and all going into Libya to be filled with fuel, which will be sold all across the Tunisian south. Some cars stop on the road as the passengers roll down their windows asking money-changers a single question, 'how much?'. Marouene turns to the customers, as his accent switches from the Ben Gardani tone to a perfect Libyan dialect, while giving them today's Libyan to Tunisian Dinar exchange rate.

That day we were sitting in the conference room of the municipality of Ben Gardane. It was not a typical day in town. It was the 7th of March, the anniversary of the commemoration of the Ben Gardane attacks in 2016, when a group of terrorists entered with weapons through Libya hoping to take over the surrounding area. The date is inscribed as a moment of local patriotism as the town inhabitants turned against the invaders and helped the military stop the attack. To commemorate the event, a think tank organized a panel under the theme 'legacies of the Ben Gardane attack'. One of the speakers discussed the difference between *irhab* (terrorism) and *tahrib* (smuggling). The two words sound similar, an irony of linguistics, yet they are different, in terms of origin and more importantly in terms of meaning. The speaker lamented that state authorities stuck in the capital and with very little knowledge or concern with southern regions confused the thriving economy with terrorism and only applied criminalization policies to the border town. 'Yes, sometimes the routes traffickers take are the same as the terrorists', evoking the intricate desert routes taken by white Isuzus filled with cartons containing smuggled goods, from cigarettes to female underwear. The panellist acknowledged that perhaps traffickers themselves smuggled illegal and dangerous objects, weapons, and drugs. Yet *irhab* was not *tahrib* and should be managed differently by the state. The linguistic slippages at play here highlight the constitutive relations between representations and reality. Much like the photographs of the customs office presented earlier, the state deploys – through devices, ranging from images to stories and expressions – representations that perceive what happens at borders as threats to the nation-state. In this state discourse, border economies become sites of lawlessness where criminals rather than traders smuggle Tunisia's wealth out of the country.

People from border regions often understand their geographies within a history of marginalization by the postcolonial state who helped develop the capital and the country's coast. Many people at the border compare the processes of surveillance they are confronted with, to the leniency toward elite corruption in the capital, which itself often mobilizes the border for wealth accumulation. In shifting from the border with Algeria to the border with Libya, I highlight how these borders interact with conceptions of the state that present border economies as inherently suspicious.

The border of a state is an essential device of territorial sovereignty to assert the nation-state. Historically Tunisia's borders were not defined, as many political units extended beyond today's borders, and were instead constituted through lineage and tribal affiliations. Both in East and West, Tunisia's borders were fixed through international treaties in the 1980s showing how the work of tracing the border-line is a contemporary ideological work, that produces the nation and the power of the state within that scale. Borders matter analytically because they are sites for the exercise of state power and have 'power effects' (Foucault 1991). Their constitutions through policing, surveillance and containment is an expression of state control. However, it is not enough to say that borders exist as ideological and performative power structures. They have been instilled socially too, as shown by the plethora of terms and expressions referring to borders. For example, the border is often named as line (*khatt*) and as limit (*hadd*). *Khatt* and *hadd* become particularly fruitful entry points to explore the contrast between borders as surface or as depth. In *khatt*, the line is surface, it is shallow and flimsy while in the *hadd* it is deep and marks a stopping point, where the border becomes a limit. The usage of the two words shows how borders can both be 'shallow' and 'deep'. The border is both surface and process, it is a line, meaning it can be traversed, but also a limit meaning it (en)closes a space, that of the nation-state.

Marouene – the money-changer in Ben Gardane – made a fuss about the usage of words that depicted the border, the region, and the economy. Sometimes the words were synonymous, the *khatt* (the line) and *hadd* (the border) playing off one another. Goods circulating were so multifarious they could not possibly all fall under the category of 'contraband good' or even 'cross-border commodity'. The list was immense as were the hundreds of warehouses, shops, and stalls that made up the urban fabric of Ben Gardane (cf. Shâfi'i, this volume). Markets filled with comforters, cloth, and furniture, shops stacking AC units and refrigerators, and warehouses with foreign chocolate or cigarette packs. The 'traders', 'smugglers', and 'traffickers' also came in all shapes and forms. Marouene pointed at different cars on the road, some with veiled middle-aged women from Sidi Bouzid smuggling fuel, while other women, well-dressed and with a driver, made their way to the main Libyan cities to buy make-up for their stores in Tunis. Men, from the thin and nervous young adults who recklessly drove Isuzus at night, to pot-bellied men with expensive watches who already made their fortune in the trade and only handled the contraband money these days. In pointing out to me the myriads of people and transactions that make border trade, Marouene was in a sense acutely aware of how representations of borders have consequences. In *Border as a Method* (Mezzadra and Neilson 2013) the authors lament the representation of the border as a wall and show how even in 'walled borders' labour and goods are constantly circulating. Rather, they wish to shift our perceptions of borders beyond the state discourses to see how borders are sites for the 'multiplication of labour' (ibid. 21). Borders constitute scales for global accumulation beyond – at times – the border regime in place. Yet, by solely dismissing the representations of borders to show the thick social lives underneath, we perhaps forget the entanglements between representations and realities. The representations of borders produce not only reactions from people living at borders but shift their very modes of dwelling in these spaces too.

Conclusion

An ethnography of circulation and exchange in a space often becomes – sometimes despite itself – a story of people. Here, Aicha, Salah, Marouene, and countless unnamed others make up the fabric of the border. The entanglements of their everyday are always co-constituted with representations – the border as lawless and threatening – that produce varying strategies to survive and thrive near borders. Using the triad of person-commodity-discourse as a theoretical device reveals what makes the political economy of borderscapes beyond hegemonic discourses on border economies. Away from representations that set border economies as sites of radical difference, ethnographic insights at Tunisia's borders show instead variegated processes that ought to be historicised and spatialised. Instead forms of circulation and exchange bring different scales together and offer new insights into processes that pass through borders but cannot be confined to them. Moreover, they highlight how border economies engage socio-political processes, people as well as state and global institutions.

Economic processes 'passing' through borders are particularly generative sites from which to study/unsettle borders. Economic processes help foreground notions of circulation, movement, categorization, and criminalization. They also reveal the overlap of scales, both scales of circulation but also ideological scales that produce spaces inside borders as 'national economy' and spaces outside as 'contra(band) economy'. The border economy encapsulates such radically different forms of circulation, actors, and objects that it bears the question of its relevance as a scale. Economic circulations are never solely across borders but rather traverse borders to pass across different sites and scales. It is by taking the border economy as an 'uneasy' analytic that we see the mutual constitution of legal and illegal, and the shifting spectrums from licit to illicit. Instead, the political economy of borderscapes reveals the power effects invested in representations that mark what happens at the border as an inversion – if not threat – of what happens within the 'national economy'. The national economy, a reified bounded unit, that produces a specific kind of knowledge and power effects, in some way loves its borders, as a site from which not only anxieties but fantasies and desires for power and accumulation are crystallized. Perhaps borders matter because they mobilize drama – through sensational representations as exceptionalised spaces – and banality – routine everyday practices – both of which make these flimsy lines into borders.

Fuel Smuggling From Libya via the Border Town of Ben Gardane

Fathi Shâfi'i

> Mokhtar, a young Tunisian at the age of 29, dropped out of school shortly after elementary level, when he was no older than 14. Because of his poor results and his wish to increase his income, the temptations of the unofficial market, which had flourished since the reopening of the border with Libya in 1988, loomed large. In the beginning he worked as an employee in one of the shops selling food smuggled from Libya to the Maghrebian market, popularly known as Suq Libya. Then he worked in a shop that sold smuggled fuel from Libya. He gained experience and built up networks of relationships on both sides of the border. After the fall of the Ben Ali regime in Tunisia and Gaddafi in Libya in 2011, the border regions entered a state of lawlessness that helped increase fuel smuggling operations, transforming it into a flourishing black market on the Tunisian-Libyan border. This period lasted until mid-2013, when Tunisian authorities resumed tightened border control in the desert, while the smuggling routes shifted from the desert to the Ras Gadir crossing. During this period, when desert routes were booming, Mokhtar managed to accumulate a capital of about 15,000 Tunisian Dinars, gain his driving license, at the age of 19, and decide to enter the prosperous market of fuel smuggling. He bought a D-MAX pick-up and generated considerable revenue that enabled him to expand his trade field. After the construction of a desert barrier and the tightening of border control since 2013, Mokhtar continued his business using the border crossing in Ras Gadir. He bought two Opel Campos in addition and finally established a shop for his smuggled fuel in Ben Gardane in 2016. He bought more cars for smuggling and had six employees working with him temporarily, while he stopped crossing into Libya and began to invest his profits in real estate and agriculture.
>
> Shâfi'i (2020: 116)

Mokhtar's story summarises and reveals the developments taking place in the field of fuel smuggling from Libyan cities to Ben Gardane, a border town of about 80,000 inhabitants in the south of Tunisia, which has flourished for more than three decades and still continues to grow (Shâfi'i 2020). Simultaneously, smuggling is expanding and with it the number of people involved from both countries, as well as the geographical area of operation and the volume of financial gain. This chapter analyses fuel smuggling practices and addresses the parties involved, as well as gains and dangers resulting from informal and illegal fuel transactions.

Libya's Oil Wealth Encourages Smuggling

The Libyan state is well known and characterised by its oil wealth. It holds the largest proven reserves of crude oil in Africa with 48 billion barrels, which is equivalent to 2.8 percent of the global reserve. Since the overthrow of Gaddafi's regime in 2011, Libyan oil production has had its ups and downs. In 2009, production reached 1.557 million barrels per day, but fell sharply to 462,000 barrels per day in 2011. Since 2017 crude oil production has gradually increased to 811,000 barrels per day and finally exceeded the one-million-barrel mark reaching 1.164 million barrels in 2021. Two-thirds of the production is exported as crude, while the remaining third is refined in Libyan oil facilities. The two most important refineries are Ras Lanouf – which is part of a larger petrochemical complex, oriented towards eastern markets – with a capacity of 220,000 barrels per day, and Zawiya, with 120,000 barrels per day. The latter covers the needs of the entire western region of the country, including the cities of Misrata, Tripoli, Zawiya, Sabrata, and Zuwara, with fuel available at a very low price level. The Libyan market is remarkable for its very low fuel prices: amounting to 0.15 Libyan Dinars (LYD) per litre gasoline and diesel, which equals 0.09 Tunisian Dinars (TND) (0.029 US$), according to the exchange rate on the black market in August 2022 (1 LYD = 0.61 TND), whereas fuel prices in Tunisia are considerably higher, amounting to 2.33 TND per litre gasoline (0.74 US$) and 1.79 TND for diesel (0.59 US$). Libya's oil wealth, its high production, and low prices, thus encourage the expansion of smuggling activities between the two countries, with the city of Ben Gardane being at the centre of these developments.

Fuel Smuggling from Libya to Ben Gardane

The operations of fuel smuggling from Libya to Ben Gardane work through multiple stages and the participation of multiple operators on a high level of specialisation according to capital and networks. The cities of western Libya from Masrata to the capital Tripoli, Zawiya and other border cities represent starting points for smuggling fuel to the Tunisian border. Trucks loaded with fuel depart from these Libyan cities towards the areas of Zaltan, 32 km from the Ras Gadir crossing, and the region of Abu Kammash, 20 km from the crossing, or even closer. According to my interviews with fuel traders commuting from Libya to Ben Gardane, the importance of these sources varies. The city of Zaltan is the first destination for Mokhtar and the rest of the traders to refuel, because fuel is always available there at low prices. Purchasing in this city, fuel trade is often combined with the trade of goods like electronic devices and food. But if they only want to trade fuel, the region of Abu Kammash or the Ras Gadir crossing is the main destination for fuel traders.

Table 1: Price of Smuggled Fuel in Libyan Cities

City	Distance from Ras Gadir crossing (km)	Official price in gas stations in Libyan Dinar (LYD)	Price of one qanouni in the Libyan black market	
			In LYD	In TND
Tripoli	170	3.3	14	Tripoli
Az-Zawiya	130	3.3	15	Az-Zawiya
Sabrata	100	3.3	16	Sabrata
El-Agelat	94	3.3	16	El-Agelat
El-Gemil	62	3.3	17	El-Gemil
Zuwara	60	3.3	18	Zuwara
Zaltan	39	3.3	19	Zaltan
Abu Kammash	24	3.3	20	Abu Kammash

Source: Fieldwork, July 2022. Note: One *qanouni* equals 22 litres. TND=Tunisian Dinar.

The prices for smuggled fuel are a lot higher than official prices in the gas stations in Libya, sometimes more than five times higher. They also vary a lot between the different Libyan cities. The closer to the border, the higher the fuel prices get. The unit used in fuel smuggling is a canister of 22 litres. In Libya it is called '*qanouni*', whereas in Tunisia it is named after the French word *bidon*. The huge difference between the gasoline prices in Libya and in Tunisia encourages multiple parties from both countries to enter the field of smuggling fuel from Libyan cities to the city of Ben Gardane (cf. Table 1).

From an historical perspective, smuggling fuel from Libya to Tunisia via the Ras Gadir crossing has been active ever since the borders with Libya were reopened at the end of the last century. In the beginning it was limited to small amounts, using specialised trading cars and for consumption requirements in the city of Ben Gardane. Since the beginning of the new century and with constant restrictions on the import of goods from Libya, the contraband trade with fuel began to flourish and was further strengthened after the collapse of Ghaddafi's rule in 2011. With the entry of Libyan parties into the smuggling process, it has taken on new dimensions and has become a stand-alone trade with an increasing number of employees. Most of the tanks of the smuggling cars have been converted in order to carry the maximum load possible, the smugglers call them *Dank*. New trucks came into action and the new capacities reached almost 600 litres for vans and more than 2,000 litres for heavy trucks, most of them Libyan.

> To circumvent Tunisian custom regulations that prohibit the entrance of these substances outside the tanks of vehicles, the capacity of the latter (light or heavy type such as semi-trailers) grew by three to four times, which allows their operators to bring in 1,000 to 1,500 litres per trip. Many sheet workers from Tataouine, Medenine, and Ben Gardane have specialised in the manufacture of this type of tank (Boubakri 2000: 43)

As a consequence of the security chaos in Libya and Tunisia after 2011 and the decline of border control, smuggling fuel from Libya through desert-tracks flourished. Joint Tunisian and Libyan markets specialised in fuel smuggling through border regions such as Karanti and Dharat al-Khas (Tunisian desert areas located near the Libyan border). From the Libyan side, heavy trucks for smuggling came into action, called *Tanta*. They are able to carry more than ten thousand litres. From the Tunisian side, light trucks with the capacity to carry almost 130 *bidon* are used. With the tightening of border-observation by Tunisian authorities from 2013, the declaration of a military buffer zone at the Libyan border, and the construction of the desert barrier, fuel smuggling in the desert regions along the border declined enormously and stopped completely after the terrorist attack on the city of Ben Gardane on March 7, 2016. They shifted to the Ras Gadir crossing instead, where the young Mokhtar and other traders continued smuggling using vans.

The Opel Campo, also owned by Mokhtar, has become a symbol of fuel smuggling in Tunisia. Most of the cars do not have any legal documents. Their transport capacity reaches more than thirty *bidon* per trip, an equivalent to approximately 700 litres. From the Libyan side Mercedes cars, some other family cars, and heavy trucks, intended for the supply of goods, are most frequently used for smuggling fuel. The volume of smuggled fuel from Libya to Ben Gardane is high, but difficult to count and still to be properly assessed. According to my fieldwork in June 2022 and statements of the police and custom services at the Ras Gadir crossing, the daily amount of fuel smuggled is close to 700,000 litres, as shown in Table 2.

As soon as the border is crossed, the prices of smuggled fuel rise, sometimes they almost double. In Batha an-Naft, a wholesale fuel market in Tunisian territory, two kilometres away from the Ras Gadir crossing, the price of one *bidon* reaches 25 Tunisian Dinars. In Ben Gardane it already costs two to three Dinars more in the wholesale market and reaches 30 Dinars per *bidon* in retail markets. In Ben Gardane the fuel trade is spread over the entire city, but concentrates on the main road to Ras Gadir, starting from the secondary school Ibn Sharaf, two kilometres away from the city centre, until it reaches the National Guard station Zakara after about four kilometres. Fuel trade takes place in fixed or temporary shops, numbering more than 400, and combines wholesale and retail trade. Shops can also be found in other parts of the city, especially on the main road to Medenine. According to my fieldwork in summer 2022, about 1,200 people engage in the field of fuel smuggling in Ben Gardane. This is more than the number of workers in the currency exchange sector, which have fallen below one thousand in the city.

According to my findings, more than three quarters of the amount of smuggled fuel from Libya to the city of Ben Gardane is diverted to the rest of the country. Its volume depends on distance and price levels. The city of Zarzis has one of the highest consumptions of smuggled fuel. My interviews in four educational institutions in the city of Zarzis during April 2022 reveal that about 80 percent of the parents of interrogated students use fuel smuggled from Ben Gardane, as do about three quarters of Zarzis' taxi and minibus drivers (*Louage*). The city of Medenine comes second in terms of consumption. Again, fuel is smuggled by both family cars and trucks (cf. Table 3).

Table 2: Daily Amount of Smuggled Fuel from Libya through the Ras Gadir Crossing

	Smuggled by vans	Smuggled by heavy trucks
Numbers of vehicles	1000	100
Load of each vehicle	25 *qanouni*	1,500 litres
Smuggled amount	550,000 litres	150,000 litres
Total		700,000 litres

Source: Fieldwork at the Ras Gadir crossing, June 2022. Note: One *qanouni* equals 22 litres.

Table 3: Daily Quantities of Smuggled Fuel from the City of Ben Gardane

Direction	Device for smuggling	Number	Load per vehicle (litre)	Total load (litre)
Zarzis	Family cars	41	400	16,400
	Light trucks	15	3,000	45,000
Djerba	Family cars	50	200	10,000
Medenine	Family cars	30	400	12,000
	Light trucks	26	3,000	78,000
Governorate Gabes	Light trucks	42	3,000	126,000
Governorate Sidi Bouzid	Light trucks	32	3,000	96,000
Governorate Sfax	Light trucks	26	3,000	78,000
Governorate Kairouan	Light trucks	8	3,000	24,000
Rest of the Governorates	Light trucks	24	3,000	36,000
Total		282	–	521,400

Source: Field work, August 2022.

Opposite to this is the demand in the island of Djerba; here, only small amounts of smuggled fuel are consumed. Smuggling possibilities are restricted due to the gate of the only connecting island bridge, which prevents the passage of trucks loaded with fuel for security reasons. After the attack on the El Ghriba synagogue in Djerba in 2001, security measures were tightened at the entrances to the island and since then have largely prevented fuel smuggling operations. Smuggling only occurs via little vans and in limited quantities not exceeding 120 litres per car.

The neighbouring cities in the Governorate of Medenine are the most important consumers of smuggled oil from Ben Gardane, due to four reasons: the geographical proximity (Zarzis 45 km, Medenine 78 km, and Djerba 100 km); the significant size of the population which accounts for part of the demand; the high frequency of traffic to and from Ben Gardane; and the simple fact that smuggling is easy on these roads. Moreover, smuggled fuel prices are low, and the quality of Libyan oil/fuel is higher than the Tunisian. The consumption of smuggled fuel in the Governorate of Tataouine is limited to the neighbouring areas, namely Samar, Qasr Oun and Beni Mhira, and only supplied on a small scale due to the small population. The whole region has no more than fifteen thousand inhabitants. The other cities of the governorate obtain smuggled fuel from the Dehiba crossing. Fuel coming from contraband trade is the main commodity which leaves the city of Ben Gardane towards the cities of the governorate Gabes. During the same fieldwork period in April 2022, I obtained the information that almost half of the fuel smuggling cars belong to owners from the governorate of Gabes, which has the second biggest demand after the governorate of Medenine. Moreover, the governorate of Sfax is also an important consumer of smuggled fuel from Ben Gardane. The respective supply structure becomes visible along the National Road No. 01, connecting the cities of Gabes and Sfax, and also in Bahri and Habib, where smuggled fuel is offered for sale in large quantities. Fuel, as an illegal commodity, also reaches most of the cities of the governorates Kairouan and Sidi Bouzid and, to a lesser extent, the governorates at the coast, such as Mahdia and Sousse. The illegal trade flourishes particularly in periods when fuel prices in Ben Gardane fall below thirty Dinars per *bidon*, while the revenues depend on the distance (cf. Table 4).

Actors in the Two Countries

There are several actors in fuel smuggling operations: gas station owners, wholesalers, retailers, truck drivers and families, to name those from the Libyan side. Before 2011, the role of Libyan parties was rather limited. There were only a few families involved, coming to Tunisia for tourism or medical treatment, some of them owning heavy trucks for commerce. At that time, most of the Tunisian traders on the other hand received fuel from Libyan gas stations in border cities. But after the political upheavals in Libya and the collapse of Gaddafi's regime, several parties entered the illegal business smuggling fuel to Tunisia and created a new reality.

Table 4: Profit Margin of Fuel Trade between Ben Gardane and other Tunisian Cities

Intended destination	Profit margin per *bidon* (TND)	Intended destination	Profit margin per *bidon* (TND)
Zarzis	1.5	Hama	3
Medenine	1.5	Sfax	4 to 5
Djerba	5	Kebili	3
Mareth	2	Sidi Bouzid	3 to 4
Gabes	2 to 3	Gafsa	3 to 4
Bir Ali	3.5	Kairouan	4

Source: Fieldwork, September 2018. Note: One *bidon* equals 22 litres.

From then on, Tunisian traders could no longer receive fuel from official gas stations. The Libyan owners of the gas stations constitute the first group involved in this trade. They started to sell most of the fuel provided officially for their stations outside the legal framework for high profits, often asking more than double the normal price. This group has been active in most cities in western Libya, from Misrata to Zaltan. According to my experiences in Libyan cities, about one third of the Libyan gas stations do not serve ordinary customers anymore, but sell literally everything to the black market. In many cases Libyans are thus forced to buy their gasoline outside the gas stations at a price that is three to four times higher than the official price.

After 2011, official gas stations in Libya came under the control of armed militias and major wholesalers, hence the majority of fuel quantities became part of the black market and the traders have a huge amount of capital at their disposal. This group specialises in smuggling fuel from cities in western Libya towards the Tunisian border. They have established extended social networks with Libyan and Tunisian parties and control the distribution channels of fuel, selling predominately to Libyan retail traders. Retail traders, on the other hand, represent the largest number of actors in the field. They work in most Libyan cities and their number increases with the proximity of the border. Most of them are found in Zuwara and Zaltan, where they run shops specialised in fuel trading. With the decline in commodity trade, their number further increased and some of them extended their activities to the Tunisian territory. They started smuggling fuel on a daily basis through the Ras Gadir crossing to Batha an-Naft, and achieved rather high incomes, up to 1,000 Libyan Dinars.

Libyan truck drivers constitute another group of actors. They are designated to transport goods to and from Tunisia legally, but usually smuggle significant volumes of fuel when they come from Libya. This is a consequence of both their high numbers and their huge tanks, exceeding a capacity of 1,500 litres (cf. Table 5), while the distance of transport itself does not consume more than one fifth of the fuel. Concerning numbers: In 2015 about 68,000 Libyan heavy trucks were registered crossing to Tunisian territory. In 2020, despite the measures taken because of the Covid pandemic and the closure of the borders for more than half the year, the Ras Gadir crossing still registered the entry of almost 25,000 Libyan heavy trucks. 'Unrequired' fuel is sold all the way from the Ras Gadir crossing to the governorate of Gabes.

The majority of Libyan families that come to Tunisia for tourism, medical treatment or trade sell the fuel out of their car tanks in the city of Ben Gardane. And although the single quantity is quite small, their high numbers contribute to a significant volume of illegally traded fuel: It accounts to about one quarter of the quantities smuggled. Since 2011, with the liquidity crisis in Libya and the large difference in prices between Tunisia and Libya, many Libyan traders and families live off smuggling fuel in order to afford food and medicine. According to my interviews during 2019 with Libyan traders that engage in fuel smuggling, the majority stressed the importance of these incomes to provide financial liquidity.

On the Tunisian side there are the traders from Ben Gardane and those from outside the city. In both cases those involved in the smuggling of fuel from Libya to Tunisian territory are highly specialised according to their field of operation. Due to the ongoing continuity of fuel smuggling over many years and the large number of workers in this field, we can distinguish between two types of actors in Ben Gardane: mobile and stationary traders. Mobile traders move on an almost daily basis between Tunisia and Libya through the Ras Gadir crossing, some of them even more frequently than once a day. Their number is not stable, but according to several personal observations and interviews between 2019 and 2022, they exceed a thousand. More than two-thirds are originally from Ben Gardane, most of whom are young adults between the age of 20 and 45 years. Most of them dropped out of school early, as more than two-thirds did not finish secondary school. The remaining traders originate from other cities of the Medenine governorate (10%), and also from the governorates Sidi Bouzid (9%), Kairouan (7%) and others (7%). These actors combine the smuggling of subsidised food from Tunisia to Libya with commodity trade from Libya to Tunisia. They make relatively high profits, sometimes amounting to thousands of Tunisian Dinars per trip and many of them own more than one car for fuel smuggling. A few of the traders from Ben Gardane also specialise in smuggling fuel to the city of Zarzis and the island of Djerba by using vans. On the other hand, there are stationary traders like Mokhtar. They run established shops for smuggled fuel in wholesale and retail markets in Ben Gardane, most of which are situated on the road to Ras Gadir. Their number exceeds 400, all of them have shops. They often work all day long without interruption and run a large number of procedures.

Since 2011, smuggled fuel has also attracted individuals from outside. They also operate from the city of Ben Gardane, but come from different regions. Their number is constantly increasing due to the significant profits and the continuous restriction on commodity trade. The largest group originates from other cities in the Medenine governorate (38%), others come from Gabes (21%), Sidi Bouzid (16%), Sfax (13%) and elsewhere (12%). Most of the traders are male, but some women, about 60, also work for different parties in Ben Gardane. According to fieldwork, the actors make varying profits (cf. Table 6).

Table 5: Libyan Actors Involved in Fuel Smuggling from Libya to Ben Gardane

Social group	Device	Quantity per device
Fuel traders	Vans	400 to 600 litres
Libyan families	Family cars	60 to 150 litres
Libyan truck drivers	Heavy trucks	1,000 to 1,500 litres

Source: Field work, August 2022.

Table 6: Capital and Financial Revenue of Fuel Smugglers

		Number of traders	Volume of capital[a]	Financial revenue
From Ben Gardane	Mobile	710	5,000 TND	500 TND per trip
	Stationary	1,000	More than 10,000 TND	3,000 to 5,000 TND per month
Governorate Gabes		126	500,000 TND	300 TND per trip
Governorate Sfax		81	500,000 TND	400 TND per trip
Governorate Sidi Bouzid		48	500,000 TND	400 TND per trip
Other governorates		45	500,000 TND	Between 400 and 500 TND per trip

Source: Fieldwork, 2019 and 2022.
[a] The high amount of capital of traders from outside the city of Ben Gardane derives from the high price of the vehicles approved for smuggling, which exceeds 5,000 Dinars. Most of them are cars acquired from rental companies, that sell new cars in instalments.

The price of fuel smuggled from Libya to Tunisian territory rises with increased distance from the border, but it always remains much lower than the official prices at Tunisian gas stations. Despite the large number of people involved in this illicit smuggling and high revenues to be earned, this trade remains unstable and dependent on the situation at the Ras Gadir crossing. The growing number of movements and people moreover contribute to the emergence of new risks.

Growing Risks

Vans are used for fuel smuggling from Libya to Ben Gardane – all of them are old, and most of them are not regularly inspected (technical, safety inspections), they do not possess the necessary legal documents, and are not registered at the Technical Agency of Land Transport. According to my interviews in 2019 with about 200 fuel traders, more than 40 percent of the vehicles do not have Tunisian license plates (81 cars out of a total of 200 cars) and were smuggled from Libya (cf. Table 7). The local expression for those cars is *rabbit*, and most of them are of the types Campo, Peugeot 505 or Renault 18, as well as the German car Jetta Volkswagen, which has a large storage capacity.

This illegal situation of fuel smuggling cars contributes to the growing level of social and security risks. The number of accidents has risen dramatically because of the lack of technical inspection and because most of the smugglers drive excessively fast and recklessly in inhabited areas as well as on the national roads. According to the same fieldwork, the intervals between technical inspections of the vehicles are more than four years for half of the respondents, and about a quarter haven't been inspected for more than ten years. On the other hand, the cars used for smuggling fuel from Ben Gardane to the rest of the Tunisian cities do have the necessary legal documents due to the large number of controls on the roads. In fact, most of the cars used within Tunisia are rather new, while most of the modified cars that are used for cross border fuel smuggling are rather old and do not comply with minimum safety conditions. Their tanks have been extended in order to transport fuel amounts of more than 500 litres. Due to this high load and long waiting times at the crossing while motors are running, cars sometimes catch fire. In 2019, the civil defence force of Ben Gardane recorded five burning cars that were used for fuel smuggling. Most of these incidents occurred on November 19, 2019, at the Ras Gadir crossing. The official website of the Ministry of Interior describes one incident:

> Ras Gadir – Ben Gardane / Five Injured among Civil Defence Forces after the Explosion of a Vehicle Tank
> *During fire-fighting operations due to a cable fire in a vehicle at the border crossing Ras Gadir, on the morning of the 19th of November 2019, the vehicle's tank exploded and five individuals of the civil defence forces of the city of Ben Gardane were injured. According to the district administration of the civil defence forces of Ben Gardane, the seriousness of the injuries vary, three individuals are in critical condition. They are currently being transported to the hospital for burn injuries and the severely injured to Ben Arous for treatment. Other injured will be treated according to their state of health in the regional hospital in Ben Gardane.*
> Source: Ministry of Interior (2019)

According to the traffic police of Ben Gardane, fuel smuggling cars (from the city of Ben Gardane to other Tunisian cities) have caused about fourteen accidents since 2016, most of them fatal due to excessive speed and the high load of fuel smuggled. Their load exceeded 2,500 litres per car. Most of the cars catch fire in these accidents, resulting in high property damage and personal injury.

Fuel shops are widely scattered throughout the city of Ben Gardane. According to personal estimates, more than 400 shops spread from the National Guard station Zakra up to the region of Jalal. Most of the shops do not comply with minimum safety regulations, and many of them are close to residential areas and to other trade shops. Many fuel smugglers in the region build stocks of gasoline when prices drop, which can reach up to 20,000 litres. Most of them are stored in iron or plastic containers, and these stocks are prone to explode when temperatures rise during summer.

Table 7: *Share of Fuel Smuggling Cars in the City of Ben Gardane (going to Libya) without Legal Documents*

	No Tunisian certificate of registration	With technical inspection certificate	With insurance certificate	With vignette
By number	81	10	15	14
Percentage	41%	5%	8%	7%

Source: Field work, 2018 (n=200).

On occasion these shops catch fire and burn down, which often leads to serious material damage and sometimes loss of life. Since 2015 the civil defence forces of Ben Gardane registered the combustion of five fuel shops, causing two deaths and many injuries. These fire-fighting operations require great efforts from the civil defence forces, who often have to request fire trucks from neighbouring cities.

Fuel selling shops also constitute a serious threat to the environment. While emptying and filling smuggling cars, high quantities of fuel are spilled and seep permanently into the ground causing the pollution of soil and groundwater. The consequences are visible in the serious deterioration of vegetation around the fuel shops. According to one of the fuel traders, every shop loses approximately five litres per day. In the case of leaking containers, the loss reaches up to twenty litres a day. With about 400 shops across Ben Gardane, the amount of leaking oil reaches up to 2,000 litres per day. This loss also contributes to a growing risk for pedestrians as well as scooters and motorcycles slipping, and where fuel leaks onto the road there is a growing risk of skidding cars and traffic accidents. This highlights the negative effects of fuel smuggling on soil and groundwater, an incident that has been repeatedly observed in the study area for more than 20 years and is more severe in the diesel trade compared to gasoline.

Conclusion

Mokhtar's story is a true story from a border city where most of the job opportunities are linked to the unofficial market and the smuggled goods trade with Libya. With continuous restrictions for Tunisians on bringing goods from Libya, the non-liquidity of banks for Libyans since 2011, because this commodity is abundant in Libya, and due to the large price differences between Tunisia and Libya, smuggling fuel appeals to many. Therefore, many social groups in the two countries engage in smuggling fuel from Libya to Ben Gardane in a first step, and then to other Tunisian cities in a second step. Whole networks have specialised in smuggling this substance. They are precisely organised and assign the parts to regions. The city of Ben Gardane has a pivotal role within these networks, which remain unstable in their activity, as it depends on the situation at the Ras Gadir crossing and on those in charge of the crossing from the Libyan side. Despite many decisions announced by Libyan authorities to prevent smuggling, it is constantly going on and generates high profits. Mokhtar and his employees remain among the main beneficiaries, but the increasing dangers associated with fuel smuggling make it an activity of multiple jeopardies, especially for road users and when it comes to human life.

Acknowledgement

[a] The information and data provided in this chapter either result from the authors' dissertation (Shâfi'i 2020) or are based on the author's own experiences in border trade, including participant observation and fieldwork between 2019 and 2022. For developments in the recent past see Boubakri (2000) and Meddeb (2016). This chapter was written in Arabic; Leonie Nückell provided a preliminary translation of the text. The translated version has then been further edited.

A 'Clean' President
Political Metaphors of Waste and Clean-Up

Jamie Furniss & Maha Bouhlel

> Apart from the dirtiness/garbage [*wasakh*] in the street, there is the dirtiness/garbage in the administration. In addition to cleaning up the country we need to clean up—the administrations, how can I put it? They are so dirty! So many terrible things happen to us. The same way you clean up outside, you have to clean up inside.
> (A woman in her 30s)

> The first thing we need is a clean mind. That's first. Next are the bribes. We need to stop giving them, in order to clean up the apparatus of the state. [...] Who could govern this country apart from Kais Saied? Everyone is talking about how clean his hands are, about how sincere and cultivated he is.
> (A man in his 50s)

> This successful clean-up campaign, if it expresses something, it expresses something about the Tunisian consciousness, it is the truth about Tunisians. About the things that need to be cleaned in this country, inshallah, if there is corruption it will be cleaned up along with the garbage and all that. About the presidential elections, they were transparent and impartial, and in that respect, we are an example for the rest of the Arab world, and even beyond it.
> (A man in his 30s)

> Interviews on: *Réalité Tunisienne*, a show known for its vox-pop street interviews.
> YouTube (18 October 2019)

For over a decade, garbage and the cleanliness of public space have had a major role in the politics of several Arabic-speaking countries in the Mediterranean, in two distinct but related ways. First, the accumulation or presence of waste due to interruptions in removal and landfilling, as well as its importation from abroad, has provoked major political crises in the region. Most famously, the closure of Beirut's municipal dump in 2015 sparked a movement that, for a brief moment, seemed like it might transform the country's political landscape (see Abu-Rish 2015; Geha 2019; Atwood 2019). The importation of

7,900 tons of waste from Italy to Tunisia in 2020 is arguably the country's most prominent recent corruption scandal (Delpueh 2021), and certainly the one where the culprits received the harshest treatment: a three year prison term for the Minister of the Environment and up to 15 years for some other involved figures (Le Monde 2023). The 2016 attempted import of 2,500 tons of waste from Italy to Morocco (Chalfaouat 2016) also resulted in a significant political backlash and criticism from Moroccans.

The second way that garbage and cleanliness have influenced the politics of the region is in moments of political transition. In particular, post-revolutionary transitions have frequently been marked by campaigns to clean and beautify public space in a highly visible and theatrical manner. For instance, the protesters who occupied Kasbah Square in Tunis organised a great garbage pickup as they vacated the space on March 7th, 2011 (Loukil-Tlili 2013: 120). In Tahrir Square and elsewhere in Cairo there were numerous movements to pick up garbage, paint sidewalks, and spruce up public parks in the aftermath of the 2011 revolution (Furniss 2012; Winegar 2016), and again in the years following (see Arefin 2019).

This chapter's goal is to explore how waste operates as a political signifier, with its removal conveying people's aspirations, and its accumulation materialising and galvanising their sense of what is wrong. Our aim is to show both how garbage acts as a way of taking the country's political pulse, metaphorically speaking, and is an instrument of expression and contention through which it is possible to intervene politically. Making public spaces orderly, literally keeping them free of waste, represents – we argue – an important dimension of governmentality. The struggles for social and political order in the public link symbolic, material, and social scapes, and reveal the political capabilities in post-revolutionary Tunisia. In order to develop our argument, we examine two case studies. The first example is a political campaign known as *hâlit wa'î* (Awakening), essentially a spontaneous and ephemeral celebration of the electoral win of Kais Saied in Tunisia's October 2019 presidential elections. It consisted of a series of initiatives to pick up garbage, paint sidewalks and murals, and tidy up parks and public gardens around the country. The second, known as the 'Sfax garbage crisis', began almost exactly two years later, and has been much more protracted, continuing at least until the time of this writing. The crisis started with the closure of the city of Sfax's controlled landfill in October 2021. This led to the cessation of waste collection and removal activities, violent clashes between police and residents who live near the dump, threats of a general strike by the country's largest union (the UGTT), a presidential order sending in the armed forces, and ultimately a genuine political crisis on a national scale.

Through the analysis of these contrasting events, we suggest that they are two sides of the same coin, two symmetrical and complementary instances of how waste became a political signifier in Tunisia, in particular with respect to Kais Saied, whose status as the 'clean' candidate (*naẓīf*, meaning mainly uncorrupt in this context) has been central to his legitimacy and success. Thus, this chapter is more about waste as a political touchstone for sentiments, including patriotic nationalism and the desire for change, rather than viewing waste as an 'environmental hazard', even if the relatively novel register of 'environmental justice' is discernible in the movement leading to the dump closure in Sfax, and some participants in *ḥālit wa'ī* participated in their capacity as environmental activists rather than Kais Saied supporters. The role of garbage in political parables of uplift and decline, its use to express critiques and aspirations, and to stage allegories of corruption and renewal, may contain a deeper point about the sphere of party politics. Our argument here is not only that trash has been politicised (cf. Bouhlel 2020), but that Tunisian politics have been 'trashed'. Voter turn-out, the rhetoric and actions of Kais Saied, and the very sentiment that carried him to the helm of the country certainly seem to confirm that the rituals, institutions, and key figures of the political sphere are perceived as trash, and either completely thrown out or in desperate need of being cleaned up. If politicisation means understanding the significance and nature of waste in political terms (rather than technical, economic, or environmental ones, and therefore as a realm of de-politicisation), what we also want to show is how trash and cleanup provide some of the most utilised and cogent vehicles through which people understand and express their feelings and thoughts about politics. If images of disease and moral offense—ulcers, cankers, mildew, drunkenness, murder, adultery, etc. —convey the rottenness of the state of Denmark in Hamlet, then this paper is about a similar role played by waste in Tunisia, and perhaps the southern and eastern Mediterranean more broadly.

A word on methods: The initial inspiration for this paper came from the visibility of the *hâlit wa'î* campaign in traditional media, social media, and public places. We began by collecting and transcribing television reports and social media material, while also interacting directly with the creators of the Facebook group *Hâlit wa'î*. We subsequently conducted two group interviews with youth from the poor and ill-famed northwest suburbs of Tunis, Ettadhamen and Douar Hicher, who were active in the campaign. It was also a theme in some broader focus group and interview work we did with approximately 30 young people who were active in civil society organisations in Bizerte, Tunis, and Utica. Our research on the Sfax waste crisis proceeded similarly with respect to media, and later involved field visits to conduct targeted interviews with key institutional actors in Sfax (National Agency for Environmental Protection, National Agency for Waste Management, Municipality of Sfax), and a group interview with activists and residents in Agareb (Sfax landfill site). While we both resided in Tunis for the entire period of the study (2019 until writing), Maha is from Sfax and her regular return trips for personal reasons provided opportunities for direct observation and more interviewing. Maha was also granted observer status as a researcher in the 'Crisis Committee' that was established in 2022 to attempt to aid in resolving the problematic situation and regularly attended its meetings, held via Zoom. Jamie also attended a conference on environmental law in Sfax in autumn 2020, with different figures from both the political and research communities. Although the event had been planned before the crisis began and was about a variety of topics, the fact that the crisis was unfolding literally outside of the conference venue coloured the discussions and provided a valuable opportunity for participant observation.

Hâlit wa'î (Awakening): Celebrating the Election of the 'Clean' President

On 13 October 2019, shortly after Kais Saied's win in the second round of the Tunisian presidential elections with more than 70 percent of the vote, groups of people began cleaning and 'beautifying' their neighbourhoods around Tunis and in towns across the country (cf. Pepicelli 2021: 51, where the moment is briefly mentioned as a 'spectacular and mediatised' campaign sparked by the 'widespread feeling of civic pride' after Kais Saied's election win). The main activities undertaken consisted of picking up trash, gardening, and painting sidewalks and walls. These actions took place during successive weekends after the elections for about three to four weeks. Despite calls to institutionalise the phenomenon and make it like the 'Umuganda' community cleanup held on the last Saturday of every month in Rwanda, the movement petered out after a few weeks. For the time it lasted, observers remarked that it reminded them of the spirit or atmosphere that prevailed shortly after the 2011 revolution. While the 'environmental' dimension and the desire to eliminate waste in the literal sense of the term was not absent, it would be a figure-ground perception error, so to speak, to foreground that element: this was not an environmental social movement of the kinds in Tunisia as studied by Loschi (2019), Robert (2021), or Pepicelli (2021).[1] The material waste and the act of cleaning were more like the plot and props for the *mise en scène* of a political and nationalistic allegory. While the 2015 waste-inspired political movement 'You stink' (*tili't rîhitkum*) in Lebanon had essentially the opposite causality (waste accumulation sparked a political movement, as opposed to a political movement sparking waste elimination), their semiotic worlds were quite similar. 'We had to make it clear that this was not an environmental issue' (Geha 2019: 84), one activist in Beirut said. Another participant in the Lebanese movement, speaking at a public meeting, noted that 'the problem was not an environmental one, but a problem of the state. [...] We are in a *political* crisis' (Arsan 2018: 400; emphasis added).

The Awakening movement is located firmly in a genealogy of regional deployments of the same idiom that transcends borders and political lines, which is not limited to the post-revolutionary clean-ups in Tunisia and Egypt as mentioned in the introduction. Indeed, the idiom was redeployed in Egypt by the regimes of the two diametrically opposed figures, Mohammed Mursi, the short-lived Muslim Brotherhood president of Egypt, and Abdel Fattah Al-Sisi, the head of the armed forces who would oust Mursi. In 2012 Mursi launched a programme called *watan nazîf* (clean nation or homeland) which invited 'citizens' (the term is significant) to pick up waste on a volunteer basis as a fulfilment of civic duty and a pro-national demonstration of their aspirations for a clean and beautiful country (Arefin 2019: 1065–1070; Karagiannis 2015: 188). Arefin's interpretation of these events is that through garbage pickup, people 'were also participating in a symbolic act: cleansing the nation of all types of corruption and negligence embodied in the waste that littered the streets' (2019: 1068). Some of the campaign's proponents described it as a way of cleansing the country of 'all manifestations of backwardness' (Arefin 2019: 1069). During this period in Egypt, political rhetoric (slogans, speech, caricatures) of all sorts drew heavily on words such as purification, clean, garbage, and remnants (*fuloul*, referring to those who belonged to the *ancien regime*) to express and categorise people and practices.

---

1   The work of the authors cited here has focused largely on developing sociological typologies of the movements, discursively analysing the terms in which they present their claims (e.g. in terms of a sentiment of injustice or of regional disparity, recasting the terminology of the revolution, rather than 'environmental' terms *stricto sensu*), and in analysing the types of social networks and connections around which the movements coalesce.

Arefin (2019) correctly observes the ongoing role of cleanliness and waste pickup in Abdel Fatah Al-Sisi's dictatorial project. To provide another example of this, in 2016 a major campaign very similar to *watan nazîf*, called *helwa ya baladî* (my beautiful country), incited the citizens of Egypt to volunteer to pick up trash, plant gardens, and paint murals and sidewalks (sidewalk curbs are painted in alternate striped colours – black and white, red and white, etc. – in Egypt and elsewhere in the region). Newspaper archives from that time, especially of Al-Akhbâr al Yûm[2] – a semi-governmental and pro-regime daily that was a sort of sponsor of the campaign – overflow with propagandistic texts posing as news stories, reporting triumph after glorious triumph of broom, wheelbarrow, and paint brush, and encouraging people everywhere to join in the orgiastic adulation of their beautiful nation.

The *hirak* movement in Algeria has also seen this metaphor employed. The *awlâd al-hûma* (residents, with a connotation of authenticity and lower social class) of neighbourhoods through which the protest marches move often organised clean ups. Similarly, some protesters, especially older women, marched with brooms as though to say that what the country needed was a good cleaning, and the country's politicians were a pack of brats who never grew out of needing their mums to pick up after them. As Safar Zitoun (2021) underscores, this was not about protecting the environment, but using the streets to stage demands for the removal of the 'pollution' and 'dirtiness' that afflict the political system. Safar Zitoun adds that lower social classes in particular have utilised this language precisely because it contests and inverts discourses about 'negative behaviours' and 'dirtiness' through which they are often stigmatised and condescended to by elites (ibid.).

Based on our observations in Tunisia at the time, participant analysis of video reportages, and as confirmed in interviews which we conducted later on, the majority of the participants were youth under 20 years of age, and for those who were above 20, the majority were students. The movement's geography was the electoral geography of Kais Saied, and skewed toward lower income neighbourhoods and peripheral areas. The campaigns were organised in a highly spontaneous fashion, without central coordination: they were not a response to a call from the leadership of any political party or established civil society actor, and they came about through a snowball effect between friends, relatives, and over social media. Some feeble attempts by established political actors to claim some part in the movement were rejected by participants, whose opinion was that classic political divisions, actors, and institutions were at the origin of the country's institutional impasse and dysfunction. This 'anti-system and anti-politicians' positioning was a shared feature with the Lebanese *tili't rîhitkum* movement, who used slogans like 'everyone means everyone', meaning that all politicians were equally responsible, and that as far as the protesters were concerned, they wanted nothing to do with any of them (see Kraidy 2016: 22; Khalil 2017: 708; Geha 2019: 85). In Tunisia, several municipalities, NGOs, and private companies supported the movement by purchasing and donating supplies such as wheelbarrows, brooms, garbage bags, or paint. According to one news report, the Ministry of Environment and Local Affairs issued a call to municipalities to support the

---

2 Author Furniss conducted fieldwork in Egypt from March to September 2016.

movement by making masks, gloves, and garbage trucks available for the effort (Brésillon 2019).

Clean (*nazîf*): no single word better crystallises the foundation of Kais Saied's electoral success, or the ongoing support he has enjoyed after his anti-democratic streak reared itself. In late 2021 and into 2022 it was common – in those superficial three or four sentence exchanges you have with not-so-close work colleagues, taxi drivers, neighbourhood vegetable sellers, etc. – for people to say there was nothing to worry about because Kais Saied was 'clean', or if they were concerned, to say something like 'things are fine now, but what if the person who comes after him isn't so clean'. This trait was accentuated by the contrast with his opponent in the second round of the elections, Nabil Karoui, who spent a portion of the campaign in prison for accusations of financial crime, and, irrespective of whether you thought he was scum or a political prisoner, inescapably acquired a reputation for being something like a Tunisian Berlusconi.

Réalité Tunisienne, a show known for its vox-pop interviews on Bourguiba Avenue, Tunisia's largest and most famous boulevard, uploaded a video to YouTube on the 18th of October, 2019, which they entitled 'After cleaning up the streets, let's clean our mentalities and eliminate bribes for a better Tunisia'. In the video they interviewed people by asking questions such as 'We are currently observing an awakening (*hâlit wa'î*) since Kais Saied was elected. Do you think it will last'? 'What do you think of the campaign to clean up and change the Tunisian mentality'?, and 'Apart from the streets, what else needs to be cleaned up in Tunisia'? To a non-Tunisian ear, the peculiarity of the video's title and the journalists' questions is revealing of the association between cleanliness and politics that this chapter hopes to convey a sense of. As represented in the opening quotes, the answers people gave consistently restated the themes of the city's physical cleanliness, the 'Tunisian mentality', and political corruption as a fluid series of interconnected, almost interchangeable predicaments.

The name that was given to these campaigns to celebrate the election of the man who was supposed to be incorruptible and sweep aside the rest of the garbage that was clogging up the political sphere, was *hâlit wa'î*. The expression, attributed by participants to Kais Saied's campaign speeches, is difficult to translate. Meaning 'state of consciousness' or 'condition of awareness', it is tempting to translate it as the 'awakening,' or even the 'elevation' or 'illumination' movement. It had a connotation of uplift, and of sudden vision or stirring. *Wa'a* is also conjugated as a verb to describe acts of moral or intellectual growth, such as to realise or apprehend, to awake, or to grasp or perceive.

True to these vague and diverse meanings, the campaign had a variety of inspirations and objectives, depending on who you spoke to. While the cleaning efforts attracted the most attention in the media, the television channel *Al-Hurra*, in its reportage on the campaign from the 20th of October, 2020, summarised its objectives as a jumble of 'promoting civilised behaviour, respect for the law, and the boycott of overpriced goods'.[3] When we contacted the administrator of the Facebook group *hâlit wa'î* to express our interest

---

3 Beginning in the summer of 2019, a few months before the presidential elections, there was an ephemeral national campaign that could be roughly translated as 'Better living by boycotting expensive prices', the aim of which was to encourage people to refuse to buy foodstuffs whose prices had recently multiplied, in particular potatoes, bananas and *zgougou* (a substance made from pine

in studying the cleanup campaign, he replied that he started the group solely to 'support Kais Saied to win the presidential elections' and had never taken part in any of the clean ups. Two young people who had participated in the original clean up campaigns and whom we interviewed in 2020 after the corona virus pandemic told us that *hâlit wa'î* was now about hygiene, and its aim had become preventing the spread of the virus. There were also misunderstandings between different participants about why they came to the cleanup events. For instance, a young woman from Utica who volunteers in an association that organises the annual Sustainable Development Goals camps for high school and university students told us that she joined other young people from her neighbourhood on the first day of *hâlit wa'î* because she was excited to see people finally picking up garbage in their neighbourhood. 'But most of them spent the whole time taking selfies to put on their Facebook', she complained:

> I said to them 'Hey guys, how about putting down your phones for five minutes and actually working a bit'!? I didn't go back the next day. After that experience, I decided it wasn't worth it. We weren't there for the same reasons.

Similar differences of interpretation of their objectives emerged in group interviews in Douar Hicher, a peripheral suburb of Tunis. A 22 year-old man explained to us enthusiastically: 'I was one of the participants in *hâlit wa'î*, which was started by young activists who supported Kais Saied, who supported the idea that he represented, as well as the man himself as a candidate for president'. As soon as he had finished speaking, another participant (male, 25) hastened to respond to this characterisation by saying:

> Politics is the thing I hate most. When I hear the word 'politics', I run for the hills! I can't even stay in the room when people start talking about politics. So as far as I'm concerned, when I saw this campaign, I was totally uninterested in knowing whether it was organised by politicians, or whoever. All I thought was: "sounds like a nice opportunity to help our country." [...] I said to myself "this is a chance to clean up some of the dirty spots around Douar Hicher, the ones everybody who lives here knows about." [...] We got up in the morning with the desire to clean up, and to draw [e.g. paint murals]. People woke up one morning and wanted to do a little cleaning and painting, that's it'.

Despite, or perhaps because of, his 'phobia' of politics, his vote in the presidential elections went to Kais Saied, he acknowledged. His sister, who would also have voted Kais Saied had she been 18 years old at the time of the elections, explained that:

> When I heard there was a 'state of consciousness' and a clean-up campaign, I decided to go. It would be good for us, and good for the country, I thought, and would show that Tunisia has been cleaned up thanks to the efforts of its youth. The meaning for me was that Tunisia was uniting itself, and that young people were doing something to make to the country a better place.

---

cones that is used for making deserts, especially those served during religious holidays). The campaign succeeded in forcing a number of food wholesalers to dispose of unbought stocks.

Toward the end of the conversation, the 35-year old president of a small neighbourhood association returned to the political meaning of *hâlit wa'î*:

> If today we repeated *hâlit wa'î* under another name – I mean if we organised another clean-up campaign but called it something other than *hâlit wa'î* – a lot of people, especially young people would take part. Because within the *hâlit wa'î* movement there were people who wanted to clean up the country, but who didn't believe in the *hâlit wa'î* label because of its association, at that time, with Kais Saied, his supporters, and the Ennahdha movement, which supported Kais Saied.

In addition to being a celebration of the election of the 'clean' candidate and an expression of the type of change to which many people aspired through Kais Saied, two additional important dimensions of *hâlit wa'î* were 'self-help' and expression of pride. Echoing the anti-establishment posture of Kais Saied, whose principal electoral argument consisted of reiterating that he had no party, no platform of policies, and no campaign organisation, many participants in *hâlit wa'î* sought to manifest their belief in the notion that public and state institutions are inoperative, and that meaningful change or improvement can only come from individuals, acting independently. The pride that they sought to express was of course nationalist, but also had a class and generational dimension. In the Bardo neighbourhood, a middle-class area to the West of Tunis, where the Parliament is located, groups of participants in *hâlit wa'î* crowded in front of television cameras in order to be filmed singing the national anthem. Elsewhere, a young man in a TV interview explained that he took part as a response to Nabil Karoui's claim, in the presidential debate, that Kais Saied's approach to running the country was a 'Walt Disney programme'. The expression was supposed to mean that it was an imaginary and unrealistic approach. 'We want to prove to Kais Saied's opponent [Nabil Karoui] and to the entire world that we are not Walt Disney. As young people, we are educated and aware', the man said. In a YouTube video with approximately 120,000 views, the vlogger Yacine Ben Osman shared his vision of *hâlit wa'î* through voice-over commentary of people cleaning the streets while waving Tunisian flags. He viewed the movement as a continuation of 2011 and a new revolution 'against the politicians who have shown us the bad side of our country':

> We united ourselves, and freely elected someone who is clean, with whom we will work for progress. People have said of us that we are dirty, and that our country is dirty, but I am here to tell you that we are not dirty. And if our country is dirty, then we will clean it, politically, and literally.

The message contained in the video's hashtag 'clean in front of your house', is reinforced by the narrator's incessant repetition of the imperative 'Clean! Clean'! The video concludes with the claim that the campaign has changed the opinion of 'those who saw us as marginalised and underdeveloped':

> Now they see us as civilised. [...] We will continue until our Arab neighbours have heard of our campaign and also become 'conscious'. Then, there will be nobody who can say they are better than us.

In summary, *hâlit wa'î* can be seen first and foremost as a political '(non-)movement' (Bayat 2010) in support of the candidate Kais Saied before he was elected, but it can also be seen as a form of political consciousness awakening in self and others, concerning corruption, the broken promises of the revolution, and the country's economic problems. Finally, *hâlit wa'î* should be considered as a festive demonstration of joy and hope in the immediate aftermath of Kais Saied's election. In its wake a number of other online groups were born, such as 'We want our country to be clean' (*nhibu bladna nadhîfa*), which had 230,000 members within three days of its creation, or 'Clean up your country' (*nadhaf bladak*). The metaphorical meanings of these campaigns, which might be seen as efforts to show and reclaim 'Tunisia's dignity' while demonstrating that the country is 'deserving of democracy' and that Kais Saied's supporters are 'serious' people, relies on the association between cleanliness, on the one hand, and civilisation, respectability, and high standing (*ruqiyya*), on the other.

The Waste Crises in Sfax: 'Something is Rotten in the State of Denmark'

So what happens to the reputation of the 'clean' President when there is a sudden and massive accumulation of actual waste in the country? In the context of waste and cleanliness as metaphors of the kind we have been observing, how can such an event be understood politically? The idea that the legitimacy of the state is challenged and potentially undermined when waste goes uncollected has been made by a variety of authors working in diverse contexts, including studies in Lebanon (cf. references below), Palestine-Israel (Stamatopoulou-Robbins 2019), Senegal (Fredericks 2014: 534), and in literature review-style pieces covering multiple sites around the Mediterranean (Bouhlel 2020; Baker 2022: 54–55). In a manner that is analogous to municipal solid waste, Arefin shows how a breakdown in the sewer system in 1980s Cairo was one of the first threats to Mubarak's newly inaugurated rule, and how getting it fixed quickly was central to consolidating his legitimacy (2019: 1062–65). The closure of Beirut's principal landfill without the concomitant opening of an alternative in 2015, resulting in spectacular accumulations of waste, was interpreted by many people in Lebanon as a quintessential demonstration of the absence of a state and the failure of public authorities to live up to their stated core attributes (c.f. Abu-Rish 2015; Arsan 2018: 369–419; Geha 2019). The knock-on effects included a national political crisis, the birth of a political movement called 'Beirut Medinaty' that presented a list of candidates in the city's municipal elections, called for the resignation of the Minister of Environment, and parliamentary elections, with some activists calling for the dismantling of the sectarian regime (Arsan 2018: 388) and the election of a new president (Khalil 2017: 708).

Several authors have sought to explore this idea in Tunisia, arguing for instance that the accumulation of waste after 2011 was a sign of the downfall of the authoritarian regime and the beginning of a period of instability (see Loschi 2019: 93; Loschi 2016). So far, Darwish has done the most to push this idea, arguing that the idiom of waste eventually became a common vehicle for expressing pessimism and critique of the rocky post-2011 political transition in Tunisia:

The phrase *balad al-zibleh* (country of rubbish) was employed in discussions about corruption, traffic, and the seemingly slow pace of political transition. Garbage became a metaphor for everything that was perceived to be wrong with Tunisia during the Transition (Darwish 2018: 68; 2020).

This was the period during which the rap artist Kafon's song *Houmami*[4] became a national hit for the way it captured the 'shit life' of people from lower class neighbourhoods. Its most famous line, 'we live like trash in the garbage bin' is still often cited in 2023.

There have been several 'waste crises' (primarily Djerba) and political scandals involving waste (the resignation of Prime Minister Elyas Fakhfakh and the 'Italian waste scandal') in recent Tunisian history. These 'runners up' – examples that could, and should, be analysed in more detail – are a reminder of an almost uncanny recurrence of waste at the core of political crises and corruption scandals in Tunisia. That is an important point for appreciating this paper's broader significance, and contextualising *hâlit wa'î* and Sfax waste crisis as involving recurrent themes. The choice to focus on the Sfax crisis derives in large part from the way it is a parallel reply, or counterpoint, to *hâlit wa'î*. The choice is also justifiable in terms of the events' significance for Tunisian politics. 'Sfax' has been the most severe of the waste crises and, significantly, the protests and mobilisations it generated were essentially the first, and so far the only, moments of real public contestation and violent clash since July 25th, 2021, the date on which Kais Saied dissolved the Parliament and began a process of dismantling political and judicial counter-powers and checks and balances.

What happened in Sfax follows a similar pattern to the cases of Djerba and Monastir. In all of these cases, longstanding grievances of nearby residents of a dumpsite were galvanised as the facility reached, then overran, its expected lifespan without ceasing operation. The residents began to protest and eventually forced its closure. At this point, the municipal collection authorities, as well as the private companies to whom the service is sometimes subcontracted, have nowhere to put the waste they collect. Then begins the dumping of waste in allegedly 'unowned' land, dry riverbeds, marshes, and wetlands. This situation usually continues until authorities manage to reopen the old site by promising that it is a 'temporary', 'exceptional', and 'emergency' measure: unavoidable until a new dumpsite is ready. However, in Monastir, the waste has continued to be dumped in a protected wetland for over a decade. In Djerba, the original site has been caught in a cycle of reopening and re-closing every few years, with no lasting alternative having been found. The way the authorities claim to always be somehow 'caught off guard' by such events, so that they only begin working on creating a new landfill – a process that takes years – with the closure event of the old one often makes these cases seem senseless and avoidable. There is a real parallel here with the governance situation in Lebanon, described by Arsan as 'focused entirely on the short-term, the exceptional and the temporary – on the next six months, the next year – but utterly uninterested in, or incapable

---

4   A *houmami* is someone from a *houma*, meaning a 'popular' (*sha'abi*) neighbourhood. The word means something like hoodlum, both in the sense that it refers to people from the hood, and connotes young thugs.

of, devising dispensations for the long run' (Arsan 2018: 372), except that Tunisia lacks the historical factor of civil war that Arsan uses to explain Lebanon's short-termism.

The landfill for the greater Sfax area is located approximately 20 km to the West of the city, near the town of Agareb (pop. approx. 15,000). Since 2017 residents of Agareb have been protesting against the presence of this dump, notably via a campaign they call 'I am not a dump' (*manîsh msab*), a slogan that along with, 'close the dump' (*sakker al-msab*), has been used widely in Tunisia in recent movements against landfill locations, and other forms of pollution too, such as industrial wastewater (cf. Robert 2021). The movement began to get some national media coverage in 2019 (for a detailed, chronological, treatment of this social movement, see Moulin 2022: 103–104), but what was to become the 'Sfax waste crisis' in the minds of the public and in national and international media has its origins in the dump's closure in the fall of 2021. Without an alternative site, waste began to accumulate in the streets. Attempts by authorities to reopen the dump in Agareb were met with redoubled protests from nearby residents. Clashes were at times violent, resulting in a police station being burned and the death of an activist. Consistent with the Ministry of Interior's approach to avoid stoking up conflict and social movements in recent years, the police withdrew. Then, as a sign that things were 'serious,' the military was deployed on presidential decree to re-establish order. The dump was never reopened, however. While this represented a real victory for local residents, it resulted in a regression to the waste disposal system that had existed before the opening of the Agareb landfill in 2008, which meant the dumping of waste in dozens of uncontrolled sites (allegedly unowned land, dry riverbeds, etc.) throughout the agglomeration. For want of a better alternative, the city's two former dumps, one in the industrial zone of Thyna, and the other on the seafront in the city's port, were reopened. A significant amount of waste collection was stopped entirely, with municipal authorities at times making efforts to move it from the centre to more peripheral areas, to maintain some appearance of cleanliness and order in the core neighbourhoods. Residents affected by the waste accumulations filed cases before the administrative courts, resulting in injunctions ordering the municipalities to remove the waste, but still in a context where there was no designated or controlled facility for receiving it.

There are many angles through which to approach these events analytically. For example, the 'crisis committee', established in the summer of 2022, tried to facilitate solutions to the ongoing situation, and whose work Maha Bouhlel was able to follow as an observer, provides an interesting insight into the functioning and limits of local governance and participatory models in the context of the push for decentralisation in Tunisia. In a more advocacy-oriented spirit, the dump's location and management has been criticised as a form of 'systemic ecological terrorism' that is 'produced naturally by the global economic system and national political systems' in Tunisia (Moulin 2022: 105). The thread we wish to pull out of this tangle concerns the manner in which the 'Sfax waste crisis' became a national affair involving Kais Saied and the largely political interpretation it was given, foremost by the president himself. Rather than consider it a local or regional matter, Kais Saied quickly entered the fray himself, gathering the Prime Minister and the Minister of the Interior on 8 November 2021 in order to sermonise to them in these terms:

> I am meeting with you today to examine the issue of waste removal in Sfax, in the knowledge that it has an objective aspect, but also that the accumulation of causes, which over many years led to the environmental issue of which everyone is now aware, is also – we must inform Tunisians – a matter that has a staged and artificial aspect, since those who history rejected are searching for garbage and waste, since they are, after all, themselves in history's dustbin.

His terminology here is rich in meaning and difficult to translate for both linguistic and contextual reasons, as well as reflecting the speaker's reputation for his idiosyncratic use of perplexing and tangled language. Two points are worth further discussion here. First is the juxtaposition between the terms, objective (*mawdou'î*) and artificial (*mustana'*). The first of these two terms signifies that which is objective, but also impartial and non-partisan, whereas the second is an adjective that can be applied to anything that is artificial, theatrical, or made up. The President thus implies that the situation in Sfax has been amplified and artificially manipulated for partisan ends. Whether this sort of insinuation that the country's problems stem from plots, conspiracies, un-Tunisian activities, and so forth is the result of genuinely held belief or is deliberate manipulation, it remains a recurrent motif in contemporary Tunisian politics. The second point concerns the phrase about the people who are consigned to the rubbish bin of history. This phrase was much-commented upon in the country, and many Tunisians found it amusing. It is immediately recognisable as a way of designating the political movements and actors who oppose Kais Saied, in particular the 'National Salvation Front,' a kind of anti-Kais Saied block. It wonderfully illustrates the weaving of an entire thread of political thought through references to waste as a substance and metaphor, in which both Kais Saied and his ostensible opponents vie to chuck one another in the garbage as a form of unappealable political discredit. Once consigned to the dustbin by history, Kais Saied's political opponents emerge trying to dirty his image by fabricating a scandal around garbage collection, ultimately confirming that they themselves are trash, reaffirming the initial verdict toward them.

Kais Saied employed similar phrasing once again in 2022 when a fire broke out at one of the 'temporary' landfills that was reopened at the beginning of the crisis. Summoning his Minister of Environment, Leila Cheikhaoui, he spoke to her in these terms in a video published online by the official channel of the Presidential Palace:

> The issue is environmental, and everyone knows that this affair is about the environment. [...] So whoever talks about the possibility of overthrowing the state[5] is delusional and is, once again, in the garbage dump of history. His place is amidst the waste that he has been letting accumulate for weeks and months.

It is precisely the de-politicising insistence of the 'environmental' dimension of the crisis that tells us what is really at play here, with that something being highly political. Defining reality in a manner that is consistent with the interpretation for which he is arguing, Saied sees his opponents' symbolic place in the garbage bin of history as confirmed by

---

5 It is interesting how he speaks of their aim of 'overthrowing the state', carefully avoiding the word 'regime', which has too many close and negative associations with pre-2011 governance structures.

their physical recourse to waste as a political weapon. In other words, the waste crisis in Sfax is but a concrete realisation of his opponents' trashiness, quite the opposite of impugning the president's governance.

Kais Saied's take is of course but one spin on events, and through our interviews and fieldwork we can typologise the rhetorical positions or framings of the issue into three categories. The first stance belonging to employees of various levels of government and the public sector (Agence Nationale de Protection de L'Environnement, ANPE, and the Agence Nationale de Gestion des Déchets, ANGED) for the most part describes the crisis as technical in nature: the landfill had reached its capacity (or not). If these actors accepted to engage in discussions about the political nature of the crisis it was often by allusion, or 'off the record' once our formal interview had ended. Next, the activists of Agareb themselves sought to characterise their movement as being based on the need to protect people's health, and to protect the environment. They also developed a discourse around 'environmental justice' which included a strong dimension of equity. Finally, a number of activists articulated an explicit awareness of the implications for their struggle of the different positionings, for example one activist told us:

> Environmental causes are noble causes, like the fight against racism. The whole world defends the environment. When a problem is environmental, people all around the world will support you, but when you have a political problem, nobody is interested.

However, a number of people we spoke to, without necessarily being Saied supporters, did believe the argument that the residents of Agareb were seeking to amplify the crisis for political ends and in particular in order to damage Kais Saied's image. For instance, one former elected parliamentarian explained that according to him:

> The movement was not 100 percent innocent. Even if it contained an element of social protest, it was also instrumentalised. As I explained to you, many people have deep conflicts with Kais Saied, his government, and his political direction. They took advantage of this situation, and had no real desire to resolve the problem.

According to this way of seeing things, the residents of Agareb, who mostly support the Nahda and Karama political parties, which are of Islamist leanings, have been seeking to get 'revenge' against Kais Saied since 25 July 2021 when the president stripped parliamentarians of their immunity from judicial proceedings and dissolved the Parliament. Hicham Mechichi, the Prime Minister at the time, was a member of the Nahda party, and since Nahda and Karama, with support from Qalb Tunes, formed a Parliamentary majority at that time, Kais Saied's 25 July actions were considered as having sealed the conflict between the president and these Parliamentary blocks.

Conclusion

The political meanings of cleaning and waste, within and beyond crises actually involving garbage in the material sense, provide some interesting insights into how many people in Tunisia think the sphere of politics and public administration is fundamentally put together, what is wrong with them, and how these problems might be addressed. Thus, the actual physical stuff of waste has a particular capacity to materialise – that is to make visible and give physical existence to – what is wrong in the country, (i.e. corruption, bad governance, and so forth). It metaphorically opens up two meanings. While cleaning up trash is one way of speaking about getting rid of the rubbish physically, it also hints at the political transformation required: to establish societal order, to organise space, and to discipline citizens, in order to make them fit for a modern and ordered state. While there are significant conflicts of interpretation over who is responsible for 'rottenness' of the state/politics and how it can be rectified, the underlying diagnosis and idiom for its expression is quite widespread and certainly recognisable by all. In that sense, this chapter is about inequalities and contemporary Tunisian politics, and underscores the importance of notions of decomposition, stench, rejection, and the efforts to overcome them as part of the unfolding political forces at play in the country.

Barbéchas – Waste Collectors
Margins of Society or Centre of a Circular Economy?

Hanen Chebbi

> Khira: 'I'm a widow [...] my husband didn't leave me any pension or anything. I don't have a care book (health insurance), my son is unemployed and still lives with me. I collect bread, a few plastic bottles and aluminium cans to earn between five and eight Dinar a day. You know, like today's young people, my son doesn't want to work with me. He's even ashamed of me. When he sees me in the back streets of the neighbourhood, he ignores me [...]. Look at the state I'm in, but what do you want me to do? [...] I don't talk to anyone, I just work, staring at the ground with my mouth shut, and I go home. I don't like the neighbours to see me carrying a big bag full of plastic'.
>
> Khira, aged 71, collects plastic and old bread in the Ennassim neighbourhood

The current Tunisian context is characterised by increasing unemployment and poverty. This deteriorating socio-economic situation is fuelled by factors extrinsic to the local context, namely the political, economic, health and environmental crises, such as the Covid-19 pandemic, the war in Ukraine and climate change. Greater Tunis, the largest fast expanding urban space in Tunisia, is marked by environmental problems and social inequalities that challenge the social landscape. Since the 2011 revolution, there has been growing awareness and mobilisation around environmental issues, particularly in relation to poor waste management (cf. Furniss/Bouhlel, this volume). Alongside visible mobilisations, other more invisible practices, particularly among marginalised sections of the population, who make a living from collecting and recycling waste, are fighting exclusion and poverty. The Tunisian government has been implementing a waste recovery and management system since the 1990s. This system is dominated and governed by the state through the coordination of actions between municipalities and national institutions. In recent years, however, the problems associated with waste management increased, and induced political debates and growing tensions between civil society, citizens and public authorities (ibid.). On the one hand, conflicts have fostered demonstrations and collective actions that in turn have challenged government policies, for example in Djerba, Galléla or Sfax (cf. Weißenfels, this volume). On the other hand, the problems and debates also highlighted another group of stakeholders of prime importance for waste management and, particularly, for the circular economy in Tunisia: the waste pickers, or *barbéchas* in the Tunisian dialect. These are individuals living on the fringes of society, carrying out waste collection activities informally. Plunged into oblivion through social invisibility (Le Blanc 2009: 1) they are nonetheless highly active in the urban space, in Tunisia as in other cities in so called developing countries (Florin/Alix 2016).

In urban situations, characterised by social inequalities, poverty and exclusion of vulnerable groups, *barbéchas* interact, scavenge, recover and sell recyclable waste abandoned by city dwellers. Although they are stigmatised and regarded as the weak link in the waste recovery chain by state institutions, such as the national waste management agency ANGED, they are nonetheless at the heart of a circular economy. Conceptualising a circular economy as a model of production and consumption, that involves sharing, reusing, repairing, refurbishing and the recycling of existing materials and products as long as possible, in order to extend the life cycle of products (Hobson 2016), the *barbéchas* are the essential suppliers of recyclable waste in Tunisia. But their everyday practices come at a high social cost, particularly as their recovery activities are neither regulated by legal or institutional frameworks nor supported or protected by any third party – in this sense they are part of asymmetric economies (Gertel/Audano, this volume). Through an analysis of the social context, the organisation of their recycling activities, and their spatial practices in the city, this chapter reveals a form of 'ordinary resistance' that the *barbéchas* engage with in relation to their stigmatisation and social invisibility. Daily resistance, engaging in a constant struggle against life's constraints, requires skills, the ability to act, and to negotiate (Gertel/Grüneisl, this volume). This aspect will be analysed in this chapter in order to deconstruct the social and cultural realities of these marginalised people. Deconstructing their realities will reveal their ways, means and strategies for accessing and appropriating the resources required to improve their conditions and preserve their dignity. It also aims to answer the question of whether the *barbéchas* represent the margins of society, or are found at the centre of a new circular economy.

To tackle these questions, I carried out an ethnographic study using life stories and participant observation with *barbéchas* in Greater Tunis. I accompanied *barbéchas* in the Ettadhamen district during their working day and took part in the collection and sorting of certain types of waste. As well as in the Mnihla commune in the district of Ettadhamen, I also worked in the commune of Soukra in the Ennassim district. Another part of my survey was carried out in the officially controlled dump spot at Borj Chakir, but this was interrupted when ANGED refused to grant me authorisation. Nevertheless, some empirical data collected at Borj Chakir will support the analysis presented in this chapter. The choice of the two districts – Ennassim and Ettadhamen – was prompted by the concentration of a large number of *barbéchas* in these two working-class areas. About 250 *barbéchas* live in Soukra and almost 800 *barbéchas* in Mnihla (c.f. International Alert 2020). The group of people I interviewed was made up of women, men and also couples engaging in waste recovery activities together. I interviewed three couples, eight women and seven men from the two neighbourhoods. Their age ranges from 45 to 70 years. This variation in age and sex allows me to compare the different experiences and life trajectories of waste collectors.

The chapter is divided into three sections. The first describes the social context of their lives in order to identify and understand important and significant moments. In the second section the focus is on their practices and know-how of their work. Finally, I address and analyse the spatial dynamics and reconfigurations of the living space and the neighbourhood in relation to the waste collection activities.

The Social Context of *Barbéchas*

Capturing the history and social context of the *barbéchas* makes it possible to understand their lived experiences and to scrutinise the links between the different fragments of their social life, as well as to understand the logics of action that fuel their choices. Their personal narrations are characterised by a feeling of exclusion, of rejection from social life, which takes the form of marginalisation in the urban space while also being neglected by state institutions. The *barbéchas* interviewed all originate from families who migrated from rural areas to the capital Tunis in the 1960s and 1970s. As former farmers confronted with the poverty and hardship of rural life, their parents moved to the outskirts of the city to build neighbourhoods such as Ettadhamen, Ennassim or Ennour near the Borj Chakir dump site. Because the public authorities consider these areas to be illegal settlements, living in them carries a stigma. What is more, the lack of legal recognition creates a state of rupture, discontinuity and even rejection in relation to the city. Their precarious living conditions and weak infrastructure also translate into practical difficulties, like accessing public transport. This is a major constraint to fluid mobility and prevents the creation of close links and affinities with others in the expanding metropolis, while also fostering a sense of enclosure and confinement to the neighbourhood, which reduces the chances of socio-professional mobility (cf. Bouzid, this volume).

The low cultural, economic, and social capital of *barbécha* families has contributed to the social reproduction of insecurity and precarity. In relation to the argument of Castel (1994: 13), the absence of relational networks and the lack of work, push *barbéchas* and their family members from the 'zone of vulnerability' to that of 'disconnection'. Zina, aged 61, a *barbécha* in the Ettadhamen neighbourhood, talks about her experience:

> I'm originally from Béja, and my father and mother came to Tunis when I was 20, and we were poor, so we moved here and stayed with family members in Ettadhamen. [...] Precarity and I know each other very well [...] I can even teach people how to live in poverty and insecurity.

In the same context, Sayda, aged 45, adds:

> I'm from Le Kef, there are eight of us in the family, we came to Ettadhamen when I was eight years old. [...] My father was ill and couldn't work. [...] I didn't go to school. It was misery.

Although the life stories of the *barbéchas* diverge, they are similar in the description of unbearable experiences of misery, accompanied by a degrading and devaluing perception of themselves. Their feelings of isolation, confinement and rejection reflect the negative image of their social life. This image of low self-esteem is captured by Serge Paugam as being the result of a context where 'success is transformed into a value in societies, and where, within the justifying and dominant discourse of wealth, poverty becomes the symbol of social failure' (2006: 16). He further adds that most of their life and energy is invested in maintaining the biological existence of their exhausted bodies (ibid. 119). This also perfectly applies to the situation of the *barbéchas*. One man, aged 54, who works at the Borj Chakir rubbish tip, explains:

> I've spent my whole life in the rubbish, my father was an alcoholic, and I've been collecting rubbish since I was 12 years old. [...] You call that a life, don't you [...] nobody thinks about us, neither the state nor the political parties – nobody [...] I can't take it anymore.

Another man working in Borj Chakir added:

> People are afraid of us, they look down on us, classify us as *hogra*, (meaning contempt, repulsion in the Tunisian dialect), they think we're – you know – criminals, thugs. When you go to ask for a job in a factory or a company, as soon as they find out we live in the Ennour neighbourhood (next to the rubbish dump) they get suspicious.

Social stigmatisation and neglect by state institutions (by social services, care services, public health centres) has led to a feeling of helplessness and powerlessness among the *barbéchas*, who have neither the resources nor the tools to develop projects that would enable them to move up the social ladder. This repulsion, the imprisonment in a sphere of exclusion, has given rise to a perception of social existence that is reduced solely to the biological significance of survival. In 'Sources of Shame', Vincent De Gaulejac (1996) shows that poverty becomes humiliating when several factors come together, such as degrading living conditions, stigmatisation, and abandonment by institutions. This relation between the effect of shame and poverty reflects the unease of the *barbéchas* about their living and working situations. This shame often takes the form of withdrawal and invisibility in the space of social interaction, such as in the neighbourhood, or in relation to neighbours and relatives – as exemplified in the introductory quote. A man aged 65, living in the Ettadhamen district, further exclaims:

> I often work at night so as to be safe from the contempt of the inhabitants of upper-class districts like El Manar and El Menzeh, you see. [...] I'm always surrounded by rubbish and bad smells, but what can I do, eh – nothing. They treat us as if we were a virus. The other time a woman in El Manar kept a bag of plastic bottles for me, you know, she opened the door of her flat and suddenly threw the bag out, the bottles scattered, it hurt me, but I picked them up. One time a woman threatened to call the police, because I was rummaging through the rubbish – she said it was noisy.

Despite this stigmatisation of the *barbéchas* – linked to their professional activity of collecting rubbish – their autobiographical accounts also bear witness to the many strategies they use to resist poverty, and even destitution. Their involvement in the survival economy (*economie de débrouille*, Ayimpam 2014; 'hustle economy', Thieme 2017) shows that, in a context of crisis, poverty and exclusion, individuals who lack resources – not just material resources, but also cultural, social and symbolic capital – choose to struggle through, in order to gain a degree of social recognition and to give meaning to their lives.

During the interviews, the *barbéchas* recount short stories that illustrate their experiences with the world of hustling, the search for opportunities and the continuous management of risk (Thieme 2017: 537). It was through *tadbir rass* (hustling) – for example, accepting odd jobs as bricklayers, hairdresser apprentices, stocking goods at a grocer's or selling sweets outside schools – that the *barbéchas* managed to provide for their families before joining the waste recovery sector. The quest for small, exhausting and underpaid jobs is a way of coping with uncertainty and socio-economic instability (cf. Gertel 2018a). Getting by 'to survive', 'to feed the mouths', and 'to feed my children' are expressions that recur in the life stories of the *barbéchas*. The search for new means of survival is often triggered by events such as the death of one of the parents – especially the father – the start of a family, or caused by the husband's low income.

What's more, people's perceptions of these odd jobs reflect a whole concept of work and self. According to them, working for someone else is seen as degrading for oneself, even humiliating, and working in waste recovery therefore represents a choice for them.

> My father was a farmer, I love the land, the greenery, but we moved here to Ettadhamen in the hope of improving our lives. [...] Farming doesn't pay as much as it used to. [...] I worked in a Hairdresser's. I earned from day to day, but not too much – it's hard. As time went by, I couldn't stand being humiliated in front of customers or offended by an inappropriate look or word, so I gave up. [...] I prefer to be isolated and free, which is why I chose waste collection. It's true that it's tiring, but no one tells me what to do.

A 45-year-old woman at the Borj Chakir dump site exclaimed,

> Before coming to the dump, I worked as a cleaner. It's tiring and at a certain point you can't take the humiliation any more. So, I started collecting bottles and tarpaulins here at the dump. [...] Well, it tires me out but it's better that way.

A woman in the Ettadhamen neighbourhood adds,

> When I was 25, I started working as a cleaner here in Ettadhamen, but it doesn't earn me anything, people are poor here and they can't afford to hire a full-time cleaner, sometimes I earn three or five Dinars for mopping. In the summer, I make a bit of couscous and spices that I sell. But at the age of 45, I stopped doing this kind of work, my body aches all over. So, I started collecting bottles and bread to help my husband, he works day to day. It's hard, but hamdulillah.

The social life of the *barbéchas* is a succession of ordeals that push these players to reinvent their social realities by resisting poverty and exclusion. The *barbéchas* may see themselves as marginal, invisible or even disqualified 'but they are also free actors capable of adjusting their actions to the situations they face' (Nachi 2006: 56). These individual trajectories retrace similar collective experiences that show how the *barbéchas* act, interact with those around them and mobilise a network of local actors to implement a socio-economic dynamic based on the activity of collecting and selling waste as a survival strategy. By collecting waste, they expand their mobility in the neighbourhood, and sometimes even in other neighbourhoods, which enables them to escape from their isolation. This spatial mobility, going beyond the neighbourhood, also enables them to become part of the network of actors involved in the collection and sale of waste. The *barbéchas* interact and forge links with small wholesalers and collectors with lorries (cf. Grüneisl 2021). Sometimes, they choose to socialise with their neighbours so that city dwellers will buy waste and recyclable objects from them. This unregulated activity is carried out informally and is organised according to standards, working practices, and rules that are the result of negotiations, conflicts, and arrangements between the protagonists of this recycling economy, thus conveying a unique socio-cultural dynamic, including, of course embodied costs and risks threatening their health and limiting the prospects of a fulfilled life.

Waste Collection: Practices and Know How

The characteristics of waste collection activities in Tunis reveal that access to this practice is not governed by fixed social norms and is not reserved for a particular social, religious, or ethnic group, as is the case in Egypt (c.f. Assaad/Garas 1993/94). In her study of the Zabbâlin, the garbage collectors in Cairo, Bénédicte Florin (2015) notes that the government neither runs a rubbish collection system nor operates a waste recovery system. The collection of recyclable waste is carried out exclusively by a group of Christian Copts, living in the rather marginalised Manshiat Nasser district of Cairo (Tekce et al. 1994), handing down the profession from father to son. Women are not involved in this activity of collecting waste from public spaces and households. The same is true of Morocco, where women only take part in sorting activities, but not in waste collection (Florin 2015b).

Women in Tunisia, in contrast, collect and sell waste both inside and outside controlled dump sites, and they engage in socio-professional mobility, as will be detailed later. Based on my participant observations, I distinguish between two modes of work for the same activity, the first being collection of waste at the central dump spot of Tunis, Borj Chakir. There are more than 900 *barbéchas*, active men, women, and children that are working at the site. The work consists of collecting the waste deposited by the municipality's skips, sorting it and selling it on or off the site. What characterises this activity is specialisation: each *barbécha*, man or woman, specialises in a type of waste, such as plastic, aluminium, wood, iron, foam padding or cardboard. This specialisation is organised according to gender, as gender relations have had an impact on the division of labour in the landfill. This can be seen in the way the territory is divided up and the objects appropriated: men collect more varied types of waste than women (plastic, tarpaulin, wood, iron, copper, cardboard) and have greater freedom to move around the landfill. The women, feeling dominated by the men, collect, for example, clothes and upholstery foam, which they renovate and sell in the neighbourhood. Faced with this situation, the women have adopted a strategy of withdrawal and have appropriated an isolated corner near the platform where the waste is deposited. Here they can do their sorting and sell their waste to the buyers who come with their lorries at the end of the working day (about 2 pm). In addition, collection and recovery work at the dumpsite is highly hierarchical. In fact, I observed a pyramidal and hierarchical structure of relations with the following configuration: lorry owners who transport the waste, workers who work on their behalf and recover the waste, and groups of workers (about 10–15 persons) that specialise in a specific type of waste, and finally, the individual *barbéchas*.

The second mode of work, the work of collecting and recovering waste by the *barbéchas* outside the Borj Chakir site, is completely different from the first. This work allows greater flexibility and freedom in terms of work processes and the choice of recovery areas. The *barbéchas* are autonomous in the way they organise their working day, working hours and days off. The choice of territory is not governed by strict rules, although there may be conflicts over territories, as will be explained below. The work process consists of collecting or digging up and selecting the rubbish in their neighbourhoods and vicinity. *Barbéchas* can also extend their working territories, often by forging affinities with neighbours or acquaintances who would keep their waste for them. The vehicles for the trade are generally objects that have been abandoned by city dwellers, such as pushchairs or shopping trolleys taken from shops to transport recovered waste. Some *barbéchas* invest considerable amount of capital, borrowed from family and friends, to have (push) carts built by blacksmiths. Others, lacking the financial means, use their bodies to carry the large filled bags on their shoulders or heads. Another group of *barbéchas* use motorbikes or small pick-ups rented for the day costing between 10 and 15 Dinar. When it comes to exploring and digging, *barbéchas* construct their own tools from discarded objects, such as screwdrivers and small iron bars that they use to rummage through rubbish containers or uncontrolled landfill sites. This enables them to avoid abrasions and injuries during the search.

The next phase of the work process is sorting, which mainly takes place in private homes. Sorting is governed by criteria such as the cleanliness of the goods or their condition, which qualifies objects for resale or re-use. The selection methods are part of a strategy to build buyer loyalty: offering good quality goods improves stable demand and enhances profitable sale prices. The *barbécha* men and women who use carts, wheelbarrows or motorbikes travel to storage depots, often identical to semi-wholesalers, to sell their goods. Although (valuable) waste is often collected in unregulated ways, its purchase and sale prices are determined by the international recycling market (e.g. Turkey, China, etc.) and price trends. For example, the purchase price of plastic tripled from 2020 to 2022, while aluminium prices have risen by fifty percent in the same period. There are also fluctuations, such as price variations determined by wholesalers and recyclers. The *barbéchas* have developed a strategy to sell at the most profitable price. They mobilise a network of players (other *barbéchas*, semi-wholesalers, etc.) to collect information on variations in selling prices, and choose and negotiate by making 'arrangements' (Nachi, 2001: 92) with the semi-wholesaler who offers the best price.

While price setting is generally a peaceful way of solving trade conflicts, at the Borj Chakir dumpsite, conflicts also arise over valuable waste recovered and the space used for recovery, i.e. the objects and resources of exchange itself. For example, the *barbéchas* of Borj Chakir consider the owners of lorries originating from Sidi Bouzid as intruders. To resolve these kinds of disputes, the antagonistic players adopt strategies to compromise. The *barbéchas* of Borj Chakir sell types of waste such as mattresses, plastics and packaging to the lorry owners, who spend between two and three months at the dump collecting waste to sell in Sidi Bouzid. Negotiations also revolve around selling and buying prices between the semi-wholesalers and the *barbéchas* outside the landfill site. On this subject, Sayda, a *barbécha* in Ettadhamen, explains:

> I don't have any friends in the trade. I sell to whoever offers me the best price. I get information, I go round the neighbourhood to see what's going on, you see. I make a good selection and I offer a good price. [...] At the moment I'm selling to a woman who has a storage depot, we work things out and I sell to her on credit and she offers me a good price.

Sales also depend on the means of transporting the goods, which determines the quantity of waste collected and therefore the profit. *Barbéchas*, who do not have the resources for transporting their own goods to a wholesaler, forge a link with a collector – the owner of a lorry – who comes to buy and collect their goods. These *barbéchas* opt for a strategy of withdrawal and concession, in order to keep the business going. Lacking the material resources to improve their work tools or to increase their earnings, they collect valuable waste by storing it at home, often up to a week. This type of sale involves relationships of power imbalance. These *barbéchas* do not have enough resources to negotiate with peers, which manifests in an asymmetrical balance of power, largely advantageous to the buyer. In this context, a *barbécha* man explains:

> I'm old. I have no means of transport, so I put my bottles in this big bag and at the end of the day I wait here under this post for a man I know to come and buy them. He doesn't weight the bottles, but he gives me five Dinar, sometimes a bit more. [...] I can't complain, you know.

A 35-year-old woman from Ettadhamen adds:

> I have nothing to carry my goods in. I wait for the man to come and get them. He gives me a sum of money without weighing the bag. He knows that I can't refuse, which is why he exploits me – I can't do anything. [...] Yes, he's the one who contacted me in the street while I was rummaging.

These testimonies demonstrate the power imbalance that was also present in the hierarchy of waste collection and recovery work at the Borj Chakir dump site. The organisation of work, the choice of working hours and of the sales method depend on the type of waste, its availability and the skills required for collection. Additionally, the position in the *barbécha* hierarchy also depends on the type of networks, skills, and knowledge about waste that they can mobilise. The development of these skills depends on forging links with 'connoisseurs' and those who know 'the tricks of the trade', who pass on their experience to the *barbéchas*. Skills development also involves enrolment in recycling courses. These skills and knowledge are a prerequisite to explore new areas and new types of valuable waste: Sayda tells me how she rubs shoulders with recycling plant workers, who taught her how to use a magnet to check the metal recovered. She also learned how to burn electricity wires to extract the copper. Sayda has also learned how to take apart a fridge motor or a washing machine to extract profitable materials (copper, spare parts, etc.). She assures me that she keeps her knowledge a secret. Zouhaier, another *barbéche*, has learned about the types of objects desirable for resale and re-use, such as kitchen utensils, screws, motorbike chairs, lamps, and old taps through observing and engaging with the sellers of re-use items at the weekly markets. Since then, he has been collecting these items during his working days and selling them at the Sidi Abdeslam market in the Tunis medina on Sundays. He has even attended recycling training courses in the hope of setting up his own recycling unit. The development of skills, the weaving of networks, and bonds of sociability make it possible to achieve social mobility. This can be seen in the transition from *barbéche* to semi-wholesaler. Zoubaier, a semi-wholesaler based in Soukra, describes his own path:

> Times were hard, I worked night and day as a *barbéche*, collecting everything I could sell, and I saved a bit of money after a big sale of copper. Then a recycler who trusts me loaned me money, so I was able to rent out this depot, and it's working.

On the same subject, Sayda explains:

> Sometimes, I still go out to collect when I don't have a customer. [...] You know, I took a risk, but it's worth it to get ahead. I borrowed 500 Dinar from a friend – God bless her – and I rented this little depot. I know it's difficult, given the competition, but I'll hold out and I intend to set up a small plastic crushing unit and buy a more sophisticated scale.

For *barbéchas* who are professionally mobile, interactions with other players in shared spaces, such as the neighbourhood or recovery areas, reinforce both, social transactions and conflict relations, often through gender differences. Women are sometimes forbidden to rummage in areas that have been appropriated by other male *barbéchas*. Hence, they adopt other forms of sociability with their neighbours: neighbourhood residents who keep the rubbish – bread, plastic bottles – or solidarity by collecting together and sharing the proceeds.

The collection of waste by the *barbéchas* can be seen not just as a survival strategy, but also as a means of 'resistance' (De Certeau 1990), as an answer to processes of social marginalisation. Resistance tackles institutional (i.e. state driven) and social exclusions. Ordinary resistance is practiced by those who are considered weak, but who still do not give in. It takes the form of grassroots opposition in a globalised world, and includes the ability to take action in everyday life 'to resist the demands of instrumental rationalisation made by the market system' (Dobré 2002: 6). It is thus on the basis of 'their daily lives, their little struggles, that these ordinary acts can be described as resistance' (Florin 2016:

100). Resistance is a capacity, a skill that the *barbéchas* build every day to achieve their ultimate goal of living in dignity (Nussbaum 2011), which they see as intimately linked to their economic independence.

Resistance and conflicts are entangled: Major conflicts have arisen around waste collection, illustrating the vital importance of controlling the routes and territories involved. These conflicts exist between the *barbéchas*, as well as between the *barbéchas* and the municipal workers who also collect waste. For example, objects left in trashcans take on a new meaning for these players, as its appropriation becomes a central issue. The municipal refuse collectors have assets and resources at their disposal to exercise their powers and appropriate the object. They have the transport means to move around quickly and can fill several big bags at once. Lacking the assets and resources to negotiate or settle, *barbéchas* often opt for the strategy of withdrawal to mitigate disputes. They adjust their collection times before the public refuse collectors arrive. They collect from early morning until 8 am, in the evening before 8 pm, or after midnight. Conflicts also arise between *barbéchas* over the objects they collect. The *barbéchas* then adopt a preventive strategy of reducing the flow of information between them so as not to divulge the 'tricks of the trade'.

Gender relations are also an important factor, reflecting the power relations and disadvantaged position of women *barbéchas*, both inside and outside the dumps. Women earn less than men, on average they receive between 5 and 15 Dinar a day. This precariousness and low incomes are not due to a reduced amount of work compared with men; it is linked exclusively to a social construction resulting from unequal power relations between the sexes in the workplace (Maruani 2005; cf. Garraoui, this volume). At the Borj Chakir dump site, these relations materialise in the appropriation of space, where women, as a form of resistance, have staked out a small area for themselves away from the collection area in which to sort waste in peace. Lacking the resources to buy a means of transporting the waste (cart, wheelbarrow, motorbike), the women made arrangements with the buyers to sell directly at the dump. Outside the dump, women are also sometimes assaulted or humiliated by men. To protect themselves, they develop bonds of affinity and cooperation between themselves, but also adopt strategies of withdrawal to make themselves less visible to the men and avoid conflict. On this subject, a *barbécha* woman in Ettadhamen exclaims:

> Four years ago, I was collecting at 2 am when I was attacked by two men. They hit me on the head with an object and I was seriously injured. [...] I was left traumatised. [...] Look, now I have this iron bar and I put it under my pushchair to defend myself [...] and sometimes my neighbour and I go out together to collect at night. She has no means of transporting her goods and I have a pushchair and trolleys, so I offer her a means of transport and we share the winnings.

In addition, a sense of belonging and a strong identification with their activities have developed among *barbécha* women. In their work on *cartoneros* (waste pickers) of Buenos Aires, Laura & Sainz (2007) describe the forms of solidarity that emerge between the actors, evolving in relation to the organisation of trade, in order to improve their situations and assert their identities. A similar situation can be observed in Tunis, even if the *bar-*

béchas' expectations were initially somewhat divergent. Between 2015 and 2018, engaged *barbéchas* in the Ettadhamen district founded an association (Association des Barbéchas de Tunisie) with the help of GIZ and the municipality of Mnihla. Since, collective actions have been organised within this framework in order to better structure and organise the work. A primary recycling unit has been set up as part of the projects related also to a state induced project, the Circular and Solidarity Economy. This unit has brought together former *barbéchas* who sorted, recycled and marketed the goods. Other *barbéchas* in the neighbourhood also contributed to the project by collecting and selling their goods to the recycling unit. However, the project eventually failed, due to problems linked to poor sorting, and problems of responsibility in the context of shared agency. Workers had sometimes put non-recyclable waste in the shredding machines, which lead to returns of goods from the buyers (i.e. the processing plants). That contributed to generating a financial deficit. These problems ultimately led to the closure of the unit and the workers had to go back to their old jobs: being again 'unemployed' *barbéchas*.

As part of the activities of the Association des Barbéchas de Tunisie, the members of the association, whose elected president is a *barbécha* woman living in Ettadhamen, have organised selective sorting awareness campaigns for households in the district, offering badges stuck on the doors of residents who commit to sorting in their homes. The municipality of Mnihla initially provided the association with premises, but in 2018 began using the premises themselves . Since then, the members of the association hold their meetings in a youth centre in Ettadhamen. The president of the association explains:

> It was like a dream come true, and it's very rewarding to be part of this association. We've done a lot of work and since then my life has had meaning. But since the local council took over the association's premises, we're not as active as we used to be.

A sense of belonging and identification with the recycling activity also emerged in the players' discourse. A cognitive perception built up an image as *barbéchas*. Those who collect waste using a lorry, or building caretakers, are not perceived by *barbéchas* as people in the trade. Belhassan, a *barbéche* in the Ettadhamen district, proclaims:

> Now they're everywhere with their big lorries and their 60,000-Dinar D-Maxes ... and what's left for us? [...] It's our livelihood.

This non-identification of the *barbéchas* with the threatening newcomers is the basis for the construction of their own professional identity, despite the fact that it is not officially recognised. These norms of belonging and recognition as a *barbéche* are similar in Borj Chakir, where *barbécha* work is often passed down from father to son. The *barbéchas* of Borj Chakir perceive people from Sidi Bouzid and Kasserine as intruders who threaten their professional activity, which has been rooted in the dump spot for generations. A 54-year-old man exclaimed:

> I've been a *barbeche* since I was 12, and I'm exhausted ... Today I'm taking my 14-year-old son with me, so that he can learn the job and take my place. This dump is my life

and there are those who come from 'who knows where' to dig and leave again, [...] what do I do with my years of working experience.

This professional identity is based on learning and passing on the know-how and experience of elders, including tricks of the trade, such as applying successful criteria for assessing recyclable waste or the skills to identify which skips could contain the most valuable waste. This self-identification is linked to a dimension of self-representation. A dual self-perception emerges from the *barbéchas*' discourse, tipping the balance between self-recognition and a strong sense of exclusion, or even contempt for oneself. On the one hand, they see themselves as excluded, unwanted and invisible. Collecting waste by rummaging through other people's rubbish is demeaning and does not fit in with social norms. On the other hand, self-recognition and self-worth are the result of a long struggle against marginalisation and surviving poverty by the sweat of one's brow. The *barbéchas* thus value the fact that they manage to provide for themselves in a situation of social rejection and non-recognition by the public authorities.

As a result, *barbéchas* see themselves as 'outsiders' through the exclusionary and discriminatory eyes of others. And yet, they are contributing to developing the circular economy sector and thus to solving part of the problem linked to urban waste and the saturation of landfill sites in Tunisia. This is what Bénédicte Florin (2015: 89) describes as the 'perverse inclusion' of the *Bouâra* (waste pickers in the Moroccan dialect) in a study carried out in Morocco, because they are both useful and undesirable in the city. Zouhaier, a 48-year-old *barbéch* in the Ettadhamen district, explains:

> Although it's my livelihood, it bothers my daughter, and she's become very sensitive and depressed, because I collect rubbish. She's ashamed of me. But I love what I do, it's my job, I feel in control of myself and nobody tells me what to do.

A *Barbéche* woman, aged 61, adds:

> Sometimes the way people look at me, kills me; they look at me as if I'm not a human being. But it's my job, I earn my living with the sweat of my brow, I don't steal from anyone *hamdulillah* and I feed my family and help my husband.

Socio-Spatial Dynamics: Use and Reconfiguration of Space

The use of space and the anchorage of the *barbéchas* in the urban territory, i.e. the spatial dimension of their practices, is central to understanding their work and everyday strategies of resistance. These socio-spatial dynamics can be understood in two stages: firstly, through their appropriation of the collection territory and the conflicts that ensue; and secondly, through the special configuration and use of the *barbéchas*' living space.

The isolation and compartmentalisation of the *barbéchas* in their neighbourhoods, which constitute the outskirts of the city, reinforces the social inequalities and segregation created by the disengagement of the public authorities. And yet, the mobility of *barbécha*-residents from poorer to wealthier neighbourhoods to collect waste shows the important role they play in solving waste problems. Numerous daily routes link the *barbéchas*' neighbourhoods with the more affluent areas of Tunis as the waste produced there represents a potential source of wealth for them. Moreover, these movements enable ways of reestablishing their connections with the city and escaping from the confinement of their neighbourhoods (Cirelli & Florin 2015: 14). The choice of route is never arbitrary; on the contrary, it follows a well-defined rationale, and requires great dexterity and know-how. The *barbéchas* first familiarise themselves with the area by walking through the streets, alleys, and neighbourhoods near where they live, to identify areas rich in rubbish. They generally choose densely populated neighbourhoods and the choice is influenced by the search for more profitable waste, such as aluminium or copper, which are rare materials. Little by little, the *barbéchas* then extend their collection territories to more affluent neighbourhoods where consumption is higher. This strategy of identifying and mapping out routes eliminates uncertainty and ensures that the work is well organised. The routes taken by the *barbéchas* depend on the type of waste collected. Objects that are suitable for reuse are often disposed of in illegal landfill sites.

Waste collection by the *barbéchas* has prompted residents to reconfigure the space in front of their houses: the window fronts are used to hang bags of sorted waste and bags with bread, while large bags of sorted bottles or utensils are placed on the small pavement in front of the house. This use of objects and space reflects a bond of sociability that has developed through the daily itinerary of the *barbéchas*. The daily passage through the neighbourhoods has helped to create a network of actors who are a component of the system and 'this is the very principle of an action without which the system would not exist' (Passeron 2002: 21). The *barbéchas* make arrangements with residents who keep high-value waste such as old engines, irons, hairdryers, new utensils, etc. for them. Sayda, a *barbéch* from Ettadhamen, has built up a network of residents whose homes she visits every Saturday to collect bottles and other items free of charge. Sayda's itinerary starts in Ettadhamen, and extends from there to the Intilaka neighbourhood, and the middle-class Ibn Khaldoun district. Zouhaier, also a resident of Ettadhamen, follows a route that starts from his neighbourhood, Intilaka, towards the affluent neighbourhood of Jardin Elmenzeh, and extends as far as the road leading to Cebalet Ben Amar.

The routes and their expansion raise another problem, namely the rift between practical and legal appropriation of a collection area. The collection areas are public spaces, which leads to conflicts between *barbéchas* and municipal waste collection companies. The municipal companies see themselves as the only institutional and legal actors that represent the proper application of the law, which imposes the prohibition of informal waste collection; their representatives and workers are convinced that only they have the right to dispose of the waste. The public companies mobilise this return to institutional norms, because what is at stake is the negotiation of legitimacy and territorial access. In this situation, the *barbéchas* opt for a strategy of withdrawal, as they are an erratic group with no assets to negotiate collectively (Crozier/Friedberg 1977). Internal conflicts, generated between the *barbéchas*, are resolved however differently. In fact, the *barbéchas* have developed norms that regulate relations and organise social transactions in cases where their routes cross, when digging in an unauthorised dump, or in a street. One man in Borj Louzir underlines:

When we meet in the same place while we're working, we change places straight away, I go the other way. It's better than arguing over a bottle or a bag of bread.

The other problematic aspect is the measures put in place by local authorities to encourage residents to sort their waste at home, in particular the installation of closed bins in neighbourhoods and apartment blocks. According to the head of the health and environment department at the Soukra municipality, these measures have been introduced to restrict access to the area by *barbéchas*, who are perceived as pests and troublemakers by the authorities and some city dwellers. *Barbéchas* consider these devices as obstacles, excluding them and threatening their access to their territories; so they have cut holes in the boxes to be able to remove the bottles collected inside. This calls into question the government's environmental protection reforms, which totally ignore the vital role played by *barbéchas* in sorting and recycling valuable waste in Tunis.

Waste collection involves, however, a complex recovery process, with activities taking place both in the public space (the collection site) and in the private space (the living space). The home takes on a new meaning, and changes the way it is perceived by its users. The homes of the *barbéchas* are often refurbished for a series of activities that complement waste collection. This involves dedicating a room to one of the activities, such as sorting, storing, or maintaining work tools. Sometimes *barbéchas* are creative and make savings. They build their own space by adding a room or a small garage where they store or sort merchandise and make small sales. A couple of *barbéchas* in the Ettadhamen district divide up the tasks as follows: suffering from a chronic illness, the wife has set up a space in the hall of the house to receive the rubbish brought in by neighbours. Another corner of the hall is reserved for sorting the goods collected by her husband. In the same space, reused objects destined for sale at markets are piled up against a wall. In the Ennassim neighbourhood, the 26/26 housing estate hosts a very poor population and most of the inhabitants work as *barbéchas*. The interiors of their half-built houses are filled with plastic bottles, chairs and other collected objects. Their trolleys and pushchairs are placed on the ground floor or hang in front of the houses with an iron chain and padlock. In Cherifa's house, which she rents for 150 Dinar a month, the unfinished space is used as a storage area. Additionally, in a small hall between the two bedrooms of the house, she reserves a corner to keep an old motorbike from which she will extract spare parts that she will sell, and a washing machine from which she will extract copper in times of need.

The studies carried out by Florin in Manshiét Nasser in Cairo reveal the emergence of a whole autonomous recycling circuit. In the neighbourhoods of Tunis, semi-wholesalers' and primary recyclers' depots were set up in residents' places, in garages or abandoned premises. These places have become primary recycling units or storage depots in the heart of residential areas. Their location is strategic, as they must first and foremost be included in the itineraries of the *barbéchas*.

Arranging one's home can be seen as a strategy for making oneself less visible and protecting oneself from the scornful gaze of neighbours. A 71-year-old woman in the 26/26 housing estate explains how she had built a small room at the back of her house so that she could bring in her large bags of rubbish discreetly, away from the neighbours' gaze. Making oneself invisible in the neighbourhood by rearranging the living space is thus also a form of resistance to a degrading and stigmatised self-image. A key problem resulting from these living conditions are health risks. The *barbéchas* are continuously exposed to the (toxic) smells of the waste stored at home, and during excavation work. Moreover, smelly and sometimes poisonous vapours escape from the illegal dumps located near the poor neighbourhoods where they live. This is due to the disengagement of the local authorities and the malfunctioning of official waste management in the capital. This again represents the inequalities between poor and well-off neighbourhoods, although the *barbéchas* play a central role in maintaining the waste circuit of the city.

Conclusion

In this chapter I investigate the work of waste collection and recovery of valuable materials by an emerging professional group that self-identifies as *barbéchas* in Tunisia. Paradoxically, the crisis context characterising Tunisia today has led to the expansion of informal and unregulated work, which is proving to be an opportunity and a resource for securing livelihoods for marginalised people. Through activities linked to the collection of household waste this vulnerable social group, often invisible to the public authorities, use waste as a resource and transform it via their work into a commodity. The *barbéchas* are the essential suppliers of recyclable waste, extend the life cycle of products, and thus contribute to a circular economy. While they live a form of ordinary resistance against inequality, injustice and contempt, the professional engagement of the *barbéchas* and their role in the community does not come without social costs.

Their life trajectories are characterised by processes of marginalisation, exclusion, and stigmatisation rooted in their histories, feelings, and social interactions. This is exacerbated by the failure of state institutions and local authorities to recognise their need for support and integration into the formal labour market. The lack of recognition of this group has given rise to survival strategies based on asymmetric economies that takes the form of unregulated entrepreneurship. The working practices and know-how of the *barbéchas* inside and outside the dump spaces are marked by conflicts over the appropriation of territory, materials, and objects. Live and work are inseparable. Even the intimate living space of the *barbéchas* is configured through waste collection and the recycling activities that emerge from it. The chapter thus shows how the *barbéchas'* value-creation activities shape its social world in the city. It is characterised by distinct norms and logics of action, and is reflected in new meanings attached to urban territories and networks of actors. Simultaneously, *barbéchas'* aspirations reflect ordinary resistance and the striving for recognition and dignity. Through their identification as a professional group that contributes to urban waste management, they claim a right not just to survive, but to live fully in society and to be recognised as equal social individuals. This reveals the complexity of Tunisia's waste management system – a sector proving to be problematic: involving, as it does, dysfunction at a policy and management level, and tensions between public actors and associative and local actors, as corroborated in following chapter.

Self-Governance
Collective Resource Management in Jemna and Awlad Jaballah

André Weißenfels

> EL-MECHRI: 'Raising cattle in this region used to be profitable.
> It provided [the farmers] with a decent living wage.
> Recently, the profits decreased, but they held on to cattle-raising and to their lands.
> What they defended was their way of making a living.
> Cattle-raising is how they pay their bills, their children's education, etc. This is how
> they make a living. They revolted because that was taken away from them'.
>
> Interview with El-Mechri (2021)

Two agricultural communities in Tunisia, Jemna and Ouled Jaballah, have taken action against long lasting marginalization and exploitation through centralized authorities; namely, the French colonial administration and later the postcolonial Tunisian nation state. After the revolution in 2011 they have engaged in collective management of their local resources, while practicing and experimenting – at least in part – with self-governance. The two cases show features of 'commoning' (Bollier/Helfrich 2015) and employ anarchist practices (Bamyeh 2009) manifesting in their tendency towards direct participation, consensus decision-making and voluntary compliance with those decisions. In this explorative chapter I aim to show that such movements exist in Tunisia, and with them the lived possibilities for participatory self-governance and collective resource management as an alternative to a state-centred governance structure. My analysis is based on literature research as well as on semi-structured interviews with spokespeople of both movements in October 2021 in Jemna, and in November 2021 in Monastir. This empirical basis does not allow me to draw final conclusions, instead it represents a starting point for more detailed research, interpretation, and further theorization. There also exists a considerable gap between the information available about the famous and widely published case of Jemna and the more recent and barely known case of Ouled Jaballah. Both movements are still in the making, I thus do not aim to finally assess the role they play in post-revolutionary and post-coup Tunisia, but to open up a perspective.

Jemna: On January 12th 2011, two days before the resignation of then president Ben Ali, a group of rioting young men occupied a date farm in Jemna, an oasis in the governorate of Kebili in South Tunisia (Kerrou 2021). The land on which the farm stands, the men felt, belonged to them. It had been taken from them first by the French colonizers and later by the post-colonial Tunisian nation state. During the protests a nearby station of the national guard was burned down. The mobilization around the occupation of the farm led to public discussions in the oasis and while some wanted to divide the land among different families, a public gathering of men ultimately decided to keep the farm intact, its territory undivided and to manage it through a collective body. For this purpose, they decided to establish a committee – Comité de Protection de la Revolution – which, among other tasks, was responsible for the management of the farm. The committee consisted of representatives of the different districts of the town and worked, according to the people involved, without hierarchies and offices (Kerrou 2021: 49, 83, 115). When the committee was dissolved after the Tunisian elections for the constituent assembly in October 2011 (Etahri 2021, interview), the Association for the Protection of the Oasis was created in March 2012 in order to assume the management of the farm. This association is a registered body with an official management board. The latter was first established by a consensual decision among the men of Jemna (Kerrou 2021: 112) and later elected through a ballot vote (Etahri 2021, interview). Even though the current association is more hierarchically structured than the committee used to be, the management of the farm continues to be a public issue in Jemna and contains important elements of consensual decision-making. All decisions concerning the use of profits from the farm and the handling of conflicts with the state are taken collectively in a public space (Etahri 2021, interview). This collective management of the date farm has, so far, yielded impressive results. Profits improved massively and they have been partially reinvested in the local infrastructure: in a roofed market place, a football court, also in renovations and expansions of primary schools. Notwithstanding an ongoing conflict with the state authorities over the occupation of the land, the association has become the legitimate representative of the movements' interests in the negotiation with state authorities: the Ministry of Public Domains and the Ministry of Agriculture. So far, however, no legal solution has been agreed on.

Ouled Jaballah: On January 10th 2021, dairy farmers and activists in the village of Ouled Jaballah, located in the governorate of Mahdia held a sit-in at a roundabout in the centre of the village. They were protesting the rising fodder prices that pushed many small farmers out of business. While the state had fixed the price of milk, three big enterprises held a monopoly on the fodder and raised the farmers' costs of production, which effectively made small scale farming unprofitable. As a reaction, the farmers had blocked the nearby road between Jebeniana and Ksour Essaf. They had stopped and hijacked the trucks from the fodder companies that were profiting from their misery. That afternoon, 24 police cars from Mahdia arrived to reoccupy the trucks that had been highjacked. This resulted in a massive violent clash in which many of the roughly 5,000 people living in the village fought with the police and forced them to withdraw. Over the next few days, the protestors clashed repeatedly with the police, who returned regularly to reclaim the trucks (sometimes successfully, sometimes not), while the protestors continued to stop and confiscate new ones (El-Mechri 2021, interview). On February 13th, the protestors formed a committee to coordinate and represent their movement. This committee – Coordination of Small Farmers – started negotiating with the governor of Mahdia and the regional council about reforms that should be implemented in order to end the protests. The negotiations resulted in a reduction of the soy price and put an end to the monopoly practices of the big fodder companies. Meanwhile, the news of the protests in Ouled Jaballah spread and farmers in other villages in the region also started organizing and voicing their opposition to the functioning of the fodder market (El-Mechri 2021, interview). During the sit-ins the activists and dairy farmers in Ouled Jaballah decided to found a cooperative in order to cut out mediators who skim off profits from the transport of fodder and milk and take a big margin away from the farmers. A group of protesters organized the necessary legal procedures and in July 2021 the governing body of the cooperative was being elected through ballots. At the time of my research, in late 2021, the cooperative had written its statute and almost every farmer in Ouled Jaballah had signed up to contribute money to establish the cooperative's basic capital.

The two cases of Jemna and Ouled Jaballah, I argue, represent examples of anarchist practices and commoning patterns. They connect joint resource management with practices of self-governance. As such, they continue to raise the same questions that were important drivers of the 2011 revolution: who in Tunisia has access to local resources, and who holds the authority to decide about access to land and the use of resources? Thus, Jemna and Ouled Jaballah show that inequality is always multidimensional and should be understood as unequal access not only to material resources, but also to decision-making processes and collective world making. Before I compare and discuss different aspects of both movements, I want to highlight that, as will become clear later, in the two cases the relationship between men and women inside the movements is very asymmetrical. Speaking for others in public, as well as the actual 'formal' leadership of both movements has so far been reserved for men. Another asymmetry concerns labour and pay beyond the gender level, for example, inequalities between members of the community and seasonal workers. The point is therefore not to show that all forms of exploitation have been abolished, but rather that the creation of equal opportunities involves an ongoing process of negotiation.

Social Movements in the Context of Historical Marginalization

While the movements of Jemna and Ouled Jaballah deal with different problems, both address the consequences of a flawed agricultural policy that has been implemented since colonialism, has continued after national independence, and deepened inequalities with the export-oriented policies of the last 50 years.

In the case of Jemna, as Mohamed Kerrou (2021) has shown, the date farm and the related conflicts about land, have their roots in the time of colonialism. During colonial occupation, formerly collectively used land had been appropriated by the authorities and transferred to a French investor who founded the date farm and exported its produce to Europe and the USA (ibid. 132–138). In 1938, the farm was sold to a Belgian investor; and after independence the Tunisian state took control over it. In 1963, the people of Jemna wanted to buy back the lot and paid the governorate of Gabes half of the requested price for it as a deposit. However, the state used the capital to finance a range of economic projects and did not return the land to the Jemniens, but rather nationalized it in 1964, allowing the state owned national Tunisian company for the dairy industry to cultivate it (ibid. 16; 114). Decades later, when the company went bankrupt, the state rented the land in 2002 for a suspiciously low price to two businessmen with close ties to the regime (ibid. 140). Under their management, the land was insufficiently cultivated and yielded meagre profits (ibid. 115). During and after the revolution, when state administration and security forces were temporarily weakened, the people of Jemna took control over the farm, reorganized it and turned it into a model for successful collective management.

While the case of Jemna, today, is an exceptional example for collective management, it was, in the beginning, only one of numerous (post-)revolutionary occupations, as in 2011 individuals and groups all over Tunisia occupied state lands. As in Jemna, those people felt that they had a long-standing historical claim to the land and that the state had stolen it from them. Thus, they re-occupied the land and started cultivating it. At first, the state authorities let most of them continue to work the land. But with the power of the state institutions growing, especially after 2016, the state started to re-dispossess people of many of the occupied areas (Gana/Taleb 2019: 31–48). In the course of this development, the State Secretary of Public Estates froze the Jemna association's bank accounts in October 2016. But, with the help of national and international activists and media support, the local association was able to withstand this pressure and forced the government to re-open their accounts in July 2017 (Kerrou 2021: 380–381).

Similarly to Jemna, the dairy farmers of Ouled Jaballah were the victims of a long history of dispossession and agricultural mismanagement (Ayeb 2012). In Jemna, first state management and later privatization had cut off the town from the profits of the oasis. In Ouled Jaballah, the farmers had been slowly pushed out of business by the monopoly structures of the fodder market. Farmers feed their dairy cows with soy imported from the US. According to Bilel El-Mechri, the spokesperson of Ouled Jaballah's coordination committee, it used to be imported and distributed by the state's Cereal Office until, in 1997, it was handed over to a private company owned by the Ben Mokhtar family which had close ties to the Ben Ali regime. This company sells soy exclusively to three major fodder factories – Poulina, Alfa, and Alco – who formed an oligopoly and raised the fodder price dramatically (El-Mechri 2021, interview). Thus, while the state had fixed the price at which farmers could sell milk, costs of production increased. This is why many of the smaller dairy farmers had gone out of business (ibid.).

The dairy farmers' problems are part of an overall trend since the 1970s, when the government opted for export-oriented liberalization policies, and even more so since the 1980s implementation of neoliberal structural adjustment programmes. Increasingly, the Tunisian administration has steered the agricultural sector towards trade based and capital-intensive farming (Ayeb/Bush 2019: 86). As a consequence, small scale farmers have problems keeping their businesses profitable in the face of the competition from private investors and corporations that have privileged access to resources like loans and subsidies, water, land, or agricultural imports like soy (Fautras 2021: 109; 115; Ayeb/Bush 2019: 90–91). In Jemna and Ouled Jaballah the protestors signalled that they were not willing to continue living under these circumstances.

This indicates a moral economy, in the sense that both movements felt morally entitled to access to particular economic resources (Thompson 1971: 76–136). In the case of Jemna, it is about access to a particular plot of land, legitimized through an inter-generational ownership logic. As Tahar El-Tahri, former president of the association and long-term union activist, put it: 'On this day, the 12th of January, they have burnt down the police station and they have reclaimed the properties that they had always considered to be theirs; it is the plot of land that belonged to our ancestors' (El-Tahri 2021, interview). In the case of Ouled Jaballah, people feel they are entitled to making a decent living as dairy farmers, as the opening quote of this chapter highlights. Rather than the right to mere individual economic stability, this implies the right to a way of life.

When the state, often in conjunction with the private sector, blocked access to what people felt morally entitled to, the movements in Jemna and Ouled Jaballah sought alternative ways to guarantee their access through contentious politics and collective management of resources. Thus, the movements should be read as a critique of the socio-economic status quo.

Institutions: The Economic is Always Political

The movements in Jemna and Ouled Jaballah are based on two complementary and connected dynamics. On the one hand, they organize themselves politically by establishing forms of collective decision making. On the other hand, they organize themselves economically though the collective management of common resources. However, there are important differences between the two cases. In the case of Jemna, the whole movement is centred around the collective management of the date farm. The political structure built around the management of the farm, the Association de Protection d'Oasis de Jemna, organizes the work, markets the product, distributes the profit, and continues negotiations with state authorities about the legal status of the farm. In the case of Ouled Jaballah, the structures of collective decision-making and representation, embodied by the Coordination of Small Farmers, addresses a wide range of economic policies and functions as an interest group, almost like a union. The cooperative is an offspring of this broader political movement and is not at the centre of the conflicts and negotiations with state authorities. Also, both movements face different obstacles in establishing collective management structures. While in Jemna the juridical status of cultivating the farm is in question, the cooperative in Ouled Jaballah operates in a clear legal framework. However, the dairy farmers' cooperative needs more capital for investing in equipment and infrastructure, while the date farm in Jemna can be profitable without much new investment. Furthermore, the cooperative in Ouled Jaballah involves many more people directly, because most of the farmers are a part of it. In contrast to this, the date farm in Jemna involves fewer people and the community profits indirectly since they have a say in the use of the profits. Thus, the institutions of collective self-management function differently in Jemna and Ouled Jaballah.

Nevertheless, there are important similarities. First of all, both cases of local collective resource management have the same target: to localize economic returns. The creation of the association in Jemna, as well as the cooperative in Ouled Jaballah, are ways to cut off private companies from their access to agricultural profits. The association in Jemna took the farm directly out of the hands of private companies and has since then made sure that profits would stay within the community. It also plans to build a factory to process and export the dates, and thus control other parts of the value chain in order to keep even more profits in Jemna. The same is true for the cooperative in Ouled Jaballah. Here, the necessary capital for the cooperative will be paid by the members themselves, the dairy farmers, and this is aimed at cutting out the middlemen who make their profits from transporting milk and fodder between the farmers and factories. Their long-term goal is to invest in a local fodder factory to provide cheaper inputs and sideline the big companies.

Parallel to the structures of collective resource management, protesters in Ouled Jaballah and Jemna have established, via public assemblies, representative bodies to organize their action and to represent their movements when interacting with state institutions. The coordination committee in Ouled Jaballah consists of one spokesperson, Bilel El-Mechri, and seven members. The committee coordinated protest actions by making sure that some farmers took on the necessary daily work while others protested and confronted the police. It has also taken on the task of negotiating with state institutions about reforms. In the same way, the association in Jemna, consisting of ten council members, not only runs the date farm, but also deals with state authorities on questions of its legal status.

Both representative bodies directly report back to the people they represent and decide any further course of action with them . In Jemna, the association convenes an assembly whenever there is an important decision to take. A person with a loudspeaker informs the people, and usually between 100 and 200 men[1] show up to participate in the assembly. If they agree on a course of action, the association is entrusted with its implementation. However, according to Ali Ben Hamza, the treasurer of the association, the assemblies have become less frequent since 2019. When it comes to the day-to-day running of the farm, the association council has the mandate to make autonomous decisions, sometimes with the foremen's input (Ben Hamza 2021, interview).

In Ouled Jaballah, the coordination committee functions similarly. According to Bilel El-Mechri, '[t]he most important fact is that the committee never makes decisions alone, even though it is an elected entity' (El-Mechri 2021, interview). The coordination committee gathers the farmers at the central roundabout in the village when they have to report updates from government negotiations or in order to discuss new steps to be taken. Like in Jemna, the coordination committee works more like an executive body enforcing the decisions that have evolved from the public meetings.

As will be discussed below, the members of the association in Jemna and the coordination committee in Ouled Jaballah have a powerful role in the decision-making process. However, on a procedural level, those gatherings establish a direct link between the representation of the movement and the local society (i.e. the movement itself) as it evolves with the problems and questions at hand and through ongoing public discussion. In

---

1   In this case study, it is always the men who speak in public, which is in line with local customs. The extent to which they speak on behalf of the women depends on their individual positioning, but remains unclear here.

both cases, we find a direct link between economic (re-)distribution and collective decision making. This indicates that inequality is not only expressed in access to material goods but also in access to political procedures and to the collective shaping of realities. Therefore, a comprehensive understanding of the movements in Jemna and Ouled Jaballah requires a multi-layered approach to inequality that takes into account the close links between all those dimensions.

Consensuses and Un-imposed Order

The collective decision-making processes in Jemna and Ouled Jaballah are based on a range of similar principles. Firstly, both cases display a clear preference for direct participation (as opposed to representation) and consensus (as opposed to majority votes) as the basis for collective decisions. In the two communities, votes are being used to elect the representatives in official (state recognized) bodies, but not used in public gatherings. When I asked my interview partners how they resolved differences in those gatherings they told me:

> There are usually many opinions, but we filter them out and pick the best ones until we arrive at a unified point of view. It's a democratic process. At the end, when a decision is taken, everyone has to support it because it's the group's decision. That is why the police forces were not able to break the sit-in despite their large numbers (El-Mechri 2021, interview).

> Even if the decision is not the one somebody prefers, he has seen that the majority is supporting it – therefore he accepts it. He might have tried to defend his point of view, but unfortunately for him, he has not been convincing enough (El-Tahri 2021, interview).

Consensus, thus, does not mean that everybody shares the same opinion, but rather that everybody supports a collective decision because they can participate in the process of forming an opinion. My interview partners highlighted the importance of the fact that every single person can speak and be heard at the public gatherings. That means that every (male) person feels heard and his voice respected, but also that everybody gets a good idea of why the group make certain decisions. An example: In their negotiation with state authorities, the representatives from Ouled Jaballah agreed on a ten days 'ceasefire' during which the protests were supposed to stop and the regional council would have time to talk to the ministry about the protestors' demands. When the representatives from the coordination committee reported this back to the protestors in a public gathering, some of the farmers were against halting the protests. After a heated discussion, the farmers agreed to accept the 'ceasefire', partly because the reasons convinced them, but also because the coordination committee agreed that they, as Bilel El-Mechri put it, would be held accountable if their strategy did not work. According to El-Mechri, those discussions were intense but very productive. In such a process, decisions don't need to be imposed because everybody supports them, which is what Mohamed Bamyeh, in his attempt to systematize anarchist thought and practice, calls 'un-imposed order' (Bamyeh 2009: 27).

Un-imposed order requires a continual process of interaction in which the people involved have the chance to inform themselves and others, discuss and find common ground and a collective course of action for every new problem, situation, or question that comes up. Both in Jemna and Ouled Jaballah the public gatherings provide such an opportunity. This, however, requires participants to be able and willing to continuously take a position on different issues, revise their position in the course of public discussion, and finally come to a collective understanding and decision. This means that the gatherings require a 'willingness to become' (Bamyeh 2009: 30), to permanently change yourself and others in a collective process.

In Jemna in 2012, for example, some members of the association, among them Tahar Etahri tried to found a company that could have taken on the management of the farm. When they could not generate a consensus among the people in Jemna, they went through with establishing the company anyway. Even though the management of the company was supposed to represent many different parts of the oasis's society, the whole affair created resentment among the community and the company had to be closed soon after its foundation due to public opposition. In our interview, Tahar Etahri told me:

> We proceeded stupidly and members of the association, three members [...] first of all I take my responsibility [...] me (and two others) made the decision after a meeting with the former Tunisian Minister of Agriculture [...]. When we came to Jemna and told the people that we would establish a company, we did not find mutual agreement among the people. This is why we acted alone. [...]. That was the big mistake that we made (El-Tahri 2021, interview).

In this instance, the ongoing and living process of the movement in Jemna outweighed the attempt to create new institutional structures (based on private interest), the development of which was made possible by the movement itself. While more centralized institutions have a tendency to become rigid and follow their own logic, the movements in Jemna and Ouled Jaballah represent living processes that can challenge and revise existing strategies and institutions on the basis of collective decision making.

Power Relations: Authority and Trust

In the two communities, representation is only used when it is necessary, which is mostly the case when state authorities need a 'recognizable' body to negotiate with. But how do those formal bodies of representation influence the power relations inside the movement? How is authority established and legitimized in movements that have a preference for direct collective decision making? Both, the association in Jemna and the coordination committee in Ouled Jaballah, were founded *ad hoc* in turbulent situations to fulfil particular purposes: to organize movements and to represent those movements in dealings with the state. In both cases, the people of the movements chose representatives. In

Jemna, the members of the association were later elected through ballots. In both cases, people with activist experience convinced other protestors to establish organizational structures and to manage local resources collectively.

In Jemna, it was an old guard of well-respected men who convinced the protestors to keep the farm intact and not divide the land among different people. This was a group of teachers and educators, most of whom had experience as activists within a union; some of them later became the spokespeople of the movement and initiated the foundation of the association (Etahri 2021, interview). Their experience is why many of the young people who also occupied the farm valued their opinion and trusted them. According to Ali Ben Hamza, the trust in the association, apart from the social and cultural capital of the people involved, has been enhanced as much by the fact that the members of the association personally make no money, as by the positive economic outcomes (Ben Hamza 2021, interview).

In Ouled Jaballah, a group of activists convinced farmers to hold a sit-in. They suggested founding a coordination committee, explained the advantages of it, and then gave the farmers time to think about it. When the latter agreed to the idea, the activists asked them to choose representatives that were trustworthy and competent:

> I explained these two conditions to them because they are the most important ones in my opinion. The members have to be competent enough to deliver the demands, able to negotiate, and trustworthy. [...]. As you know, many people are opportunistic bureaucrats. They deliver the demands and then they serve their own interests (El-Mechri 2021, interview).

The protestors then identified seven representatives during public meetings and nominated Bilel El-Mechri to be their spokesperson. When I asked Bilel, why the farmers trusted him, he told me:

> Trust is the result of experiences. It can increase or decrease. During that period, there was pressure from police, authority, etc. We were under several threats. I never fell back and I never hesitated. I think that this increased the farmers' trust in me (El-Mechri 2021, interview).

Overall, there are both: positions of authority and subsequent power inequalities that exist inside the movements of Jemna and Ouled Jaballah. The association and the coordination committee have the power to make small decisions by themselves and to lead negotiations with state authorities. They also can decide whether or not and when to convene public meetings with the wider movement. Also, certain individuals are more powerful, have more social capital, and have more influence on decisions. This is the case with Tahar Etahri and Bilel El-Mechri. Mohamed Kerrou, in his comprehensive study on Jemna, identifies Etahri's role as a teacher, his activist past, and his belonging to an old family as the basis of his authority. He characterizes him as a 'consensual and democratic leader' (Kerrou 2021: 124). This reveals the constitution and importance of personal positions of authority inside the movements. However, those positions rely on continued efforts to build trust and respect. Their individual authority is under regular scrutiny as long as the movements are driven by permanent collective and direct interaction. But how and why are the people in Jemna and Ouled Jaballah able and willing to partake in a continuing process of collective negotiation and action?

Solidarity: The Economic and Political are Always Cultural

The representatives of the movements emphasize how important the culture of discussion is to their projects. It seems that the movements enable people to interact in a way that further empowers mutual understanding and collective action. As Bilel El-Mechri describes it: 'the dairy farmers have the energy to intensively and respectfully discuss issues because they went through collective experiences which forged solidarity'. When I asked him why the heated debates in the gatherings did not turn violent, he reasoned: 'Solidarity exists between them, and the solidarity has been created by the police attacks. Everyone fought together. Together we were exposed to teargas. Everyone became a target and could get shot' (El-Mechri, 2021, interview). Solidarity, then, can be understood not only as a condition for collective decision-making and action, but also as its result. One constitutes the other – and *vice versa*. Existing experiences express themselves in cooperation and cooperation creates new experiences. Thus, the explanation for the success of both movements might not lie outside the movements but within them: to a certain degree, the movements made themselves possible. For both communities the immediate reality of the movements brought into being the development of new cognitive tools, a new mode of interaction, and opened up a process of collective becoming. A becoming that is not a realization of some basic existing truth like a 'tradition' but something new, adding to the existing forms of interaction. In this way, decision-making processes (politics) and material resource management (economics) are always also tied to individual and collective world making (culture) – the open ended and continuous becoming of individuals and communities.

A concept that lends itself to understanding the connection between those three dimensions is the notion of 'commons' in the way Silke Helfrich and David Bollier define it (Helfrich/Bollier 2015, 2019). Commons describe forms of production that are collective and oriented towards the needs of a community. Helfrich and Bollier identify three categories of commoning 'patterns': commons provisioning (economic), peer governance (political), and social life (cultural) – all of which the movements of Jemna and Ouled Jaballah exhibit to a certain extent. In terms of commons provisioning, both cases are characterized by 'collective production and use' of local resources (ibid. 159). In terms of peer governance, they exhibit 'transparency in places of trust' (ibid. 125) and 'deciding with a collective voice' (ibid. 129). In terms of social life, both movements are 'cultivating shared intentions and values' (ibid. 99), 'working through conflicts in a way that preserves relations' (ibid. 108), and 'establishing collective rituals' (ibid. 100). This notion of commoning corresponds to the multidimensional understanding of inequality mentioned above. It is a set of practices that address economic, political and social inequality at the same time.

Examples of comprehensive, full-fledged commoning are hard to find. When we analyse examples of commoning, a variety of patterns exist or are absent in different cases (ibid. 91). This is certainly the case in Jemna and Ouled Jaballah where important inequalities persist. Most obviously, the people directly involved in the movements are predominantly men. In Ouled Jaballah, women have been involved in the protests and public discussions, but it is men who take the leadership of the movement. In Jemna, women have been involved in providing food for the protestors but are not part of the public discussions. When I asked Tahar Etahri about the absence of women, he explained: 'This is a question of mentality. Perhaps, there are a lot of female activists in the cities. But in the villages, this is rare. The association does not have to take responsibility for the absence of women' (Etahri 2021, interview). Another limitation, besides the male dominance of the movements, is that, so far, sustainability has not played an important role. This is mostly because, in both cases, the management of local resources still functions according to the constraints of profit maximization, even though those profits might be socialized inside the community, as is the case in Jemna.

What about the State?

Mohamed Kerrou has shown that the movement in Jemna prioritizes legitimacy over legality and thus questions the 'bureaucratic organization of economy and society' (Kerrou 2021: 18). This distinction between legitimacy and legality is one that Bilel El-Mechri also mentioned in our interview:

> There are necessary legal procedures like legally registering the association so that it appears in the Official Gazette of the Republic of Tunisia. I do not care for that. What really matters to me is that something was created by the farmers and that they considered it real. That's all. That's what matters to me (El-Mechri 2021, interview).

Because existing legal bodies lost their legitimacy, the institution of 'coordination committees' spread fast. The farmers' union, according to Bilel El-Mechri, had lost the trust of the farmers:

> We established coordinating committees in other regions like Ksour Essaf, Ferchich, Gharayra, Ouled Bousmir, Bouzayyen, Oueslatia, Hajeb Laayoun, etc. The farmers were all convinced that the farmers' union does not represent them [...]. When we started this thing, the idea spread. We contacted some farmers. Others have adopted the idea by themselves (El-Mechri, 2021, interview).

Thus, both movements question the legitimacy of existing state institutions and offer alternative processes of establishing legitimate (self-)governance through direct participation, consensus decision making, and collective resource management. As such they have a complicated relationship with the state. In the case of Jemna the state is mainly perceived as the force that dispossessed their ancestors of their land and secured the accumulation of capital through appropriation of local resources. In Ouled Jaballah the state is experienced as the force that organized the liberalization of the fodder market in a corrupt way, and, again, secured the accumulation of capital through appropriation of local resources. When both movements tried to reclaim a part of their resources, the state turned out to be an obstacle, represented, for example, by the security forces. While in 2011 in Jemna security forces were overstrained and hesitating, the police in Ouled Jaballah (ten years later) had a clear strategy, one that had been developed in clashes with protestors in other parts of Tunisia. Bilel El-Mechri emphasized that shortly before the police forces entered Ouled Jaballah, the same policemen had been deployed in Hay Ettadhamen in the capital, where a well-known series of riots in disenfranchised neighbourhoods had recently occurred. The police, according to him, used the same strategies as they had in Ettadhamen, firing tear gas at houses and estates that were not involved in the protest. This 'random violence' discouraged the bystanders and protestors in the capital, and finally the protests were dissolved. However, Bilel El-Mechri takes pride in the fact that this strategy did not work in Ouled Jaballah:

> The Ouled Jaballah sit-in is the only one in the entire country that the police have failed to dismantle. [...] . When they attacked people's homes here, the people went outside and fought back, even those who have never hit a cop before. We showed the people of Ouled Jaballah what had happened in Ettadhamen and how the cops attack everyone regardless of who they are. We advertised those events in our favour and the people showed solidarity (El-Mechri 2021, interview).

Thus, the violent clashes with the police did not end the sit-in but furthered the solidarity amongst the protestors, which was one of the key factors that allowed the movement to develop in the way it did towards collective organization. However, even though in Jemna and Ouled Jaballah protestors questioned the sovereignty of the state, they still address government institutions with their demands and thus accept the state as a negotiation partner. In Jemna, negotiations about the legal status of the land and how it should be cultivated have been ongoing since 2011. Relationships with the authorities have had their ups and downs, resulting in a series of conflicts since 2016. However, like in Ouled Jaballah, when conflict with the state intensified, the people in Jemna seem to have closed their ranks: 'There are people who are against the association, but they are very few. But in 2016, even those who were against the association came with us to confront the state' (Etahri, 2021, interview). Nevertheless, the association is looking for a way to collaborate with the state, not to replace it, as long as the profit from local resources stays in Jemna. Similarly, in Ouled Jaballah, the movement has clashed with state authorities, only to address their demands later to the governor of Mahdia and the regional council. The farmers don't want to do away with the state but rather hope to change both its economic policies and the political channels to address them. Instead of the farmers' union, they want the coordination committee to represent them:

> The coordination is not judicially legal. But for us, this is not a judicial matter. It is about the *status quo*. The governor kicked out the farmers' union, which is an organization that has been active since 1982, and kept us in the room (El-Mechri, 2021, interview).

Conclusion

The self-governed movements in Jemna and Ouled Jaballah can be understood as anarchist practices (Bamyeh 2009) and forms of commoning (Helfrich/Bollier 2019). They create access to resources, to meaningful participation in decision-making processes and to collective world making – combining capabilities and aspirations (Gertel/Grüneisel, this volume). They are a reaction to a long history of regional and sectorial marginalization that can be traced to colonial times and has been exacerbated since the 1970s. As such, they encourage us to think about inequality as multidimensional. They suggest that the widespread public discontent with the economic and political order after 2010/2011 might not only be grounded in material inequality but also in inequality of possibilities to participate and to collectively shape the world. This is why Mohamed Kerrou understands Jemna as a successful manifestation of the Tunisians' revolutionary demands for 'work, freedom, and dignity' (Kerrou 2021: 52). The experiences of Jemna and Ouled Jaballah reveal that alternative forms of governance and economy are suited well to address the inequalities that many Tunisians are facing today.

Mobilities.
Aspirations for a Dignified Life

Introduction

Ann-Christin Zuntz

> MOHSEN LIHIDHEB started his personal migration museum in Zarzis (southern Tunisia) in the 1990s. A former postman, he used to find messages in bottles on his local beach and reply to the senders, and also send his own messages. Later, he began to pick up migrants' belongings, alongside shells and fishbones. Occasionally, he has found human bodies, which he has buried. Over time, his collection, the Musée de la Mémoire de la Mer et de l'Homme (Museum dedicated to the Memory of the Sea and of Humans), has grown to fill an entire building and the courtyard of his house. Although Lihidheb is not a trained archaeologist, he catalogues his findings, trying to infer information about migrants' stories. He speculates that a shoe with a worn sole might have belonged to someone from Sub-Saharan Africa who crossed the desert on foot. He uses the found objects to raise awareness on two issues that are intertwined in Tunisia's coastal regions: environmental pollution, and dangerous, often deathly, migrations. The material traces of the mobilities crisscrossing Tunisia, whose owners are usually absent and unknown, point to a paradox at the heart of the country's migration landscape (cf. El Ghali 2022): the (in)visibility of Sub-Saharan Africans who figure prominently in European and, more recently, in Tunisian policy discourse, but who try to remain unnoticed in everyday life to avoid violence at the hands of Tunisians and local authorities.
>
> Interview with the author (October 2021)

The following chapters shed light on the nexus between (im)mobility, border policies, and (in)visibility in Tunisia: commuting in Tunis, begging in Sfax, Sub-Saharan African and Syrian migrations to North Africa, as well as the forced return of young Tunisians. Drawing on a wide range of data – from large-scale surveys and ethnographic research with aspiring and actual migrants, to urban planning documents and key stakeholder interviews – they highlight intricate entanglements of (in)visibility in policy discourse and on the streets. Neither mobility nor immobility are inherently bad. Rather, as proponents of the 'regimes of mobility' approach (e.g. Glick Schiller 2013) have argued, people's ability to move or stay put is shaped by their positioning within exclusionary power structures. In the chapters, powerlessness may translate into stuckness – for example, when low-income fringes of Tunis are excluded from public transport networks (Bouzid, this volume) – or into forced mobility. By way of illustration, young Tunisians hope to overcome barriers to social mobility – e.g., access to decent work – by moving from the country's poorer interior regions to coastal cities, and, for some, across the Mediterranean (Kreuer/Gertel, this volume). In a similar vein, precarious mobilities might force people on the move to conceal their presence, but some, like the Syrian women begging in Tunisia's big cities, also become exposed to the public eye (Zuntz et al., this volume).

Considered a country of emigration for Tunisians before 2011, Tunisia has since turned into a hub for diverse migrations and mobile populations, hosting 59,000 migrants, mostly from Sub-Saharan Africa (Institut National de la Statistique/Observatoire National de la Migration 2021), and more than 12,000 asylum-seekers and refugees registered with the United Nations High Commissioner for Refugees (UNHCR 2024). Domestically, the country's migration and asylum legislation perpetuate a 'patchwork of laws, bilateral agreements, exemptions and informal practices' (Natter 2022: 144). Tunisia signed the 1951 Refugee Convention and its 1967 Protocol, and its 2014 and 2022 Constitutions acknowledge the right to political asylum, but this has not yet been translated into domestic asylum law (Ben Achour 2019; Amnesty International 2022). For most migrants, and even for refugees with protection status, there is no clear pathway to residency permits and access to the formal labour market, let alone Tunisian citizenship (Nasraoui 2017; Geissler 2019). Internationally, Tunisia has concluded a series of bilateral agreements, for example with Italy and France, and accords with the European Union (EU), receiving development funding in exchange for hardening its borders (for an overview, see Martini/Mergisi 2023). In 2023, Tunisia signed a Memorandum of Understanding with the EU, securing 105 million Euro to fight people smugglers and around 15 million Euro for humanitarian organisations to facilitate 'voluntary return' of migrants. Almost immediately, the Tunisian government announced that it would not accept as returned migrants Sub-Saharan Africans who had passed through Tunisia on their way to Europe (Doyel et al. 2023). Meanwhile, members of Tunisia's security forces, paid by EU funding, routinely beat and sexually abuse migrant women (Guardian 2024).

In European policy discourse and media, Tunisia is now framed as a 'transit country' for Sub-Saharan Africans and as the EU's new frontier. This is partly borne out by statistics: Tunisia has recently overtaken Libya as a main country of departure in the Central Mediterranean, and since 2022, more Sub-Saharan Africans than Tunisians have arrived in Italy (Martini/Megerisi 2023). After the hate speech of the Tunisian president and ensuing racist attacks, boat crossings departing from Tunisian beaches were at a record high in summer 2023 (Doyel et al. 2023). Yet, such framings are highly political in themselves, as perpetuating a narrative of uncontrolled EU-bound migration serves to justify the further enhancement of bordering measures (Düvell 2012; Crawley et al. 2017). Both the Tunisian state and the EU have taken a securitised approach to migration, portraying Tunisia as a prime target for combatting smuggling and human trafficking (El Ghali 2022; Natter 2022; Meddeb/Louati 2024). Significant protection gaps, and state and community violence against migrants in Tunisia are well documented (e.g. Badalič 2019; Bisiaux 2020; El Ghali 2022). Indeed, the lived reality of border violence is discussed in multiple chapters in this collection: blatant deception, in the form of forced returns and empty promises of assistance for deported Tunisian emigrants (Garnaoui, this volume), but also, less conspicuously, through lack of urban governance in low-income neighbourhoods with a significant presence of Sub-Saharan African migrants (Kahloun/Frische, this volume).

Besides being painted as 'criminals' and 'security threats', migrants, especially women, are also portrayed as 'victims'. Since 2011, security-oriented approaches to migration management in Tunisia have been complemented by 'soft' bordering measures, as international donors have engaged with Tunisia's newly emerged civil society to increase migrants' protection – but not their rights (Cassarini 2020; Cuttita 2020; Dini/ Giusi 2020). Two chapters in this collection attend to migrants' newfound humanitarian visibility: while some local governments have been praised by international donors for their pragmatic and welcoming approach to migration, Ben Media and Sha'ath's contributions remind us that some European border policies present themselves as 'progressive'. Their chapters capture the recent trend in foreign assistance for supporting localisation efforts and participatory development. However, conflicts arise when there is little room for meaningful participation for irregular migrants, and despite good intentions, municipalities remain enmeshed in multi-scalar structures of migration management, through which they take part in monitoring migrants on their territory.

On the ground, productions of invisibility are the flip side of migration management. Several chapters address the entanglements of (im)mobilities and invisibility, suggesting that deliberate unknowing is a strategy of the powerful to deny the presence and rights of marginalised populations. Despite Tunisia's international commitments, migrants and refugees are absent from its domestic legal frameworks, and there is little coordination between state authorities and civil society actors providing assistance to mobile populations (Ben Media, this volume). These intentional absences allow the Tunisian government to refuse being turned into a more permanent 'host country' for Europe's unwanted migrants against its will. On the city level, the needs of migrants are not reflected in urban planning documents (Kahloun/Frische; Sha'ath, both this volume), and municipalities know little about undocumented local residents. However, visibility can also be reclaimed by migrants themselves. During the Covid-19 pandemic, unprecedented forms of civil society support alerted Tunisian municipalities to the presence of vulnerable migrants on their territory (Sha'ath, this volume). At times, visibility can be tactical: in Bhar Lazreg, Tunis, Sub-Saharan African women set up street stalls and open hair salons targeted at Sub-Saharan African customers (Parikh, this volume). In a context in which access to decent labour, accommodation, childcare, and even public space is shaped by race, these women challenge racial fault lines by asserting their presence in the public eye. Meanwhile, in big Tunisian cities, Syrian women beg at central roundabouts, while Syrian cuisine has become popular among upper-class circles, and Syrians open restaurants, cater to weddings, and even dance in talent competitions on Tunisian television (Zuntz et al., this volume). In a nutshell, migrants in Tunisia may be forced into exclusionary forms of (in)visibility that make it difficult for them to make a living, but they also creatively engage with visibility, at times flying under the radar, at times making their presence seen and felt.

On a final note, the chapters in this volume broaden our understanding of Tunisia's borders: besides the country's sea and land frontiers, there are other borders resulting, for example, from unequal capabilities (Gertel/Grüneisl, this volume). Invisible and unofficial, but sometimes just as efficient, these borders divide the more affluent coastal cities from the impoverished interior of the country, and upper and middle-class areas in the capital from low-income neighbourhoods in flood-prone suburban zones with poor sanitation and informal housing. While media reports and policy discourse focus on spectacular sea crossings, the chapters reveal mobilities of various magnitudes, including urban and regional. Often, mobilities cut across scales: Bhar Lazreg, a neighbourhood of Tunis studied in two chapters (Kahloun/Frische; Parikh, both this volume) is home to significant numbers of undocumented Sub-Saharan African migrant workers – it is also bypassed by transport arteries connecting different parts of the capital. Many migrants experience both lack of access to mobility within cities and stuckness in Tunisia, as they can neither return to their home countries – due to Tunisia's penalty system imposing huge fines on those who overstay their visa – nor cross the borders of a highly securitized European Union.

Our comparative study of mobilities towards, within, and emerging from Tunisia shows that poor and marginalised people travel for longer, are forced to take detours, end up paying more, and their movements are potentially riskier. Commuters in low-income areas in outer Tunis have to wait and pay more for private transport to access schools and workplaces, and women feel unsafe at night (Bouzid, this volume). In a similar vein, Syrian refugees have used dangerous and costly smuggling routes across the Sahara to reach Tunisia. Adopting a cross-scalar perspective helps us connect the dots between waiting for a bus on the outskirts of Tunis and waiting to cross the Mediterranean. While public discourse in Tunisia and Europe plays out 'migrants' against 'citizens', we show the similar bordering logics at work, restricting, delaying, and circumventing the movements of Sub-Saharan African migrants, Tunisian emigrants, and suburban travellers (cf. Cassarini 2020). Such insights help us denaturalise migration policy categories, asking instead what processes 'migrantise' mobile people from the Global South and even marginalized Tunisian citizens, i.e., turn them into vulnerable migrants (Anderson 2019). Hence, the study of (im)mobilities in Tunisia turns out to be a diagnostic of systemic, interlocking factors that stifle mobile people's aspirations for a dignified life: of hardening EU borders and allegedly 'softer' approaches to migration management across the Mediterranean, but also of issues affecting the general population, including changed labour relations, increasing precarity, und urban sprawl.

Shattered Trust
Aspirations for Emigration among Young Tunisians

David Kreuer & Jörg Gertel

> YASSINE: 'I took part in the Tunisian revolution, and I was impressed and touched by what we experienced then. But later I became frustrated because of the economic situation and the political corruption. I no longer believe in political work because my efforts were in vain. Now I'm indifferent to how things develop, almost selfish. I only care about my personal affairs.
> We are no longer able to buy meat because of its high price, nor vegetables and vegetable oil, the price of which has risen sharply. All food has become more expensive, and this is made worse by the low purchasing power of Tunisians. My income and that of my family are not high enough to cover the food costs. Sometimes I go hungry, I cannot cover my food needs. I eat anything just to survive. We don't have a clear strategy; we try to adapt to the situation. Sometimes we stretch our food that was meant to be for one day over three days. When I experience such situations of inequality, I feel hatred and the desire to leave the country'.
>
> Yassine, Summer 2022

YASSINE, a 26-year-old doctoral student from the coastal city of Sfax, is not alone in wanting to leave his country. Given the enduring mood of crisis and the lack of legal options for migration, many young people currently see clandestine migration across the Mediterranean as the only way out of their economic and personal predicament. In fact, Tunisia has witnessed a 'soaring rise in *harga* numbers' (Mnasri 2023:1038) in recent years. *Harga*, the colloquial Arabic term for clandestine migration, denotes the 'burning' of papers and, metaphorically, borders. What is more, even those young adults who remain in place often dream about a better life elsewhere. Why do so many young people want to leave Tunisia? What kind of experiences and frustrations fuel this aspiration? There are no simple answers, as we must take the complexity of livelihoods into account.

In this chapter, we explore migration aspirations of young people in Tunisia. Asked about his experiences of inequality, Yassine guides us through the chapter and shares his thoughts and reflections as of late summer 2022. He emphasises the role of the Tunisian state, the situation of the middle-class, and his personal expectations of life. We will situate his experiences in the context of quantitative interviews that were conducted in the country. Special emphasis will be placed on socio-economic capabilities, but also on the political grievances of aspiring young migrants and on the crucial role of regional inequalities within the country (cf. Gertel/Grüneisl, this volume).

The chapter is structured as follows: first, we give a brief introduction into mobility dynamics and summarise the interview methodology employed. Then, we present survey findings, combined with further interview quotes, concerning the young generation's economic situation, their loss of trust in the state and its institutions, regional patterns of inequality, and how all this affects their aspirations to international mobility. Capabilities and aspirations of young people in Tunisia have changed in a very short time; in the final sections, we discuss these findings and their implications.

Background

People, things, and information are constantly on the move. When people are mobile, this can take the form of spatial displacement between locations (for example as commuters or migrants), but also of social mobility as movement within groups (including social ascent and descent); even identity narratives of individuals should be considered mobile (captured, for example, as on-going narration of a coherent self) (Gertel/Breuer 2011; cf. Zuntz et al., this volume). Spatial movements of people, which are the focus here, are often related to social formation processes and identity dynamics. They take place in a polycentric world that exerts specific temporal and spatial powers. The European Union and its member states north of the Mediterranean interact – for example through different trade and security agreements – not only with North African countries like Tunisia, but also with transnational corporations and globally active tech companies, each in their own way. These interactions unfold through different layers including national, but also local and individual levels in Maghreb countries. Simultaneously, these relations are subject to permanent change and different temporalities: intergenerational socialisation processes, for instance in Tunis or Sidi Bouzid, shape individual values in the long term, such as group-specific attitudes towards mobility; multi-year legislative processes, linked to electoral cycles, define desirable and undesirable individuals for national spaces (e.g. specific groups of migrants such as Sub-Saharan Africans; cf. Parikh, this volume); and the algorithm-generated pricing processes for wheat, the most important staple food in North Africa, take place in the nanosecond range and are increasingly responsible for food insecurity and hunger, which in turn induce migration and flight (Gertel 2023).

Which different groups are we talking about when migration is understood as a process? On the one hand, this refers to the spectrum of potential migrants – those who express the desire or the aspiration to migrate, and those who are making concrete preparations but are still in the country of origin (cf. Saib Musette/Maamar 2024). On the other hand, there are actual migrants, i.e. all those who have travelled to a new country, irregularly or legally. In the case of legal migrants holding a visa, this often includes highly qualified workers (who by leaving contribute to a 'brain drain' of their country). Then, there are those who arrived at their intended destination irregularly but were subsequently recognised, as well as those who arrived irregularly and remain so. Finally, one should not forget those who tried to migrate but did not make it. They might have been arrested after an attempted departure, drowned during crossing the Mediterranean, or been deported or 'voluntarily returned' (cf. Garnaoui, this volume). We thus have to be precise when we speak about migration. This chapter focuses on the first group: potential migrants who have not left Tunisia.

Unfortunately, there is no comprehensive data that provides comparable figures for all categories of Tunisian migrants. However, we know that, depending on the sources, between 30 and 92 percent of Tunisians are estimated to be potential migrants (i.e. those who intend to emigrate). But only three per cent of all North Africans have concrete and active migration plans or visa applications (i.e. are actually preparing to leave the country), according to Gallup and Afro-Barometer data (Saib Musette/Maamar 2024: 257). This reflects the large gap between migration aspirations and the actual planning of migration. The achievement of such plans is further complicated as the proportion of rejected North African visa applications was on average between 25 and 40 percent in 2019, depending on the country. In 2020 and 2021, a total of 35,040 irregular migrants tried to leave Tunisia – two thirds of them Tunisians – but were intercepted by Tunisian security and defence forces. On the other side of the Mediterranean, the Italian authorities registered 34,124 immigrants coming from Tunisia in the same period – again overwhelmingly Tunisians (Herbert 2022: 5–8). The number of irregular migrants evading both the Tunisian and Italian security forces is not known, but is likely to be considerable.

The spatial significance of Tunisia as a migration corridor has been growing recently (cf. Matri/Zuntz, this volume). Frontex states that in 2022, the largest increase in irregular migrants arriving by sea to Europe from North Africa came from the Libyan-Tunisian area (Frontex 2023: 15). However, as we know, not everybody survives the crossing: around 3,000 migrants drowned on average per year in the Mediterranean between 2014 and 2021 (ibid. 15). Even a successful sea crossing may not be sufficient for completing the migration journey: in 2021, the rejection rate for asylum applications in Europe from people with a Maghrebi background was 54 percent, with the highest proportion for people coming from Tunisia (Saib Musette/Maamar 2024: 257). Successful migration projects to Europe have not become any easier after the Covid-19 pandemic.

From a political perspective, two objectives define the European Union's cooperation with partners in the southern Mediterranean, namely promoting democracy, and liberalising trade. So-called Mobility Partnerships have been considered a key instrument of the 'North' for shaping mutual relations after the Arab Spring. They were implemented as a new agenda for the Mediterranean region in Morocco, Jordan and Tunisia in order to curb irregular migration and forced displacement, and to put a stop to smugglers and traffickers. However, when evaluating the data of the last decade on migration, programmes of financial support and visa issuance, Panebianco/Cannata (2024) remark: 'Despite the political rhetoric concerning democracy promotion and assistance in the Mediterranean, for several years the EU had been *de facto* cooperating with powerful authoritarian leaders to achieve political stability and avoid insecurity' (ibid. 75). Accordingly, they consider Mobility Partnerships a disappointment, criticise the lack of credible incentives, and suggest it would be more appropriate to talk about immobility instead.

Disconnected from local needs, the Partnerships 'were at times more advantageous for the EU than for its partners' (ibid. 85). This context is important to keep in mind for the following discussion.

Methodology

In this chapter, we will juxtapose Yassine's personal narrative with the quantitative information of two cohorts of young people, aged 16 to 30 years. They were interviewed in Tunisia in 2016 and 2021, respectively, in the context of larger youth studies in the MENA region (Middle East and North Africa) that were commissioned by the Friedrich-Ebert-Stiftung (FES), a German political foundation, and conceptually guided by Leipzig University (Gertel/Hexel 2018; Gertel et al. 2024a). Specifically, the data stem from a standardised, quantitative survey of about 150 closed questions on security, economy, politics, personal values, consumption, mobility, and related topics. During each of the two surveys (FES 2016 and FES 2021), about 1,000 young Tunisians were interviewed by a local polling organisation in face-to-face encounters through the means of computer-assisted personal interviews of about one hour each. The sampling points were spread out across all Tunisian regions, and steps were taken to randomise the selection of respondents as much as possible. After fieldwork, the data were checked for errors and inconsistencies, and subsequently weighted by gender, age group, and region to be representative of the country's total population distribution regarding these criteria. Moreover, the quotes given throughout this text are based on twenty qualitative, semi-structured interviews with young men and women as part of the same survey, carried out in summer 2022 by academic partners from Tunisia (cf. Melliti 2023).

Relying chiefly on the 2021/22 data set, but drawing comparisons to 2016 where appropriate to highlight dynamics over time, we start with a description of socio-economic characteristics of the young people in the sample to establish who speaks here, and adopt a resources/capabilities perspective. We then move on to the political disappointment and resulting attitudes they profess, take a more specific look at regional patterns of economic inequality, and finally present the young peoples' assessment of their own mobility aspirations with a focus on international migration – including, but not limited to, clandestine *harga* – and the related aspects of identity and imagination.

Capabilities in Crisis

Young people do not live in isolation; they are members of a family. In other words, they are part of a dynamic and ever-changing reproductive unit, usually a household, in which resources and risks are redistributed to a certain extent, for example between people who are able to work and children or elderly people who are not yet or no longer able to do so. The 2021 survey suggests that the vast majority of young Tunisians in the 16-to-30 age bracket – more than three quarters (85%) – live with their parents; they are cared for by them and have hardly any economic responsibility of their own. In contrast, only a small proportion of respondents, just eight percent, have already started their own independent households or families. This group is primarily made up of women (76%), as in the MENA region women tend to marry earlier than men.

When asked about their perception of their families' economic situation, two thirds of young people say it is 'quite good', which may be surprising at first glance, but can partially be explained by the 'borrowed security' experienced by all those still living with their parents (Gertel 2018b, 161). Moreover, when a stranger (such as the interviewer) asks about personal issues, the socially expected response is often simply *al-hamdu li-llah* (Praise be to God), which while it can be interpreted as 'quite good', is first and foremost a polite answer. Conversely, those who say their situation is quite bad (23%) or very bad (8%) can be assumed to be in financial trouble. A clear overall economic decline is visible in comparison with the 2016 study. Back then, no less than 80 percent had assessed their families' economic situation as quite good, with only twelve percent declaring it as quite bad and two percent as very bad. The proportion of young adults who feel that their families experience economic difficulties has thus more than doubled, expanding from 14 to 31 percent within five years.

A complementary insight is provided by young peoples' perception of class affiliation. The majority see themselves as part of the middle-classes, with one in four respondents (27%) placing their family in the upper middle-class and more than half (59%) in the lower middle-class in 2021. One in eight youngsters (13%) consider their families to be poor or destitute. Compared to the 2016 survey, the self-perceived upper middle-class has shrunk considerably (by 17 percentage points), with more families having dropped down into lower classes (Gertel/Ouaissa 2018: 163). In a complementary approach, we calculated a MENA-wide strata index based on criteria such as the father's education level, home ownership, and the presence of certain items that could indicate wealth (air conditioning, internet access, or a vehicle) in a family (Gertel et al. 2024a: 412). The five strata are distributed as follows in the Tunisian sample: 6 percent fall into the highest stratum, 19 percent are in the upper middle stratum, 28 percent belong to the middle stratum, 26 percent are in the lower middle stratum, and 21 percent in the lowest stratum. This latter group has increased by nine percentage points since 2016, mostly at the expense of the middle stratum (minus six); the others remain stable. That is, some resources, such as home ownership and the educational background of the parents' generation, have evidently not deteriorated at the same speed as income loss and perceived class attachment. Yassine, who is determined to leave the country, emphasises:

> The middle-class has eroded, it has become a poor class. Even teachers who belonged to the middle-class have become poor. The middle-class has shrunk a lot. To belong to the middle-class in Tunisia, you need a monthly salary of more than three thousand Dinars. That is a rarity in Tunisia. Ministers in Tunisia have become members of the middle-class. I myself belong to the class of the poor because sometimes I can't meet all my daily needs for food, clothing and entertainment.

Slim, 30 and single, a factory worker from Tunis, adds more examples:

> The middle-class no longer exists in Tunisia! The Tunisian middle-class consisted of public sector employees and bank employees, but now this group of society is no longer

able to fulfil all the daily needs of their families. For example, a teacher now works in the private sector in addition to their job in the public sector. This is because their income from working in the public sector is no longer enough to cover their daily expenses as it was in earlier years. I myself belong to a class that has no name. I don't consider myself poor, I belong to a class that is even below the class of slaves. It's as if you have no existence, I can compare my situation to worn-out shoes that people use and then throw away.

Salma, 25, a single university student in Tunis, describes polarisation dynamics:

I don't see a middle-class in Tunisia, I see a wealthy class and another at the lower end of the scale, especially given the high cost of living. Wages are limited by laws that change every day; life is getting more and more expensive. I don't see a middle-class! As long as I live in a family where only my father works and my mother is a housewife, while my father can barely provide for us, he can't even buy my siblings most of their school supplies… It is clear that his salary is less than his labour. That is exploitation. He works between eight and twelve hours and can't feed his family!

In terms of the young generation's personal and social orientations in life, the data reveal a surprisingly big shift in the five-year period from 2016 to 2021. When asked to pick the one thing that was most important for their personal future among four options, most chose a good job. In contrast, having a fulfilled family life and, for young women, the ambition of a good marriage, have clearly become less important (Figure 1). However, gender inequalities start in school and do not stop at labour relations, within family constellations, or in politics. Salma continues:

We're in an Arab Tunisian society, gender inequalities are clearly visible, even though girls and women are more successful in their studies. They work and prove themselves as able to provide for everyday life and support their families honourably, while the boys huddle together in the cafés. They refuse to work at anything. Girls are more successful in class. In a class of 29 students there are four boys, the boys only think about *harga*. The graduates today are girls, normally they should be better qualified and better paid, and yet in our society the mentality is different.

Yassine complements:

We live in a patriarchal society. Most inequalities in Tunisia are based on gender. A transgender or homosexual person cannot become a minister or president of the republic in Tunisia, as is the case in Western countries. Society does not accept this. Gender inequality is also reflected in the salaries that men and women receive in Tunisia. Women receive less pay than men. For example, in agriculture, men's wages are still higher than women's wages. It is a prevailing mentality that sees women always settling for less. This is related to a male mentality that always despises women, even if they hold prestigious positions. And religion feeds this mentality by saying, 'Men are the caretakers of women'.[1]

---

[1] This is a quote from the Qur'an (4:34).

Figure 1: Most Important Aspect for Personal Future

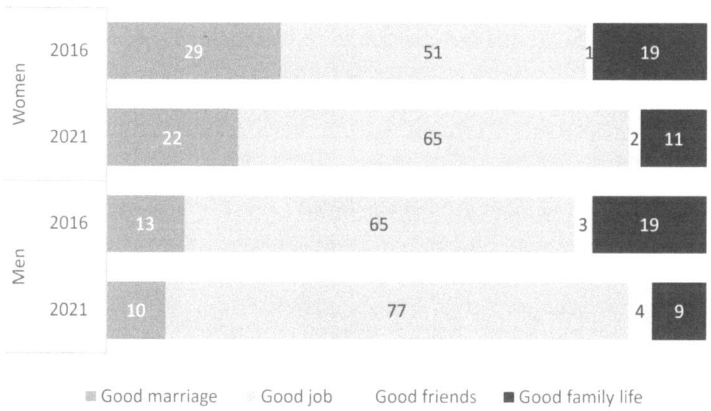

Source: FES 2016 & 2021. Note: All numbers are given in percentage points (n = 1,000).

Economic concerns and gender inequalities are related, but distinct from expressions of dwindling trust in the political field. The latter, however, also crucially contributes to mobility ambitions and will be examined in the next section.

Loss of Trust

A local scholar has interpreted the FES Youth Study data as an indication that 'the interlude that started with the revolution is now definitively over' and underlines the extent of political disillusionment this has produced (Melliti 2023: 29). Indeed, a dramatic loss of confidence in the state and its various institutions has taken place in the span of five years among young people in Tunisia (Figure 2). It had not been high in 2016 to begin with, but the percentage of those who still trust their government, parliament, the legal system, or the police has almost halved. Even the relatively respected military has suffered from this trend, falling from almost three quarters to just over half of the respondents expressing trust. What is more, confidence in one's own family – by far the most highly trusted institution on the list – has equally gone down, from an impressive 92% in 2016 to only 78% in 2021. Speaking of shattered trust, therefore, is not an exaggeration, and it concerns all institutions of society. Yassine is definitive in his judgement:

> After independence, the nation state tried to reduce inequalities, but currently there is no attempt whatsoever. The state instead increases economic inequalities and widens the gap between rich and poor. Inequality is reflected in the fact that university and professional degrees are no longer a guarantee of employment in the Tunisian labour market. Inequality also exists on a spatial level, between regions in Tunisia and even between neighbourhoods in a city. Several laws in Tunisia ensure equality but are not sufficiently implemented, while other laws are regulations that perpetuate inequality, as the Tunisia's inheritance law does.

He further explains the prevalent mistrust:

> I don't like political life and membership of political parties because most people involved in political activity in Tunisia are individuals pursuing personal interests, often they try to escape from justice. The political field in Tunisia is a corrupt field.

Other young adults similarly quote persistent 'corruption and fraud' (Slim, a 30-year-old factory worker from Nabeul) as fundamental reasons they have 'no confidence in politicians' (Nourhene, 26, a housewife from Kasserine). However, loss of trust not only relates to the executive branch (parliament and political parties), the judiciary and police also have low scores and have lost a great deal of support over the last five years.

For a long time, moreover, many young adults considered falling out with their family almost unthinkable. On the economic level alone, there are often no other institutions that could cushion uncertainties, something that has become all the more serious due to almost non-existent government support during the last few decades. Trust in the family as a social and economic security system, correspondingly, used to be very high (Gertel 2018a). Yet, even families as key social institutions in Tunisia have lost trust, accompanied by 'a process of individualisation that has been underway for decades and continues apace' (Melliti 2023: 29). Insecurities in the labour market, livelihood deterioration, the limited financial buffer capacities of their parents, and the continuation of dispossession processes that undermine equal opportunities, have left many young Tunisians frustrated. Mobility options thus become more attractive – particularly for young males.

One additional finding testifies to the extent of desperation and resignation among young Tunisians: the importance young people give to values in general has clearly gone down over the past few years. Their 'openness to change', one of four basic value dimensions we have identified elsewhere (Kreuer/Gertel 2024), seems at a low point, but so does its counterpart, the orientation towards 'conformity' (in the sense of preserving the existing order). On the other hand, values related to 'self-enhancement' are ranked higher than in neighbouring countries, whereas 'community orientation' is very low (ibid. 275). In this view, there is little energy left for community engagement, and many young people are focused on their own interest or even survival. Yassine explains his position:

> Honestly, I don't care and I don't believe in social participation, I work on my personal development in my free time. I don't believe in political and social engagement, I believe in myself, that's enough for me. I don't care about this society; my goal is to leave Tunisia.

This sentiment is widespread, as the 'institutionalised political sphere [has become] devoid of any interest to the young people' and other forms of engagement and collective action 'appear completely useless to them'; instead, young Tunisians seem committed to 'a resolute quest for personal salvation' (Melliti 2023: 29).

Figure 2: Trust in Institutions

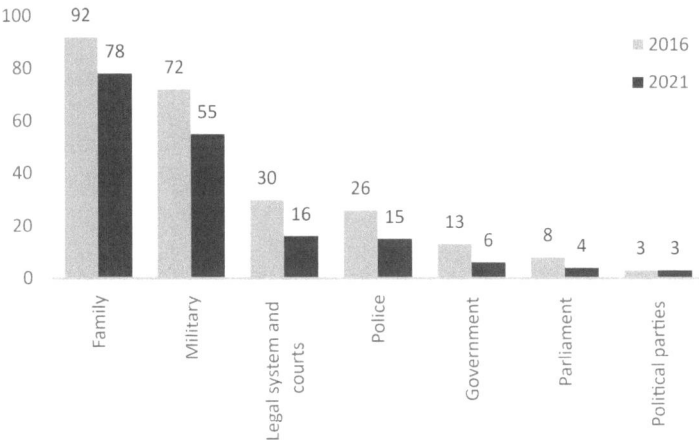

Source: FES 2016 & 2021. Note: All numbers are given in percent (n = 1,000).

Figure 3: Preferred Political System

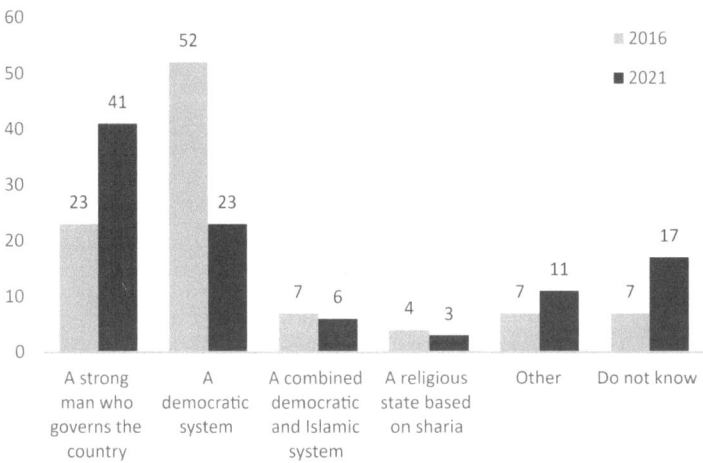

Source: FES 2016 & 2021. Note: All numbers are given in percent (n = 1,000).

A further significant change has taken place in the young people's preference for a political system (Figure 3). The predilection for democracy, which was shared by the majority just five years earlier, has plummeted to less than one quarter of respondents. In terms of alternatives, an authoritarian form of government appears most attractive (and indeed matches the development of Saied's presidency), but the share of young adults who no longer know what political system to aim for has equally grown. This group, one in six respondents, is at a loss at best, and has completely stopped caring at worst.

In what may seem like a paradox, young people overwhelmingly express a wish that the state play a larger role in their daily lives. While this sentiment has fallen from 90 percent in 2016 to 78 percent in the 2021 survey, this is still a vast majority and comparable to other countries in the MENA region. This should not be understood as a way of approving of the government's performance, however. Quite to the contrary, the glaring absence of a functioning state is contrasted to an imagined ideal situation where the administration would actually provide and safeguard public service, infrastructure and education, healthcare and freedom of expression, safety and security. Amine from Souss, 26 and married, comments:

> There is no equality in the legal system or the police. There are increasing inequalities in all public areas. I think the situation is getting worse in the interior compared to the coastal areas. Relations with the Tunisian administration depend on your relationship capital, if you have relationships within the department, you will get your service easily and quickly. I was the owner of an industrial equipment maintenance company and it took me a month and a half to prepare a work permit, there were many bureaucratic procedures. In the end, I wouldn't have been granted it if I hadn't had the sympathy of one of the employees who finally helped me.

In sum, the dominant perception of young Tunisians is that the state does not serve them the way it should. These grievances are often compounded by regional inequalities, as Amine alludes to, which we will now explore. We assume that they, too, affect mobility aspirations.

Inequality between Regions

The issue of regional inequalities is pronounced in Tunisia, its relatively small geographical size notwithstanding. Broadly speaking, the coastal regions in the east are where industry and tourism have been concentrated, which has long made them more attractive for (domestic and foreign) investment; they are also better connected through seaports and airports. On the other hand, the backcountry in the western part of Tunisia lacks infrastructure and opportunities on many levels (cf. Kahloun/Frische, this volume). This situation has a long history and is 'rooted in the government's political and economic choices since independence' (Abidi 2021: 1). Looking below the national level could help elucidate the spatially differentiated manifestations of shattered trust and aspirations for mobility.

Table 1: Strata Distribution by Region in Tunisia (2021)

	Lowest	Lower middle	Middle	Upper middle	Highest
East	16	26	28	22	8
West	32	27	28	12	1

Note: All numbers are given in percent. The strata index (see Gertel et al. 2024: 412) is calculated based on four aspects: father's education, family's financial situation, home ownership, and prosperity indicators. Based on these four indicators, each respondent can reach a total score of 3 to 14 points; they are then divided into five groups of similar size.

Table 2: Civic Engagement by Region in Tunisia

Region	No engagement	Occasional engagement	Frequent engagement
North East	40	7	53
North West	81	6	12
Centre East	41	30	29
Centre West	54	24	22
South East	15	9	76
South West	61	14	25
Total	45	16	40

Note: All numbers are given in percent (n = 1,000).

Our subsequent analysis is based on the six regions used by the National Institute of Statistics (Institut National de la Statistique 2012: 9), which we aggregate into East and West here. The East (near the coast, where 71% of respondents live) and West (hinterland, 29%) display a number of stark differences. For instance, almost three out of four young people in the East assess their families' economic situation as very good or quite good (73% combined), while only 58 percent in the West do so. Further, the distribution of strata according to the FES Youth Study strata index (which is based on a combination of different criteria, see above) shows a clear East-West split in the two highest strata as well as the lowest stratum (Table 1), although the lower middle and middle groups are similarly distributed. This skewed distribution paints a picture of a certain polarisation in wealth: well-off Tunisians tend to live near the coast, while some of the most disadvantaged groups are found in the more remote, rural areas of the west.

This tendency closely corresponds to patterns of civic engagement across the six regions, which show massive discrepancies between the coastal regions and the hinterland (Table 2). Young respondents were asked whether they regularly or occasionally engaged in a range of societal issues. The difference is especially pronounced when comparing the North West (the region with the lowest engagement levels, where four out of five respondents never engage in any civic issues) and the South East (which has the highest engagement levels with three out of four respondents frequently engaging in some form). This finding corroborates observations of low engagement in marginalised regions (Rennick 2023) and is reflected in the testimony of Melek, 30 years old and married, who works as a public service agent in Nabeul (North East) but previously lived in a provincial setting:

> I notice a great inequality between the regions in Tunisia. I lived in the south of Tunisia, in the city of Gafsa [South West], for two and a half years. There is no investment there and therefore no job opportunities. The only employer is the phosphate company, everyone wants to work there. Compared to the north, there are no entertainment options in Gafsa either, which has an impact on your psyche. The young people who live in the southern regions always want to migrate to the northern regions.

Such stories indicate that internal mobility from the peripheries to the capital region can be a first step in a personal mobility career; international migration may follow later if conditions do not improve. This escalation of scale reflects similarly engrained structures of inequality between regions on the one hand, and countries on the other.

Migration Aspirations

When asked about their own migration aspirations, the respondents were asked to choose among four possible responses the one that came closest to their current feelings. Once more, the shifts that have occurred within just five years are remarkable (Figure 4). Only one in five young Tunisians can currently rule out migration as an option for themselves, while more than half of this generation appears willing to leave. Compared to the 2016 survey, only half as many are still sure they will stay, but twice as many young Tunisians are sure they will leave. Their preferred destination region in 2021 remains Europe by a wide margin, which is not surprising given the geographical proximity as well as the long history of close, if unequal relationships across the Mediterranean – including migration episodes within many young people's own families.

A gender gap is evident: young men are more prone to considering emigration as an exit strategy. However, young women are catching up and, just as we showed above for the importance given to marriage versus employment, have now reached the levels their male peers had five years earlier.

Figure 4: Own View Regarding Emigration

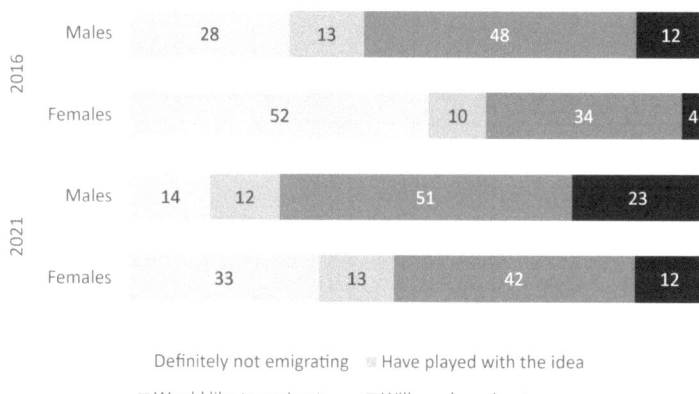

Source: FES 2016 & 2021. Note: All numbers are given in percent. For 2021, the 'No reply' answers (12% of the total) were excluded from the percentages in order to compare the findings with those from 2016 when this response option did not exist.

Figure 5: Migration Aspirations by Region

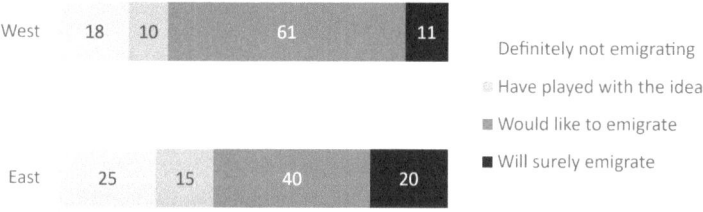

Source: FES 2021. Note: All numbers are given in percent. 'No reply' answers (12% of the total) were excluded from the percentages.

Ines, 28, a teacher from Ben Arous in the Tunis metropolitan area, belongs to the largest group who is inclined towards migration but has not taken any concrete steps. She muses:

> Years ago, I was against *harga*, but today I tend to agree with young people who choose to leave. When I think about my own situation, I tell myself that if I had the opportunity to leave, legally or illegally, I wouldn't hesitate to do so!

In contrast, Ahlem, 26, a saleswoman in a bakery in Matmata in the southeast, summarises a more critical view of migration:

> There's a difference: today's young people aren't trying to study, to work hard, or to find a job. They're only looking for *harga*, whereas previous generations were looking for work.

Adam, a 20-year-old farmer from Cap Bon (North East), who struggles with his livelihood and aspirations, has experienced migration in his immediate surroundings:

> Life was better for the generations before us. The wage I receive as a labourer does not guarantee me a decent life, as all my income is wasted in the face of rising expenses. Many young people from our neighbourhood have preferred to migrate clandestinely to Italy, as the economic and social conditions for young people in Tunisia have deteriorated.

To obtain a more comprehensive picture about young people's preparedness to accept life changes, we calculated a Flexibility Index, merging three challenges of social mobility: family, work, and marriage (Gertel/Wagner 2018: 200). It appears that young people's overall flexibility ('High') increased dramatically within five years between 2016 and 2021 (cf. Table 3).

Such thoughts are in fact somewhat more prevalent in the coastal East of the country (Figure 5), where young people are more likely to be determined either to stay or to leave. An absolute majority of those in the interior regions, however, state that they 'would like' to emigrate. This relationship between place and aspiration is never simple and straightforward, but deserves more detailed study.

Spatial movement of people, particularly their migration career, is often related to social formation and identity dynamics. Questions about the self, dealing with new networks and dependencies, and emerging new uncertainties during the migration journey change aspirations and imaginations, as they affect one's relation to the world. Mobilities are complex constellations.

Table 3: Flexibility Index

	2016	2021
High	25	40
Quite high	28	27
Quite low	31	16
Low	15	11
Missing	2	6

Note: All numbers are given in percent (n = 1,000).

Discussion

A decade after the revolution, Tunisia seems stuck in permanent crisis mode. The national economy is frail, worsened by the Covid-19 pandemic and its aftermath. At the same time, the political system has become increasingly authoritarian, more so as 'Saied's administration has failed to reverse political turmoil or economic decline' (Ben Jelili 2023: 1). Young people are disproportionately affected and constitute a 'sacrificed generation' (Rennick 2023: 15) without adequate opportunities to find employment, develop a career, start a family, have a say in politics, or live a fulfilled life. Their opportunities have thus been curtailed, and many of their aspirations have turned into desperation so deep that a perilous migration attempt seems the only remaining viable option for some. An enormous chasm appears between aspirations and actual possibilities – between 'what is' and 'what could have been'. We have analysed this as a situation of dispossession (Gertel et al. 2024a).

Yassine's statements indicate great disappointment with the revolution and its outcomes. In the years after 2011, there was a genuine belief among young Tunisians that the economic problems could be solved politically, with new actors and new rules of the game; that belief has completely eroded. Even the last bit of trust in state institutions and democratic processes is now gone. By contrast, the economy is on everyone's mind – much more so than family, marriage, or friends – with a clear perception of decline and injustice. The perceived economic situation and class affiliation of young Tunisians worsened dramatically between 2016 and 2021. Their relatively declining desire for a larger role played by the state also indicates disappointment and resignation. At the same time, young people are still comparatively optimistic: in a recent study based on the Arab Barometer surveys, Tunisian youth 'exhibited the highest level of support for democracy' in comparison to other age groups (Ben Jelili 2023: 15). However, democratic government systems are no longer fashionable in the region overall: our data reveal a dramatic decline even in Tunisia, which had become the democratic hope for North Africa and beyond after the 2011 revolution.

The self-centring of young people that we found in the data, as well as the low prevalence of 'community orientation' values and civic engagement, also tie in to the meritocratic if misleading neoliberal mantra that everybody is responsible for their own successes and failures in life (Pettit/Ruijtenberg 2019). On another level, the current penchant of young Tunisians for populism and authoritarianism has parallels in many parts of the world. Intensifying crises often give a boost to populism, especially when it is 'embodied by a political outsider' such as Kais Saied used to be (Fulco/Giampaolo 2023: 29). Part of the explanation why the young generation seems largely acquiescent to autocratic tendencies could be that the Ben Ali regime, which was ousted in 2011, may already be too far in the past for these young people who barely remember experiencing it (Rennick 2023).

By such mechanisms, dwindling and shattered trust has contributed to a new migration wave of young adults from Tunisia. The country's role as a migration nexus, which was for some years dominated by foreign nationals who used Tunisia and Libya as hubs for transit migration, is again changing towards a source of local emigration with a nationwide catchment area. Importantly, (existential) mobility is not laden with negative emotions only: it is linked to hope. Even attempting a risky *harga* seems for some groups better than doing nothing, because at least they experience agency. For many young Tunisians, the rest is up to God anyway. Immobility, on the other hand, is connected to depression and dejection (*ikti'ab*) (Pettit/Ruijtenberg 2019).

While 'imagined futures are important for why and how people move' (Wyss et al. 2023: 574), this does not mean that migration hopefuls are naïve about their prospects. Migrants typically experience 'a continuous oscillation between a sense of existential mobility and immobility, between the hope that they [are] moving towards a better future and the depressing sense of being stuck in life, with moments of fear, doubt, joy and distraction emerging in between' (Pettit/Ruijtenberg 2019: 739). In the current situation, however, even if a migrant ends up in precarity or in illegal activities (e.g. as drug trafficker) in Europe, there may be less social pressure and scrutiny than there would be back home, as long as they manage to send back some money occasionally. Even this prospect may seem more attractive than the complete lack of opportunities experienced in Tunisia these days. Imagining alternative futures has become almost impossible, especially for the younger generation.

At the government level, one persistent problem is that the country has become trapped 'in cyclic phases of decision-making stalemate [that fail to] address the rampant social inequality and regional disparities' (Fulco/Giampaolo 2023: 36). One macroeconomic goal should be to break loose from dependency on the International Monetary Fund, although it is not easy to find funding alternatives (Ben Rouine 2023). Taken together, it appears that 'the problem of *harga* can only be handled efficiently by devising an economic strategy based on a reconsideration of the country's growth model' and tackling all forms of corruption (Mnasri 2023: 1042). Yassine from Sfax, whose statements we have quoted throughout this chapter, shares this diagnosis and sums up the bleak current state of affairs:

> The government is incapable of changing the deteriorating situation, and corrupt politicians have impoverished and robbed the Tunisian people. I don't see any more solutions, so I want to leave the country.

Our investigation of the links between trust, inequality, and mobility aspirations of young Tunisians suggests that an entire generation feels excluded, frustrated and hopeless. A reduction of economic inequality, including between regions, and an increase in real choices and opportunities seems to be the only way to rebuild a minimum level of trust in the state and its institutions. In turn, this could affect the young people's (mobility-related) aspirations and turn them into more diverse and hopeful directions instead of being fixated on leaving the country at all costs. This, however, is a colossal task.

Coping with Disparities
Urban Development in Tunisia

Hatem Kahloun & Johannes Frische

THE MAYOR OF LA MARSA, M, considers himself a patriotic citizen and a devoted politician, but he leaves no doubt that, by training and professional socialisation, he is first and foremost an urbanist.
His reasoning and perception are profoundly influenced by urbanist thinking. This allows him to keep the big picture in focus while drawing connections with public policy. Balancing his many hats and roles, he shows himself as a mediator who delicately juggles multiple commitments with public institutions such as ministries and the administration, foreign donors, private agencies, consultancy companies, civil society actors, and the local population.
Throughout his career, M. has gained intimate knowledge of urban planning processes, the functioning of the central state and various local disputes. This led him to the conviction that crucial planning issues and their legal implications are often insufficiently understood. As he admits, it is still unclear how decentralisation, local power, and participation play out in territorial development. His most urgent concern is to upgrade deficient infrastructure and integrate deprived areas – such as Bahr Lazreg – within the boundaries of his municipal district and into the surrounding urban fabric. As an expert for urban development issues, he has criticised that the challenges of urban projects have been left in the hands of private developers and investors for too long. More than ten years on, the legacy of Ben Ali's crony capitalism still looms large. M. is among those who became actively involved in reshaping local politics in line with national policy reform and new legislation, the adoption of the new code of local authorities being the most prominent case.

Field notes, based on an interview with the mayor and president of the municipal council of La Marsa (June 3, 2022)

The neighbourhood Bahr Lazreg, which is situated within the municipal district of La Marsa, one of the seaside suburbs in the northeast of the Greater Tunis region, illustrates very well how an urban development project comes with many conflicting priorities and a high degree of uncertainty. According to M., the mayor and president of the municipal council of La Marsa, the city must address infrastructural deficiencies in this utterly deprived zone, where approximately 50,000 residents live. As parts of the public highway have no sewer connection, regular floods obstruct plans for upgrading the road system and public utilities. Makeshift drainage systems are only a temporary solution for flooding problems. As the mayor stresses, there is an urgent need to take action in order to avoid further degradation. Even if his entire budget for this community were used, it would not be sufficient to tackle the challenges in this zone. The total cost of such a comprehensive development project is impossible to afford for the municipality by its own means. A consultancy company has been commissioned to conduct a full analysis of planning needs in the Bahr Lazreg zone. However, as the mayor points out, the funds for conducting this study have not yet been made available.

Bahr Lazreg is not covered by an urban land use plan, which not only hampers the implementation of an urban development project, but, according to the mayor, also makes it impossible to find a solution for unauthorised or non-conforming housing. A study commissioned by the Ministry of Equipment (2020), which outlines an operational approach to urban intervention and restructuring in the localities of Bahr Lazreg (La Marsa) and El Matar (Sousse), demonstrates that non-conformity of habitat can take a variety of forms, for example housing in commercial areas or in green spaces. The study argues that instruments for legal intervention and regulatory urbanism, such as an urban land use plan, are not adapted to informal neighbourhoods; in fact, they undermine any operation for restructuring informal housing. While acute violations of the legal framework and of construction regulations are often attributed to land tenure issues, the land available for urbanisation is mostly in the hands of private developers who engage in speculation and hoarding outside the scope of institutional norms and regulation (ibid. 20–24).

In face of this problem, the mayor has pledged on several occasions to review the urban land use plan of La Marsa and adapt it to the realities of the urban terrain. He is very critical about the fact that the state has withdrawn from any national strategy for access to housing, so it is not surprising that struggles of marginalised people for housing have become more acute in terms of claiming the right to a territory, even if this disregards regulations. Since the outbreak of the Covid-19 pandemic, the number of refugees and migrants residing in this zone, many of them from Sub-Saharan Africa, has greatly increased and their housing situation is often very precarious, especially sanitary conditions. Among them are workers, students, and young families who have to contend with different forms of exclusion and racism (cf. Parikh, this volume). Due to the urban morphology, population density, and the modes of transport available, urban zones like Bhar Lazreg have also proven to be particularly sensitive to the challenges of the pandemic.

Municipal governance thus faces problems and disparities on very different levels: financial constraints, environmental risks, social vulnerability, legal uncertainty, and governmental and political instability. While a longstanding economic crisis over the last decade has had a negative impact on the middle-classes and their income situation (Kreuer/Gertel, this volume), failed attempts to install a mode of governance that supports the inclusion of vulnerable groups and poor classes have proven even more devastating. The pandemic crisis, which came on top of this, laid bare the vulnerability of cities being dominated by a centralised system, which, as we will see, does not favour the transfer of competencies to the local level. The legislative mandates of municipalities are too limited to manage societal problems and disparities within their district autonomously.

Starting from this specific case, the chapter offers an introduction and analyses of urban development and disparities in the Tunisian context. Our argument develops as follows: We start with addressing the emergence of regional and urban disparities from a long-term perspective. We then contextualise urban development and planning. In a next step we scrutinise the Programme for the Rehabilitation and Integration of Residential Neighbourhoods (PRIQH) as a recent urban development programme driven by vested interests. We finally illustrate respective socio-ecological and political implications in particular localities, including the neighbourhood of Bahr Lazreg. The chapter's method is based on a critical and comparative analysis of implementation and evaluation reports, available publications, as well as scientific studies of urban development programs in Tunisia. The findings are combined with qualitative interviews with key actors involved in urban development.

Emerging Regional and Urban Disparities

The debate on the preconditions of the Arab Spring addresses spatial inequalities as a major cause of the protests in 2010 and 2011, which eventually led to the political uprising in Tunisia (Daoud 2011).[1] Territorial inequalities manifest themselves in social and economic forms of disparity that have become pronounced between north and south, coastal and inland, centre and hinterland, and border regions, depending on one's point of view. According to Meddeb (2017: 2), the lagging behind of the country's periphery is not solely due to neglect, but it is also the result of a targeted policy of the Tunisian central state over several decades. The protracted crisis that finally brought about the political uprising of 2011 is not least a crisis of the state's ability to act and of its poor integrative capacities at the local level. This finding can also be applied to processes of 'city-making'. To the extent that urbanisation primarily concentrated in coastal regions, key economic sectors such as industry and the service sector primarily developed in the cities located there. Under the Ben Ali regime, the central administration of Tunisian territory was no longer run by state institutions but directly subordinate to the then president, or outsourced to foreign investors, developers and land speculators, who built large-scale tourist facilities, commercial and industrial enterprises, residential complexes and shopping malls (Bouraoui 2011).

In times of advanced globalisation, spatial policy shifted its focus to increasing the international competitiveness of Tunisian cities by embracing metropolisation. The three coastal cities of Tunis, Sfax and Sousse were to be developed into regional attraction poles by bundling political functions and economic activities there. Even after the uprising of 2011, the majority of Tunisian and foreign companies are mainly active in coastal areas. In 2012, 85 percent of Tunisia's gross national product was generated in

---

1   This section is adapted from Johannes Frische's doctoral thesis published as a German-language monograph (Frische 2022: 68–85).

the three cities of Tunis, Sousse and Sfax and 92 percent of all industrial firms are within an hour's drive of these three cities (World Bank 2014: 282).

In order to respond to the problem of territorial inequalities, growing disparities, and marginalisation of regions in the interior of the country, known as shadow zones (*zones d'ombre*), several social programmes and social policy instruments were introduced. The related measures were able to provide basic social welfare by means of financial assistance, and partially integrate particularly vulnerable groups into the social system; however, the causes of unemployment and economic disintegration were not addressed (Destremeau 2009: 147–49; Laroussi 2009: 111). Against the backdrop of a growing territorial divide, it is no coincidence that the waves of protests in late autumn 2010 spread rapidly across the periphery of the country and moved then from the marginalised regions, particularly the southeast and southwest of Tunisia, to the metropolitan centre of Tunis.

After the uprising of 2010/2011, the problem of regional disparities was officially recognised; however, concrete development measures were only hesitantly undertaken, or postponed. The second transitional government, which worked under the leadership of Béji Caïd Essebsi, prepared a white paper that analysed the root causes of regional disparities. The study evaluated previous spatial planning policies and made recommendations for improving public infrastructure in the areas of health and education, social housing, as well as legal and administrative reform concepts (Mattes 2016: 4). In addition, the problem of regional disparities was recognised in the Tunisian Constitution of 2014 and included in the State Development Strategy; henceforth, the principle of 'positive discrimination' was to be applied in favour of balanced regional development. However, the implementation of development measures failed again due not only to a lack of budgetary funds, but also to the delay of the decentralisation process. In fact, the legal framework for decentralisation was established as late as April 2018 in the run-up to the local elections.

Short-sighted government policies and unbalanced socio-economic developments have created an asymmetrical geography in the country, which furthered inequities between the centre and the periphery at different levels. This also applies to Greater Tunis, which, as the most important urban centre in Tunisia, is both a driving force behind national developments and in turn is exposed to them. Over a period of eighty years, the rate of urbanisation in Tunisia has increased steadily, from 28 percent in 1925 (under the French protectorate) to 65 percent in 2004 (under the Ben Ali regime). Large and medium-sized cities have developed mainly along the Mediterranean coast; already in 1994, 68 percent of the Tunisian population were concentrated here (Chabbi 2006: 219). Moreover, rural areas also experienced a profound transformation. After political independence the aim was to modernise agriculture by setting up cooperatives. Chabbi explains how this project failed. Small farmers were relocated by force and their landholdings incorporated into the cooperatives. Threatened by poverty, many heads of households had no choice but to move, with or without their families, to larger cities, first and foremost the Tunisian capital (ibid. 30).

In the Greater Tunis region, precarious residential areas, known as *gourbivilles*, were built from temporary, self-built dwellings. Throughout the 1960s, these *gourbivilles* became more and more widespread, as the authorities were unable to provide accommodation for poor internal migrants. Instead, the state sometimes destroyed temporary dwellings with bulldozers and deported the inhabitants back to their region of origin or placed them in resettlement camps (ibid. 14f). To escape these measures, many migrants moved to the Medina, the old city centre of the Tunisian capital. Due to the large number of internal migrants and the lack of financial resources, the state was unable to counter or control these unpredictable dynamics with planning measures. Increasingly the living conditions in the *gourbivilles* deteriorated and led to an 'urban exodus' (ibid. 22): migrants who had previously found shelter in the overcrowded city centre or in the *gourbivilles* moved out of the urban core into housing projects at the peri-urban fringe. In these zones, precarious housing named Habitat Spontané Péri-Urbain (HSPU), became increasingly widespread. They differ from the *gourbivilles* in the urban origin of their inhabitants, the solid construction and the prior purchase of the land by the residents. The expansion of these informal settlements was thus not so much driven by rural-urban migration from the countryside to the city, but rather from population movements within the growing metropolitan area of Greater Tunis. It was not until the 1970s, in the wake of the beginnings of economic liberalisation, that a new urban planning policy emerged, aimed at upgrading precarious housing, improving transport systems, and creating government housing programmes to cope with the worsening housing conditions.

With the new urban planning law of 1979, urban construction measures were supposed to enable better control of the spatial expansion of cities. However, it was primarily the (upper) middle-class that benefited from social housing projects, as almost half of the Tunisian population lived in extremely precarious conditions and could even not afford state-subsidised housing. They had no choice but to acquire land on the black market, which prospered due to the high demand (Chabbi 2012b: 102). The process of so-called *péri-urbanisation*, i.e., the development of informal settlements on the peri-urban fringes of the city and ever-expanding the city limits, is largely due to this dynamic. Between 1975 and 1980, the surface area of these informal settlements doubled each year and by 1980 they extended to an area of 400 hectares within the Greater Tunis region (ibid. 97). On the western outskirts of Tunis, the two suburban areas of Ettadhamen and Douar Hicher were created in this way. By far the largest number of precarious housing residents was concentrated in these two suburbs. By the late 1970s, a quarter of the country's population lived on the periphery of the Greater Tunis region (Mansouri 2002: 66), whereas the population in centrally located neighbourhoods, especially in the old city, decreased from 160,000 in 1966 to 95,000 in 2004 (Chabbi 2006). Due to spatial expansion and a higher housing density in peripheral areas, property prices rose considerably between 1975 and 1995, so that by the turn of the millennium scarce housing became a serious problem again.

Administratively, the Greater Tunis region – the metropolitan area – consists of four governorates: Tunis, Ariana, Manouba, and Ben Arous. This metropolitan area is very heterogeneous in terms of history, population and layout. The Governorate of Tunis, which is located in the vicinity of the northern Lac de Tunis (Lac 1), contains the traditional city centre, the Medina, and the modern extension, the former colonial city. It stretches from the northeastern coastal strip (including the upscale suburbs of La Marsa and Gammarth) to the western shore of the salt-lake Sebkhet Séjoumi in the southwest of Greater Tunis (with the adjacent neighbourhoods Sidi Hassine-Séjoumi and Ezzouhour). While the governorate of Tunis constitutes the core of the metropolitan area, its adjacent urban periphery consists of the three other metropolitan governorates: Ariana (to the north and northwest), Manouba (to the west and southwest), and Ben Arous (to the south and southeast). In the north, there are mainly affluent residential areas such as the El Menzah zone and the coastal districts of El Kram or Sidi Bousaid, while the south and southwest contains mainly middle-class districts, industrial areas and the commercial port of Radès, an important hub for national and international trade. In the west and northwest, there prevail residential areas of the lower income groups and middle-classes, such as Sidi Hassine, Séjoumi, Douar Hicher and Ettadhamen, which emerged as informal settlements (Lamloum/Ali Ben Zina 2015).

Since the turn of the millennium, the Greater Tunis region has expanded considerably. On the one hand, this has led to a reduction in population density, and on the other hand, created or increased commuting times. With longer distances between the place of residence and economic centres or workplaces, many city dwellers are required to use urban transport systems in order to be able to overcome physical distances (cf. Bouzid, this volume).

For urban politics and urban planning, the territorial expansion of the Greater Tunis area and its internal fragmentation proved to be major challenges. In the context of advanced globalisation, Tunisian urban policy increasingly followed an efficiency-oriented market logic, and at the same time subscribed to international flagship models of innovative urban planning. As early as the 1980s, a first project was launched to upgrade the Berges du Lac district, with the aim of constructing high-calibre new residential complexes, and expanding infrastructure (Barthel 2008). With the increasing orientation of the Tunisian economy towards the world market, the so-called 'urbanism of large-scale projects' experienced an increased boom after the year 2000. Considerable investments have been made in the implementation of ambitious projects like in the vicinity of the Great Lakes in Tunis, such as shiny waterfronts, sports facilities, technology parks and upscale residential districts, which were financed by private investors and foreign holding companies, especially from the Gulf States. These large-scale projects were no longer directly under state control but were instead left to the management of urban planning companies and foreign investors. However, the financial crisis of 2008 saw a decline in capital flows; some investment projects were abandoned. Ben Othman Bacha and Legros (2015) argue that these large-scale projects produced ambivalent effects: on the one hand, they enabled the upgrading of peripheral areas and promoted their integration into the urban system. As poles of attraction, they created new dynamics that benefited – albeit only partially – the urban economy of the Greater Tunis region. However, since these spatially isolated large-scale projects were aimed exclusively at the middle-classes and the wealthy, they also deepened marginalisation of other urban spaces and furthered socio-spatial polarisation.

The power vacuum after the uprising of 2010/2011 led not only to a temporary loss of state control over national territory, illegal land occupations and informal housing also expanded. Since self-constructions were not officially approved, it was not possible to apply for housing aid and the dwellers were often not connected to the electricity grid or drinking water networks (Hibou et al. 2011: 29). At the same time old established planning structures have had an enduring legacy: after the introduction of an urban planning policy in the 1970s, which led to the creation of the Tunisian Urban Rehabilitation and Renewal Agency (Agence de Réhabilitation et de Rénovation Urbaine, ARRU), several restructuring, upgrading and rehabilitation measures were carried out in the urban periphery to improve infrastructural and sanitary conditions in informal settlements. These measures served not only to alleviate poverty, but also to regulate social problems. Although nowadays decentralisation and privatisation dominate the urban planning agenda, the central state still indirectly intervenes in urban peripheries through the mediation of NGOs and local associations. It is crucial to understand if neo-liberal strategies can deliver on their promises of overcoming poverty and precariousness, promoting economic initiatives, and reducing socio-spatial exclusion, or if the state will need to step in, but this aspect exceeds the scope of the chapter.

Urban Development and Planning

Engaging with issues of urban development and planning inevitably raises questions about the nature of public intervention and the role of the state in these functions. In fact, these issues are part of a larger historical continuum which Hibou (2015: 148) describes as the 'social and spatial asymmetry of state formation'. This asymmetry can be considered a root cause of the perpetuation of uneven development, despite efforts to counterbalance regional disparities. The attempts of the 1970s to promote rural development and curb internal migration from rural areas and small towns to big cities eventually gave way to more integrated development schemes for improving local living conditions. Public intervention at the local and regional level increasingly shifted its focus to urban areas, but the projects remained modelled after the state-led development approach first applied in rural areas. The implemented measures were mostly targeted to a sector, and they pursued a particular objective, such as the social integration of working-class populations in the periphery of the Tunisian capital. Small cities and towns were largely excluded from this field of intervention.

Under the regime of Ben Ali, regional planning as a technical process that gave priority to the development of Tunisia's coastal governorates was closely intertwined with the international development cooperation apparatus (ibid. 118). These planning processes remained, however, to a large extent centralised, often – as mentioned – directly subordinated to the then president. As municipalities lacked both financial and administrative autonomy investment decisions were usually imposed from above in a technocratic style of government that catered to the interests of private investors and real estate developers. The technocratic model that dominated urban policy-making was tied to an image of the state as an urban developer, commissioned to provide technical solutions for different forms of 'underdevelopment' (Chabbi 2012a: 214). However, what Chabbi considers a strategy of 'rationalising urban development' (ibid. 205) led to little more than the creation of planning tools, planning documents and operationalised procedures, often without practical components for the actual implementation of projects in urban agglomerations. Institutions capable of coordinating planning processes were largely absent, and if local government authorities had a role, it was mostly passive. According to

Chabbi, the sectorial approach for upgrading infrastructure hampered any effort to build coherence through local planning instruments (ibid. 205–206).

Nowadays urban development and planning should be understood as being embedded in a process of decentralisation that puts greater emphasis on participatory approaches. However, so-called integrated approaches of previous development schemes, which were established as part of the national strategy to fight poverty and social exclusion, still constitute the prevailing logic of interventions, often with a regional or local focus. As will be shown below by the example of the programme to upgrade residential neighbourhoods (PRIQH), these interventions address the interplay between urbanisation and economic development through different components (such as providing basic infrastructure, creation of productive activities and employment opportunities, socio-collective equipment) with the goal of fostering social and territorial cohesion. Yet, even a decade after the Tunisian revolution, the long-lasting impact of these state-led urban development interventions, suffer from uncoordinated, incoherent planning policies, and risk to undermine power-sharing as well as counteract the support of and for local government authorities.

Operational Implications of an Urban Development Project

The Programme for the Rehabilitation and Integration of Residential Neighbourhoods (Programme de Réhabilitation et d'Intégration des Quartiers d'Habitation, PRIQH) was first launched in 2012 by the French Development Agency (Agence Française de Développement, AFD) as part of the Support Programme for City Policy (PROVILLE). It works as a strategy for enhancing urban management across national territory. Exploring the design and implementation of this programme allows us to inquire into the challenges of urban development and planning in the context of urban disparities, the impact of governmental instability and of constrained financial resources. We will illustrate our argument by referring to case studies from Sfax and Gabes, but we will also come back to Bahr Lazreg in Greater Tunis.

The original impetus for this programme came from the French Development Agency, which was convinced by the integrated character of the earlier programme, Programme de Promotion des Quartiers Populaires dans les Grandes Villes (PPQPGV) and determined to offer a follow-up.[2] On the one hand the initiative can be seen as a strategic move by the AFD to reassert its role in urban development while creating synergies with other fields of action, namely energy transition, resource management, innovation, and governance. Moreover, the AFD offers technical support to the Tunisian government and its city-oriented policy. For the Tunisian state, on the other hand, the

---

2   PRQPGV was first initiated in 2007; it emerged from acknowledging the limits of an eradicative approach vis-à-vis informal neighbourhoods. In situ upgrading and the improvement of living conditions became established as new priorities. Reaching out to 26 neighbourhoods in 17 municipalities,160,000 urban residents and 32,000 housing units, this program was financed with a budget of 114.5 million Dinar. It was followed by a supplementary program in the period 2010–2012 that drew on an investment of 149.715 million Dinar, covering 56 neighbourhoods and 200,000 residents (Ben Jelloul 2013: 6).

PRIQH provides an opportunity to explore a new mode of operation that relies on a multi-actor approach within a participatory public policy framework. It is subsidised by the Tunisian state and refinanced by the French Development Agency, the European Union and the European Investment Bank. The structure of foreign donors suggests that the public aid provided for this programme serves two major purposes: promote European Union neighbourhood policy and offer a contribution to the achievement of global developmental agendas (first and foremost the SDGs).

The first generation of this urban development programme (PRIQH1), which ran from 2012 to 2024, reached out to 155 neighbourhoods in 100 selected municipalities and 24 governorates. Its preoccupation was to overcome spatial seclusion of neighbourhoods, especially within urban areas in the interior regions of Tunisia, by upgrading basic infrastructure and building sport areas, as well as activity zones and industrial facilities. The programme covered both so-called popular neighbourhoods as well as rural agglomerations. Public service networks became extended to create a safer and cleaner environment, better living and housing conditions, as well as new employment opportunities (both direct and indirect). The programme resonated with the strategy to tackle both regional disparities and territorial disparities between neighbourhoods.

The second generation of the urban development programme (PRIQH2), which, from 2019–2024, extended to 161 neighbourhoods and 100 municipalities, aimed to replicate the positive impact of previous upgrading projects (implemented as part of the PRIQH1 for residents of informal neighbourhoods labelled by ARRU as *quartiers anarchiques*). Being aligned with Tunisia's five-year development plan, the programme comprises four stages, each one lasting two years. The originally calculated total costs amounted to 1.2 billion Dinar, which were reduced to approximately 700 million Dinar, because otherwise the Tunisian state would not have been able to finance its share (covering value added tax and the costs for housing rehabilitation; ARRU 2022). The funds provided by the Tunisian state have been complemented by co-finance (both credit and grants) from foreign donors, namely the European Investment Bank, the French Development Agency, and the European Union. Within this total envelope, allocation across different regions was decided according to the development index, i.e., by calculating a budgetary quota for each governorate. While the number of implemented projects varies from one governorate to another, the method of allocation does not privilege one region of the country over another.[3] The programme explicitly aims to improve living conditions in disadvantaged urban zones, providing better access to basic services and enabling the socioeconomic integration of their residents, who can be considered 'beneficiaries in the lower part of the wealth distribution' (Morabito et al. 2021).

Urban development projects are, however, complex undertakings that take place in a particular environment and are often also confronted with unfavourable environmental conditions. Flooding, as for example in the governorate of Sfax, caused by a rise in the water table (like in the zone of Essaltnia-Zanket in Sakiet Eddayer) can have an extraordinary impact on buildings, roads, and infrastructure. Here, a rainwater drainage system had to be installed to resolve this recurring problem. Another example would be

---

3   This information was conveyed during an interview with a representative of ARRU, December 2, 2021.

unsafe housing construction in hazard zones of natural depression such as the *Sebkhas*, highly saline aquatic systems. According to the AFD, tackling such risk factors impacts the project budget heavily. But there are also significant trends of improvement, for example the installation of a potable water system in Debdaba el Hamma in the governorate of Gabès, which has led to a lower hepatitis B contamination rate. These examples illustrate how social and environmental vulnerability become intertwined, especially in risk prone areas within poor or deprived neighbourhoods. Though urban development projects involve a variety of institutional stakeholders with their vested interests, these projects are only one aspect of urban transitions. At the same time, they are likely to raise questions about the interplay between socio-ecological impacts and longstanding processes of urban transformation.

New evaluation approaches thus put stronger emphasis on the economic, social and environmental impact before and after the implementation of a specific urban development project. To this end, several consultancy companies were engaged to produce a longitudinal analysis. In many cases, the implementation of such projects faces a number of operational challenges, including sluggish administration procedures and a lack of knowledge about the existing infrastructure among the public service concessionaries.[4] They also face the more profound problem of discerning whether the issue at hand is merely upgrading and rehabilitation or if there is a more far-reaching need for adapted spatial planning and comprehensive bottom-up development. The urban management approach is supposed to address this very problem. However, attempts to regulate irregular or dysfunctional processes are likely to produce new loopholes, haphazard processes or cutting of corners. Dysfunctional processes seem to be an inherent part of ongoing urban development processes and are to some extent deliberately tolerated by public authorities in order to deal with existing inequalities.

The case of Bhar Lazreg mentioned earlier is particularly instructive because it provides an example of how urban development processes are embedded in specific socio-ecological spaces and how they articulate local expertise with different temporalities. The latter emerge, for example, under conditions of uncertainty such as the instability of the governmental and legal framework, an economic crisis exacerbated by the Covid-19 pandemic and a complex mix of socio-ecological problems. The profound challenges for the Bhar Lazreg neighbourhood have repercussions at the municipal level. Local affairs are particularly susceptible to political interference. One example of this is the disagreement between representatives of different political parties in the municipal council, which led to serious tensions and affected cooperation between the technical administration of the municipality and the elected committees. The mayor, however, is keen to underline that as an independent political figure he considers the work he does as both patriotic and non-partisan. What he has in mind is the implementation of a large project for Bhar Lazreg, and he is determined to bring in more expertise in urbanism from abroad. Due to his understanding of public policy issues, he presents himself as a person that mediates between involved stakeholders and prevents conflicts between local institutional actors and civil society representatives. In any case, he is determined to push his municipality to the centre of collective efforts for building a new city strategy. In addition to

---

4   Field notes based on an interview with two representatives of ARRU, June 1, 2022.

government programmes, it is therefore also personalities at local level who ultimately shape urban policy. It remains to be seen to what extent mediators, such as mayors, who could strengthen municipalities against the abuse of power by the state, private interests and external interventions, represent a new opportunity for a fairer and sustainable urban policy in the future.

Conclusion

This chapter has offered a multidimensional understanding of urban development in Tunisia by providing a long-term perspective – from providing historical insights into emerging urban disparities to discussing the recent PRIQH2 programme for upgrading residential neighbourhoods. Urban development, as a paradigm, which eventually came to replace an interventionist approach geared towards restructuring, has fed into a broad range of upgrading and rehabilitation projects in varying scope and investment size. Context-specific conditions of access to land, housing, and facilities highlight the problem of territorial inequality that is constitutionally recognised but insufficiently addressed by territorial planning and decentralisation policies. While changes in the legislative and institutional context have reconfigured local governance, further capacity-building in public agencies and municipalities is required to foster participatory approaches, inclusive governance mechanisms, and a solid institutional framework. For now, urban development in Tunisia reflects a wider trend of how the democratisation of public action in the vast domain of international cooperation faces profound challenges (cf. Ben Medien; Sha'ath, both this volume).

Our analysis of the urban development programme for residential neighbourhoods (PRIQH2) revels that the sectorial approach and municipal interventions are not yet fully compatible with each other. It shows that there is a need for further alignment of urban development with decentralisation goals, local participation, and the empowerment of municipalities. In particular, land management issues require concerted action when it comes to the implementation of planning, urban development, and housing projects. The urban land-use plan is significant in confronting deregulation, over-regulation and informal urbanisation. However, it appears to be merely a policy instrument that extends regulation and promotes hurried catch-up urban development within a short-term time frame. An alternative would be an adapted planning tool for long-term-focused planning processes, which would be more suitable to anticipating ongoing urbanisation trends.

As concrete cases of urban development project or plans thereof demonstrate, the potentials and perils of upgrading and rehabilitation could better be grasped by methods, which take into account the project environment and a variety of socio-ecological and political implications that affect local governance strategies to facilitate interventions. These strategies are developed or improvised under constraints that are financial, political, or environmental in nature. In view of these constraints, local institutional actors may develop their own approach for addressing territorial inequality and conceiving a city strategy that is not, from the start, predetermined by an institutional framework.

Daily Mobilities
Young People in the Urban Periphery

Souhir Bouzid

> MUNDHIR: 'After graduating from university, I managed to find the right job for me in a private company in Megrine [an eastern quarter of Greater Tunis – 36 kilometres away]. Nevertheless, the daily commute from Burj al Amri to Megrine is very arduous. This forced me to quit my job and then look for another, closer option. For me, as well as for the majority of young people in Burj al Amri, the first criterion for choosing a job is proximity. So, living in Burj al Amri means struggling in terms of daily mobility because we don't have a transport system that meets our needs'.
>
> Mundhir Jlassi, 31 years old, Burj al Amri

This chapter examines how the requirements of daily mobility are transforming everyday lives, and – accelerated by the forces of modernity – are changing family contexts and creating new social landscapes. This is argued from the perspective of young people in Burj al Amri, a growing peri-urban town, located 25 km southwest of Greater Tunis. My argument is based on three dynamics: First, on the transformation of work-relations in the Maghreb. This relates to profound changes in the Tunisian economy, which was dominated for many centuries by agriculture and subsistence production, and now is characterised by low-paid industrial work, precarious labour in services, and dependent export production – all based predominantly in urban spaces. During recent decades, rural and agricultural livelihood systems have changed and caused large-scale rural-urban migration processes – especially to the Greater Tunis area, while university education and graduation increased, without a corresponding labour demand. Graduate unemployment is thus high and rising in Tunisia (Garraoui 2023). This development is compounded by regionalisation, the second dynamic. Regionalisation reflects the constitutive process of economic and socio-spatial restructuring, which constantly produces new links between the local and the global, and is exemplified here by commuter activities – the everyday movement between suburbs and inner-city places for purposes of education or work. The constant renegotiation of social relations be it in the family or between friends, as well as in the community, together with shifting borders of mobility, constitute the third dynamic, the production of new social landscapes. The latter is characterised by a variety of departures, in both senses of the word: physically, as individuals set out on new daily routines, as for example commuting to work; and in terms of deviation from an accepted, prescribed, or usual course of action, such as engaging in new encounters, that may be uncertain, but may change local social contexts and offer new opportunities.

In the chapter, two central terms – everyday life and mobility – are discussed in more detail. I first refer to the term everyday life, which in Giddens's sense is largely structured by routines ([1984] 1990a). Routinisation refers to 'the habitual, taken-for-granted character of the vast bulk of activities of day-to-day social life; the prevalence of familiar styles and forms of conduct, both supporting and supported by a sense of ontological security' (ibid. 376). According to Giddens, routines are constitutive for the continuous reproduction of the personality structures of the actors in their everyday actions as well as for the reproduction of social institutions. Complementary to routines is a dynamic perspective of everyday life. Following Scott (1991) this can be captured by the notion of experience, as a constructivist conception:

> Subjects are constituted discursively, but there are conflicts among discursive systems, contradictions within anyone of them, multiple meanings possible for the concepts they deploy. And subjects do have agency. They are not unified, autonomous individuals exercising free will, but rather subjects whose agency is created through situations and statuses conferred on them. Being a subject means being "subject to definite conditions of existence, conditions of endowment of agents and conditions of exercise". These conditions enable choices, although they are not unlimited (Scott 1991: 793).

Actors are hence not simply at the mercy of discourses. Although actors are bound by concrete conditions, they have the potential for action (agency) that opens up choices for them, even if these are not unlimited. It is this aspect that marks a central interface in the argument of Scott (1991) and Giddens (1984): Both tie the ability to act back to access to resources. The access to resources thus shapes the potential for action of individual actors. The space where the possibilities of access to material and immaterial resources interlock again and again is the acting individual (Gertel/Breuer 2011). In the wake of these dynamics, the conditions of experience-making and thus of the construction of one's own biography are increasingly fragmented, even for the inhabitants of the seemingly peripheral places, like in Burj al Amri. Based on these considerations, my focus is on everyday practices. This raises questions about the reference of experiences: whether they refer to a place, to a feeling, a routine or to an active being-in-the-world (Gertel/Grüneisl, this volume). All combinations seem possible. I therefore comprehend experience as an interface between space, power and identity.

My understanding of mobility fits into this notion. Based on the fact that mobility is generally understood as the movement of people, goods and information (Urry 2007), the emphasis here is on movements of people. Three forms can be distinguished (cf. Gertel/Breuer 2011: 13): First, the spatial mobility of individuals and groups moving between places. In Tunisia, migrant workers embody this in particular, but also commuters, pilgrims, tourists, and other travellers. Secondly, social mobility, which refers to movements of people within and between groups – i.e. changes in positions in the social structure. This applies to upward social mobility such as successful entrepreneurs, but also to downward mobility such as marginalised casual workers. Thirdly, identities are not fixed entities, but rather mobile composites: these include changes in self-constructions in many ways, i.e. the possibilities and the way in which people shape their biography; they negotiate their identity positions in a changing social structure. These mobility dynamics interact to create new social landscapes and new processes of identification.

Burj al Amri serves as a case study. It is a small suburban town that has been transformed by rapid urban sprawl. Influenced by its proximity to Greater Tunis, the town has become increasingly attractive and has undergone various socio-spatial changes. On the one hand, it is confronted with changing land uses, namely the extension of private housing (legal and illegal) and new housing estates often built on fertile agricultural land, including the development of road networks connecting Burj al Amri via Mornaquia and La Manouba to Greater Tunis. On the other hand, it represents a typical urban fringe (Taleb/Sallemi 2015), where land and labour shape the economic development and the rural-urban transformation. The objective of this chapter is hence to explore the consequences of the mobility practices in Burj al Amri, based on semi-structured interviews in June 2022 with commuters, predominantly young people, and other local actors in the municipality. The aim is to highlight the interaction between the local practices of mobility in a peri-urban area, and the livelihood perspectives of young people who suffer from mobility restrictions and non-spontaneity of their movements.

Burj al Amri

Burj al Amri represents a specific type of urbanisation, namely the development from a small rural village, dating back to the colonial era, to a sprawling peri-urban city that attracts real estate operators to profit from the housing needs of the rapidly expanding capital Tunis. Even today the most important commercial, administrative and industrial activities are located on both sides of the main street, the RN5, connecting Mournaguia / Tunis in the east and Mejez El Bab / Beja in the west. Along this route, the first nuclei of settlement and trade activities appeared during the colonial period. The small centre along this road was originally called Massicault, in tribute to Justin Massicault, Resident General of France in Tunisia from 1886 to 1892. Established by Beylical decree on 17 December 1904, it began life as a village inhabited by French settlers who grew cereals and wine. For a long time, it remained a small spot. In 1961, when the last French settlers departed, it was renamed after Burj al Amri an ancient fort. In 1975 only about 1,664 inhabitants lived in village, after which population growth accelerated until the mid 1990s as a result of both natural growth and migratory inflows. At the beginning of the 1980s, the municipal limit was extended and Burj al Amri absorbed precarious housing in the surrounding areas. From there some people were transferred to new housing estates within its urban setting, particularly to El Intilaka in the northern part of Burj al Amri. In 1994, there were about 5,523 inhabitants (INS 1994: 14). While population increase slowed down for almost two decades (6,519 inhabitants in 2014), with the communalisation of the national territory in 2016, the municipality of Burj El Amri was extended again and integrated three peripheral locations and, compounded by population growth, it reached 19,072 inhabitants in 2023, representing about 4.6 percent of the population of the governorate of La Manouba.

However, urban development remains restricted. The lack of housing in Burj al Amri can be attributed to issues with land ownership. Developments are generally carried out in an irregular manner on agricultural land, and the majority of this land in Burj al Amri are plots without individual title. This hinders planned urban development. The land tenure situation of agricultural land – allegedly inherited from the colonial period, is therefore a real obstacle to the development of the municipality. People are forced to buy un-serviced plots on agricultural land and build their homes without a building permit. This led to the expansion of unregulated housing and a lack of formal housing options. Mongia Jlassi, 45 years old, who works as technical service person for the municipality, explains:

> Unregulated housing has invaded our territory, and the municipality with its limited means cannot solve this problem alone. We have begun to settle the situation of those who have previously purchased their parcel of land from the commune. For the rest of the lots, we need help from other actors and it takes a lot of time.

Public intervention or even on the ground controls have been ineffective due to the lack of local authority resource and the inadequacy of urban planning. Public actors, central decision makers and local implementers, have therefore accepted irregular buildings as 'admissible' by default, in particular by including these unplanned localities in urban planning studies, new development plans, and by gradually planning for infrastructural projects (roads, sanitation, drinking water, etc.). New housing developments occur piecemeal, scattered around the edges of Burj al Amri, and increasingly encroach onto agricultural land. The physical spread of housing locations is a major constraint to taking action on making sure the developments are regulated and up to standard. As state intervention has remained limited, and often only has focused on the rehabilitation of roads and other infrastructure, the gap of unequal living conditions between the core and the periphery in the Burj al Amri municipality is widening, even in this small town.

Agricultural fields often separate low-density peri-urban areas surrounding Greater Tunis. In these sparsely populated peripheral areas, such as in Burj al Amri, public transport is often not efficient and does not meet the travel needs of the residents. Subsequently socio-spatial inequalities prevail, as the core of the municipality including the main axes is privileged over peripheral localities: most services and facilities are concentrated here. People living in the periphery, in contrast, do not have many transport options. They need to walk or otherwise travel into local urban centres in order to connect to anywhere else, by bus or collective taxi. As in Burj al-Amri this, of course, adds the burden of extra time and higher transport costs.

Transport Options

Transport networks are a crucial tool for any city, facilitating the movement of people and goods, connecting locations of production and consumption, and those of education and work with local homes, spaces of reproduction and recreation. In his analyses of the superimposition of the lower ('traditional') by the upper ('modern') urban circuit Santos (1979: 19) identifies the transport system as crucial for facilitating exchanges between the two circuits of the urban economy (cf. Gertel/Audano, this volume).

> Urban transportation organisations and the use of private vehicles are important in explaining the forms taken by both complementarity and competition in the commercial activities of both circuits. Transport facilities are sometimes so limited that certain individuals, even if they have money available, do not have access to products sold by the commercial upper circuit (Santos 1979: 141).

Moreover, urban labour markets, supplied from actors of the lower circuit are, for example, equally dependent on a suitable transport infrastructure. Each city produces its own transport networks – consisting of private and public operators – and is largely shaped by them (Dupuy 1991; Wachter 2004).

In Greater Tunis, the Tunis Transport Company, also known as TRANSTU, a public transport company created 2003 from the merger between the Tunis Light Rail Company (SMLT founded in 1981) and the National Transport Company (SNT founded in 1963), is responsible for the management of passenger transport. However, transport to and from Burj al Amri is shared between public and private operators: TRANSTU public buses serve the municipality via three different lines and also via school buses. But Burj al Amri is poorly served, as all lines only go down its main road, National Road 5. This is, of course, very inconvenient for residents who live far from the main road. They are forced to walk a considerable distance to reach public transport.

Private contractors operate shared taxis, responding to the shortcomings of public transport. They ensure the transport of people from the town to rural localities and also provide transport options for people to La Manouba or Denden. Shared taxis including microbuses, that can accommodate up to eight passengers, can access into dense urban quarters where the roads are narrow or poorly communicated. In suburban areas, they thus represent a vital segment of the economy and transport system (Bouzid 2020): they provide speed of travel, as well as flexibility in service and schedules, and adapt to the needs of users who travel collectively. Using them is simple: vehicles are grouped together at stations, departure and arrival points, and follow precise routes to predefined destinations. As collection points, the private transport stations are located either at central urban locations, at locations with secondary centrality or at the most frequented places on the outskirts of the city. According to the regulations, shared taxis must only serve inter-municipal connections (i.e. interurban transport crossing municipal boundaries). However, in larger Greater Tunis area, shared taxi lines are tolerated by public authorities for use within communities like Burj al Amri because the public bus services are not sufficient.

Public school buses provide the transport for students to Burj al Amri High School (the first is at 8 am and return is at 5 pm). For lunch, students do not have buses to go home. They are forced to either stay in Burj al Amri or return home by taking the shared taxi or a public bus, if they have enough time. While students who live near the RN5 can take the TRANSTU bus, pupils living in localities far from the RN5 can only take a shared taxi, paying, of course, a higher price. However, even public-school buses have a lot of problems, such as delays in the morning and on rainy days.

Daily Mobility of Young People

> Being mobile is not simply traversing landscapes, mobility is not wandering or drifting. It is the extension of the limits of the self and multiple anchoring, for better or for worse (Le Breton 2015, own translation).

Everyday mobility differs from other forms of spatial mobility in that it is repetitive, reminiscent of everyday routines. It is inscribed in short temporalities and in habitual practices. On a day-to-day basis, mobility is the product of more or less constrained residential, professional and family strategies. Unlike one-off trips linked to the satisfaction of a rare need, work-related mobility is an unavoidable structuring axis of everyday life around which all the trips of an individual or a household must be organised. These trips are sometimes supplemented by other trips that can modify usual patterns of mobility. We are then faced with two situations: the first where the place of residence merges with that of work or study, here active individuals have a low mobility. In the second, workers or students have to travel outside their place of residence. In this situation, their mobility practices generate significant flows in terms of commuter mobility. The public transport network is not suitable for travel within or beyond Burj al Amri given its unequal urban housing dispersion throughout the community. Even for those who can access the TRANSTU bus lines, buses are slow, take many detours, come infrequently and are not punctual. Public transport is not attractive. As explained above, this has led to the use of shared taxis for daily mobility, especially for residents of peripheral localities, despite their higher cost.

In peri-urban areas, public transport quickly becomes restrictive in terms of frequencies and schedules. Meeting the mobility demands of young people often is problematic, particularly that of adolescents who are in the process of acquiring spatial autonomy (Thomann 2009). This spatial autonomy is important in terms of identity formation and social inscription. It is therefore interesting to focus on this sensitive and fragile segment of the population that is often not directly targeted by public policies. In territorial terms, middle and high schools are not well distributed throughout peri-urban areas. In the Burj al Amri community, the school map has not been changed since the 1980s and it no longer meets today's needs. But schools are not only locations for education: they are also local hubs for social life; being important for all young people, schools represent a strong element of identity formation.

Young people from Burj al Amri developed their own mobility practices to access their schools, whether primary, secondary or high school. Their mobility is often higher than of the average population in the peri-urban community of Burj al Amri. This can be explained by 'study' reasons, requiring two daily round trips, since the majority of young people go home for lunch. Among young people, those who live in the community's centre use public buses more frequently, as already mentioned, they only have to walk short distances to access cheap public transport.

Mobility practices have also different temporalities: All rural areas of the Burj al Amri municipality have primary schools. All trips to school can be made on foot due. Going to school thus allows children to acquire their first spatial autonomy. Only children living in non-regulated housing centres far from anything else, and outside the municipal boundary have to travel long distances to school. Teenagers, sometimes at the beginning of middle school, but more likely at the beginning of high school, see their daily lives reoriented towards the city and their spatial practices expand considerably. When teenagers change schools, they have to take new modes of transport. New friendships are forged between teenagers from Burj al Amri and teenagers from elsewhere. Shops, cafés, restaurants, the youth centre, the cultural centre, the public library and other urban establishments can become the medium for leisure and sociability of high school students. The space for leisure and sociability is expanding, while the links with the neighbourhood of residence are weakening. The question of mobility for leisure and social activities therefore quickly arises acutely and is often a primary factor of conflict in the household. It is frequently teenagers in peripheral peri-urban areas who suffer the most from the inadequacy of public transport.

The interviews underline the considerable attractiveness of shared taxis for young people living in the periphery. This is due to the inefficiency of school buses in relation to delay, overload, discomfort, and distance to public bus routes. During visits to Burj al Amri High School, there were huge groups of young people waiting to go home. The principal of the high school explains that the delay is caused by the school bus. This delay can be up to an hour and in some cases, buses do not come at all and young people have to find alternatives. Chaima Hammi, 18 years old from Mehrin comments:

> As a captive of public transport, I am not at all satisfied with the public transit offer, particularly school transportation. The school bus is always late, which causes me problems with the school administration. The school bus should normally come at 7 am to be able to bring us to school until 7:35 am, but in reality, it comes either very early or very late. So, I have to take a shared taxi. In addition, I live away from the bus station, so it takes me a walk of 15 minutes to get to the station. I missed two exams last year because of the bus delays, I got two zeros (failed marks) and the high school administration didn't believe that my tardiness was due to the bus delays.

Jihan Benur, 17 years old, from Burj Ennur adds:

> Burj Ennur is very quiet, but we lack facilities and more reliable public transport. I would prefer to live in a busier, more dynamic city. I'd prefer to change my place of residence and live in an environment that offers more amenities to its inhabitants, such as the municipality of El Mornaguia. And I want to live close to schools and extracurricular facilities in order to avoid costly and painful daily commutes, which have a detrimental effect on students. In Burj Ennur people know each other so we

don't live in peace: we live in a very controlled area; as a girl I don't feel comfortable and free to choose my clothes, for example.

The use of public transport by teenagers is contradictory, on the one hand it is restrictive, setting their travel times according to the schedules of the school buses, and on the other hand it positively affects their ability to socialise. Spatial mobility is important for young people because, as Kaufmann and Flamm state, 'the emancipation of the child and then the adolescent is built around the autonomy of movement' (Kaufmann/Flamm 2002: 3, own translation). For these young people who live in peri-urban areas, the gap between their perceptions of mobility and their real experiences is not without consequences. Transport difficulties lead to a strong desire to go somewhere else, which very often manifests itself in the desire to live in the city. Kaufmann and Flamm summarise the process of empowerment among young people as follows:

> It begins with learning to walk, continues with the authorisation to go and play alone at friends' houses, then to move alone during the day, then in the evening, each time with negotiation [...], negotiation whose terms are differentiated between boys and girls (Kaufmann/Flamm 2002: 17, own translation).

Spatial independence should thus increase with the age of the adolescent, while girls are often more controlled and monitored than boys. Seventeen year old Jihan from Burj Ennur comments: 'I can't do extracurricular activities because I have to go home no later than 6 pm, the time of the last bus'. A crucial factor influencing the mobility of young people is thus their residential location. Activity of household members, and consequently the daily mobility of young people, is also shaped in a gender specific way.

Transport problems moreover relate to the labour market: The municipality offers educational and other facilities, but it cannot provide sufficient jobs to its young graduates. The majority of the latter are thus forced to move outside the municipality in order to find suitable jobs. The key problem in terms of daily transport is the movement from Burj al Amri to the Slimane Kahia feeder station in La Manouba, where passengers can change buses or even means of transport. There are no direct lines to Tunis or other destinations: passing through La Manouba is mandatory. Mundhir Jlassi, 30 years old, from El Griaat in Burj al Amri, whom we know from the opening quote, explains his situation:

> Our problems in Burj al Amri lie in the lack of public transport, services and facilities. If I had a private car, my life would be better. I'd prefer to change my place of residence and live in an environment that offers more comfort to its inhabitants. I consider that Burj al Amri is the *delegation* [i.e. district] least served by public transport in Greater Tunis. In addition, living in the outlying localities of Burj al Amri is doubly problematic. In short, people here struggle a lot because of the lack of public transport and this especially during the school holidays since the frequency of bus runs decreases. In addition, living in Burj al Amri means being far away from the places where jobs are concentrated.

Another young person, Naim Chlagou, 32 years old, who lives also in Burj al Amri, in Entilaka housing estate, has an similar assessment:

Burj al Amri is very quiet, but we lack facilities and more reliable public transport. I would prefer to live in an environment that offers more services to its residents. And I want to live close to leisure and community facilities and industrial areas in order to avoid expensive and arduous daily travel. For example, I can't look for a job in the Lake area [35 km away, located on the opposite, western side of Greater Tunis] because it's impossible to commute to the [affluent] Lake area. I think that the distance of Burj al Amri from Tunis has a direct effect on the growing unemployment rate of young graduates of Burj al Amri.

The girls who live in the outlying localities of Burj al Amri have a feeling of being stuck far from urban areas. They have a lot of free time, especially during weekends and holidays; and experience boredom and residential isolation in the suburbs. They face serious problems of insecurity: they cannot move around in the evening as they live in a socially highly controlled peri-urban space. Manal Guesmi, 27 years old, from Mehrine, illustrates her experiences:

I take the bus daily from Griaat, where I live, to Burj al Amri and then to La Manouba where I work. I struggle daily with public transport, which remains insufficient in relation to demand. I can distinguish two major problems here for a girl: the first is that we can't dress in a free and independent way, people know each other and survey each other a lot; and the second is that you can't move easily because the buses are always overcrowded and, in the evening, they become unsafe.

These interviews show that transport and residential location strongly influence the daily mobility practices in peri-urban areas. They limit the professional opportunities of young people from disadvantaged households who are concentrated in peripheral areas. Inequality particularly affects women. For them, living in a place like Burj al Amri reduces the likelihood of finding a job. The place of residence can then have a decisive effect on access to employment and satisfaction with life.

Conclusion

Burj al Amri has experienced considerable spatial and demographic sprawl. On the one hand, rural exodus attracts many people from the countryside to urban areas in search of work and better living conditions. On the other hand, cities are forced to find spaces to establish new residential areas. But very often the new urban population does not find housing opportunities in the city that match their income. The situation on the urban fringes was illustrated with the case of Burj al Amri. Here two types of peri-urban spaces, namely its centre and its peripheries were distinguished. Each space has its own characteristics and transport facilities that determine the lifestyles of families living there. The investigation of mobility practices reveals that social and spatial conditions combine to constrain daily mobility, and limit the accessibility of services and opportunities to disadvantaged households, especially those in peripheral areas outside the community core. Young people in particular suffer from mobility restrictions and the non-spontaneity of their movements, which ultimately impacts their livelihood prospects, their social advancement and consequently their socio-spatial integration. Teenagers are often victims of inequalities in transport options, complicating their access to schools and other facilities. Young graduates are disproportionately affected; especially women dependent on public transport. They are forced to look for jobs everywhere in Greater Tunis and are often limited in their choices by a question of transport accessibility or by restrictive working hours, such as is the case for those who work in clinics and hospitals with changing working shifts. However, the role of rural and shared taxis is considerable and of growing importance – and needs to be taken into account by the authorities. Transport networks and services are also important for another reason: private and public stakeholders are increasingly making location decisions for the settlement of households, companies and facilities that depend on the availability and reliability of transport infrastructure. If we want to better plan the spatial development of urban spaces today and to create sustainable social landscapes, we might be well advised to focus on good transport accessibility for peri-urban areas.

The Dream of Integration
Civic Participation of Sub-Saharan Migrants in Tunis

Olfa Ben Medien

> FATOU: 'I'm here to listen. I live in hope of being accepted, working, and finding shelter'.
>
> Fatou, a 38-year-old Ivorian migrant who has been living in Tunis for eight years

With this sentence, Fatou begins her speech at a participation workshop that is part of the Tunis City Development Strategy (SDVT) in 2022. Initiated after the revolution in 2011, this strategy was developed for application in urban settings (Kahloun/Frische, this volume) and is based on the cooperation between Tunisian municipalities, civil society, and international organisations. The SDV strategy in Tunis is part of the overarching ASIMA Tunis: Strategic Planning and Improved Governance for a Resilient City project. The SDVT strategy is also part of the Medinatouna[1] ('Our City') initiative, and has organised two consultation workshops with Sub-Saharan migrants living in Tunis. Like many migrants who have entered Tunisia, either legally or irregularly, to settle or transit to Europe, Fatou – Fquoted above – is driven by the hope of a better, more stable and secure future. For years, Tunisia has been a country of immigration for Sub-Saharans, fleeing wars, environmental, political, or economic crises in their countries of origin. Fatou took advantage of the Tunisian authorities' 2014 abolition of visas for nationals of several Sub-Saharan countries. Between 2014 and 2019 a stay of less than 90 days for nationals of several African countries, like Côte d'Ivoire, Senegal, Mali, Niger, Burkina Faso, Zimbabwe, Botswana, and the Central African Republic did not need a visa. However, as people fled economic misery in their countries of origin, they came to Tunisia with the hope of finding work and then paying for a journey across the Mediterranean to Europe, aspiring to a dignified life and better future – but many stayed. This journey thus represents the dream of thousands of Sub-Saharan migrants for whom Tunisia is a transit country. For

---

1   For further information about these initiatives see the online presentations (cf. https://medinatouna.com).

others, it has become a final destination where they must settle down due to lack of other options (INS et al. 2021).

Sub-Saharan migration to Tunisia dates back to 2003, when the African Development Bank transferred its office from Côte d'Ivoire to Tunisia. This relocation led to many civil servants and their families moving to Tunisia. Moreover, Sub-Saharan students frequently enrol in Tunisian universities following bilateral agreements linking Tunisia with other African countries. With the opening of several private universities in Tunis, Sfax, and Sousse, the number of students, often attracted by the French-speaking environment, further increased. In 2011, a new migration dynamic began with the Tunisian revolution, making Tunisia an increasingly attractive territory for Sub-Saharan migrants (MMC 2021). Indeed, the political and regulatory context, shaped by a very dynamic, post-revolutionary civil society working for the protection and integration of migrants, has resulted in Tunisia being perceived as a safer country than its neighbours: In Libya there is little protection for migrants, while Algeria carries out mass expulsions of irregular African migrants. The civil war in Libya has also prompted many Sub-Saharans to leave the country and instead make a new attempt at (irregular) emigration from the Tunisian coast to Italy (Nasraoui, 2017: 159). Finally, the 2014 opening of visa regulations for several African countries has contributed to the growth of Sub-Saharan immigration to Tunisia. Thus, the number of registered migrants in Greater Tunis has increased from 7,200 migrants in 2014 to 21,466 in 2021 (INS et al. 2021).

The United Nations Department of Economic and Social Affairs (UNDESA) estimated there were 57,000 Sub-Saharan migrants – including registered refugees and asylum seekers – in the capital Tunis and Tunisia's major cities (UNDESA 2019). However, this number does not represent the entire migration community given the difficulties in identifying informal migration networks and the choice of many migrants not to report to the Tunisian authorities for fear of paying fines (that accumulate per day of irregularity). The Observatoire National de la Migration (ONM) focuses its studies on internal migration and the migration of Tunisians abroad. It is limited to data on migrants who entered Tunisia through official channels or who have taken steps to legitimise their situation. Therefore, the ONM also underestimates the actual number of Sub-Saharan migrants in Tunisia. The National Institute of Statistics (INS) also does not collect data on this demographic. As a result, the Tunisian authorities have no meaningful statistical picture of the migrant population. Can we then claim that 'migrants do not exist in Tunisia', as they are absent from official statistics? (El-Ghali/Chemlali 2022: 84)

Researchers prefer to speak of a 'Tunisian non-migration policy' on two accounts: firstly, because of the absence of the right of asylum and refugee status in Tunisian official texts; and secondly, due to a fragmentation of the architecture for the protection of migrants' rights, distributed over a multitude of national bodies, local associations and international NGOs, without any real collaboration and harmonisation. When it comes to the integration of migrants in the city, local governance is the 'echo chamber of national policies' (Belmessous/Roche 2018: 21). Faced with the Tunisian non-migration policy at the national level, what should local action look like, and what kind of impact can we expect in the absence of regulations regarding the protection and integration of migrants?

This chapter thus addresses the connection between the enforced immobility of Sub-Saharan migrants and their situations of il/legal and socio-economic instability. These migrants, driven by their hopes for dignity and a better future, now often find themselves 'stuck' in irregularity in Tunisia. In the following, I will focus on local action of the civil society, which strives for the welcoming and integration of Sub-Saharan migrants in Tunisia. I assess this topic in the context of a Tunisian democratic transition that places the issue of human rights, and in this case those of migrants, at the heart of the political debate at the national level, as well as more recently at the local level.

Since the 2011 revolution, Tunisia has faced a series of transformations, also in relations between government and citizens. The territorial dimension and causes of the uprising, the call for more spatial equity between regions, and the inclusion of marginalised territories in development policies quickly placed decentralisation as a major pillar of the reforms carried out. Furthermore, the legal framework has been changed with the implementation of the Local Authorities Code (Organic Law No. 2018–29 of 9 May 2018). This law confirmed the new principle of subsidiarity and reduced control over local governments. Indeed, in this period participatory approaches in the design and implementation of local policies or projects have become a main feature of municipalities' activities and projects. Thus, encouraged – or pushed – by NGOs and donors, several municipalities, directly elected since 2018, have begun to integrate their migrant populations into the process of citizen participation.

My aim then becomes to answer three questions: Why is this migrant population, which has remained 'invisible' in national statistics and policies, becoming the focus of municipality action? What is the role of international donors in these campaigns to involve migrants in local affairs? And what is the reasoning of local actors and their positioning in relation to operating methods imported and dictated by international actors? I address these questions in the context of the SDVT migrant participation workshops, by investigating the reasoning of the different actors, including the participating Sub-Saharan migrants. These workshops took place on the 9th and 10th of June 2022. Migrants, who have suffered racism, illegality, precariousness, and exclusion in the capital's neighbourhoods are suddenly called upon by the municipality of Tunis to participate in a reflection for an inclusive city, ensuring the 'right to the city' for all its inhabitants. However, the question must be asked, what are their expectations from these consultation workshops and are they being met? What are the difficulties and limitations of this process of involving migrants in citizen participation around the SDV in Tunis? To answer these questions, I favoured a qualitative approach based on interviews with migrants, carried out on the sidelines of the consultation workshops organised by the municipality of Tunis. These interviews were conducted at the beginning and end of two focus groups, one with Sub-Saharan students enrolled in universities in Tunis and the other with irregular Sub-Saharan migrants. Other interviews with associations promoting the integration of migrants in the city, stakeholders from the SDVT project in Tunis, representatives of the municipality, and international donors complement this research.

Expectations of Migrants and Objectives of the Workshop: A Gap

While the team of stakeholders of the SDV of Tunis and the municipality need the migrant populations to help them develop proposals, and plan a set of projects and programmes to develop the capital, the migrant participants – students and irregular migrants – came to the workshops with a different set of expectations. Migrants on the one hand, came with an attitude of 'listening', expecting to learn more about their own status and how to manage insecurity. On the one hand, many students expected to receive information to facilitate the paperwork process of becoming 'regularised', as they often face problems with administrative procedures in Tunisia. They deplore the lack of a virtual or physical space that centralises information on the granting of a residence permit, services, or cultural and sporting events for students: 'I am involved in community life, I come to find out how to improve the situation of Sub-Saharan students and to benefit our brothers and sisters and to pass information on to others' (Marie, Cameroonian student). The group of irregular migrants in contrast, came to participate in the SDVT consultation in the hope of finding information or new regulations that could improve their daily lives. In addition to this, they wanted to explain to local authorities how their daily lives are characterised by racism, violence, and precariousness. The discourses of planners on public spaces, the development of the metropolis, or the rehabilitation of the central axis are therefore far from their reality, and distract from their essential and urgent needs. From the beginning, the discrepancy between the expectations of the workshop organisers and the expectations of these migrants is glaring. In response to 'we came to listen' to migrants, one of the so-called experts replied 'we are the ones who are listening to you!'

When they took the floor, the migrants explained their discomfort in the city, their lack of rights; from difficulties in finding housing, precariousness of work, insecurity in public spaces and transport, difficulties in accessing public health services, to the challenges of enrolling a child in a nursery. In response to the question: 'What projects can the municipality propose to improve your situation and your living environment?', those present asked for a regularisation of papers and a change in the mentality of Tunisians, who are often seen as very hostile to their presence. Very quickly, the migrants understood that the municipality and its representatives had nothing to offer them and, vice versa, the organisers of the consultation soon realised the limits of the municipality's ability to act in the face of the migrants' situation.

Indeed, in Tunisia, many of the issues raised, such as laws and regulations on migration and the organisation of work, are the responsibility of the central government. Similarly, there is no local housing policy in Tunisia and the municipalities are drastically lacking in resources. The scope of local action is thus limited to the provision of spaces for cultural exchanges, awareness-raising programmes, reception and information centres, or for training and learning the Tunisian language. In this sense, during the consultation workshops with civil society, associations (e.g. community groups, unions, NGOs, religious organisations) taking care of migrants in Tunisia recommended improving access to housing, transport, public spaces, and services in the city for all inhabitants of Tunis regardless of their origins. For better social integration of migrants, the associations advise against residential projects or public spaces that exclusively target migrant populations, as this would risk further isolating them in the city. For these associations, comprehensive action to improve the living environment in the city would reduce tensions and hostility among locals towards migrants.

Sub-Saharan students who are in their final year of high school or at the end of their studies say they have very little interest in the city and its development. As one workshop participant explained: 'We are here for a year or two, but the important thing is that I can attend today, because we as Sub-Saharan students lack information and thus have a lot of problems' (Charles, Cameroonian student). These students do not show a connection to the city because they have no plans to stay there after graduation. The other group of students, who aim to study and settle in Tunis – often for reasons of the quality of its universities, affordable study fees, and living costs – have, however, found it difficult to integrate into the city. Some stress, they stick to the community where they live and rely on solidarity among Sub-Saharans. Others live in university accommodation and only socialise on campus. In Greater Tunis, many students thus only know their particular community or the university, its premises, its students, its teachers, and its cultural and sporting events. During the rare opportunities they have to travel around the city, they experience discrimination and racism both in the means of transport and on the streets. This experience strongly influenced their perceptions, practices, and their lack of attachment to the city. 'If I feel marginalised, I don't even want to learn the language and try to integrate', says Marie, a Cameroonian student who participated in the SDVT consultation. Many students also confirm that they have great difficulty finding end-of-studies internships in Tunisian companies and that they do not intend to settle in Tunis after completing their studies. They speak of the impossibility for Sub-Saharans to work or create their own business in Tunisia, unlike European or Arab foreigners. Tunis is then perceived as a city of passage where, 'you come …, you do what you have to do (get the diploma) and then you leave', says Arnaud, a student from Burkina Faso. In the absence of a sense of belonging to the city, students subsequently lack enthusiasm to get involved in the design of a project for developing the capital.

The group of irregular migrants did not express a lack of interest in the city's issues, but on the contrary, they wanted the right to access the city's services. They demanded more basic rights than Sub-Saharan students, such as access to health care in hospitals without the police being notified of their illegitimate status, or being able to enrol their Tunisia born children in childcare. Irregular migrants are very interested in any change of Tunisian regulations that might grant them access to residence permits, allow them to access work in the formal market, open a bank account, and sign a rental contract – they aspire to gain these basic rights that are necessary for a stable future in Tunisia.

Most recurrent and important are however safety and security issues; this comes up in the interventions of all Sub-Saharans, even if there are vast demographic differences between migrants, such as gender, religion, and legal and illegitimate-status. The testimonies reveal that irregular migrants are more vulnerable to physical attacks and acts of racism than students. The latter are frequently in contact with Tunisian students and academics that are more often open to otherness and are accepting foreigners. These students also show a certain level of awareness and information about their rights as a result of their proximity to associations, in particular the African Students' Association. On the one hand all participants noted that women are more exposed to aggression in public spaces and to exploitation in the workplace, while on the other hand Muslim Sub-Saharan women who wear the veil say they are spared and feel safe in the city.

Local Experts: Adapting a Participatory Approach

In the following I first introduce the discourse and methodological project settings of the SDVT consultation workshops, before I discuss the interest and motivations of the municipal experts and the scope of participatory approaches. Discursively speaking, the use of the term 'expert' reflects an acceptance of asymmetrical knowledge. I therefore would rather suggest that we are all experts in the practices we perform and experience, regardless of whether we earn an income from these tasks – as foreign students, refugees, representatives of an urban policy, or stakeholders of an international organisation: different groups have specific and sometimes vested interests. Even though the methodology applied in the SDVT strategy has to be considered a travelling model (i.e. it is imported by European donors) it has been easily adopted by local experts. The latter are professionals working on a private basis who are responsible for setting up the SDVT strategy on behalf of the municipality of Tunis, and in accordance with a methodology imposed by the Medinatouna project. These experts who have studied in European or Tunisian universities (allegedly) share the same values of human rights and beliefs of an inclusive and sustainable city. The two principles – participatory approach and sustainable development – are the strategic axes of the project for Tunis. The methodology involves a participatory diagnosis of the social, urban, economic, and environmental situation in the city. The results serve as a basis for building a strategic framework with a future vision of the city that will be translated into strategic development axes, objectives, goals, and projects. The project's integrative methodology is further based on the consultation of the city's stakeholders, including institutional actors, civil society, private entrepreneurs, and citizens. It works to ensure that the Sustainable Development Goals of the Agenda 2030 are met.

Local experts should be familiar with the participatory approach, imposed by the regulations (such as the Local Government Code, Local Fundamental Law No. 29 of 9 May 2018) for local projects financed by international donors. Their understanding is that through learning processes they have overcome 'the mistrust and scepticism of the first participatory experiments giving citizens a voice in Tunisia' (SDV Tunis, coordinating expert). They now adhere to the principles of participatory democracy, which 'ensure the acceptability of actions and projects and the appropriation of the strategy by all stakeholders', as an expert involved in the consultation workshop put it. Simultaneously, they remain sceptical about the results that can be obtained from consultation workshops. One of the local experts from SDV Tunis testifies:

> Sometimes, institutional actors are very much involved in sectoral reasoning. Private actors are driven only by their own interests. They often come to take advantage of the availability of municipal officials to deal with a personal problem. The discourse of civil society is often very relevant, except when associations follow a politicised discourse.

The consultation with citizens was carried out in the form of a large questionnaire survey, which was then supplemented by more targeted focus groups. The outcomes of the first round of citizen participation have been mixed: One local expert said, 'the needs confirm the results of our diagnosis and the orientations of our strategic framework'. The expert continues:

> Residents perceive the city through the prism of their own neighbourhoods; often the proposals do not go beyond the scale of the neighbourhood and issues of proximity. They don't plan for the medium or long term and don't visualise the metropolitan scale.

The participatory approach with city stakeholders and citizens required local experts to have command of both technical knowledge, and the ability to analyse, interpret, and make use of the results. This task becomes harder when in engaging with migrants.

In the focus group discussions, the experts admit that it did not go exactly as planned as the migrants mainly talked about their own experiences and difficulties in the city. These problems are mainly related to everyday violence, limited access to housing, and racism. The cornerstone of this pyramid of precariousness and vulnerability is Tunisia's regulations on migration and the granting of residence permits. Without a regularisation of the situation, migrants can only work in the informal market. They have no social security coverage or right of access to public health services. In addition, they are often underpaid or exploited by their employer. Without a residency card, migrants cannot sign a rental agreement and risk eviction and abuse by landlords. Migrants cannot even file a complaint against their attackers with the police as they fear of paying a fine for overstaying their visa deadline. One of the experts involved in the consultation workshops with migrants explains the difficulty of getting irregular migrants interested in the city's problems:

> It's good to involve migrants, they have the right to the city like all inhabitants. But our discourse on sustainable urban development and the city's outreach strategy is very far from their needs, which are very urgent. They need to come out of hiding and build a future.

For the representatives of the municipality, the participatory approach is supposed to be an assurance of the acceptance and appropriateness of the project for the city by the citizens. Often, the mobilisation of citizens in consultation workshops gives the municipality visibility among voters and legitimisation of their action. This was the case of participatory budgets, which, despite a low level of citizen mobilisation, constituted 'an opportunity for legitimisation by involving citizens through deliberation in municipal management' (Som/De Facci 2017: 246). Moreover, the participation of citizens is often mediatised and politically co-opted by local representatives. The migrant population, however, which has no electoral clout, has difficulty making itself heard by Tunisian officials. The involvement of migrant populations in the SDVT project in Tunis is therefore first and foremost due to the recommendation of donors and international 'experts'. The local authorities have accepted this procedural obligation, but stress that there are limits to their ability to respond to the needs of the irregular population, given their logistical and financial means, and their limited powers. However, among the actions that have been proposed is the creation of local reception centres to take care of the vulnerable homeless population, including migrants, while a creation of citizenship schools would raise awareness of the values of living together and the right to the city for all.

Donors: Imported Know-how about Migrants' Participation in Local Affairs

To understand the potential participation of migrants in the management of the city, it is also important to analyse the role of international actors in policy transfers. This concerns the establishment of local governance based on participation of all of the stakeholders involved in the management of cities. Indeed, the Medinatouna initiative through the nine SDV projects exports a city model (labelled sustainable and inclusive) and a modus operandi to include all stakeholders. In addition, the SDV in Tunis is part of international cooperation focusing on local governance for the integration of migrants, an MC2CM project (Mediterranean City to City Migration project) implemented by the ICMPD (International Centre for the Development of Migration Policies), and funded by the European Union and the Swiss Development Cooperation (cf. EU 2023) happens alongside. The main objective and slogan of this support project is: 'Leaving No One Behind: For an Active Participation of Migrants in the Strategy of the City of Tunis' (MC2CM project, Tunis, 2022). This project focuses on the capacity of cities to improve the living environment of migrant populations, even if the basic problem – especially in relation to the legal status and rights of migrants – is a matter of national policies. As part of the MC2MC project, international donors, in partnership with local associations, municipalities (e.g. Sfax, La Marsa, Raoued), and Sub-Saharan migrants, have carried out cultural projects and built reception centres that aim to facilitate the inclusion of this vulnerable population at the local level. The current Tunisian context, moving towards decentralisation and local governance that favours both an inclusive and participatory approach, seems to be conducive to the development of these local actions. International actors have defined their objective as the promotion of the social integration of migrants and the enhancement of the role of migration as a driver of development. This starts with the active involvement of migrants in the SDV of Tunis and in local affairs, and this has given rise to the establishment of focus groups organised with Sub-Saharan migrants as part of the citizen consultations.

In order to succeed in mobilising the vulnerable population and groups at risk of exclusion, including migrants, to participate in the SDVT, and to strengthen the role of Tunisian cities in the involvement of migrants in sustainable urban development (expected results of the MC2CM project), the local experts of the municipality were closely supervised by international experts during each stage of the project. The international experts speak of a mission to provide 'methodological and technical support to the teams of the municipality of Tunis'[2]. The trainings then aim to strengthen capacities in urban

---

2   MC2CM Project Presentation Note: 'Leaving No One Behind: Towards Active Participation of Migrants in the City Strategy of Tunis', Component 2 (2022).

planning, the Sustainable Development Goals, and participatory processes. More specifically and in terms of the inclusion of migrants, a specific 'training in social inclusion and taking into account the needs of marginalised populations, including migrants in the SDVT' (Interview with the SDV Project Manager in the Municipality of Tunis, 2022) and a webinar 'Migration and Integration' with the objective of exchanging good practices between cities on the participation of migrant communities in local planning processes and local affairs, were carried out for the benefit of SDVT local experts. Because of the adaption of the imported methodology by local experts and the municipality, some political scientists fear a forced modernisation of local governance in the countries of the South by the importation of standardised modus operandi without sufficient adaptation to the local specificities, and the social and political contexts of the different countries. This critique is not new: Allal, for example, reflects on international development actors in Tunisia:

> [They] use specific rhetoric to promote the adoption, in the countries where they operate, of instruments and knowledge that they consider to be international standards. They act as import-export entrepreneurs of 'good practices' in different fields [democratisation, good governance, sustainable development, citizen participation] and propose to the governments with which they cooperate model reforms aimed at modernising the different sectors of the state (Allal 2010: 98, own translation).

Other political researchers question the interests governing international donor activities for the integration of Sub-Saharan migrants in the countries of the southern shore of the Mediterranean. Beyond the application of the SDGs for inclusive and resilient cities and beyond the granting of the right to the city to all inhabitants despite their origins, is there not the desire to 'better settle' these migrants far from European countries (cf. Garnaoui, this volume)? Chemlali/El Ghali (2022) denounce a European policy of externalising borders that makes Tunisia a good student in terms of security migration policy (cf. Sha'ath, this volume). Indeed, for Geisser (2019), Tunisian politics in recent years has seen a return to the security paradigm implemented by a government elite that develops good relations with donors and European states. Such Tunisian decision-makers are trying to meet European requirements for border control and the fight against irregular migration. This kind of security policy is a step backwards for Tunisia, which has enshrined the right to asylum in its 2014 constitution, without however, translating it into an asylum law. At the same time, the post-revolution democratic effervescence of 2011 has led to a de-tabooisation of the debate on migrants' rights. The issue has thus been reappropriated by a Tunisian civil society driven by an openness to otherness and acceptance of foreigners (Geisser 2019: 6–7).

The role of international donors in the indirect application of a security policy aimed at protecting other maritime borders from the flow of Tunisian and African migrants has tarnished the image of international and even humanitarian organisations acting for the protection of migrants on Tunisian territory. This perception is strongly influenced by a general political climate in Tunisia that is positioned against any external interventionism under the leadership of international organisations. The issue of migrants is particularly sensitive, since Tunisia is both a host and a country of departure. Like Sub-

Saharans, Tunisians are drowning in the Mediterranean, and are victims of racism, and clandestine and precarious situations in the countries of the North.

Conclusion

The global economic crisis, exacerbated by the Covid-19 pandemic, the war in Ukraine, climate change, as well as national political instability, has affected the most vulnerable in Tunisia, particularly the young and the poor, who are now increasingly seeking to move to Europe. With rigid border controls and the near-impossibility of obtaining a visa, these young people attempt illegal journeys, braving all dangers. This same desperation has made Tunis a departure point not only for its youth, but also as a transit country, and even as a forced final destination for thousands of Sub-Saharan migrants. This chapter, by analysing the process of migrant participation in the urban development strategy of Tunis, captures a moment of freedom and hope for a better future in an inclusive city, offering the right to expression and mobility for all. The consultation workshops offered a space for mutual listening that translated for some migrants in an experience of regained dignity.

However, the participation of Sub-Saharan migrants in local affairs, or in this case more so in the drawing up of a development strategy for the capital Tunis, is clearly the result of a recommendation from international donors, based on vested interests. These actors have ensured the application of a methodology designed and tested in developed countries. But the implementation of participatory processes in the Tunisian context has shown clear limitations. First, Tunisian municipalities do not have the means to meet the specific needs of migrants in terms of housing and services. Indeed, in Tunisia, several issues such as housing, health, and access to work and security are in the responsibility of the central government and not the municipalities. Secondly, the current migration policies and regulations fail to facilitate the integration of migrants (e.g. via granting residence permits or changing labour laws). Finally, the hostility of the local population towards migrants has been aggravated as a result of the economic crisis and high unemployment rate in Tunisia. However, personal encounters in workshops made it possible to bring together the city's stakeholders to discuss the often precarious and vulnerable situation of Sub-Saharan migrants who are currently mainly concentrated in Tunis. While the Tunisian authorities often seem to deny the existence of this population (inadequacies in terms of data, strategies, and laws) and adopt a migration policy based on a security model, the municipalities in contrast are beginning to implement more concrete actions for the integration of migrants, with the support of local and international associations. Local authorities, who are often directly confronted with the difficult situations of migrants, are called upon to act and integrate these groups in the urban setting.

Improving the situation of migrants can therefore begin with the creation of places of information and reception for migrants, places of cultural exchange and sociability, and safe and inclusive public spaces. In the absence of reliable statistical data or official information, the workshops enabled representatives of the city to better understand the difficulties of migrant populations. The participation of migrants in the consultation workshops has therefore achieved one of its main objectives, namely to give 'visibility' to a migrant population that is rarely heard. This, in turn, could be a first step towards strengthening a sense of belonging to the city – and having a voice in local development – among a population that often feels excluded from political decisions. As Fatou, the Ivorian migrant and participant in the consultation workshop, explains: 'I came out of curiosity, I come back with the satisfaction that there is someone who is worried, who is fighting to find a solution for me'. Marie, the Cameroonian student and participant, explains: 'I appreciate the initiative, you are taken into consideration somewhere. It all starts with a round table. I hope that the statements can be applied'. While the results of the consultation process remain uncertain, the dialogue established between the municipality and migrant populations potentially opens up avenues for participation and collaboration that could establish relationships of trust in the future.

Municipalities and Migration Governance
Ambiguous Surveillance and Assistance in Tunis

Hiba Sha'ath

> SAMUEL: Even before Covid, migrants did not go to their local municipal offices because they did not know there were services available for them there […] if I tell you, for example, there is the United Nations Population Fund, UNFPA office – which provides healthcare, many migrants do not know that these services are also available to them and if this information is not communicated to them, they will be unaware and not go.
> Some, as long as they are not reached [by us], will continue their precarious situation, and their status – of irregularity.
> Their fear will prevent them from accessing available services. Hence, the importance of community leaders. The municipalities have this idea of recruiting us as leaders of migrant associations, to be community liaisons with whom they can work in relation to conduct outreach to migrants in their districts. We are also here to address a certain number of issues, issues that migrants face in Tunisia: related to work, access to residence permits, integration, and in particular racist behaviour [from locals], which persists, even though the law has been passed [against it].
>
> Interview with Samuel, former head of a migrant association (July 8, 2021)

In recent years, cities have been at the forefront of challenging securitised approaches to migration deployed by their national governments. While states have usually seen migration through the lens of national security, regulating migrants' access to territory and legal status at a national level, local governments have been more concerned with the day-to-day aspects of migrant integration policy. This can be attributed to the fact that migrants' everyday struggles to access housing, decent work, and healthcare mostly take place in cities, with local authorities being most directly impacted when migrants are unable to meet their needs. Furthermore, city spaces are places of encounter between residents and foreigners, and city streets are where local and national migration policies are implemented, negotiated, and contested.

As a result, policy discourses surrounding the involvement of local authorities in migration governance have typically been celebratory: local governments are seen as progressive, pragmatic, and unburdened by the focus on national security. They are considered more willing to address the practicalities of improving migrants' living conditions without being pre-occupied with issues of legal status. While cities have indeed contested restrictive migration policies in certain contexts and have deployed more welcoming policies towards migrants, this humanitarian, caring approach to migration at the local level can also reinforce the premises upon which the national state bases its restrictive national migration politics. As scholars have recently shown, humanitarian techniques of government, while providing assistance and care, can often operate through benevolence and charity rather than through a defence of human rights (Fassin 2007; Ticktin 2011; Topak 2019). In Tunisia, some local governments have become more involved in assisting migrants. The types of assistance provided, while filling a critical need, do not contest the underlying legal and political principles determining migrants' access to legal status. This leaves migrants in continuous dependence on the benevolence of local governments (and their donors) to obtain support while residing in Tunis. At the same time, the key problem of their lack of access to legal status remains unresolved and depoliticised amidst the focus on social assistance and care. Thus, with the growing involvement of local government in migration issues in Tunisia, it is important to critically examine the role these local authorities play in the surveillance and containment regime against migrants.

In this chapter, I analyse the work carried out by two municipalities in the Greater Tunis Area – La Marsa and Raoued – with migrants[1] from Sub-Saharan African countries through two initiatives: first, the provision of vouchers and essential supplies to migrants during the Covid-19 pandemic; and second, the set-up of information help-desks for migrants within the framework of the programme Inclusion, Migration, Integration and Governance[2] (I-MIGR). Through a close-up examination of these initiatives, I argue that it is premature to interpret local governments' involvement in migration work as necessarily liberatory, or as a positive development for migrant rights per se. Rather, I show how the work of these municipalities is enmeshed within the multi-scalar, multi-actor border regime that targets migrants in North Africa and seeks to contain their transnational mobility towards Europe. As this chapter demonstrates, local governments are not outside the state: they are an extension of state power that seek to shape migrants' conduct through positive reinforcement of desirable behaviour. Rather than presenting a promising avenue for defending migrants' legal rights, local governments' role in migration governance works in tandem with the control tactics deployed at a national level. Rather than using coercive measures, municipalities adopt the approach of managing

---

1 In this chapter, I use 'migrant' as an all-encompassing term to refer to those who travelled to Tunisia to study, work, claim refuge, or join family, regardless of legal status.
2 The help-desks were set up through project I-MIGR – Inclusion, Migration, Integration and Governance (Raoued and La Marsa) (ICMPD et al., n.d.). The project ran in two phases: the first was funded by the Italian Agency for Cooperation and Development and ran from late 2019 to late 2020 and the second phase (2022) was funded by ICMPD through its Mediterranean City-to-City Migration (MC2CM) programme (ICMPD et al., n.d.).

migrants' aspirations in relation to onward mobility. By working with migrants to change the conditions in which they live to make staying a more viable option, while also counselling them against the dangers of the Mediterranean crossing, municipalities reshape migrants' relationships to the migratory possibilities they have ahead of them. In this way, they engage in the borderwork that seeks to curb irregular onward migration to Europe from Sub-Saharan countries. The ultimate result, however, is that migrants remain in a precarious legal situation with their access to their rights curtailed, while relying on the local government's benevolence to access assistance on an *ad hoc* basis.

This chapter draws on data from my doctoral research that was carried out in Tunis in 2020 and 2021. It consists of semi-structured interviews with 41 migrants, activists and professionals working on migration, of informal conversations and observations in migration-themed events, along with a review of project reports and documents related to migration and migration governance in Tunis. The following section will elaborate on the tensions and continuities in migration governance between the national and local level. I will then outline the growing role of municipalities in migration governance in Tunis, against a background of growing securitisation of Sub-Saharan migration to the country over recent years. Finally, I will examine the two afore-mentioned initiatives undertaken by some municipalities of Tunis, exploring their merits and limitations in improving conditions for migrants in Greater Tunis.

Migration Policies at the National and Local Level

The growth of sanctuary and solidarity movements around the world in recent years has signalled a willingness on the part of some local authorities to push back against draconian national immigration policies criminalising migration. Sanctuary cities have held promise for migrants as spaces of refuge, safety, and distance from the violence of borders, securing their rights to work, education, and services regardless of legal status. These movements have taken different forms, some of which involved a refusal to cooperate with national authorities in order to protect refugee claimants or illegalised migrants (San Francisco being one of the earlier and more famous examples; cf. Mancina 2012); others adopted a policy of not collecting migrants' legal status in spaces and services where identification is usually required, or not sharing that information with national authorities (Bauder 2019). While not fully effective in protecting illegalised migrants from the risk of detention or deportation, these policies have discursively created a culture of welcome and acceptance towards newcomers. On the other end of the spectrum, some cities – one example being Phoenix, Arizona (Varsanyi 2008) – have been hostile towards undocumented migrants, as demonstrated by their support of intensified policing and surveillance of migrants, contributing to the latter's' socio-economic and geographic marginalisation (Gilbert 2009; Coleman/Stuesse 2014; Stuesse/Coleman 2014; Bauder 2019).

With migration increasingly being seen through a prism of security, there are a variety of ways through which the state governs the perceived threats posed by migration: the state categorises migrants, contains them, pushes them back, confines, and finds other ways to govern migrant populations through ambiguity, opacity, and other grey areas that do not neatly fall into Foucault's biopolitical binaries of 'making live or letting die' (Tazzioli 2021: 3). Surveillance in various forms becomes a central element to finding, categorising, filtering, and governing populations of migrants; state surveillance deployed against migrants in the form of monitoring and data collection renders them more visible and knowable to the state, and therefore easier to manage. Through an awareness of being watched, and known, migrants regulate their behaviour, keen to show displays of 'good citizenship' – through civic engagement, labour market participation, minimising confrontation with law enforcement or local citizens – in the hope that this will eventually improve the state's perception of them, potentially leading to easier access to a residence permit.

To understand how these modes of governing migration are deployed, experienced, and contested, we look to cities to examine the tensions and contradictions between the national and local level. Cities are where the state's policing of migration takes place, but – as with sanctuary and solidarity movements – the nation state's techniques of migration governance can also be challenged at the local level. 'The city may become a space for a politics of critique relative to the state, a politics that refuses specific forms of governmentality – most notably the abjection of those displaced' (Darling 2017: 192).

Cities and Migration Governance in Tunis

In spite of its long history, the migration of Sub-Saharan nationals to Tunisia has become a politicised issue in the last decade. While Tunisia has been a destination country for Sub-Saharan students, workers, and visitors for a long time, the country has traditionally focused on its emigration flows, which have been much bigger in number, rather than immigration flows. Its legal framework regarding immigration, most of it based on legislation from the 1950s, is highly restrictive with regards to migrants' access to work authorisations and long-term residence permits. For students intending to stay and work in Tunisia following graduation, and for workers in construction, agriculture, domestic work, hospitality and other industries, obtaining a residence permit or a work permit is nearly impossible, leading to a high level of informality among Sub-Saharan migrant populations. Foreigners from the Global North are subject to the same legal restrictions in theory. However, elements of race and class have led to a double standard in which their lack of legal residence has not been criminalised in the same way as that of Sub-Saharan migrants.

Although not occurring in a systemic way or on a large scale until 2023, workplace raids, arrests due to lack of papers, detentions, and deportations of migrants carried out by national state authorities take place frequently in Tunisia, producing an everyday condition of deportability (De Genova 2002) among Sub-Saharan African migrants. This makes them more vulnerable to exploitation by landlords, employers, and other actors taking advantage of their limited abilities to pursue livelihoods under such restrictive conditions. Undocumented migrants are legally entitled to public healthcare and primary education for their children – yet many fear seeking those services due to concerns that providing identification might make them more visible to authorities, increasing their list of being captured and deported.

While these conditions have been due to national state policy and practice, migration issues carry a transnational dimension due to the EU's heavy financial investment and political interest in preventing migrants' onward migration to Europe (Raach et al. 2022). Since 2015 in particular, Tunisia has thus witnessed a rapid growth in budget for a number of humanitarian and development programmes focusing on migration funded by the European Trust Fund for Africa (EUTF) and the Swiss Development Cooperation. At the same time, Europe has pressured and funded Tunisia to strengthen its border security, enhance its surveillance capacities, and reinforce its fight against irregular migration.

Humanitarian and development funding has mostly gone to international NGOs, UN and intergovernmental organisations, and has mainly supported the delivery of migrant protection and assistance programmes. Seeing that cities have tended to be more willing partners than national government counterparts, international agencies have increasingly designed projects targeting municipal authorities as implementing partners or as beneficiaries (cf. Ben Medien, this volume). One of the largest EU-funded programmes focusing on cities and migration is Mediterranean City-to-City Migration (MC2CM), implemented jointly by the International Centre for Migration Policy Development (ICMPD), United Cities and Local Governments (UCLG), and the United Nations Human Settlement Programme (UN-Habitat). The programme ran in 22 cities across two phases, from 2015 to 2022. In Tunisia, the cities of Tunis, Sfax, and Sousse were the main sites of intervention for programme activities (ICMPD, n.d.). Targeted city actions were developed through a call for proposals aimed at local or regional governments, local or international NGOs, associations, and networks, urging applicants to focus their interventions on 'contributing to foster rights-based urban migration governance and advance social cohesion in the region' (UN-Habitat, n.d.).

While this was the main programme promoting greater municipal engagement with migration issues in Tunisia, the International Organisation for Migration (IOM) and the UN High Commissioner for Refugees (UNHCR), with EU funding, also supported municipalities' participation in regional forums on cities and migration, and in the provision of material assistance to migrants, such as supermarket vouchers, hygiene kits, and other in-kind assistance, particularly during Covid-19 lockdowns in 2020 (Mixed Migration Centre/UNHCR 2022).

These programmes must be understood in the context of the Tunisian municipalities' transformation through a process of decentralisation and the promotion of local governance as part of 'good governance' reforms taking place during the country's democratic transition over the past decade (Amara-Fadhel et al. 2020). This has encouraged some municipalities to include migration governance within their mandate and to design programmes for the humanitarian assistance to and integration of migrants in their respective cities. The points of contact between migrants and local authorities had traditionally been restricted to civil administrative procedures, such as the legalisation of a home rental contract, or the registration of a birth or marriage. However, municipalities have expanded their outreach to migrants to include information help-desks, mediation services[3], language classes, and integration programmes, in addition to the humanitarian drive to distribute essential supplies that municipalities were involved in during the Covid-19 pandemic. However, municipalities have no authority over residence and work permits for migrants, nor do they have any say on health, education, and security policies. The national ministries of interior, employment, health, education, and social affairs thus remain the primary authorities responsible for these aspects of migrants' lives in the country.

Initiatives in Greater Tunis

The following two examples elaborate in more detail on two initiatives carried out by some municipalities in Greater Tunis for Sub-Saharan African migrants in recent years.

(a) Assistance to Migrants During the Covid-19 Pandemic

During the Covid-19 pandemic, Sub-Saharan migrants were among those most acutely affected by restrictive lockdowns imposed by the government between March and June 2020. Most migrants lost their sources of income, putting them at greater risk of hunger and eviction from rented accommodation (Mixed Migration Centre 2020). During this time an exceptional sense of collective solidarity emerged in Tunis. Local associations and NGOs worked together to collect donations of food, money, and hygiene kits for distribution to migrants and others most acutely affected. Local authorities also emerged as prominent actors in these efforts. In La Marsa – a municipality in the north-eastern suburbs of Tunis that has become home to a large Sub-Saharan worker population – supermarket vouchers were distributed to migrants, who lined up for hours outside the municipal office to obtain them.

In addition to providing direct assistance and coordinating other aid efforts, local authorities also engaged in negotiations with landlords in situations where migrants were threatened with eviction from their homes as they were unable to pay rent (UNHCR 2020). In my conversations with community activists I also learned that some municipalities acted as intermediaries with employers who had withheld migrant workers' wages, negotiating agreements to pay their workers what they owed them.

This sustained and direct engagement, local authorities said, brought them into closer contact with the migrant populations living in their jurisdictions. In a conference organised by Médecins du Monde – an international NGO – and La Marsa municipality in July 2020 entitled 'The Rights of Migrants and the Role of Municipalities during the Covid-19 Crisis', representatives from several municipalities noted that providing such direct assistance to migrants allowed them to gain better insight into the numbers, demographics, living and employment situations of Sub-Saharan African migrants. They

---

3   As further explained below, mediation services here refers to the work that municipality representatives undertook to negotiate between migrants and landlords or employers in cases of disputes where migrants' wages weren't paid, or where they could not afford to pay rent and were threatened with eviction.

could now quantify, profile, and categorise the migrants in their jurisdictions, making migrants visible as a category of concern, and as a target group. At this conference, local officials were keen to discuss their responsibilities towards their Sub-Saharan 'brothers', as the mayor of La Marsa referred to them in his opening remarks. His and other representatives' speeches were marked by sentiments of compassion, as they made a humanitarian case for why local officials should get involved in migrant assistance (cf. Kahloun/Frische, this volume).

Later, in an interview with Mira, a professional involved in designing and running migrant assistance programmes with an international organisation, I learned that voucher distribution initiatives were organised and financed by international organisations working on migration in Tunis. They chose municipal authorities to be the face of these distribution efforts, she told me, in order to build migrants' trust towards the Tunisian state, especially as migrants had become increasingly distrustful and hostile to any initiatives they knew were initiated by international organisations (Interview with Mira, June 5, 2021).

The work of municipalities during the Covid-19 pandemic however also demonstrated the limits of their potential for enacting systemic change. With a very limited budget, they were wholly reliant on the funding, capacity, and will of international organisations to support them in delivering such support to migrants. Meanwhile, the mediation work they were able to accomplish worked as a temporary relief measure, but it did not address the root of the problem: violations of migrants' rights as workers and tenants. Finally, while these two actions did provide some help, they also contributed to the intensification of surveillance against migrants, as municipalities systematically gathered information that they did not previously have. This data could facilitate state security practices against migrants, such as home and workplace raids, arrests, and detentions, in the future.

(b) I-MIGR Help-Desks

In 2019, two municipalities in Tunis – La Marsa and Raoued – set up information helpdesks in government offices that were dedicated to providing information to Sub-Saharan local residents in French and referring them to other organisations providing relevant migrant-specific services, based on their needs. These help-desks, advertised as 'Guichets d'Information et d'Orientation' (rlfmedia, 2020) were set up with the input of the NGO Centre d'Information et d'Éducation au Développement (CIES Onlus) Tunisia in partnership with the UTSS (Union Tunisienne de Solidarité Sociale) and Médecins du Monde Belgique.[4] During my fieldwork, I spoke with two people – Wanda and Hala – who had been involved in either the planning or the day-to-day operation of the helpdesks. Wanda – a project manager from Europe who was based in Tunisia – worked with one of the organisations designing and funding this initiative. Hala – an activist who had been involved in migrant rights and anti-racism advocacy – volunteered both as a help desk agent and as a team coordinator.

---

4   For more information about this project, see the information sheet published by ICMPD et al. which funded the second phase of the project.

The project's stated aim was to reinforce the capacities of municipal bureaucrats so that they were better equipped to work with and assist non-Tunisians in accessing their rights. Wanda, who oversaw aspects of the project planning, mentioned that the focus on working with municipalities, and the choice of placing these help-desks in government buildings was to build migrants' trust in local authorities, and to show local governments' openness towards assisting migrants, regardless of their legal status in the country.

Through the establishment of these municipal help-desks, the team gathered information on the types of assistance migrants sought from their local governments. Some of the requests were straightforward: referral to health services, or questions about access to residence permits. In the case of more complicated requests for which an answer wasn't readily available, Wanda told me that the project team set up an Emergency Committee composed of representatives from the UTSS, the local municipality, and the CIES team, in order to decide how to resolve the issue the migrant faced. At the same time, the programme team set up agreements with universities so that international students of Sub-Saharan African origin could staff the help-desks in a volunteering capacity, in a further attempt to gain the trust of the migrant workers who came to seek assistance.

This setup did not do much in terms of increasing Tunisian municipal bureaucrats' exposure or experience in working with migrants given that the help-desk agents and project planners were external to the local government, leading to limits in knowledge transfer or the development of institutional memory about better serving the needs of Sub-Saharan local residents. Further, the help-desks created parallel structures within the municipality that dealt with Sub-Saharans' concerns separately from everyone else's – in a similar mannter to the delivery of Covid-19 assistance measures. Nevertheless, the help-desks served another purpose, related to surveillance.

Sub-Saharan migrants were encouraged to come to the help-desks both to seek information and to share their experiences related to the problems and frustrations they'd experienced in their time in Tunis. According to Hala, the basic information collected by the agents prior to assisting migrants included their full name, their marital status and family situation, the length of time they had spent in Tunis, and their reason(s) for coming to Tunis in the first place (Interview with Hala, August 15, 2021). In conversation that ensued, migrants would inevitably talk about the difficulties they've had, and the reasons why they came to seek support. In response, they received positive reinforcement in the form of advice, counselling, referrals to other organisations providing the services they were seeking (such as health services, for example, legal assistance, or voluntary return), and the attentive ear of a fellow migrant with better access to people in power who could potentially change processes or provide resources that could make a positive impact on their life. In the meantime, this gave the state and the affiliated organisations an opportunity to learn more about – and perhaps eventually intervene in – elements of migrant family and community life that it did not have access to prior.

Wanda underscored the value of this information, mentioning several times during our interview the comprehensive database the help-desk agents had built over time: a database that was accessible to her organisation, the municipalities, and the other partner organisations in the programme, and that they used to better understand the profiles of migrants seeking assistance. Notably, it wasn't the information itself that was the most important aspect; it was the means through which it was gathered. As she told me:

> There is an indirect psychosocial function that is very important, where there are peer educators who are listeners. That really allows one to enter into the personal, familial dimension, where a service run by a Tunisian, or a non Sub-Saharan [origin] person would not have the same impact (Interview with Wanda, June 19, 2021).

To her, this information, and the method of gathering it, was a valuable means to know more about migrant populations, and perhaps to have an entry point for engaging them in a dialogue. To Wanda, it appears that migrants thus lowered their guard, despite being in a situation of vulnerability. Once this relationship of trust was established with their help-desk counterparts, it could potentially make them more receptive to advice and direction. She continued:

> The fact that there is this trust, allows [us] to really be an outlet to resolve problems. Because everyone who comes to see them [the help-desks] is in a situation of vulnerability; so being close to understanding this vulnerability with a psychosocial and anthropological vision, that allows [us] to resolve [the problem] and find solutions together (Interview with Wanda, June 19, 2021).

Here, the motivation for setting up the help-desks becomes clearer, echoing similar reasoning to the Covid-19 supports provided. In both cases, local governments are seeking to become trusted sources of information and support to migrants, using this leverage to exert greater control over migrants through counselling and advice, in what Wanda euphemistically referred to as 'finding solutions together'. This is an important element of borderwork. Whereas peoples' ability to migrate and their desire to do so are key drivers of migration, aspiration is also an important element underpinning peoples' migration decisions. This goes beyond having positive feelings towards moving: aspirations are also influenced by social norms in which migration is seen as a positive step, perhaps to self-fulfilment or socio-economic progress. Migrants' aspirations are shaped and reshaped through their interactions within their socio-economic and geographical context (Carling/Collins 2018; Carling/Schewel 2018). Thus, by intervening to change the conditions in which migrants live in Tunis, while reframing the option of onward movement as dangerous and irresponsible, municipalities manage migrants' aspirations in an effort to contain and curb irregular movement towards Europe. The psychosocial and anthropological vision Wanda referred to is crucial, as local authorities seek to gain more insight into migrants' decision-making and behaviour that goes beyond numbers and statistics.

Hala confirmed that the help-desks have helped dispel misinformation that spreads through migrant communities, overcome administrative hurdles, and access healthcare (Interview with Hala, August 15, 2021). They addressed a gap that hadn't been filled by other actors, and helped uphold migrants' access to their legally guaranteed rights. At the same time, she was also critical of their limitations, which she saw as a lack of sustainability. Hala told me there were significant barriers to the help-desks' ability to make a difference: budget limitations meant that they could only operate for short periods of time, with no substitute service available when funding was depleted. This was due to the fact that a separate service had been created to address migrants' needs that was wholly dependent on outside funding and whim, rather than equipping existing bureaucratic structures to better serve migrants and resolve their specific issues in a more sustainable manner.

This calls into question the sustainability of such endeavours, and relatedly, municipalities' long-term commitment to integrate migrants and to govern them as equal to national citizens. Neither migrants' legal status (or lack thereof), nor the basis upon which it is conferred, are challenged in the help-desk model, nor by extension, by the municipalities themselves. Help-desks are not facilitating migrants' access to residence documents, arguably the only thing that will make a material, long-term difference in their quality of life as foreigners in Tunisia. Instead, migrants are left with the exhausting position of fighting for – and having to justify their right to access – any basic service needed, from healthcare to education to housing, work, and financial services.

Further, the securitised surveillance of migrants through fingerprinting, identity checks, and policing carried out by the national arm of the state is complemented by these other forms of 'humanitarian' surveillance carried out at the local level. The state is using its proximity and closer access to migrants 'on the ground' to influence migrants' conduct, modelling desirable behaviour by influencing them to come to the state with requests for assistance individually, rather than demanding systemic change collectively through political mobilisation. Problems of lack of access to services, or exploitation, are taken up as administrative rather than political concerns: one-off errors to be addressed rather than symptoms of underlying fundamental inequalities. In this way, demands for legal status as a means of guaranteeing rights are depoliticised.

Conclusion

In this chapter, I have discussed some of the ways in which municipalities in Greater Tunis have engaged more directly with urban migrant populations and their governance over recent years. While international organisations started supporting local governments in engaging directly with migrants prior to the start of Covid-19, the pandemic provided more reasons and opportunities for these municipalities to expand their outreach in migrant communities, providing services, while gathering more information about this population which they knew little about beforehand. Growing numbers of municipalities are setting up help-desks, providing information to migrants about their rights along with some basic support services such as mediation with employers and landlords.

This however has not yet developed into a systematic and collective undertaking across cities in Tunisia. Rather, in my interviews, certain municipalities' openness to supporting migrants was attributed to the personal characteristics or politics of local decision-makers who were characterised as 'progressive' and 'open-minded'. It could also be the case that certain municipalities worked harder at obtaining funding for international programmes. One of my key informants, Wanda, who has worked on one of these programmes, acknowledged that internationally funded organisations have not coordinated well in choosing which municipalities to work with, leading to duplications and overlaps of work with one or two municipalities in the city (La Marsa and Ariana in particular), while others have remained excluded.

When available, direct assistance and information services to Sub-Saharan African migrant populations are important and positive developments as they offer opportunities for migrants to learn more about their legal protection and about how to navigate the opaque bureaucratic system in Tunisia. However, despite the promising character of such interventions at first glance, there are reasons to be cautious about the extent to which such initiatives could sustainably improve the living conditions of migrants, or even challenge or overturn the status quo regarding the governance of migration in contemporary Tunisia.

The ad hoc funding structure for these programmes, and municipalities' dependence on foreign donors with their own time-limited agenda prevents the development of an autonomous and long-term vision and strategy on the part of Tunisian municipalities. As seen with the I-MIGR help desk project in La Marsa and Raoued, all project activities stopped when a gap occurred between phases of the programme, with no indication given to migrants on whether municipalities were working on building a more sustainable and self-sustaining structure or not. Similarly, during Covid-19, municipalities were chosen by international organisations to be the face of social assistance provided to migrants. However, the municipalities' ability to extend assistance and targeted programming to vulnerable migrants is limited, and can thus only occur in response to situations when external funding becomes available.

Until recently, municipalities' autonomy and legal mandate regarding migration have been quite limited, as a legacy of Tunisia's centralised system. While the process of decentralisation taking place in the country might give municipalities more power over certain aspects of decision-making, key areas where migrants' rights are restricted or services are not easily accessible – work, residence, health, education – remain largely within the purview of the national government. Barring sustained demands for legal reforms, or challenges to the securitised approach to migration being undertaken by the national state, the ability of municipalities to instigate systemic change to improve the living conditions of migrants in their jurisdictions remains quite limited.

At the same time, the type of work that municipalities engage in with migrants contributes to making them more visible to all levels of the state through various surveillance practices. Long frustrated with the lack of information on the number of undocumented migrants in the country, municipalities have used these initiatives to gather more data on the numbers, locations, nationalities, and demographic characteristics of the migrants they have assisted. State surveillance was thus enacted under the cloak of 'humanitarian' concern. As local authorities lent a listening ear to migrants' preoccupations, with the declared aim of providing assistance, they also promoted a model of the ideal migrant subject as one who comes to the government to request support rather than one who works in a collective to challenge the legal basis upon which these rights are selectively distributed.

As these initiatives fail to challenge the existing legal framework through explicit demands or alternative practices, they reinforce the securitarian approach to migration already in place at a national scale. They risk becoming what Ticktin (2011) refers to as 'regimes of care', centring empathy and compassion at the expense of collective mobilisations for rights, thus risking depoliticising certain issues through one-off technocratic solutions and occasional charity. Ultimately, migrants remain in a precarious legal situation, vulnerable to exploitation, and dependent on ad hoc benevolence to access their basic rights.

'Too many Africans'
Racialising Urban Peripheries in the Face of Tunisia's Economic Precarity

Shreya Parikh

YVONNE, who 'came on a plane'

'I came on a plane to vacation here with a *frère* [a fellow Ivorian man]', Yvonne tells me, 'but then, he died and I didn't have any money and so I stayed'. Yvonne has lived in the Bhar Lazreg neighbourhood of Greater Tunis since she came here in 2018, finding comfort in the presence of other Ivorian migrants like her. Sitting before her, next to where her table selling so-called African products is spread out, I wonder if 'vacation' is a form of euphemism for transit or guestworker migration? Yvonne's insistence that she 'came on a plane', unlike other Ivorian migrants in the neighbourhood who arrived via land from Côte d'Ivoire, may reflect symbolic class differences within the migrant community – those who can afford a flight ticket versus those who cannot! It may also represent an attempt at regaining dignity while their collective status as undocumented migrants implies continuous marginalisation and humiliation in Tunisian society. When I speak to her in October 2022, Yvonne is 34, a practicing Christian, and has little formal education. She worked as a domestic worker until recently when she gave birth, making it physically impossible for her to continue working while caring for an infant. She inherited a stock of so-called African products from another Ivorian woman who left Tunisia recently– food items and toiletries brought in from Côte d'Ivoire. She sits on the pavement of the main road in Bhar Lazreg almost every day, from 11 am to around 4 pm, selling her merchandise to other Sub-Saharan migrant women and men. The neighbourhood of Bhar Lazreg, around 15 kilometres away from Tunis city centre, is described often, in popular narratives, as a working-class neighbourhood increasingly inhabited by Sub-Saharan migrants mostly from Côte d'Ivoire.

Like Yvonne, many other Sub-Saharan women also sell products, brought in from their home countries, on tables set up informally around the main crossroad of Bhar Lazreg. Yvonne tells me that she earns around 20 Dinars (or around six Euro) a day, after accounting for the cost of the products. Most of her clients are Ivorian women; over the afternoon I spent with her, four women and a young man from different Sub-Saharan communities pass by her table, asking for spices, dried fish, and plastic sandals. Over the months that I spent walking around Bhar Lazreg (February-November 2022), never once did I see a Tunisian stopping at one of these tables. I do not spot Yvonne's baby and ask her where she leaves them. She tells me that there is an Ivorian-run place where women leave children and pick them up after work. I suspect that this might be a part of the network of day-care centres that are informally run by and for the Sub-Saharan migrant community in Bhar Lazreg. I ask her where she plans to send her baby to school in the future, and she tells me that the schools teaching in French are private and expensive, while the public schools in Tunisia only teach in Arabic. Children of migrants end up without schooling because of this linguistic gap; most Sub-Saharan migrants do not speak Arabic and see no incentive in educating their children in Arabic because of the assumed temporariness of their stay in Tunisia. Yvonne hopes to have left Tunisia by the time her child is old enough to go to school. I ask her if she hopes to go to Europe, implicitly implying her taking a clandestine boat, and I find myself facing silence. I ask her what she wants to do later? She tells me that she does not really know what she will do; she might stay in Tunis because her family in Côte d'Ivoire does not have money, neither to pay for her to return nor to pay for her to go on a boat to Europe. She tells me that she is *en penalite* (in penalty), meaning that she has undocumented status and would need to pay the penalty charges of staying in Tunisian 'illegally' before being allowed to leave the country; Tunisian border police levy a charge of 20 Dinar (around six Euro) per week of overstay, or around 310 Euro per year. This penalty is a part of Tunisian state's migration control policies enacted under pressure from the European Union in return for economic support. I asked Yvonne if she has faced racism, either at or outside work. She tells me that she has had no problems either while doing domestic work or while selling her products. I sense that maybe the term 'racism' that I used in the question is too negatively connoted to induce the desired response – the recounting of experiences of racism. So, I ask her what she does in her free time. She tells me that she works and then she goes back home because she is scared that the Tunisian men on the streets will 'snatch her bag or bring out a knife'. She tells me that there are always cases of aggression against migrants like her.

YAYA, who 'came by land'

Yaya is 22 years old and came to Tunis in March 2022 via land from Algeria where he had spent around six months. He fled Algeria because of 'too many problems with the police', he tells me. From Côte d'Ivoire, his home country, he had made his way by land to Algeria with neither passport nor other identity papers with him. Bhar Lazreg has been his home for most of his time in Tunisia. Yaya wears short dreadlocks with white sea shells braided in and a goatee that has been coloured blonde. I meet him in October 2022 while waiting in a queue in front of a Tunisian fast-food stand in Bhar Lazreg. Throughout our interaction, Tunisian men gaze us at with suspicion. I have known this gaze before; every time I walk around with a Black Tunisian or Sub-Saharan man (both assumed to be non-Tunisian by society), I (as a brown Indian woman) am assumed to be a Tunisian woman involved in a romantic relationship with them. The gaze over my body reflects an accusation of being a race-traitor – of having refused Tunisian men by having accepted a romantic relationship with a foreign Black person.

Before we leave the fast-food stand, around four young Tunisian men corner Yaya; I sense a beginning of a fight, which, fortunately, dissipates. I invite Yaya for coffee, and he takes me to an almost empty café. Like most cafés across Tunisia, this café is *shaabi* implying that its clients are working-class men. After we sit down and order sodas, Yaya tells me that he left Côte d'Ivoire after the death of his father, because he felt 'bizarre'. Back there, he never finished secondary school and had never worked before arriving in Algeria. He tells me that his mother is aging and his two siblings do not work. I ask if he is the one financially supporting his family and he says no. For the first four months that he was in Tunis, Yaya worked for a *patron* (boss) whom he had met through a fellow Ivorian man and for whom he painted and repaired walls with putty. His Tunisian boss abruptly announced that he no longer had work for Yaya and that he would call him in case he needed a hand. The call never came!
Since then, Yaya has struggled to find work and does day jobs whenever he finds them. He has an injury that he doesn't fully disclose to me, but adds that he cannot do physically straining work that is asked for at the construction sites that are scattered all around Bhar Lazreg and its neighbouring region. Working-class Tunisian men, many from the neighbourhood, work on these sites along with Sub-Saharan migrant men; yet, the former group is paid more than the latter. Yaya tells me that he is paid 30 Dinars (around nine Euro) for a day of work, while wages are higher for Tunisian men. I ask him if he knows the amount, and he responds saying that discussions among Tunisians happen in Arabic, which he doesn't understand. He doesn't know the exact amount.
I ask him what his future goals are and he mumbles something that I cannot decipher. I reframe and repeat my question, thinking that maybe the question itself was not clear. Yaya mumbles again. I feel a bit anxious about directly asking him whether he is trying to go to Europe on a clandestine boat like every other Sub-Saharan migrant I know, because I am aware that the claim itself is enough for the Tunisian police to put anyone (including Tunisians) in prison. He nods a yes when I whisper a question about taking the boat. I also ask Yaya if he has faced any form of racism in Bhar Lazreg, and he tells me that while 'there is always a lot of harassment on the streets', he has personally never faced any. In the many conversations I have had with Sub-Saharan migrants, I have noticed that most start by saying that they have not faced any problems but have heard of fellow migrants facing problems. Later, Yaya tells me that he has faced 'a lot of provocations' from Tunisian men on the street, the goal of which are to anger him and to get him to act violently. For example, a Tunisian man would come up to him on the street and ask '*mon ami, donne-moi un Dinar!*' (my friend [a term used to refer to Sub-Saharan migrants in Tunisia], give me one Dinar) and a refusal to give money would result in a fight. Yaya tells me, repeatedly, that there are many *bagarres* (brawls) all the time between Tunisians and Sub-Saharan migrants, and that he tries to avoid them by not going to cafés or walking around in the streets; he goes out to eat or do groceries, and stays in his rented studio for the rest of the time.
I ask Yaya if he gets support from the significantly large Ivorian community that lives in Bhar Lazreg. He tells me that there is a difference between those who came '*par vol*' (by plane) and those like him who came to Tunisia by land. Unlike him, Yaya adds, they (like Yvonne) have stamped passports. He does not specify if this potential class difference between migrants implies that there is little intra-community solidarity.

On a late afternoon in March 2022, Aymen and I are walking around Bhar Lazreg, his neighbourhood of birth and residence, when we spot two young Sub-Saharan men walking in the opposite direction. He points to them and tells me 'they are everywhere'. He adds that, usually, two migrants rent a room somewhere in the area and 'then, suddenly, eight of them show up' from their country of origin. Aymen, in his early 30s, makes pastries for private hotels and runs a small tour company. He tells me with pride that his family is one of the oldest families living in Bhar Lazreg, having farmed on its land since the 1940s when the neighbourhood was still an agricultural village. As we walk, he describes the dilapidation of urban infrastructures in his neighbourhood, like all over Tunisia, because there are 'too many *Africains* [Africans] everywhere in Tunisia now: in Tunis, as well as in Sousse, Sfax, and Monastir'. Africans, in Tunisian vernacular, refers to the Sub-Saharan populations; it reflects the racial othering of Blackness and Africa, both seen as synonymous, in a country that is a part of the African continent.

When I started my fieldwork in Tunisia, the neighbourhood of Bhar Lazreg often came up during informal discussions when I presented the topic of my dissertation research – the study of Blackness in Tunisia. During my conversations with residents of Tunis, I was often told that in *'Bhar Lazreg ... il y a beaucoup d'Africains qui sont là!'* (Bhar Lazreg ... there are many Africans there!). For quite some Tunisians living in and outside Bhar Lazreg, Sub-Saharan migrants like Yvonne and Yaya are a part of the 'too many Africans' who have come to reside in the urban peripheries of Tunisia; this includes Ariana, Aouina, and Bousalsala neighbourhoods in Greater Tunis, and El Ain, Gremda, and Sakiet Eddaier neighbourhoods in Sfax.

This chapter takes as its object of study the description of 'too many Africans' employed by Tunisians to refer to certain neighbourhoods in the periphery of Tunisian cities, hence racialising (or giving racial meaning) to urban space. I do so by focusing on the racialising discourses that construct Bhar Lazreg neighbourhood as a uniformly black 'African neighbourhood'. I patch together site observations, in/formal interviews, and media reports that I collected in Tunisia between September 2020 and December 2022 to analyse the socio-economic context and the content of these discourses. I point to two interlinked structural processes that re/produce these racialising discourses: on the one hand to the shifting national and international migration regimes and on the other hand to the increasing economic inequalities that worsened during the Covid-19 pandemic. I show that the designation of a neighbourhood as 'African' is negatively connoted, and is discursively presented and framed as a 'problem'. In addition, while the discourse of 'too many Africans' reflects racial prejudices against Sub-Saharan migrants, it also reflects the latent sentiment of labour-market competition among working-class Tunisians in relation to Sub-Saharan migrants. In many urban peripheries like Bhar Lazreg, working-class Tunisians and Sub-Saharan migrants work the same jobs, leading to a feeling among the Tunisians that the migrants are taking away Tunisians' jobs. The narrowing of labour market opportunities exacerbates the feeling of dislike towards 'Africans' – a dislike that reinforces the already existing racist stigma towards people classified as black.

In the context of this chapter, I choose to use the term 'racialisation' to name the process by which a body and/or space 'come[s] to be seen as 'having' a racial identity' (Ahmed 2002: 46). Bhar Lazreg is not homogenously populated by black migrants as the discourses of 'too many Africans' or 'African neighbourhood' portray. At the same time, it is precisely the study of these discourses that allows us to capture the mechanisms of racialisation and stigmatization of working-class neighbourhoods like Bhar Lazreg. The local case highlights a broader process occurring in southern and eastern Mediterranean coastal cities, where transiting migrants have settled in such neighbourhoods on the urban peripheries; this settlement process contributes to fuel a discourse of 'urban blackening' in the context of Sub-Saharan migration.

Bhar Lazreg as an Urban Periphery

Bhar Lazreg is a part of La Marsa municipality, which itself is a part of the Greater Tunis region (cf. Kahloun/ Frische, this volume). The district of Bhar Lazreg was set up as an official entity in 2018, hence no official district-level data for the neighbourhood exists in the last census conducted in 2014. Given the presence of informal housing and undocumented Sub-Saharan migrants, the local public institutions have faced challenges in enumerating the total population. According to a journalistic estimate, there are about 50,000 inhabitants in Bhar Lazreg which account for half of the La Marsa municipality's population (Galtier 2020). The name 'Bhar Lazreg' in Arabic translates to 'blue sea'. During my fieldwork in the neighbourhood, its Tunisian residents noted that the name refers to a metaphorical sea of blue flowers of *gnaouia* (okra in Tunisian Arabic) historically grown in the agricultural plains that surrounded the area. Unequal urbanisation meant that the neighbourhood of La Marsa (that later became La Marsa city centre) developed as a residential site for the French during French colonisation of Tunisia (1881–1956). Meanwhile, Bhar Lazreg remained largely agricultural.

Like in the case of many agricultural lands located in or around the growing urban centres, Bhar Lazreg witnessed drastic demographic changes after Tunisia's independence in 1956. In this period, many families began to migrate from south and northwest Tunisia to Tunis in search of work, and settled in agricultural lands around Greater Tunis. These informal settlements were a response to lack of accessible housing in the city, and often developed close to urban centres where human labour was needed (Chabbi 1988). Tourist-attracting neighbourhoods along the coast of La Marsa and Carthage became sites of employment for these internal migrants settling in Bhar Lazreg. Over time, differences in socio-political histories of its inhabitants have translated into differences in urban development of Bhar Lazreg in relation to La Marsa city centre. During my fieldwork, inhabitants of Bhar Lazreg often complained of roads filled with potholes, flooding after rainfall, lack of a local police station and post office, and absence of public parks; they contrasted these with the relative abundance of resources in La Marsa city, less than two kilometres away from Bhar Lazreg. They also talked often about the absence of reliable public transportation; most residents depend on a clandestine network of transportation (called *grand-taxi*) to get to La Marsa city centre from where they take shared taxis or light rail to Tunis city centre.

In the public imagination, La Marsa city centre, which faces the sea, is constructed as white and European, while Bhar Lazreg, which is more inland, is constructed as 'African' and Black. Parts of this imagination come from the fact that a significant area of the city centre in La Marsa is occupied by the French ambassador's residence, and is surrounded by villas inhabited by European-origin migrants. In addition, one regularly sees white Global North migrants and tourists walking around and sitting in La Marsa's restaurants and cafés; one rarely sees Sub-Saharan African-origin individuals in these spaces, except as servers or cleaners. In Bhar Lazreg, Sub-Saharan migrants are hyper-visible in public spaces – in cafés, in markets, and on the streets. Tunisians regularly describe La Marsa by words like 'chic' and 'classy' while Bhar Lazreg is depicted as 'dangerous'. While they often talk about the 'many' Europeans living in La Marsa with pride, associating their presence in the neighbourhood with Eurocentric ideas of modernity, they refer to the 'too many Africans' in Bhar Lazreg as a problem, associating the presence of Sub-Saharan migrants with 'criminality'.

Who are the 'Africans' in Tunisia?

In the Tunisian vernacular language, *les Africains* (the Africans) is a French-derived term used in both French as well as Arabic-only conversations to refer to Sub-Saharan African migrants. In contrast to Tunisia's location in the African continent, this terminology reflects the racial othering of Blackness and Africanness (both of which are seen as synonymous). When asked about what Tunisianness refers to, many of my non-Black Tunisian interlocutors would mention ethnic, religious, and regional identities like Arab, Muslim, Mediterranean, and Maghrebi, with negligible mention of African or Black identities.

According to the Tunisian National Institute of Statistics (INS) data on 'resident foreigners', Sub-Saharan migrants numbered 21,466 in 2020–2021. This figure does not fully take into account those migrants who are undocumented, necessitating a reliance on estimates that seek to account for this undocumented population (cf. Ben Media, this volume). According to estimates by United Nations Department of Economic and Social Affairs (UNDESA), there are currently around 57,000 Sub-Saharan migrants living in Tunisia; a majority are undocumented guestworkers, and around 7,000 are students (Ayadi 2021; Boukhayatia 2022). There exists a small number of Sub-Saharan guest workers with work permits, but they remain a minority compared to those who are undocumented (Nasraoui 2017). Most Sub-Saharan migrants come from francophone countries in western or central regions of Africa, with a majority coming from Cote d'Ivoire. Since the start of the war in Sudan in 2023, there has also been a growing Sudanese migration to Tunisia.

Before Tunisia's independence in 1956, Sub-Saharan migration to the region took various forms; many were brought there as enslaved migrants, and others arrived as merchants or political refugees, or moved to North Africa looking for work. Since Tunisia's independence, and over the last two decades, there has been a visual and numerical shift in migration flows from Sub-Saharan Africa. In year 2003, the African Development Bank (AfDB) moved its headquarters to Tunis because of civil war in Côte d'Ivoire, its primary location. This prompted migration of its employees and their families, most of whom were socio-economically privileged Sub-Saharan citizens. Their socio-economically privileged position, as visible from the chauffeured cars they moved in, contrasted with the popular Tunisian imagination of 'Africans' as uniformly poor (Mazzella 2012).

After the bank's departure in 2014, the Sub-Saharan student population became more visible across Tunisia's urban centres that host universities. The increase in their numbers from the early 2000s was attributed to the rise in private higher education institutions that provided internationally recognised diplomas (Mazzella 2009); this private sector flourished partly because of the high tuition fees paid by these international students. The growth in student population corresponded to the growth in civil-society organisations run by and for these students; the Association of African Students and Trainees in Tunisia (AESAT) set up in 1993 is one key example. These organisations and associated individuals became vocal about the racialised violence faced by the Sub-Saharan student communities, calling for political changes to protect their rights. For example, the mobilisation around the near fatal attack on three Congolese students in Tunis in December 2016 prompted the then-Prime Minister Youssef Chahed to publicly support the passing of a law criminalising racial discrimination; the law was passed in 2018 (Parikh 2021).

Since the 2011 revolution, the image of an 'African' has shifted from being associated with AfDB staff and students to being linked to poor and undocumented black migrants on the move. The contemporary increase in the presence of Sub-Saharan African migrant communities across Tunisia is linked to two factors: firstly, the easing of visa regulations for citizens of many Sub-Saharan countries in the early 2000s (Msakni 2020), and secondly, the externalization of European Union's border in the Greater Mediterranean region (cf. Sh'ath, this volume). Since early 2000s, citizens from Côte d'Ivoire, Guinea, Mali, Senegal, and Niger (among others) benefit from a 90-day visa-free policy in Tunisia. Yet, this ease in entry requirements was not accompanied by changes in regulations governing access to residence or work permits. Tunisian lawyer Ahmed Messedi, who works on cases involving Sub-Saharan migrants in Tunisia, noted during a personal communication that most im/migration laws date from 1968 and are unable to respond to changing contemporary migration patterns. At the same time, contemporary practices of migration governance in Tunisia, like those across the Mediterranean region, have come to be dictated by policies and politics of European Union's border externalisation. This includes the 2013 decree that penalises undocumented stay in Tunisia, which many, like Yvonne, experience as an additional burden in an already precarious legal and economic situation.

The externalisation of European borders onto the southern and eastern coasts around the Mediterranean has led to a dramatic halting of migrant flows originating and transiting through these coastal countries (see Garnaoui, this volume). Externalisation refers to the process of outsourcing border control and migration management to non-EU countries by EU countries, starting early 2000s. As scholars like Casas et al. (2011) note, an increase in internal mobility within the EU ran in parallel with the moving of border control to the edge of this area and, later, outside it. According to them, the border externalisation process 'involves the emergence of a series of new border practices, border actors and institutional arrangements in these neighbouring countries: from detention centres; to funds for police training; to establishing programs of circular temporary labour migration' (ibid. 77).

The drastic immobilisation of migration into Europe has led to a form of transitory settling of migrant communities in 'border countries', often in cities and towns where they begin to reside over longer periods, building and forming diaspora communities.

These include Syrian, Afghan, and Pakistani migrants in Istanbul; Ivorian, Malian, and Senegalese migrants in Tunis and Rabat; or Sudanese and Eritrean migrants in Cairo. In many cases, they come to reside in neighbourhoods of the urban periphery with close proximity to urban centres hosting employment opportunities. This is the case of Bhar Lazreg.

Hyper-Visibility of Sub-Saharan Migrants in Bhar Lazreg

The majority of Sub-Saharan African migrants I met here during my fieldwork come from Côte d'Ivoire. The length of their stay in Tunisia varies; some have been in Tunisia for less than two months, while others have been here for four years or more. Deteriorating political and economic conditions in countries like Côte d'Ivoire, Burkina Faso, Republic of Guinea, and the Democratic Republic of Congo have pushed many to take land or air routes to arrive in North Africa, with hopes of seeking refuge in the region and/or traveling on to Europe through clandestine routes.

Bhar Lazreg is not the only neighbourhood in Greater Tunis where Sub-Saharan migrants live in larger numbers; a significant number also reside in Aouina, Ariana, Bousalsala, Lafayette, and Soukra. However, the migration status of the majority of Sub-Saharan migrants living in Bhar Lazreg is different from that of those in more middle-class neighbourhoods like Soukra, Ariana, and Lafayette; in the former, most of them are irregular (or undocumented) migrants while in the latter, a large proportion of migrants are students, which relates to the proximity to universities or professionalising institutes in these neighbourhoods. Migration status differences overlap differences in socio-economic and legal status; most Sub-Saharan students come from socio-economically more privileged backgrounds and have more transparent paths to procuring residence permits compared with that of guestworkers or transit migrants.

As in the case of Bhar Lazreg, the presence of Sub-Saharan migrants in these neighbourhoods is visible in the public space. Yet, the stigmatising appellation of *'quartier des Africains'* (an African neighbourhood) is carried most intensely by Bhar Lazreg. This is linked to Sub-Saharan migrants being hyper visible in Bhar Lazreg compared with other neighbourhoods, which are socio-economically more privileged than the former. This difference is partly linked to differences in urban infrastructure that determines the population density of public spaces. Almost all neighbourhood activities of importance in Bhar Lazreg are concentrated in a rather narrow space – along Rue Charles de Gaulle starting at the main crossroads to the intersection with Rue Amilcar. The cafés, grocery stores, butcher, public primary school, and the large vegetable market are all concentrated along a 400-meter-long strip of this road. The road is barely wide enough to let two vans pass simultaneously, and pedestrians compete with formal and informal stores (like Yvonne's table shop) as well as vehicles for space to move. In contrast, the population density in public spaces is less in more middle-class neighbourhoods like Aouina and Soukra, since residences and cafés are spread out, and roads and pedestrian streets are wide.

During my walks around Greater Tunis neighbourhoods hosting significant Sub-Saharan migrant populations, I noticed three socio-urban structures in Bhar Lazreg that I found either absent or comparatively rare in other neighbourhoods: firstly, informal table-shops, like the one set up by Yvonne, which sell so-called African products on pedestrian streets; secondly, Tunisian and Sub-Saharan men occupying café chairs laid out on café terraces that extend into pedestrian streets; and finally, restaurants or hair salons run by Sub-Saharan migrants, which display posters of trending hair-styles or foods from their countries of origin. The visible presence of these structures contributes to the hyper visibility of Sub-Saharan migrants in Bhar Lazreg. While *shaabi* or working class cafés serve as legitimate sites of social leisure for both Tunisian and Sub-Saharan men, there are no such socially legitimate leisure sites for women in Bhar Lazreg. To fill this gap, Sub-Saharan women in the neighbourhood use table-shops (like Yvonne's) set up along the pavements as well as 'African' hair salons as sites for socialisation and leisure.

In Bhar Lazreg, informal stands selling 'African products' are concentrated along the 400-meter strip of Rue Charles de Gaulle (where I spotted four during peak week hours); a few can also be found along Rue Amilcar. These stands are composed of plastic tables, an umbrella to shelter from the sun, and an assortment of herbs, teas, peanut butter, dried chillies, and broth cubes. The hair and beauty salons that are run by and which cater to Sub-Saharan women are concentrated along Rue Amilcar; there are also Sub-Saharan men-only salons but in lesser frequency). In addition to table-shops and hair salons, I spotted two Ivorian-run restaurants that serve as visible gathering space for Sub-Saharan migrants. There are no official churches in the area, but I recurrently heard stories of attempts by a Sub-Saharan man to set up a church in his apartment in Bhar Lazreg. While not being visible, these stories and rumours about Sub-Saharan migrants' religious practices (which stand out in a majority Muslim country) contribute to the feeling of there being 'too many Africans'.

The presence of these formal and informal institutions, which are run by and for Sub-Saharan migrants, points to a degree of integration of these communities in the socio-urban fabric of Bhar Lazreg. As they integrate, they create socio-spatial structures that extend onto or around those already present; for example, informal table-shops like Yvonne's imitate those run by Tunisians along Rue Charles de Gaulle.

Yet, the integration of these communities is not complete, as reflected in the rarity of interactions between Tunisian and Sub-Saharan inhabitants of Bhar Lazreg. The only occasions during which I noticed intergroup interactions was when Sub-Saharan migrants were buying groceries from Tunisian grocers or ordering food from Tunisian cafés or restaurants. While many Sub-Saharan men hang out in cafés that line Rue Charles de Gaulle and which are frequented by Tunisian men, both groups sit around tables among themselves; never during my fieldwork did I notice two groups sharing a table. Both Tunisian and Sub-Saharan men move around each other in these cafés in a way that avoids verbal interactions or possible brushing of arms while navigating through packed tables. Both groups move through the same space without acknowledging the presence of the other. The tensions between Tunisian men and Yaya that I witnessed while speaking with him point to the fact that my interaction with Yaya in front of a fast-food store broke two norms that govern socio-spatial behaviour in Bhar Lazreg – first, I (assumed to be Tunisian) interacted with a Sub-Saharan migrant, and, second, I (a woman) interacted with a male stranger. My spending time at Yvonne's table also resulted in curious gazes from passing Tunisians but did not escalate into tensions.

Economic Precarity: Motivating Discourses of 'Too many Africans'

In urban peripheries like Bhar Lazreg with relatively cheap rent compared to that in urban centres like La Marsa city or Tunis city, Sub-Saharan migrants rent homes and build visible community infrastructures like restaurants and stores selling 'African' products or services from their countries of origin. This increasing visibility of Sub-Saharan communities has led to a sentiment among local populations of being *envahie* (invaded) by 'too many Africans'. For example, one comment (in French) under an article describing the precarious situation of Sub-Saharan migrants in Tunisia notes that 'one should not be manipulated by these migrants who can work in their own country instead of invading North Africa, which is experiencing its own health and economic crises' (see comments section in Business News 2021).

The sense of competition felt by the Tunisian residents of Bhar Lazreg towards their Sub-Saharan neighbours manifests in the discourses among Tunisian residents that portray migrants as willing to take any job and for less pay than Tunisians, making it more profitable to employ Sub-Saharan migrants over Tunisians. As in the case of Yaya, Sub-Saharan migrants are employed for lower salaries and with more insecure contracts than those given to their Tunisian colleagues. In another case, one Tunisian man in his 60s, who had worked for most of his life as a 'day labourer' in local factories around Bhar Lazreg, said to me that Sub-Saharan migrants accept 15 Dinar (around five Euro) for jobs that Tunisians would not do even for 25 Dinar (around eight Euro). In addition, commercial activities by Sub-Saharan migrant communities are seen with suspicion, which is justified using racial tropes present in Tunisian discourses about Black and Sub-Saharan individuals. For example, Imen, a Tunisian woman in her thirties who sells dried peppers, indicated that the overpriced 'African' peppers that the Sub-Saharan woman on the other side of the street was selling were Tunisian. Imen noted that she felt cheated by the commercial activities of her Sub-Saharan neighbours, reflecting the larger discourse describing Sub-Saharan migrants as 'criminal' and prone to cheating (see Draouil/Jmel 2022 for more details). In another case, a Tunisian colleague and I visited the table-shop held by Mireille (in her thirties) from Côte d'Ivoire; she explained to us that the herbs in different plastic sachets cure stomach problems, as well as 'ejaculation issues', and can also be used 'for cutting pregnancy' or abortion. My Tunisian colleague, a young middle-class woman, looked at Mireille and her activities with suspicion and noted that she corresponds to the trope of a Black witch in the Tunisian imagination.

Beyond the gendered trope of 'Black witch' associated with Sub-Saharan women, other racialised discourses about Sub-Saharan migrants are present among Tunisians living in Bhar Lazreg (as among Tunisians elsewhere). One such discourse is that which constructs all Sub-Saharan migrants are 'uncivilised'. During the time I spent in Bhar Lazreg, Tunisian residents would often complain that Sub-Saharan migrants did not know how to use a kitchen or a toilet, or that they have bodily odours. For example, Mokhtar, a Tunisian man in his 60s, used these tropes to justify his decision to never rent an apartment to Sub-Saharan migrants (Draouil/Jmel 2022). I also noted contradictory discourses about the financial status of Sub-Saharan migrants – while many Tunisians told me that the migrants would do any job for meagre pay, they would later add that the migrants get money from international organisations or other richer

Sub-Saharan migrants. In addition, like Aymen (presented in the introduction), many Tunisians mentioned that 'too many Africans' live in rooms made for two or three people. Tunisians use these discourses to justify the comparatively elevated rents charged on migrants. Overall, the structural precarities that the residents of Bhar Lazreg, like in other 'African' neighbourhoods, face are interpreted by their Tunisian residents as being a result of their neighbourhoods being 'invaded by Africans' rather than reflecting a failure of the Tunisian state to address inequalities. This discourse often justifies acts of aggression like the kind noted by both Yvonne and Yaya.

The 'too many Africans' discourse would take a violent political turn in early 2023. On 21 February 2023, President Kais Saied made an anti-Sub-Saharan migrant statement that politically legitimised vernacular discourses like the discourse of 'too many Africans': He stated that Tunisia was being 'invaded by hordes of illegal migrants' who seek to 'change the demographic structure of Tunisia and make it African', implying an imminent social, racial, and moral degradation of the Tunisian society (see Parikh 2023). Saied's statement was followed by state- and civilian-supported violence against Sub-Saharan migrants, including police harassment and arrest, deportation and expulsion into the desertic borders that Tunisia shares with Algeria and Libya, sexual harassment and rape, as well as refusal of emergency medical services. While there is no quantitative data about these violent occurrences, anecdotal data suggests that violence was more elevated in neighbourhoods like Bhar Lazreg that are discursively constructed as *quartiers des Africains* or 'African neighbourhood', compared to other urban neighbourhoods not seen as 'African' despite hosting significant Sub-Saharan populations. Following Saied's statement, many Tunisians took it upon themselves to follow his call to rid Tunisia of Sub-Saharan migrants (see Matri/Zuntz, this volume). In the months following the statement, my Facebook feed was filled with videos of Tunisian men in mobs looking for Sub-Saharan migrants in 'African' neighbourhoods of Tunis and Sfax, beating and robbing those they found hiding, leading (in a few cases) to the death of these migrants. It is true that the neighbourhoods that come to carry the vernacular appellation of 'African' tend to be working-class; the stigmatisation of 'African' neighbourhoods, as well as the experiences of violence against migrants who live in these spaces, are governed by the entanglements of class and race. While it is difficult, with current data, to disentangle class and race, I hope that this chapter will motivate future research to expand the study of these discourses that link race, class, and migrant/citizen inequalities to space.

Conclusion

With the externalisation of European Union's borders onto the southern and eastern shores of the Mediterranean, potential onward migrants like Yvonne and Yaya find themselves spending more time than planned in these regions where European border control is now outsourced. As these migrants stay longer periods in Tunisia, Morocco, Turkey or Egypt, they also create visible communities in urban peripheries like Bhar Lazreg, which offer cheaper housing options and access to urban centres where jobs are concentrated. They take up jobs similar to those held by working class citizens of their host countries.

While racialising and inferiorising stereotypes associated with Blackness remain the basis for a general dislike and non-tolerance of Sub-Saharan migrant populations, the already-precarious economic conditions in southern and eastern Mediterranean countries add to the sentiment of labour-market competition and resulting dislike for the black migrants. This dislike itself manifests in and is justified through racialising discourses. Although Sub-Saharan migrants share sites of employment, as well as experiences of unemployment and financial precarity, with working-class Tunisians living in Bhar Lazreg, this has not created class-based solidarities across the two groups. For example, both groups work as cooks or cleaners in cafés and restaurants, as domestic workers (usually women), or as construction workers (usually men) in and around the neighbourhood. Yet, the increasing presence of Sub-Saharan migrants in Tunisian's mostly informal 'low-skilled' labour market has generated a sentiment of competition among many working-class Tunisians who fear that these migrants are taking away their jobs. This sentiment is fuelled by the collapsing economic conditions in Tunisia, as manifested by the decreasing number of employment opportunities. For example, over June 2021 as well as following Saied's 2023 statement, Tunisians living in the city of Sfax (south of Tunis) organised protests against migrants for 'taking away [Tunisian] jobs' (see Matri/Zuntz, this volume) The discourse of 'too many Africans' living in urban peripheral neighbourhoods like Bhar Lazreg is used as evidence for larger conspiracy theories – claiming that Black migrants will replace the Tunisian population. In January 2023, an ex-minister interviewed on a popular television channel IFMTV said that 'if the migration of Tunisians [to Europe] continues, Africans will come and marry [Tunisians] and replace [Tunisians]' (Papillon [@Papiillon] 2023). According to such conspiracy theories, the racial blackening of Bhar Lazreg and other 'African' neighbourhoods is expected to spread all over Tunisia. With a worsening economic and political climate in Tunisia, these kind of stereotypes and prejudices will unfortunately become more popular and fuel increasing violence against Sub-Saharan migrants.

Working Lives
Syrian Refugee Women's Intimate Labour and Mobilities in Tunisia

Ann-Christin Zuntz, Asma Ben Hadj Hassen & Marwen Bouneb

> NAHLA: 'On Friday, people help us'.

> UM KHALIL: 'In the past, our house was always open to guests, whoever was there was invited to eat and drink'.

During the Syrian refugee crisis, humanitarians have focused on putting women to work. In the absence of more structural solutions to ending many Syrians' economic precarity, refugee women are praised as a shadow workforce and budding entrepreneurs that could be enabled through vocational training (e.g. Turner 2019). 'Work', in this sense, means paid work, and ideally creating one's own business. The reality of female refugees' work, however, is more complicated, and employment is not automatically a pathway to 'female empowerment'. In truth, displaced women can take on multiple roles and experience new forms of agency and of oppression, including in the workplace (Fiddian-Qasmiyeh 2014). Access to work is also complicated by refugees' lack of labour rights in many host countries. By way of illustration, Tunisia is a signatory of the 1951 Refugee Convention and its 1967 Protocol, and both its 2014 and 2022 Constitutions recognise the right to political asylum. However, this has not yet led to domestic asylum legislation (Ben Achour 2019), and there is no clear legal pathway for refugees, or for migrants more generally, to access the Tunisian labour market or citizenship. On major roundabouts in coastal cities, begging women, often accompanied by their children, embody Syrian displacement in this North African country. In November 2021, we met Nahla, a Syrian beggar, on the outskirts of Sfax. At around four in the afternoon, she was squatting on the pavement of a dusty arterial road, clutching a faded photocopy of her Syrian passport. She was surrounded by her young children, including an eight-year-old boy standing guard over his mother. We started to chat and later visited Nahla at her home. Mobile labour at various scales has always played a major role in Nahla's life: she used to work as a peddler in her hometown Hama before the 2011 Syrian revolution, and after displacement as an agricultural worker in Lebanon. An odyssey through Mauritania, Mali, and Algeria later brought her to Tunisia. In Sfax, her mobility inside the city has now turned her into her family's main breadwinner, although she politely refuses to call begging 'work'.

Displaced Syrian women tell themselves and others complex stories about when what they do is considered 'work', especially when they make a living through commodifying aspects of motherhood. The protagonists of this chapter are Nahla, a Syrian beggar, and Um Khalil, a Syrian grandmother-turned-entrepreneur. While Um Khalil resides in an affluent neighbourhood in Tunis, Nahla dwells in abject poverty in Sfax. We conducted interviews with these women as part of a three-month study of Syrian refugees' complex flight trajectories to Tunisia, for which we interviewed 21 Syrian households in various locations in Tunisia in autumn and winter 2021. With around 2,700 people, Syrians make up one quarter of Tunisia's registered refugee population (UNHCR 2022). Before the Syrian conflict, Syrians could enter Tunisia without a visa. In February 2012, Tunisia expelled the Syrian ambassador and cut all diplomatic ties, in solidarity with the Syrian revolution (Boubakri 2015). In 2012, former Tunisian President Marzouki announced that all Syrian refugees would receive humanitarian protection, but the promise never materialised. Today, most Syrians in Tunisia are registered as 'asylum-seekers' with the UNHCR, with their application for refugee protection pending (cf. Garelli/Tazzoli 2017). As the UNCHR does not publish gender- or age-disaggregated (or other more detailed) data on Syrian refugees in Tunisia, it is hard to know whether working women are the norm or the exception for this small community. However, available qualitative insights indicate that many Syrian women in Tunisia live in multigenerational households and have caring duties for young children and the elderly, which might make it harder for them to take on paid jobs (UNHCR 2014). Their profile is thus different from that of other migrant women in Tunisia, notably Sub-Saharan African women who tend to leave their children with family members in their home countries, thus enjoying greater freedom when it comes to finding work abroad (Ben Hadj Hassen 2024). Evidence from other refugee-hosting middle-income countries in the region also suggests that Syrian women's labour market participation rate is very low (e.g. below ten percent in Jordan; cf. UN Women 2017). What we do know, however, is that the Syrian refugee community in Tunisia is not homogeneous (Zuntz et al. 2022). In our wider research, we found that Tunisia is home to two Syrian populations with different socioeconomic standings, travel routes, and legal status in the host country: Syrians with and without pre-war ties to Tunisia. The protagonists in this chapter were selected to illustrate experiences from both groups. They entered Tunisia through different routes and now have different livelihood strategies. Before 2011, some middle-class Syrians like Um Khalil established connections to Tunisia through the transnational trade and educational migration of their spouses and were later able to mobilise these networks to get to safety and rebuild their lives in exile. Nahla, by contrast, comes from a working-class background and had no initial ties to Tunisia. She only arrived in the country after a long and fragmented journey through multiple Middle Eastern and North African countries. Nahla is still waiting for her asylum claim to be processed, while Um Khalil bypassed the asylum system, quickly securing Tunisian residency, and later even citizenship, through alternative legal routes.

What does it mean to be 'Syrian' to these women from different class backgrounds and with different forms of legal status in their host country? We chose to contrast these women's experiences not to reify their 'Syrianness', but rather to explore the different ways in which they have turned the combination of Syrian identity and motherhood into an asset. Together, they exemplify the public faces of gendered 'Syrianness' in Tunisia:

as a begging mother on a roundabout, representing suffering and refugeeness, and as the talented housewife and chef, the personification of traditional Middle Eastern hospitality. Looking at their activities as 'intimate labour' helps us highlight commonalities between their disparate experiences of life in displacement. By 'intimate labour', we understand 'work that involves embodied and affective interactions in the service of social reproduction' (Boris/Parreñas 2010: 7). This type of labour includes managing relationships and is associated with the home, body, and family. What Um Khalil and Nahla have in common is that both contribute paid and unpaid services to their families, including cooking, childcare, but also sang-froid when finding their way through war zones and unknown urban territory in Tunisia. Even though humanitarians like to imagine displaced women as future individualistic entrepreneurs, the reality of their and many other women's work is that it benefits their entire family, fits around their caring duties as mothers and wives, and complements, rather than replaces, male family members' jobs (cf. Rabo 2008). The Syrian protagonists of this chapter are either mothers or grandmothers, tending to their husbands' and (grand)children's immediate and more long-term material and emotional needs. In both cases, the husbands cannot fulfil their role as breadwinners anymore, but continue to impact what kind of work women can do and whether they get recognition for it.

'Syrianness' and, in particular, ideas of 'Syrian motherhood', come into play because maternal ideals and practices inform both women's travails but have also been commoditised: as home-made Syrian cuisine that appeals to wealthy party planners or as the stylised image of the suffering refugee-mother that can elicit the sympathy of passers-by. We do not aim to paint our subjects as 'natural mothers'. Rather, we ask how refugee women perform motherhood to different audiences and what opportunities these performances afford them. We show that women's labour may be taken for granted and devalued, as doing chores is understood as a part of a mother and wife's 'natural' role. But it can also be assigned new monetary value when it supports the household income of dispersed families. As Zelizer (2005) famously argued, monetising one's intimate relations is far from straightforward; it does not simply empty them of affect or make them less authentic. In practice, people constantly mix up economics and intimacy, and our protagonists' talk about labour brings together economic rationality, family values, emotions, and memories. We look at the 'complicated stories and practices [that Syrian refugees develop] for different situations that mingle economic transactions and intimacy' (Zelizer 2005: 12); for example, when Nahla declares her begging 'not work' or Um Khalil frames her catering service as 'family work'.

Through exploring the link between refugee women's gendered labour and mobilities, this chapter expands existing debates on what counts as 'intimate labour'. Previously, feminist scholars have studied intimate labour in the context of transnational migrations, e.g. for sex workers, care workers, and surrogate mothers, problematising distinctions between the 'local' and the 'global'. Existing research connects the dots between multinational corporations and transnational flows of Big Data and Big Money, and the everyday acts through which people sustain their livelihoods, and which place them in local and global economies (Mountz/Hyndman 2006; Pratt/Rosner 2012). A constant theme in all these cases is workers' mobility, including border-crossings and aspirations of social mobility for oneself and one's loved ones. Refugees, of course, experience different forms of movement, as well as stuckness, but they seldom have the time to plan ahead. Syrian refugee women in Tunisia make for a fascinating case study because policymakers and the media tend to think of Tunisia solely as one step of South-North migrations to Europe. In truth, however, Tunisia has long been involved in circular South-South migrations, and in recent years, restrictive European bordering practices have also turned Tunisia into a forced destination for refugees and migrants (Garelli/Tazzioli 2017). This is not to say that all refugees experience movement in the same way. Often, the worst affected victims of conflict are not those forced to leave, but those who lack the resources to escape and thus have to stay put (Lubkemann 2008). As this chapter shows, displacement can combine experiences of forced mobility and forced immobility; for example, we look at Um Khalil's decision to work from home, but also resume international travel, and Nahla's sense of stuckness in the streets of Sfax, but also inside Tunisia's asylum bureaucracy. Studying Nahla and Um Khalil's commodification of Syrian motherhood in concert with their decision-making power over their movements helps us appreciate the agency, or lack thereof, that shapes what forms of intimate labour women engage in. The chapter looks at the factors that curtail our protagonists' social and spatial mobility, and also at how our subjects carve out new forms of mobility for themselves in times of displacement. It shows that refugee women's mobilities are shaped by class, family dynamics, pre-war experiences of travel, legal status in Tunisia, as well as by women's own expectations of what counts as a good life. In doing so, we challenge simplistic assumptions about a direct link between female mobility and professional careers. Contrary to humanitarian assumptions, some women may experience mobility as precarious and, conversely, staying at home as more conducive towards economic activities that can be combined with family life.

Methodology

We met Um Khalil in Tunis through a Tunisian refugee support organisation. Our contact with Nahla came about through a chance encounter at a bus stop in Sfax. Women's consent to participate in the research was obtained verbally and repeatedly, first on the phone and then in person. Both women were interviewed inside their own homes, in the presence of various family members. As we discuss in the remaining sections, observing which family members tell women's stories, and who has to remain silent, gave us information about our interviewees' status in family hierarchies. At the same time, it made following the conversations more complicated. In Um Khalil's case, she and her husband did not agree on the exact chronology of their travels to Tunisia; in Nahla's home, the narration was taken over by her older sister-in-law. As ethnographers, it is not our job to resolve these contradictions, but rather to acknowledge that narratives of displacement are complicated, especially when they involve multiple people. Ethnographic research involves a delicate balancing of interviewees' self-representation, half-truths, and stories full of holes (cf. Saleh 2017). For the Syrians we interviewed, seeking refuge was always a family project, and this is reflected in the sometimes-discordant mixture of voices in this chapter. In our research, this was as true of wealthy Um Khalil, who was unwilling to provide details of her business deals, as of poor Nahla, whose mendicity is discussed by her family only in euphemistic terms.

All interviews were conducted in Arabic by the two female team members. One of the interviewers was a native speaker of Tunisian Arabic, the other fluent in Syrian Arabic. Remarkably, the interviewees' choice of dialect oscillated between Tunisian and Syrian Arabic; this 'migrantisation' of their language hints at their more or less stable position in Tunisian society. Ironically, Um Khalil, who secured residency in the host country, spoke eloquent Syrian Arabic. Nahla used a working-class version of the same dialect, with some Tunisian words. Our Syrian interviewees' diglossia highlights the importance of taking migrant and refugee women at their word, quite literally, to understand the complexity of their lives. It indicates that the social experimentation that characterises their intimate labour rewires not only their kinship relations, but even their vocabulary.

Nahla: Work or Charity?

On the day of the interview, it rained heavily in Sfax. Our taxi struggled to make its way through the flooded streets of the suburb where Nahla, who looked like she was in her early thirties, lived with her family. In the street, her oldest son greeted us. Despite the biting November cold, the boy wore sandals without socks. Inside the apartment, Nahla, her much older husband, his sister, and seven children of kindergarten and primary school age, were huddled up around the flame of a gas cooker in an empty, damp room.

Nahla and her family come from Hama, a city on the banks of the Orontes river in western Syria. Before the Syrian conflict, her husband worked as a blacksmith, and Nahla bought make-up in the city centre of Hama and then resold it in rural areas. Her sister-in-law recalled how Nahla would knock on doors and sell mascara to Syrian housewives. Nahla's family also used to migrate to Lebanon to work in agriculture; her never-ending hustle is typical of the precarious situation of many circular Syrian migrants before the war (Chalcraft 2008). Unlike Um Khalil, Nahla thus brought to Tunisia pre-war work experience outside the home, after a lifetime of menial mobile labour. In 2011, her family fled Hama and spent three years in an informal settlement in northern Lebanon. During this time, Nahla and her husband returned to working informally in the harvest. In 2014, the family boarded a plane to Mauritania; they transited through Tunis airport, even though they only decided to move to Tunisia three years later. In Nouakchott, Mauritania, Nahla's family joined other Syrian families in crossing the desert in Mali and Algeria, along the established West African Migration Route. In Algeria, they lived for three years in Béjaïa, a port city, before arriving in Tunisia in 2017. Nahla's lengthy and fragmented journey to Tunisia is relevant here for several reasons: first, it exemplifies the legal predicament that Syrians experience in Tunisia. Unable to enter Tunisia by plane, many Syrians have been forced to undertake increasingly dangerous routes, during which families like Nahla's incurred multiple costs for plane tickets, bus journeys, and smugglers. Other Syrians in Tunisia who had travelled along the same route told us that they could only finance their trip by repeatedly borrowing money from relatives and local acquaintances. It is thus highly likely that Nahla's family arrived in Tunisia with substantial debts.

Second, during their flight, the family grew dependent on the international humanitarian system – but aid has not proven a secure source of income. Nahla's family registered with the UNCHR in Lebanon, Algeria, and Tunisia, countries that are either not signatories to the 1951 Refugee Convention (Lebanon) or have signed the Convention but not translated it into domestic asylum legislation (Algeria, Tunisia). In Lebanon, Algeria, and Tunisia, the family received financial assistance from the UNHCR, and the aid agency also covered the hospital bills for the delivery of Nahla's younger children in Algeria and Tunisia. But their registration did not protect the family from violence at the hands of locals and even state authorities. In Lebanon, they suffered frequent racist attacks from the host community. In Algeria, the brother and cousin of Nahla's husband were deported to the desert between Niger and Algeria, in contravention of the Convention's principle of non-refoulement. In Tunisia, they had been registered as 'asylum-seekers' since 2017. While financial assistance had stopped several months before our interview, Nahla's other established coping strategies did not work either. As her sister-in-law explained: 'She cannot sell make-up like she used to do in Syria. In Tunisia, people buy in shops'. In urban centres in North Africa, opportunities for petty trading or agricultural work are much rarer than they are in rural areas in the Middle East. Without formal qualifications and childcare, it was unlikely that Nahla could find a job in Tunisia's professional retail sector. Nor did Nahla have any domestic skills or social capital that she could turn into an income-generating activity in Tunisia. In Sfax, the family lived an isolated life and did not socialise with Syrians or Tunisians, except for close relatives like Nahla's sister-in-law. The situation was made worse by the fact that livelihood opportunities for refugees and migrants, through the Tunisian Association for Management and Social Stability (TAMSS), rarely take into account women's particular needs: most jobs are offered to men, as they are considered the head of the family, even though Nahla's case shows that women may also become breadwinners. The employment on offer consists of blue-collar jobs that often require candidates to move to other regions, such as Djerba or Zarzis, thus tearing families apart. What is missing is vocational training, for example as pastry chefs or in the textile industry that could be acceptable to females. Lack of humanitarian assistance, together with Nahla's insecure legal status and the absence of other job opportunities, thus compelled her to beg. After our interview, her situation was exacerbated even more when the local office of the Tunisian Refugee Council in Sfax was closed for several months in 2022: the very infrastructure of the Tunisian asylum response became not only inaccessible, but also physically absent from her life (Personal communication, Marwen Bouneb, January 2023).

The micro-economy of begging is a sensitive issue. As Nahla's sister-in-law exclaimed, 'her situation is very difficult'! In Sfax, Nahla earned between 25 and 40 Dinar (around 8–12 Euro) per day, i.e. around 125–200 Dinar (around 40–60 Euro) per week. By comparison, Tunisian minimum wage for a 40-hour week is around 390 Dinar (around 121 Euro) per month (Votre Salaire 2022). At first, Nahla's monthly income may thus look relatively high, but she did not go out on rainy days and paid six Dinar per day to take a taxi from her suburb to Sfax's more central roads. And, more importantly, she was the family's sole breadwinner, as her husband was too sick for manual labour; her begging barely covered the monthly rent of 260 Dinar (around 81 Euro). Most days, Nahla stayed outside between 9 am and 4 pm. While she usually brought her youngest child that she was still nursing, on holidays and weekends, she was also accompanied by her oldest son – the boy we saw protecting her in the street. This type of work is in the public sphere, but it is also incredibly intimate: Nahla put her body on the frontline, exposing herself and her young children to heat and cold, dirt, and the glances and potential aggressions of passers-by. We would have liked to hear from Nahla whether she felt uncomfortable on her own in an unfamiliar city, but her husband replied for her: 'There are people in the street, she is safe'.

It is noteworthy that when we politely questioned Nahla about her 'work', she and her family preferred the euphemism 'people help us'. For example, we asked Nahla whether she had approached local mosques for support and she replied: 'On Friday, people help us' (this refers to the common phenomenon of people begging outside mosques after the Friday prayer). Throughout the conversation, it emerged that this was not the first time that the family had relied on charity. Comparing her life as a refugee in Algeria and Tunisia, Nahla explained that the family had had a better life in Algeria 'because people helped us there'. In Sfax, their Tunisian neighbours brought them food during Ramadan. Even though begging took up most of Nahla's time and generates an income, it was thus not recognised as 'work' by either herself or her family. Rather, our interviewees redirected our attention to other people's – their benefactors' – actions. Despite the multiple activities it involved, begging was framed not as an active process, but rather as something that was done to Nahla as the passive receiver of other people's charity. In pre-war Syria, Nahla and her family had been part of the struggling working class, getting by through menial labour, petty trade, and circular migrations to neighbouring countries. In Tunisia, they entered the social hierarchy even lower, at the very bottom, using grifting, begging, and support from strangers and neighbours to cope with entrenched precarity. And there is another reason why Nahla might have avoided the terminology of 'work': as a Syrian lawyer in Tunis, himself a long-term migrant and co-founder of a support organisation for his compatriots, told us, the established and affluent Syrian diaspora in the country did not consider beggars such as Nahla 'real Syrians'. Given the lack of interaction between middle-class and working class Syrians in Tunisia, it is unlikely that Nahla would have been aware of such prejudices. Still, framing mendicity as 'charity' in line with Islamic values might have made her activities more acceptable to the wider public, to neighbours, fellow Syrians, and perhaps herself.

Nahla's experience challenges simplistic assumptions about the link between female mobility and access to better livelihoods. Nahla was far from being a home-bound housewife, but for her, freedom of movement did not translate into better professional opportunities, or, in the eyes of her family, a 'job'. On the contrary, her high degree of mobility at the urban level did nothing to end the family's social isolation, as Nahla's encounters with benevolent passers-by were always short-lived. While begging, she was also exposed to extreme weather and perhaps even violence, while her children missed out on school. Her presence in the streets of Sfax was thus not a remedy for, but rather a symptom of her precarity. At the same time, Nahla's newfound role as the family's main provider has not changed her precarious positioning inside her own family. When listening again to the recording of our interview with Nahla, we noticed a curious thing: although the interview was about her and the begging she did for a living, we rarely heard her speak. Instead, her husband and older sister-in-law, who was visiting from Tunis that day, told her story. The fact that her young children, who frequently demanded her attention, surrounded Nahla also made it difficult for her to take part in the conversation – indeed, her baby's crying frequently interrupted our interview recording. The literal absence of Nahla's voice points to her subordinate position in the family, even though she has now become their only source of income.

Um Khalil: The Family is the Business

Um Khalil, a Syrian housewife-turned-entrepreneur in her mid-sixties, graciously welcomed us into her living room in Menzah, an upscale neighbourhood in Tunis. However, it was difficult to keep her attention for long. Our conversation was punctuated by multiple phone calls from clients and acquaintances, testimony to our host's economic success and standing in the small, but affluent 'old' Syrian Diaspora in Tunis. On her phone, Um Khalil proudly showed us pictures of Syrian dishes on the Facebook page of her catering business: *shanklish* [Syrian cheese], *mansaf* [a Syrian-Jordanian lamb dish], *labneh* [Syrian yoghurt], *kabsa* [a Syrian rice dish]. As we were getting ready to leave, Um Khalil insisted we stay for dinner. One of her daughters-in-law started to cover the family's spacious dining table with traditional Syrian food. Soon, there were several types of salad, yoghurt, hummus, and meat. Three generations of Um Khalil's family, including our host and her husband, various sons, daughters-in-law, and grandchildren, gathered around the table. This Syrian dinner, prepared under the watchful eye of Um Khalil herself, signalled to us the family's identity, values, and sense of belonging, and Um Khalil's role as the group's matriarch. In Tunis, this type of food had also become key to the family's economic success.

Before the war, Um Khalil used to be a housewife in Damascus, taking care of her husband and six children. To her, hospitality and food were a way of life: 'In the past, our house was always open to guests, whoever was there was invited to eat and drink. The more people ate [at our home], the happier we were'. To Um Khalil, home-made food was associated with tradition and her role as a mother. In the city centre of Damascus, her family inhabited an old building. 'I have always preferred historical places, not "Dubai-style" living. That's why I always cook, in the same spirit [of traditions]'. However, her sense of rootedness used to go hand in hand with an intermittently mobile life. Before the war, her husband worked as a trader and together, they visited Tunisia regularly. Later, they capitalised on their pre-war knowledge of travel routes and social networks to seek refuge in Tunis: in 2013, the family boarded a bus and travelled through Jordan, Egypt, and Libya, to reach Tunisia. Um Khalil's familiarity with Tunisia and travelling was central to how she makes sense of her displacement and multiple losses. She was adamant that she had come to Tunisia not as a 'refugee', but as a 'tourist', and in Tunis, she never registered with the UNHCR. Still, she occasionally used her Syrian citizenship to claim 'refugeeness' and access funding; a small start-up grant from Terre d'Asile, a non-profit organisation that supports refugees and migrants, allowed her to open her catering business. Um Khalil managed to pay back the grant after only a couple of months. With a core team of only six people, all of them family members, she has since provided catering for the Jordanian ambassador in Tunis, the Institut Français (i.e. the French cultural institute), weddings and funerals all over the country, as well as Syrian restaurants in Tunis, Hammamet, and Zarzis. At a wedding party with several hundreds of guests, her family makes a net gain of 2,000 Dinar (around 620 Euro); Um Khalil works multiple such events per month. That makes her business a part of the vibrant Syrian hospitality scene that has blossomed in Tunisia in recent years, encompassing restaurants, fast food eateries, bakeries, and catering services. One of her sisters also owns a restaurant in Tunis, a son works as a chef in an upscale Syrian restaurant close to the family home, and another son is a member of a traditional Syrian dance group, run by a young Tunisian-Syrian man, that was even featured in a talent show on Tunisian television. For Um Khalil, there was a direct link between her economic success, legal security, and cross-border mobility. Through her business, she quickly obtained residency permits and later Tunisian passports for her entire family. This is highly surprising, as Tunisian citizenship remains unavailable even for spouses of Tunisian citizens. While Um Khalil was deliberately vague about the circumstances of her naturalisation, she underlined her close ties with foreign ambassadors, other affluent Syrians, and longstanding Tunisian friends. What is clear, however, are the practical advantages of acquiring a Tunisian passport: having Syrian and Tunisian citizenship enabled her to travel more freely than registered asylum-seekers. Some years ago, when her son fell in love on social media with a girl in Syria, she went back to her home country to meet his fiancée, hand over her dowry, and organise the girl's trip to Tunis. Visiting an active war zone was only possible because she used her various passports to travel to Syria as a Syrian and return to Tunisia as a Tunisian.

Um Khalil's work blurs the boundaries between home, family, and business, as well as paid and unpaid labour. On the one hand, cooking is a 'labour of love' and Um Khalil discussed her own role and hardship as a wife and mother in food-related metaphors. Having got married at the age of 16, she compared her life to *makdous* [pickled aubergine]:

> We receive the aubergine when it is still fresh and then we add salt. Life becomes bitter. In a similar vein, women get married young and live through a lot of pain, until their bodies become hard. But still, they love their husbands in their heart and they protect the family.

In this regard, her current life as an entrepreneur is not a break, but rather a continuation of her pre-war existence as a housewife. Holding on to traditions – such as early marriage, traditional family structures, and home-made food – has helped Um Khalil deal with changes in her environment, but also inside her own family. Despite her economic success and comfortable living situation, Um Khalil expressed a strong sense of alienation: 'We integrated into Tunisian society [economically], but I don't feel Tunisian. I told you, this morning I cried'. Much of her loneliness comes from the lack of more mundane, un-commodified hospitality that she associates with Syrian culture: 'Here, we live the European way: no one [from the Tunisian neighbours] ever comes to visit'. Even though Um Khalil's sister and her own children live in Tunis, she misses the daily chats with female neighbours that she was used to in Damascus. New lifestyles have also changed family dynamics. Um Khalil married off her older children when they were still teenagers. 'This is how I was brought up, and my mother, and my maternal aunt. But my son wants to study and my daughter wants to study and take the plane'. Her children's new ambitions of social and spatial mobility threaten the family as a homogeneous unit, as well as established ways of securing intergenerational transitions. As marriage plans and cohabitation do not seem attractive to the young generation anymore, Um Khalil has had to find alternative ways of holding the family together, including through offering employment to her adult offspring.

This is only possible because, on the other hand, cooking is business. Just like Nahla, Um Khalil sells a particular form of Syrian motherhood associated with home life and devotion to one's family. But while Nahla's begging showcases refugee suffering, Um Khalil has managed to turn into a commodity a form of Syrianness that is more appealing to affluent Tunisian audiences: home-made Syrian cuisine. And to be clear, Um Khalil understands cooking as hard work, both for herself and for others. While the *makdous*, for example, serves as a metaphor of her family and gendered identities, it is also a material object that requires manual labour. As Um Khalil explained, 'by the way, this [*makdous*] is hard work'! While her food is home-made, it is also produced in large quantities. To cater to huge crowds, Um Khalil's team prepares huge amounts of deep-frozen food in advance. For example, several fridges in their apartment always contain 2,000 pieces of *kibbeh* [Syrian meatballs]. As the head of the company, Um Khalil never takes days off. 'There is no retirement, people from the Middle East say, when we retire, we die'. While she does not pay a permanent salary to her sons and daughters-in-law, she pays each of them 250 Tunisian Dinar for a two-day wedding (around 78 Euro), turning loved ones into employees. From an economic point of view, Um Khalil cannot afford to stop working because her business covers all the household expenses of their multigenerational family. Still, as her home is also her workplace, commercial cooking blends in with other unpaid caring tasks. Every Friday, for example, one of her daughters brings over her three young children, whom Um Khalil watches over the weekend, and while cooking.

Just like Nahla's example, Um Khalil's 'labour of love' complicates how we might think about work opportunities for refugee women. Um Khalil deliberately decided against opening yet another Syrian restaurant in Tunis; instead, she prefers running a catering business from her own kitchen. Her decision was partly economically motivated, as working from home allowed her to save rent. But it also allows her to be surrounded by her beloved children and grandchildren and be there for her ailing husband. For herself and her daughters-in-law, staying at home does not hinder their professional projects, but rather provides the stage for a successful business in line with family values. In return, this highlights the complex relationship between social and spatial mobility. Just like Nahla's case, it shows that women's income-generating activities outside the home are not a simple recipe for addressing precarious refugee livelihoods. Being on the street makes Nahla more vulnerable, while Um Khalil has found a job – or rather created a job for herself – that allows family members from two generations to work together from home and even includes free childcare. Yet, we should take Um Khalil's praise of her home-bound existence with a grain of salt. However much Um Khalil likes to emphasise her secluded life, as the matriarch, she leaves the house, and Tunis, much more frequently than her daughters-in-law. Her superior standing in the multigenerational household, not her gender alone, determines her greater freedom of movement.

In recent years, Um Khalil has teamed up with an event agency in Zarzis, in southern Tunisia, to find clients all over the country. One summer, she spent the entire season without her family, working in a pastry shop in Zarzis. Once, she taught a cooking course at a fancy hotel in Sousse to a women-only class. While the younger women of the family rarely leave the house, Um Khalil works with other mobile women. In Tunis, for example, she relies on the services of a female taxi driver who delivers her food. With a smile, Um Khalil explained, 'I don't work with men, they always try to interfere'.

Conclusion: Ambivalent Femininities, Ambivalent Mobilities

In this chapter, we discussed the relationship between different types of 'intimate labour' and mobility for Syrian refugee women in Tunisia. During displacement, commoditising motherhood can turn into a livelihood strategy for women on the margins of the formal labour market. The intimacy of our protagonists' activities comes from the embodied nature of their work, the extension of domestic practices such as cooking and nursing one's child into the public sphere, and the rewiring of kinship relationships: while Nahla's children are part of the stage-managing of her suffering, Um Khalil has united her grown-up children around her as employees. However, their stories are hardly straightforward examples of female 'emancipation'. Rather, they illuminate the complexities of the social production of femininities in refugee contexts. Acts of cooking and feeding may cement stereotypical views of women as home-makers; a mother's ability to nourish her family may be regarded by herself and others as a way of 'succeeding' at motherhood (cf. Cairns/Johnston 2015). At the same time, the commoditised version of motherhood is more than the on-going legacy of patriarchal oppression in refugee women's lives. Um Khalil, with her cooking classes all over Tunisia, behaves not unlike other celebrity chefs. In truth, in a neoliberal context, in which commoditised motherhood can enable female entrepreneurship and generate money, such performances simultaneously reaffirm, but also challenge gendered inequalities.

As refugee women's performances of Syrian motherhood are ambivalent, so are their experiences of mobility. Our ethnographic findings highlight that the ability to *choose* movement, rather than movement itself, continues to shape refugee women's lives after the initial displacement, long after they have settled in host countries. In this regard, our research adds to debates on 'intimate labour' and mobility: for refugees, unlike migrants, movement is rarely (at least initially) a project to improve their lives. However, there is not one homogenous way in which mobility is experienced. Multiple factors shape whether displacement makes women more or less mobile and what types of paid and unpaid labour they engage in. Class, women's positioning in multigenerational households and shifting family dynamics, pre-war connections to Tunisia, and legal (in)security together affect whether refugee women experience mobility as empowering or as precarious. Women like Um Khalil, who are the head of their families, with middle-class social capital and business acumen, can choose whether to lead mobile or sedentary lives. Um Khalil, for example, enjoys working from the comfort of her own home, but also travelling all over Tunisia as a businesswoman, while Nahla has no say over her movements: she takes to the streets because begging is her only source of income. Conversely, agency over one's movements also shapes one's ability to make a home: Um Khalil, securely established as an entrepreneur in Tunis and surrounded by her children, has no interest in moving to Europe. To her, Tunisia has become a country of permanent settlement. Nahla, by contrast, dreams of resettlement in Europe, as her family see no future in Tunisia. Different forms of intimate labour, it seems, are thus inversely linked together: Um Khalil's catering business has allowed her to establish a lasting home. Nahla's begging, however, may keep the family alive, but only entrenches her feelings of alienation and poverty, thwarting attempts at home-making.

On a final note, policymakers tend to look at refugees as disconnected from host country economies – but Um Khalil's experience hints at a broader story about the migrantisation of female domestic labour. Among scholars of displacement, there is a growing interest in the political economy of displacement and refugees' positioning in global capitalism. There is now a greater awareness that the exploitative labour that many refugees' experience is not simply the by-product of bad humanitarian governance or refugees' lack of economic integration in host countries, but rather illustrates broader dynamics that affect people across the Global South: movement control, euphemised as 'migration governance', and labour exploitation go hand in hand. Around the world, the displaced join a reserve army of other structurally marginalised workers, including migrants, women, and youth (Bhagat 2020; Rajaram 2018; Ramsay 2022). While most studies on migrant and refugee labour have been conducted in the Global North, our insights from Tunisia suggest that similar developments are underway in transit countries in the Global South. Labour market participation rates of Tunisian women are considerably higher than the regional average in the Middle East and North Africa (28% vs. 18% in 2021; World Bank 2022a; 2022b), and more and more Tunisian women join the workforce every year. In Tunisia, as all over the world, growing female employment will increase the demand for outsourcing food work to nannies, fast food workers, school ladies etc. – many of whom will be migrant and refugee women such as Um Khalil (cf. Cairns/Johnston 2015). In the figure of the female refugee, producing food from her home, two neoliberal narratives about individual responsibility and 'strong women' intersect: the humanitarian system's current approach to refugee entrepreneurship as a panacea to structural barriers to labour market integration, and postfeminist ideas about female empowerment through work. The latter obscures the fact that women's employment outside the home hinges on the labour of other, more structurally marginalised women. To capture this nexus, we need to understand better the social fabric and gendered dynamics that underpin diverse forms of mobile refugee labour. As our research shows, displacement perpetuates, and sometimes rewires, not only labour relations, but also intimate connections, including family hierarchies, social identities, consumption patterns, and the division of labour within households. Hence the need to redirect our focus on refugee women's mundane experiences of work and family life: such intimate labour is not made up of isolated occurrences, but rather connects women to broader economic and political processes. Syrian women's labour in Tunisia provides insights into the nexus of complex migratory systems, the international humanitarian regime, border policies, and local and globalised industries.

The Trap of 'Voluntary Return'
Forced Returns of Tunisian Migrants

Wael Garnaoui

> TAWFIK: 'I have spent 23 days in the detention centre of Bologna, going through much suffering and discomfort. I met the centre's judge. Sometimes detainees can also meet with some associations defending undocumented migrants, if they are able to pay 500 Euros to cover the fees for a lawyer and to submit an asylum application – sometimes their families send the money. I refused to do all that because I knew it was hard for me, and because I couldn't take it anymore. I had a drug conviction, so I had no chance. I caused a lot of problems throughout these 23 days. They came to wake me up to send me back to Tunisia, I was on sleeping drugs and I had a nightmare, I told them: No! I'm not going back! The security guards are always afraid of people's reactions during deportation.
> A friend of mine advised me: If you do the same thing next time, they'll tape you up and put you on the plane, take fate into your hands, it's better'.
>
> Tawfik, Tunisian Harrag (Tunisia 2017)

Tunisia is a country of origin of an increasing number of migrants on their way to Europe. Those who flee Tunisia to reach Europe are known as *harraga*. This reflects the irregular and clandestine practice of migration, termed *harga*. It is a fairly recent phenomenon that followed the closure of the European borders after the Schengen Agreement in 1985. *Harga*, translates from the Maghrebean dialects as 'the act of setting something on fire'. It echoes what these young *harraga* do when they burn their identity cards to avoid being identified by the police, and thus reducing their chances of being deported to their country of origin. The *harraga* also symbolically 'burn' the borders (i.e. ignore their meaning and enforcement). In an act of vindication of the law and embodied crossing, they traverse the Mediterranean in makeshift boats to reach Europe, an 'El Dorado', according to their collective imagination, for which they risk their lives. Examining irregular immigration means understanding borders as institutions and production devices of new subjectivities and collective imaginaries. Both national and administrative borders shape subjectivities and symbolic perceptions of those who are exposed to the violence of

Western power (cf. Sha'ath, this volume). The West presents itself as a universal model of governance and order, unleashing ambivalent feelings of both desire and hatred towards it (Garnaoui 2022). It is through these lenses that this chapter follows the trajectories of Tunisian migrants, those who are deported, and those who chose a so-called 'voluntary return' – going through the procedures of assisted return.

Policies of Externalising Borders and the 'Voluntary Return' Scheme

In this chapter, I will shed light on the hardest and most stigmatising step in the journey of an irregular Tunisian migrant, that of expulsion, sometimes referred to by NGOs as 'voluntary return', a measure implemented as part of the policy to externalise European borders. Externalisation encompasses a wide range of practices aimed at transferring part of the management of migratory flows – that would otherwise be the responsibility of so-called countries of arrival – to 'transit countries', or countries of origin, or to private operators. The externalisation of borders should be scrutinised distinctively because it unleashes a new set of tools for the repression and borderisation of space, population, and desires in the countries of origin. Subsequently, these practices raise the crucial question of the reintegration of young people who have spent many years working in risky and irregular jobs in a peaceful environment (i.e. Europe).

In 2014, the Tunisian government signed a Political Partnership Agreement with the EU, which facilitates the issuing of visas reserved for a small, ultra-qualified elite of Tunisian nationals; and committed itself to a 're-entry agreement' that would ease the procedures of returning to its soil, not only for its nationals who were deported from Europe, but also for third-country nationals who had transited through its territory (Bisiaux 2020a). This partnership is bolstered by anti-trafficking programmes, which are intended to 'protect the victims', but instead have frequently been repressive and often aim to criminalise the migrants themselves. For migrants acknowledged as victims of trafficking, the so-called 'voluntary return', organised in cooperation with the International Organisation for Migration (IOM), remains the preferred solution by authorities. In 2018, 60 victims of trafficking were reintegrated into their countries of origin with the support of the IOM (Bisiaux 2020b).

In contrast to the policies of forced return of irregular migrants (after irregular immigration or non-renewal of visa/residence permit in the European host country), voluntary return is a policy for managing migrant populations banned from residing in Europe after failing to obtain the right of residence. To encourage them to return to their country of origin, this policy offers forms of support and integration for migrants who are forced to leave European territory. It is carried out both in the country of immigration (Europe) and in the country of origin, through procedures run by immigration and foreign affairs ministries, international cooperation institutions, and civil society associations. Assisted return, integration, and reintegration schemes refer to a set of programmes implemented by the institutions regulating voluntary return, in order to assist the migrants concerned, with the aim of facilitating their 'way back' and economic integration (e.g. by covering the cost of return journey, training courses, and assistance in setting up projects, etc.). In general terms, these schemes refer to the aid granted by European countries combating irregular migratory flows, to countries providing migrants. This aid consists of building reception facilities for returning migrants, supporting the personal projects of selected migrants, financing civil society projects to support the socio-professional integration of migrants. The implementation of these various objectives of the asylum and voluntary return policy is entrusted to Tunisian state actors, such as the Tunisian Ministry of Employment and Training, the Ministry of Social Affairs, the National Institute of Statistics, National Migration Observatory, the Office for Tunisians Abroad, and foreign state actors, such as the Italian Ministry of the Interior, and the German Ministry of Foreign Affairs, or the French Agency for Development.

Methodology

To carry out this ethnographic study, I adopted the method of multi-sited ethnography, a mode of constructing a research space that assumes that the subject of study is a cultural formation produced in different spaces, and encourages us to follow the circulation of the subject through different contexts (Marcus 1995). I conducted some twenty interviews in three periods. Between July 2016 and December 2020, I surveyed three territories of immigration and emigration: Tunisia, Paris and Berlin. I mention this period as background information; it does not have a particular 'time of beginning' or 'time of ending', because these field investigations are part of my personal history, during which I came into contact with 'the migratory subject', before I began my research work on my doctoral thesis. This fieldwork was supplemented by another field survey of the families of missing migrants, of migrants who had been expelled, or of 'voluntarily returnees', as part of my post-doc research between September and December 2021. In my doctoral research, I have grasped the multiplicity of aspects of the individual journeys that the overall categories of *harraga* tend to homogenise. I have followed for each case, the different phases that shaped their journeys, namely the phases of departure, arrival, or deportation if necessary. I also have taken into consideration the immigrants' relationship with family and death, while paying particular attention, from a psychodynamic standpoint, to their fears, hopes, and representations of elsewhere.

To conduct my ethnographic fieldwork with voluntary returnees, I used two previously designed interview grids. The questions, drawn from both a psychological and ethnographic approach, aim to gather as much information as possible on the migrants' lives and their individual experiences, as well as their opinions concerning the programmes and measures in place to welcome and integrate them. Moreover, the questions also aim to identify the assets and shortcomings of these programmes. In this context, I not only interviewed migrants who had returned to Tunisia and have been integrated in voluntary return programmes, I also interviewed various state actors, and foreign actors located in Tunis, and observed their activities through participant observation.

EU institutions, working on assisted return and reintegration programmes for migrants, emphasise the economic and financial elements as means of reintegrating migrants who return voluntarily to their countries of origin. This approach undoubtedly stems from the fact that migration policies consider the causes of immigration to Europe to be solely economic, placing the blame on economic underdevelopment and material poverty in the countries of origin (cf. Gubert 2010). As a result, the proposed programmes for countries like Tunisia emphasise professional integration, project support, financial aid, and the like.

For me however, it was necessary to understand the reasons why the Tunisian migrants I met had left, even before considering the actions and proposals of the organisations that would support them when they returned home 'voluntarily'. This is a way of assessing the changing expectations concerning assistance once they return. By the same token, it is important to re-examine the notion of 'voluntary return' and to determine how and on what terms the decision, the desire, and the will to return are constituted. The question then becomes, to what extent could these mechanisms for voluntary return be generalised?

The interviews I conducted escape a homogeneous framing concerning the reasons and motives behind departures. Immigration is predominantly part of a complex itinerary, constituting a heterogeneous subjectivity (cf. Gertel/Grüneisl, this volume): often, one cannot separate the anthropological, psychological, and economic desires that determine a decision to leave. Moreover, these departures are frequently not conceived as a final immigration. The people I met did not consider their immigration as a permanent settlement in the host countries (e.g. France or Germany). Immigration is perceived rather as a quest for a better life, a life that is, however, also sought in the interstice of an unfixed mobility. As a result, the cases that emerge overlap with a plural societal background: visa applicants from all social backgrounds, job seekers who want to settle permanently, or those who want to live as workers between two societies. For the latter, immigration is a form of permanent mobility. Their subjectivities and collective lives are built around this dual identity: migrant and Tunisian.

In the following section, I present the example of a migrant who was expelled from European territory on several occasions without having gone through the assisted voluntary return scheme, with his last expulsion dating from 2012. This will be followed by two additional cases of migrants who have been part of 'voluntary return' schemes.

The Case of Tawfik: *'Take your Life in your Hands, it's Better'*[1]

The excerpt that follows is from an interview with a Tunisian *harrag* currently living in a town in the Tunisian Sahel. It is the story of Tawfik, who, in the opening quote, already shared with us the moment of deportation from the detention centre in Bologna. His insightful account (2017) depicts an experience of deportation that many other *harraga* have gone through. Tawfik has been deported three times from Europe following his multiple attempts to settle there. I chose to focus on his words first to familiarise the readers with the complexities of the individual fate of migrants on a psychological, social, and political level. To me, his situation seems to be a typical example of a deported *harrag*.

---

1   The original wording is: *'Prends ta tombe dans ta main, c'est mieux'*.

They came to wake me up to send me back to Tunisia. It happened in the morning. I was not expecting their presence and I was shocked. When I finally agreed to follow them, I gathered my belongings and they took me to the airport in Milan, where I got on the plane like any other passenger. During the journey to the airport, they were talking to me to keep me calm. I didn't want to come back tied up! However, the security guards left once the plane doors were closed. They are *gawri* (European foreigners), they come whenever they want, do whatever they please; they treated us like that because our government is screwed (*mnayeka*) and weak. Even the President of the Republic himself is an alcohol dealer. He doesn't even recognise God. Do you think a liquor salesman would worry about his people? No way! Would he care for the poor? Of course not, he's going to put all that shit in prison, they're just terrorists to him. That's what they do to us. What's more, he's closing the borders, the last chance for a poor young Tunisian like me is the harga. It's the only chance we have, I'll either die or I'll get to the other side of the shore, and even on the other side I don't know what's going to happen to me, nothing is guaranteed, neither the good nor the bad is granted. Just leave us alone, we want to try our luck, let us be! [his tone gets tense].

A lot of rich people are 'burning up' too – they also chose immigration. A friend of mine, whose father is a millionaire, chose to immigrate just for freedom's sake. He wanted to try, but his father tracked him down in Europe and brought him back. He wanted to go around, to visit, to have fun because the borders are legally closed. If you happen to be under the age of 35 and you want to visit Turkey, you have to have parental authorisation. It's just scandalous! Even this deal with Italy was made by that scumbag Beji Caied Sebsi! He makes 10 billion a year and acts as a border guard, he owns cars and boats, and so on. Harga has become a bit difficult, especially in my hometown. They installed a special police unit to control irregular immigration. The chief of the brigade however does a horrible job of control, he applies too much pressure, you must know that the best departure point is my hometown, there was only one accident that happened in 2014 and it was the police that caused the death of these people; the boat was overturned by the waves from an intervening coastguard boat.

WG: How was the welcome in Tunisia following your last deportation?

Two policemen welcomed me, and then the language changed. I started to regret my return, I'm sick and tired of being told bad words. They asked me a few questions like 'why did you migrate'? etc. I had to give them a bribe (*baksheesh*) to set me free on the same day. But then they didn't let me free, they brought me instead to the centre of Tunis to the headquarters of the border administration. I spent a first night in the notorious Bouchoucha prison. The conditions are awful. In the morning, I appeared before the judge and was fined 200 Dinars. Normally, they should have given me 3,000 Euros (the amount due for each deportee), as noted in the agreement between Berlusconi and our government, but the state steals this money and fines you! Who is willing to live in this country after all of this? But then I thought: 'It's better to escape from exile'. I met people who were in Europe for five years and up to 30 years, the 'trap of exile' starts after five years, if you have not regularised your situation and you don't return before five years are up, you will find yourself spending 25 to 30 years, and the trap will get you.

Finally, I paid a lot of *baksheesh* to get out of Bouchoucha. In the next morning, they come to wake us up, by shouting, 'wake up, motherfucker'! Mothers are being degraded to rubbish bins in Bouchoucha. I'm really regretting going back to Tunisia, even the food: spaghetti with *harissa* ... it's shitty. You will only experience humiliation in Bouchoucha. They saw my wallet and wanted to pressure me into paying more bribes before releasing me, by telling me, 'you are from the Sahel, you're privileged'. However, I arrived at home late in the afternoon at about seven o'clock. I was met by my mother and by my family. I was happy. My mother's support meant a lot to me. My sisters came by, and it was a real party, nobody made me feel bad, no bad feelings. But I couldn't stand the journey from Italy to here, especially in Tunisia with the borders, the food, the police, the *baksheesh*, the humiliation, the corruption etc. I'm fed up. Things have changed a bit after the revolution though, if we were under Ben Ali's regime, they would have tortured me for migrating, they would have put me in the position of a roast chicken. I am not willing to live here any longer. If they won't pay attention to me, I'm going to get myself destroyed.

Tawfik's testimony makes visible the impact of European migration policies on the disintegration, his reshaping of and, ultimately, the persistence of his identity building narratives constructed in his country. Tawfik's story shows the ordeals he endured – the risky and painful crossing, the prison sentence, the lack of any welcome worthy of the name, surviving in the target country thanks to drug trafficking, the systematic deportation by the European authorities to his country of origin – affected his identity: all this only served to fuel the inner psychological conflicts. It reveals that, in spite of the multiplicity of failures experienced and suffered by the migrant and the disappointment that follows, the West remains an ideal that orients subjective identities: far from definitively diverting the migratory desire towards other goals, the multiple obstacles placed in the way of its realisation only serve to fuel it and idealise it as a taboo that must be defied.

The Case of Lamya: An Externalised 'Dream'

Lamya, 40 years old, from Mellassine, Tunis, is a shopkeeper who is also a 'returning migrant' with whom I was able to talk. Her story also challenges the economic conception of immigration. The decision to immigrate to Europe came at the time when she was going through a divorce. Using a tourist visa, she travelled with her two children to France to escape a situation of social pressure and relationships that demeaned and stigmatised her new status as a divorcee.

This quest is inspired by a later experience of mobility, since Lamya used to work in the commerce business between Tunisia and Turkey, and thus mobility experiences are part of her personality, as is her openness to other cultures. This can be a valuable when trying to integrate in France. However, as in several other cases, my interviewee found herself confronted with the status of immigrant in the host country, and thus constrained her ability to act and emancipate herself. Lamya and her children were caught up in the bureaucratic systems of institutions in charge of organising the reception of asylum seekers and refugees on French soil: hospitalised because of her diabetes, anguished by this separation from her children, unable to find a regular job or housing as long as her immigrant status and legal situation were not settled, she was compelled to follow the vicious circle of police and social services designed for migrants. Threatened by the Obligation to Leave French Territory procedure, which follows the logic of the anti-migration fight adopted by the French government, Lamya accepted the French Office of Immigration and Integration's (OFII) proposal, which pushed her to choose a 'voluntary' departure. Without this, she wasn't able to return to Tunisia as she could not return without proving herself somehow. She thus took the offer of financial support from the immigration authorities as an opportunity to regain a symbolically acceptable status in her native society. The OFII had promised her financial aid and assistance to start a coffee shop project in an upscale neighbourhood in Tunisia. She accepted the offer of 70,000 Dinar (approximately 22,000 Euros). However, Lamya's testimony sheds light on the scars of believing this deception, and the regret of having accepted the seeming solution of 'voluntary' return.

Crying, Lamya told me how she was greeted by an OFII agent in Montpellier and how the agent asked her: 'What is your dream'? Stunned, she replied, 'you want to know my dream?! Is that really what you want to know? I dream of having a coffeeshop in El Menzah or El Nasr'. The agent replied, 'you'll eventually get everything you desire'. And for two hours, he sketched in front of her, on a large sheet of paper, the coffeeshop and gave an estimation of the construction expenses like a 'real architect of dreams'. Lamya believed him and signed the 'voluntary return' paper. Once back, she went through long and complex procedures that at best yielded small projects (often small businesses) unrelated to her experience and initial aspirations. Finally, after two long years of waiting, she received the mere sum of 5,000 Dinars to realise her dream project. She became part of an unprecedented discourse, a 'new trap' – 'voluntary return' – that creates new migration lies about the humanitarian West. She emphasised that she had been 'deceived' by the French migration authorities and the entire chain involved in the reception process in partnership with the OFII – she never received the promised sum. In this new situation, her precarious economic conditions are added to the stigmatisation and social control she already experiences in her home country. She adds that her neighbours and relatives had mocked her. On the one hand, she returned to Tunisia 'with nothing, empty-handed' and on the other hand, her neighbours thought that she was getting a pay-check from European organisations. She adds:

> When I leave my house, they think I am going to get money from the European associations. Several people in my neighbourhood wanted to leave for Europe and return voluntarily to take advantage of the promised aid like me. I am really devastated because I got nothing, and they [those in her neighbourhood] misunderstood me.

The Case of Fadel: Psychosis of Procedures

The different experiences described by here provide us with information about the anxieties and fears that accompany returning: the fear of 'falling back into the same situation that preceded the departure to Europe', to quote Fadel, another interviewee, who returned from Germany. This interviewee's itinerary illustrates the link between the voluntary acceptance of a return and structural constraints. If Fadel accepts and signs his 'voluntary' return to Tunisia, it is because a life of relentlessly harsh irregular migration makes returning to Tunisia seem acceptable again. Like many of his fellow Tunisian irregular migrants, as soon as he arrived in Europe, he joined drug-selling networks, one of the few economic activities easily accessible to people who are not allowed to work due to their status. In Germany, as soon as Fadel was arrested, he was identified by the authorities as an irregular immigrant to deport. For eleven years, he received official letters reminding him of the obligation to leave European territory. In prison, after being identified as Tunisian through collaboration between Tunisian and German authorities, he accepted his fate: deportation was inevitable. Resisting this decision would mean perpetuating his irregularity and risking prison. Thus, the choice to return is based on the reality of a life doomed by irregularity, prison time, delinquency, and shady economic activity. Their economic activity, though often shady, is usually in the service of Europeans, especially executives and the well-off.[2] This dimension of feeling like economically useful members of society, supports the claims and demands expressed by the migrants I met: they claim rights and call for compensation, which they believe they have legitimate right to. Fadel's account reveals the conditions of irregular existence that shapes the 'acceptance' of a forced return:

> It's true, when I arrived in Germany, I didn't find the image I was hoping for. I certainly found people who welcomed me. They were Tunisian friends. But their lives were difficult: they had irregular and illicit work. I had no choice but to join them, taking on the risk of further exposing myself to the police. I had other options, such as going to Italy or to a country other than Germany, but the problem remained the same: no one would help us with the paperwork, with finding housing and a job. I found myself with people who had spent 10, 15, 20 years in this irregular situation. In a nutshell, I found something other than what I expected. The reality was all about the scramble, the endless crossing from one country to another without being able to work in any other way but irregularly. During my time in the German jail, the authorities called on Tunisians whose job was to detect other Tunisians among the arrested migrants. They recognise us not only by our language, but also by appearance. The Tunisian authorities then authorised our return. I had no choice, I was so exhausted from witnessing the injustice, and I have witnessed many of my friends suffer the worst of injustices. It wears you out. I signed my return to Tunisia in prison.

Upon returning home, migrants talk about their new strangeness and feelings of alienation in a society that had undergone much transformation while they were away. Some emphasise the loss of former social networks, which means more obstacles to securing a job and a steady income. Others point to the loss of family members or simply the loss of their former role within the family unit, which exposes them to forms of isolation compared to life before migration. It is in this sense that the people I met are subjects damaged by the experience of immigration and 'voluntary return'. And it is for this reason that the issue of rehabilitation and assistance is a matter of rights. Fadel clearly explains

---

2   This makes it possible to understand the pain of the returnees, who emphasise in their interviews that the alienation is experienced on both sides of the Mediterranean: through the loss of the relationship with their home society (after their return) and through the suffering during their (illegal) work, which is not recognised in the immigration society.

why returning home requires care, support for reintegration, and reparation for a life spent in Europe, when regularisation has failed. He adds,

> I lived for 11 years in Europe, but when I returned to Tunisia, I realised that this period spent there was wasted: I have lost the contacts that could have helped me here. Besides my family that supports me, I don't have anybody that I can turn to for help or that I can rely on. Coming to terms with the fact that that all those years in Europe were in vain was the hardest part. Over there, the only problem was the risk. I managed my life well: I had a job, I earned money, and I even was able to send some to my family. Here, I will have to start all over again if I want to get by.

The first issue mentioned by the returnees is the lack of coordination and communication between the authorities of the European deportation countries and their Tunisian counterparts. When a migrant is sent back 'voluntarily', no effective reception mechanism is put in place to ensure a smooth transition and return. Fadel states:

> When I arrived at the airport in Tunisia, I was received in a humiliating manner by an authority officer who knew nothing about my previous life and allowed himself to insult and slap me. Another person on board of the same return flight as mine had lost all of his contacts in Tunisia. When he arrived, he did not even have the address of his own parents. It felt like being thrown in at the deep end. I was fortunate that my parents accepted me and took me back in. Sadly enough, this is not the case for everybody.

'A burdensome and oppressive bureaucracy' is the catchphrase used by the returnees to describe the financial assistance procedures offered by various stakeholders to help in the economic reintegration of the selected persons. Other testimonies overlap and underline the weight of bureaucracy involved in setting up projects, filling in applications, or obtaining quotes. Ayman emphasises:

> I was promised 5,000 Euros, but I had to chase that sum for three years. When I opened my store, I had to provide billing quotations. It took three years for a project that should have taken less than a month. They won't give me the money in cash or make the procedure any easier. I had to go back and forth between several offices and associations. Nobody wanted to assume any responsibility and I got lost in the hierarchy. Just not transparent who was in charge. I had gone through hell. It's the same pace as the Tunisian administration, if not worse. Why would a file take four months to finally be transferred between two offices located in the same building or the same street? I keep on telling them that I need a single contact instead of several people who refer me to other people. We are after all just numbers, files … . What's taking so long? We are talking about a small sum of money. Why all this sprawling bureaucracy? When I got stuck in this long process, I got distracted by what I could've done on my own or together with other people. I ended up chasing, for three years, a project and an administration that consumed all my time and energy.

Another major point revealed by the interviewees is their condemnation of the 'illusory project'. Although the returnees benefitted from small amounts of aid allowed by the migration schemes, they claim to have signed their acceptance of return only after being promised assistance in setting up successful, large-scale projects. But once they have returned, they find themselves entangled in long and complicated procedures that lead, in the best-case scenario, to small projects, often small-scale businesses, that are ill suited to their skills and experience, and don't meet their initial expectations. They all condemn the lack of information, and misinformation provided at the beginning of the 'voluntary return' procedure. Another migrant, Ahmed, interviewed in Tunis in 2020 described this situation as follows:

> I had signed up for my voluntary return following a promise of support to start a restaurant. I was told that I would be granted support to practice my profession as a chef. When I returned, I was offered funding that did not allow for anything compared to the promises at the beginning. The procedures took three years. I was invited to conferences and debates that I didn't understand. I had to attend and do what was asked of me so as not to miss out on the steps that I thought would lead to the promised help. Eventually I was fired from a job only because of a trip to attend a meeting in a hotel, which at the end didn't benefit me at all.

Conclusion

According to a manager of an Italian aid project supporting 'voluntary returns', the sum of 5,000 Euro allegedly dedicated to the returnees in fact covers payment for staff working in the programme (trainers, participation in seminars and meetings, etc.), while the returnee only receives the remainder. My research on those who participated in a 'voluntary' return scheme reveals, among other things, the way in which agencies and donors, in the context of neoliberalism, do entrap irregular migrants, and simultaneously reinforce policies that externalise borders.

The people I met suffered from mental health problems due to the conditions of their return to Tunisia, as well as their migration and family experiences. The feelings of isolation and alienation experienced by these immigrants is reinforced by the fact that the people surrounding them are not aware of their true return situation and of the experience of irregular migrants in Europe. In the interviews, these migrants stated that they did not receive any kind of psychological support from Tunisian or European government agencies. Nonetheless, they believe that there is a great need for moral support, for integration, and for the recognition of the mental suffering that manifests from their experiences and new lives in a society that is hostile to them upon their return. The people I encountered suffered from acute depression, feelings of isolation, and other illnesses. One of them emphasised that he needs therapy to deal with the dark thoughts that invade him as a result of his migration experience: unable to sleep regularly because of nightmares from his past life in Europe, he cannot get rid of them without space to reflect critically on the years of irregular migration. Another explains that she isolates herself because she does not feel understood by her relatives and neighbours. She is singled out, made to feel accountable, and constantly lives with a sense of guilt. She adds that she aims to find a space where she can meet people who have similar experiences, and a place where she can reflect on her experiences and be accepted and understood. The analysis of these three personal trajectories demonstrates how the phenomena of irregular immigration and 'voluntary return' of migrants are interwoven into the social and mental spaces (imagination, dreams, psychology) of Tunisians as a whole. The sheer scale of the phenomenon has a profound effect on social representations and mental patterns, requiring both general and specific thinking about policies for managing migration and the NGOs that work alongside migrants.

The case of the voluntary return migrants shows that if despair and hopelessness grip this group of people, the repercussions on society as a whole are imminent: the frustration of returning migrants is likely to amplify the feeling of hopelessness and the migratory lie that encourages other young people to risk their lives on the irregular and dangerous routes to Europe. The migratory myth can be summed up through a particular perception of Europe, as an idyllic earthly paradise that miraculously provides a solution to all the immigrant's problems (rent, work, documentation, status, dignity, etc.). This lie is fuelled by a discourse on Europe disseminated in the countries of origin by returnees. The migratory lie is a fantasy about Europe that is out of step with the real condition of immigrants. But when they return to their country of origin, instead of deconstructing this lie, immigrants simply reproduce and reinforce it. In the current political context of externalising borders, the lie is also externalised in the sense that the discourse on assisted or voluntary return could replace the migratory discourse on Europe. Given the fact that the promise of a better life is changing places, that the promise of Europe is moving to Tunisia, often enabled by NGOs, most of those who have integrated in voluntary return schemes find themselves caught in the trap of this lie.

The fear of deportation and the concern of being sent back, taped in a plane, reinforces the humiliation both of individuals and their country of origin. In fact, many *harraga* consider that the origin of this humiliation is rooted in the marginalised and alienated status of their country in the face of European tutelage, and the political accountability that the country of emigration (Tunisia) takes on. They believe that because they are not recognised or protected by their own country, European countries can justify their belittling treatment. This situation consolidates a racial hierarchy and in turn reinforces the urge to migrate. This desire is forged in the quest for power, far away from the country whose youth are being subjugated and humiliated by the Western superpower. In turn, the reasoning behind the policies of migratory repression express this desire to subjugate countries of origin. This situation is further politicised: it gives rise to a certain awareness of life in Tunisia in order to justify the act of illegal migration. The politics of hierarchy between Europe and Tunisia are reinforced at the time of deportation. The expelled migrants then experience a situation of externalised European violence. They are aware that these policies transform their own countries into 'guardians' and protectors of the European borders by repressing the local population. They are also aware that these policies are a continuation of existing internal police repression. In short, they return to the misery they have tried to escape on several occasions. As Tawfik has told us, the humiliation experienced in the homeland has an even more bitter taste than that endured from the European police.

Most stakeholders and researchers in the Western world or in the South of the Mediterranean advocate for the reintegration of irregular migrants in their host countries or countries of origin, yet very few examine the impact of the externalisation of borders and its mechanisms, such as the 'voluntary return' scheme, on people and on their daily lives. It is therefore important that researcher apply a qualitative framework, and use an epistemology of situational knowledge and ethnographic research, as an approach to forge a space for the voices and experiences of the victims of this scheme. It is about producing a kind of knowledge addressing marginalised populations, rather than only the dominant groups and their procedures of administration and management of minority groups.

Epilogue: Mobility and Racism in Sfax and Beyond

Khaoula Matri & Ann-Christin Zuntz

> In 2023/4, Khaoula Matri and Ann-Christin Zuntz both directed projects on migrant and refugee livelihoods, and migratory policies, in Tunisian cities, funded by the UK-based Maghreb Action on Displacement and Rights Network Plus. In this interview[1], they reflect on how the racist speech of Tunisian president Kais Saied on February, 21st, 2023, and the ensuing racist attacks in Sfax in summer 2023 changed migrants' situation, and impacted Dr Matri's fieldwork. Dr Matri also situates the events in Sfax in the broader context of high-profile visits of European politicians such as Giorgia Meloni and Tunisia's 2023 agreement with the European Union, through which Tunisia secured €105m to fight people smugglers and around €15m for humanitarian organisations to facilitate voluntary return of migrants.

Ann-Christin: Khaoula, I would like to start the interview with your field experience in Sfax in the summer of 2023 because it seems to me that it was a moment when things changed for migrants on the ground. Could you begin by telling us about what kind of local situation you found in the summer of 2023?

Khaoula: My first field visit to Sfax coincided with an important political event, namely the surprise visit of the President of the Republic, Kais Saied, to Sfax, which took place on June 10, 2023. This was a coincidence that allowed me to identify changes in several social areas and to document the gradual rise of tensions (Dahmani 2023). These tensions were reflected in the discourses of migrants, but also of Tunisians. Already in early June 2023, I noticed annoyance among the vendors and traders of the Bab Jebli market in the city centre. Dismay and disappointment were widespread. Nobody was satisfied: from the informal trade of the itinerant Tunisian street vendors to shop owners, the frustration was palpable. They expected a pragmatic and effective solution to what they called, among other things, the 'problems of the city of Sfax'. The urban question was central to their discourse: the question of pollution, the chaotic building in different corners of the city, the competition that some mobile vendors encounter (some say they were not able to sell on the pavements in the city centre), and the dirt everywhere, all of which were

---

1   The conversation took place over a video call on 8.11.2024; it was transcribed, the text reworked, edited for clarity and translated into English.

caused, in their eyes, by the presence of homeless[2] Sub-Saharan people. The occupation of the park's garden, located right next to the large market in Sfax, by Sudanese who had been living on the street for two or three months at the time, seemed to arouse the anger of consumers and shopkeepers alike. Female migrant vendors who spread their goods on the road were removed from the main street. The women were angry and felt humiliated by shop owners, passers-by, and potential customers.

The atmosphere was becoming more and more tense, and you could tell that everyone was frustrated and desperate for this visit. The Sub-Saharans were hoping for a solution or, at least, a change in their situation, while the inhabitants of Sfax were waiting for an answer to their concerns: the resolution of urban problems, pollution, the settlement of these migrants around the market, etc. In addition, Kais Saied's visit came just after that of Italian Prime Minister Giorgia Meloni and the President of the European Commission, Ursula von der Leyen.

At the beginning of July, riots broke out after the death of a young Tunisian boy from the neighbourhood, killed by three presumed Cameroonian migrants. The attack was filmed by a local deputy, who then broadcast it in real time, almost live. The action seemed to represent a form of implicit mobilisation for revenge; and the situation quickly escalated from a political act or political discourse to a full-blown crisis in local society.

What had happened in Tunis in February and early March 2023 (and to a lesser extent in other cities) was essentially reproduced in Sfax: a real hunt for migrants. Groups of young people assembled to chase migrants from their homes. These riots, particularly violent, seemed almost orchestrated, like a staging of violence. Police forces were there, but without adopting a clear position. After a few days, the police were content to monitor migrants present in the public square, especially around the large roundabout in Sfax and the public gardens near the Medina. This staging of violence also raises the question of the presence of Sub-Saharan migrants, who went from being invisible, particularly in the city, to being increasingly visible through the media and social networks. I had the impression that it was a well-arranged and structured staging. The police forces were present without really understanding their role. Some migrants left the city, while others chose to sleep on the street, in the main square, protecting each other. Those who could afford to leave, left the city, but those who did not have the resources or a social network preferred to stay put. There was great ambiguity at the time: some migrants were fleeing the city, while others continued to arrive from the Algerian or Libyan borders, heading directly to Sfax. The authorities monitored, even protected, those present in the public square, in a notable official silence. In addition, other actions reinforced deportations to the borders of neighbouring countries. There were difficulties for some in getting around, bus (*louage*) and taxi drivers were forbidden to take (irregular) migrants in their vehicles, etc.

The Sub-Saharan African students were more or less spared; they remained in the background of the situation. The majority of them preferred to avoid appearing publicly, and going out or mingling with 'illegals' and undocumented immigrants. This first phase

---

2   In French the word for 'homeless' is '*sans domicile fixe*' or of 'no fixed abode', which has a slightly different connotation than the English term.

lasted about two months, from July to the end of August and the beginning of September 2023.

I visited the city several times, at least four times, and the configuration of the large square in Sfax changed considerably. At times, the number of people occupying in the Place de Ribat, just in front of the large fountain of the Grand Rond-Point, increased, while at other times, it decreased. In short, the social landscape changed as the weeks went by. At the same time, on the road, there were always migrants preparing to cross the Mediterranean. With a bottle of water and a small bag, they walked on foot, heading towards the outer areas of the city. The testimonies of some migrants were very moving, because they had not expected such violence and hostility. At the same time, Tunisians keep telling them to leave their homes, even if they were in solidarity or did not oppose their presence, as they themselves were threatened, either by the police or by their neighbours.

Ann-Christin: At that time, how were you received as a researcher?

Khaoula: It wasn't easy, both emotionally and practically. On the one hand, I never approached the people present in the public square after the July riots. I walked around like a pedestrian, stopping most of the time to listen to discussions or exchange short conversations in front of businesses, as a citizen. My presence focused mainly on observations of places, of reactions, and I was particularly attentive to the temporalities of this unusual urban landscape: the different times of the day, then in the early evening, and sometimes late at night, etc., as well as the reconfiguration of this central urban space. Over a few months there was a cycle of a rise in hostility, followed by fairly upfront tensions, then a relaxation, and the cycle began again. But at a certain point, some regulars of the city, in this case Sub-Saharan Africans, managed to reorganise their lives. We can adapt even in chaos, in the sense of developing means of survival with the means at hand. Of course, they had been evicted from their homes and lost all their (relatively modest) possessions and money, but for example, those who maintained friendly relations with Tunisians had the opportunity to go and shower at a local's home, then return to the public square, look for something to eat and then come back. Those who could afford it could sit in nearby cafes and restaurants, despite the spatial segregation, to shelter from the scorching sun, take a nap (discreetly) and charge their mobile phones, before this was banned. Others were able to find work during the day to earn a small income and spent the night on the street.

While the situation in the main square, which was highly covered in the international media and on social media, continued, there were also the peripheries, a little away from this media and political over-visibility. In the olive groves and on the outskirts of the working-class neighbourhoods, some Sub-Saharan Africans avoided being seen. On two occasions, I visited a group of about fifty people, including seven women and three children, without asking them any questions, but simply accompanying a trusted person who knew most of them. These people had nowhere to go and preferred to stay away in the olive groves, not far from a well where they could access water.

Another important aspect of this period, in July 2023, was the introduction of restrictions on money transfers. No one could withdraw money without a valid passport and a three-month visa. Moreover, a poster, present in all Tunisian Post offices, indicated that it was necessary to present a valid passport for any withdrawal of money.

I avoided mixing with other professionals, even though there were a lot of experts, journalists, and humanitarian workers on the ground. I have forgotten the exact day, but during a visit – I think at the beginning of August – there were already delegates from the embassy of Burkina Faso. The scene was almost surreal: on one side, people were sleeping on the streets on cardboard boxes, and on the other, people in neat clothes – either from the IOM [International Organization for Migration] or diplomatic delegations – were discussing and observing the situation. Simultaneously, journalists were omnipresent, which further politicised and complicated the situation. This politicisation may have contributed to transforming the image of Sfax, representing it as a more accessible departure spot for migrants. The information was circulating so quickly that other migrants may have interpreted it as an opportunity to speed up their entry into Tunisia and attempt the crossing of the Mediterranean. In other words, the information was perceived and interpreted in different ways. For example, narratives about deportations at the Algerian and Libyan borders served as a catalyst, influencing migrants' decisions and trajectories.[3]

All of this seems contradictory. Sfax seemed to be both a city where the maximum number of migrants were pushed back and, paradoxically, a point of attraction for those hoping to cross the Mediterranean to reach Lampedusa.[4] This contradiction is one of the effects of the politicisation of the migration situation in the city. On the one hand, organizations such as the Red Crescent were present, distributing meals, sandwiches, juice, and water to the people there. On the other hand, a parallel trade developed around the main square of Sfax. For example, some nearby restaurants served daytime meals only to locals and North Africans, for the most part. But in the evening, these same restaurants were more frequented by Sub-Saharan migrants than by the city's population. There was thus a form of 'appropriation' of the urban space. During the day, migrants were scattered everywhere, seeking shade around buildings. But at nightfall, the city centre in front of the Medina belonged to them in a way, since it was almost deserted by other pedestrians.

There was a very striking contrast. At night, the density of the migrants' presence was particularly visible, but their range of circulation narrowed considerably. In the evening, there were almost no migrants, especially men, outside a small space around the public square, extending no more than 150 to 200 meters. The women, on the other hand, remained grouped together in a smaller corner of the square. During the day, on the other hand, their presence was more diffuse: they were found in the vicinity of the market, behind the Ribat, in the small gardens of the surrounding neighbourhoods, etc. At night, the police presence was more marked, not only to protect the migrants, but also to avoid any confrontation, as several clashes had already taken place there.

---

3   Tunisia regularly deports migrants to the Libyan and Algerian borders. In 2024, mass expulsions into the desert continued: By March, 28th, 2024 a total of 8,664 people had been intercepted at the Tunisian-Libyan border (Al-Jazeera 2023; ARD Mediathek 2024).

4   Lampedusa is an island halfway between Tunisia and the Italian mainland, belonging to Italy, and a common landing point for Mediterranean crossings.

There was a real staging of violence, characterised by rejection and relentlessness, justified by the need to 'defend the city' against what was perceived as an 'invasion'. A discourse was circulating that these migrants 'have no morals, respect nothing, and are a threat to women'. They were considered a danger, and they had to be attacked in the name of 'honour, dignity and even virility'. It was under this banner that many young people mobilized to 'restore order'.

In this context, the Tunisian president's visit was seen as a form of state disengagement. In the absence of a clear response from the authorities, some felt that it was up to them to impose social order themselves. The authorities might have consciously played on this dynamic. It was only after the violence in Sfax that we understood that this staging might have been a negotiation strategy of the Tunisian government, targeted especially at the Italians.

Ann-Christin: Just to come back a little more to the broader context of 2023. There was the famous hate speech of Said in February 2023 (Le Monde 2023; cf. Parikh, this volume). Would you agree that this marked a turning point in Tunisia's migration policy?

Khaoula: The speech marked a turning point in the management of the Sub-Saharan African presence inisia. Indeed, all previous governments, including that of Hichem Mechichi, had adopted a *laissez-faire* approach, avoiding openly addressing this issue and seeking to manage it without making it a real political issue or a social problem that occupied public opinion. Kais Saied is the first president of the Republic to have openly raised this issue. However, by the end of 2022, Sofien Ben Sghaïer, president of the Tunisian Nationalist Party, had already launched a media campaign against Sub-Saharans. This campaign benefited, among others, Kais Saied, who took up certain elements of this nationalist and xenophobic discourse against migrants' presence. In addition, this rhetoric was instrumentalised by some deputies, especially those representing the city of Sfax. Among them is Fatma Mseddi, who continues to mobilise the inhabitants of Sfax against migrants and calls for their repatriation, as well as another member of parliament who filmed the murder scene. These events marked the beginning of a new phase in the management of Sub-Saharan African migration in Tunisia.

Ann-Christin: You might have had the opportunity to read the article by Cassarini/Geisser (2023) who argue that Saied's speech also marked a transition to a new form of identity populism. How much did Saied's speech transform politics in Tunisia beyond the management of migration?

Khaoula: The discourse itself initiated a new phase, legitimised by an emotional and reactive activation of national identity. The speech was also based on themes related to state security, conspiracy theories, and law enforcement. Afterwards, he tried to qualify his remarks by adopting a more conciliatory tone: '*Africans are our brothers, I love Africans, Tunisia belongs to Africa, etc.*' But in practice, [the speech] largely fuelled an identity-based populism with the aim of strengthening his legitimacy and mobilising the population against the presence of Sub-Saharan African migrants. This issue has thus been transformed into a societal problem, a topic of public discussion and worry, and supported by some parts of society. To properly exploit this 'problem', it was 'necessary' to activate the collective imagination by playing the identity card. It can be read as a calculated strategy to evoke the Arab-Muslim identity in this specific context. But behind this discourse was a broader agenda, particularly in connection with the agreements with Italy and the European Union on the management of migration flows.

Ann-Christin: So far, we have talked a lot about the Tunisian government, but this also happens in the context of European externalisation policies. Have the latter also entered a new phase?

Khaoula: Yes, we could say that the summer of 2023 was a phase of negotiation, especially in the relations between Italy and Tunisia, in connection with the externalisation of European borders. The figures show that during the summer of 2023, departures from the Tunisian coast were particularly high. However, in the summer of 2024, this rate dropped drastically. This data does not come from the Tunisian authorities, but from the Italian Ministry of the Interior. During my field study in Lampedusa in 2024, all local actors confirmed a significant decrease in arrivals compared to the previous year. While they were overwhelmed by migratory flows in 2023, the summer of 2024 marked a clear reduction in the number of arrivals on the island. This is obviously linked to the agreement reached with Giorgia Meloni in April 2024 [to curb migration to Italy in exchange for hundreds of millions of Euro], a politically successful deal for both leaders.

However, from the point of view of living conditions, the situation of migrants has deteriorated considerably. In Sfax, forced displacement of migrants took place in early September 2023, just before the start of the school year. Buses were used to evacuate them to nearby villages such as El Amra and Jebeniana. Those who remained or continued to arrive no longer headed for downtown Sfax but for these rural areas, where resources are limited and political representation is almost non-existent. Thus, the management of the 'migration issue' has taken a new form: in Sfax, under pressure from the locals, the authorities preferred to shift the problem rather than solve it. After a few months, the issue gradually disappeared from the media, resurfacing only occasionally and episodically.

Ann-Christin: So, is this the end of the migration spectacle in Sfax [that you described earlier]?

Khaoula: The end of the spectacle that returns. The great urban staging has come to an end, but the tensions have not dissipated. Clashes continued to break out between the National Guard and some Sub-Saharan African migrants, including when the security forces entered the olive groves to displace them, going so far as to burn their makeshift tents and rob them. New red lines have been drawn. Those who travel on the main road to these villages risk being turned back.

The city of Sfax has seen increased militarisation. After September 2023, the presence of Black migrants in the neighbourhoods decreased: they were gradually erased from the urban streets. During a field trip between the end of January and the beginning of February 2024, I went to the olive groves, accompanied by a trusted person. I met many migrants there, organised in small groups.

During these informal exchanges, none of them mentioned having experienced racism from the villagers. The majority of them organised collectively to survive. Among them, some Sudanese held refugee cards. There were migrants of various nationalities. They grouped together mainly according to their linguistic and ethnic communities, forming improvised networks of solidarity in these remote areas.

Ann-Christin: Were the UN Refugee Agency (UNHCR) and the International Organization for Migration (IOM) present on the ground?

Khaoula: UNHCR was noticeably absent from the field, and this absence was often criticised. During an exchange with a Sudanese man who has a doctorate in law, he showed me his certificate and sent it to me later on WhatsApp to testify about his journey:

> I was in Libya, I tried to cross the Mediterranean, but I failed. I was caught and sent away. Then I was in the south of Tunisia under the protection of the UNHCR, but they did nothing for me. Now I'm here only to attempt the crossing. UNHCR is doing nothing for the Sudanese. We contest our situation, but it's useless.

He was carrying his refugee card, a valuable document in his eyes, but which had no real administrative value. Unlike UNHCR, the IOM was present on the ground, as it was one of the only agencies able to identify and register migrants. In January 2024, I was told that more than 2,000 people had been identified in these areas, and IOM was distributing blankets, hygiene kits, and, occasionally, food. On the ground, I was able to observe that most of the migrants had blankets and kits bearing the logos of UNHCR and IOM. However, aid remained insufficient. At first, relations with the inhabitants of El Amra [the village near the olive groves] were relatively peaceful. A certain hospitality was evident, especially in the form of access to drinking water and electricity: some villagers allowed migrants to charge their phones or stock up on food items along the main road. One particular case struck me: that of an Ivorian woman who had arrived at the end of August (2023) after a long journey through Morocco, Algeria, and Tunisia. She knew exactly where to go and had settled directly in the olive groves. According to her, the inhabitants of the village were 'very welcoming':

> We, the migrants, can access water, there are some inhabitants who allow us to charge our phones, when we go out on the main road to buy food. There are even teenagers who have told us that there were plainclothes policemen approaching, and that we had to flee.

However, despite this local mutual assistance, the situation of migrants remains precarious, marked by uncertainty and the absence of real institutional solutions.

Ann-Christin: Are we talking about hundreds of people or thousands, and are there proper 'camps'?

Khaoula: As far as I know, it was a few thousand migrants. It all depends on what you mean by 'camp'. I took a few photos, without wanting to document everything, but they do show the presence of several makeshift tents set up by the migrants. A Sub-Saharan African, who had helped IOM distribute supplies, told me that at least 1,500 kits had been distributed and that other makeshift camps existed nearby. The Tunisian authorities have gradually restricted the space occupied by these migrants, both to better control them and to redefine borders within the city itself. This concentration of migrants also facilitated the logistical management of humanitarian aid distributed by IOM and the Red Crescent, which operated under the supervision of the Tunisian Ministry of Interior. But beyond the humanitarian aspect, this grouping also allowed for increased control. The camps were about a kilometre or less from the main road. All entrances and exits to the village were under surveillance. During my travels, by taking several roads to access it, I could see that each access point was controlled. It is also known that Italy has provided equipment and logistical support to the Tunisian authorities, thus strengthening the means of surveillance and control of these migrant populations.

Ann-Christin: At the time of our interview [in November 2024], are these people still here?

Khaoula: Yes, indeed. There was a turning point a few months ago, as the people of El Amra felt neglected and ignored, which created growing tensions, especially as the presence of Sub-Saharan migrants increased. The situation has started to spill over, and what was a purely local issue has taken on a wider dimension, not least because of the increased interceptions at the borders, especially at sea, but also at the border with Algeria, where arrivals continue. Previously, many locals temporarily employed migrants for tasks like picking olives, but the pressure of public opinion to avoid aiding migrants also took its toll. Last year around the same time, some migrants moved secretly at night, often by back routes, to escape the authorities and find temporary work – it is hard to say yet if the situation will be the same this year. Women worked as domestic servants, young men on construction sites or in the olive harvest. This allowed them to earn some money, but these opportunities have disappeared because of new movement restrictions. Bans on working, housing or renting houses, and restrictions on migrants' movement, have intensified frictions between migrants and villagers. The media discourse, fuelled by social media, has taken a vicious turn, mobilising the local inhabitants against Sub-Saharan African migrants. On Facebook pages, there were viral messages such as:

> No to the settlement of Sub-Saharan Africans in Tunisia, no to the presence of Sub-Saharan Africans, no to the externalization of European borders in Tunisia.

This is often accompanied by accusations of food theft, violent assaults, and internal conflicts among migrants. This discourse has been politicised and further amplified, in particular with the support of some members of parliament, who have taken up exclusion discourses on violence and migratory invasion. Public authorities have put in place new constraints and practices, and these positions have been widely shared on social media. Part of the local population, particularly through online mobilisation, has reinforced this opposition to the presence of migrants.

Ann-Christin: If I can just come back to the question of local authorities: we have seen that for a few years now, there have been municipalities in Sousse, Ariana and Tunis that have pursued a slightly more participatory approach with migrants, and they have also received European funding to do this. But you just said that there are also new constraints for local actors. What is the power of municipalities?

Khaoula: May 2024 was a watershed moment with increased criminalisation of the illegal presence of migrants. The discourse changed dramatically: instead of simply controlling migration flows, the Tunisian state intensified repressive measures, targeting not only the migrants themselves, but also the actors who support them. The authorities targeted those in the public administration or in civil society who were perceived to facilitate or support the integration of migrants. This has led to notable arrests, such as that of the former mayor of Sousse, who was arrested and interrogated. Similarly, the president and secretary general of the Tunisian Council for Refugees were arrested. The atmosphere has become increasingly tense, with associative actors under pressure. For example, an executive director of an organization called Afrique Intelligence, a Cameroonian, was forced to urgently flee to escape prosecution. The arrests of Sherifa Riahi, the former director of Terre d'Asile Tunisie, and Saadia Mosbah, the president of the Mnemty Association, also illustrate this repression. NGO and humanitarian actors who work for the rights of migrants are now being targeted, and it does not seem that any of these actors are safe. As a result, a climate of fear has been established, where all those who support migrants, directly or indirectly, find themselves threatened by authorities that are increasingly firm and determined to eradicate any form of solidarity with migrants.

Ann-Christin: Is it still possible to do academic research on immigration? Do researchers feel under the same threats?

Khaoula: My field strategy of being invisible and avoiding the authorities was essential for my research. This allowed me to have more relaxed and natural conversations with my interlocutors and to escape the surveillance of public authorities. In some cases, by simply presenting myself as a local, I was able to conduct my observations without arousing suspicion. Even in situations where repression was present, I managed to maintain a certain distance while obtaining relevant information. However, conditions have clearly changed, and the situation has become more complex from 2024 onwards. With the intensification of repression and increased surveillance, it has become more difficult for me to continue my work on the ground in a safe manner. Migrants in Sfax, especially those with whom I used to be in contact, are now almost immobile, threatened, and unable to leave their neighbourhoods. The repression has therefore not only reduced their mobility, but also increased their vulnerability.

Cases of ransacked houses, direct threats, and arrests of foreign journalists testify to the worsening situation and the climate of fear that is spreading. But from a distance, I continue to follow the movements of some migrants, which shows that despite the repression, some are still trying to find alternative options to living in these conditions. The situation in Zarzis, from where some migrant women are moving to El Amra, highlights the increasingly difficult conditions: the lack of work, especially during the winter months, the reluctance of landlords to rent their homes to migrants, and pressure from the authorities. This phenomenon in Zarzis, which seems to reproduce what happened in Sfax, shows that the situation is systematically problematic. The general conviction among migrants, despite their suffering, is that they are in a temporary situation, but the trap in which they find themselves seems to make any exit from the crisis increasingly uncertain. Migrants find themselves in a double-bind, with hopes of leaving but also increasing restrictions and threats where they are.

Ann-Christin: You had mentioned before that there are other groups of foreigners such as Syrians who were not affected by the current anti-immigration climate. How do you explain that there are Syrians, Libyans, other North Africans who haven't really experienced discrimination and racism in such a way?

Khaoula: The first form of discrimination observed is clearly racial, and it manifests itself mainly in facial identification. During our survey, we conducted interviews with Tunisians to understand their perception of hospitality, views on Sub-Saharan Africans, migration in general, and the presence of Sub-Saharan Africans in particular. We found that black Tunisians were arrested during police checks (in times of tension), in shared taxis, or on the street, simply because they were perceived as Sub-Saharan Africans. Some Tunisians said they felt compelled to say they were Tunisians to escape racial discrimination, verbal and physical assault, and intimidation. This phenomenon is accompanied by a normative discourse that legitimises xenophobia and negrophobia, a discourse that we do not see manifesting itself in the same way towards Syrians, Libyans, or Algerians ('supremacy' of whiteness). These groups, although foreign, share identity traits with Tunisians, such as skin colour or cultural elements, which allows them to benefit from different treatment than Sub-Saharan Africans, who are stigmatised and excluded by political actors and the media.

Syrians and Libyans enjoy particular acceptance because of their common language, Arabic, and their supposed Islamic beliefs. As far as Syrians are concerned, there is a certain solidarity that is based partly on what is happening in their country, but also on social and cultural proximity. They are perceived as close to 'us', almost as part of 'our own' sphere, in the sense of identity. Tunisians are familiar with their artistic production, such as soap operas, films, artistic figures, and even music. This makes 'them' more acceptable, unlike Sub-Saharan Africans, who are perceived as foreigners, with notable cultural and social differences. Algerians and Libyans, on the other hand, are seen as close neighbours, temporarily present for specific reasons, and part of more privileged social categories, such as the middle or upper middle class. The majority of Libyans residing in Tunisia, for example, can afford to rent houses, frequent quality hotels, tea rooms, restaurants, and entertainment spaces, thus contributing to the local economy. They can be seen in hospitals, private clinics, and sometimes in the education and service sector. Algerians, although they come mainly during the summer season, also stay at hotels and contribute to the economy as consumers. There is a certain familiarity with them thanks to informal trade, especially around smuggling and cheaper products (cf. Amri; Shâfi'i, both this volume), as well as close geopolitical ties, which have always been maintained smoothly by the Tunisian authorities.

As for Libya and Algeria, the question of their impact on the migration situation has never really been addressed by the Tunisian authorities. For example, even though the Tunisian president may have expressed concerns, he has never directly criticised neighbouring authorities. Rather, it is a logic of cooperation that reigns. Ultimately, the general rule is that the poorest, the most vulnerable, especially Sub-Saharan Africans, are the ones under the greatest pressure. That said, the Tunisian climate towards Sub-Saharan Africans mirrors the attitude towards Tunisians and North Africans in European countries.

Ann-Christin: Everything you've said is fascinating. We have to understand that this is not just a question of European pressure, there are also political dynamics that are internal to Tunisia and the region.

Khaoula: I am very critical of Europe's hypocrisy. We talk all the time about human rights, asylum, and refugee protection, but we turn a blind eye to certain crises. Take Sudan, for example: a civil war that is ravaging the country, hundreds of thousands, even a few million displaced, but it is one of the least publicised and least prioritised wars for international NGOs and agencies like UNHCR. Why? Because it does not directly threaten Europe. The UNHCR has even stopped registering new asylum seekers from Sudan since June 2024, which means that thousands of people fleeing the war can no longer access recognition of their refugee status. This is not mere negligence; it is a deliberate policy. Europe does not want to manage these flows of refugees and outsources the management of migration to countries such as Tunisia, providing it with equipment, funding, and even political legitimation to ramp up the repression against migrants.

Ann-Christin: And why is that?

Khaoula: The European hypocrisy is blatant, and Italy is a glaring example of this. They have signed agreements with Libyan militias, knowing full well what happens in detention centres in Libya: torture, slavery, human trafficking. It's common knowledge. NGO reports, journalistic investigations, testimonies from migrants – everything is documented. The same is true of Tunisia. The deportations to the desert, the racist violence, the deaths at the borders… It's no secret. It has been filmed, mediatised. Yet, Europe continues to finance these policies, to sign agreements, such as the July 2023 Memorandum, just to calm the European far right. They no longer even try to hide this strategy. What matters is preventing migrants from arriving, no matter the human cost. And then there is Palestine. The war is spreading to Lebanon, and Europe, which claims to defend human rights, all the while actively supports a brutal occupation. Double standards. We protect Ukrainians (and rightly so), but the Sudanese, the Palestinians, the Sub-Saharan Africans? Nothing.

What is new and perhaps interesting is that the issue of externalisation of borders is no longer just a scientific or political concept (cf. Medien; Sha'ath, both this volume). In Tunisia, more and more people are talking about it, understanding what it means: that their country has become a barrier for Europe, a bulwark against migrants, to the detriment of human rights and even their own sovereignty. People are beginning to say that we are subject to Italy's injunctions, that we have become the guardians of the Italian border. We are powerless in the face of this European power. That is to say, as long as there is an asymmetry in the balance of power, it is impossible to analyse the situation in Tunisia without placing it in a broader framework (Garnaoui, this volume). This includes the country's internal problems, the return to populist authoritarianism and the growing threat to civil society. We cannot understand these dynamics without considering them in the context of the externalisation of borders and the relationship of dependence between the countries of North Africa and the European Union.

Ann-Christin: This might be a perfect conclusion to the interview. It was very interesting, is there anything else you wanted to highlight?

Khaoula: I would like to come back to immobility and mobility, as well as the inequalities related to it. These dynamics can be observed at several levels. We have seen the hardening of European borders and the way in which Tunisia has reproduced them in the space of a year and a half. This perfectly illustrates the unequal power relations at play, and demonstrates that mobility is not an acquired right for all citizens of the world. This is becoming more and more evident, even in the most mundane conversations between Tunisians and in their interactions with European foreigners. This is what makes hierarchical relationships and power asymmetries even more visible and striking in everyday life.

Appendix

References

Abidi, J. (2021): Political and Economic Choices in Tunisia Hamper Regional Job Creation. Tunis: Tunisian Observatory of Economy. (https://www.economie-tunisie.org/en/observatory/political-and-economic-choices-tunisia-hamper-regional-job-creation).

Abu-Rish, Z. (2015): Garbage Politics. Middle East Report, 277. (https://merip.org/2016/03/garbage-politics/).

Adams, P. & Minson, J. (1978): The 'Subject' of Feminism. m/f a feminist journal 2, 43–61.

Agence de Réhabilitation et de Rénovation Urbaine (ARRU) (2022): Rapport d'Exécution du PRIQH1. Tunis.

Ahmed, S. (2002): Racialized Bodies. In: M. Evans & E. Lee (eds.): Real Bodies: A Sociological Introduction. London: Macmillan, 46–63.

Al Jazeera (2023): Tunisian Minister Denies Expulsion of Black Refugees. (Film). (https://www.aljazeera.com/news/2023/8/4/tunisian-minister-denies-expulsion-of-black-refugees).

Alami, I. (2021): Global Finance Capital and Third World Debt. In: I. Ness & Z. Cope (eds.): The Palgrave Encyclopaedia of Imperialism and Anti-Imperialism. Cham: Springer, 1050–1068. (https://doi.org/10.1007/978-3-030-29901-9_123).

Allal. A. (2010): Les Configurations Développementistes Internationales au Maroc et en Tunisie: Des 'Policy Transfers' à Portée Limitée. Critique internationale 3, 48, 97–116. (http://www.cairn.info/revue-critique-internationale-2010-3-page-97.html).

Allal, A. (2011): Avant on Tenait le Mur, Maintenant on Tient le Quartier! Politique Africaine 1, 53–67.

Allal, A. (2016): Retour vers le Futur: Les Origines Économiques de la Révolution Tunisienne. Pouvoirs 156, 1, 17–29. (https://doi.org/10.3917/pouv.156.0017).

Allal, A. & Bennafla, K. (2011). Les Mouvements Protestataires de Gafsa (Tunisie) et Sidi Ifni (Maroc) de 2005 à 2009. Des Mobilisations en Faveur du Réengagement de l'État ou Contre l'Ordre Politique ? Revue Tiers Monde, 5, 27–45. (https://doi.org/10.3917/rtm.hs01.0027).

Allix, E. & Florin, B. (2016): Indésirables dans la Ville, Utiles dans l'Ordure? Géographie et Cultures 98, 1–30. (https://doi.org/10.4000/gc.4434).

Amara-Fadhel, E., Ben Moussa-Jerbi, A., & Hendaoui-Ben Tanfous, F. (2020): La Municipalité Tunisienne. À Nouveaux Enjeux, Nouveaux Contre-Pouvoirs! Recherche et Cas en Sciences de Gestion 18, 2, 85–105. (https://doi.org/10.3917/rcsg.018.0085).

Amnesty International (2022): Tunisie. L'Adoption de la Nouvelle Constitution ne doit pas Entériner l'Érosion des Droits Humains. Déclaration Publique – Amnesty International, 19 Août. (https://www.amnesty.org/fr/wpcontent/uploads/sites/8/2022/08/MDE3059252022FRENCH.pdf).

Amri, M. (2023): Inflation as Talk, Economy as Feel: Notes Towards an Anthropology of Inflation. Anthropology of the Middle East 18, 2, 27–45. (https://doi.org/10.3167/ame.2023.180203).

Amri, Myriam (2025): Cash Country: A Revolutionary Biography of the Tunisian Dinar. PhD, Harvard University. Boston.

Anderson, B. (1983): Imagined Communities. Reflections on the Origin and Spread of Nationalism. London: Verso.

Anderson, B. (2019) New Directions in Migration Studies: Towards Methodological De-nationalism. Comparative Migration Studies 7, 1, 1–13.

Aouani, I., Giraudet, M. & van Moorsel, J. (2020): Urban Mixed Migration – Tunis Case Study. Mixed Migration Centre Briefing Paper. (http://www.mixedmigration.org/resource/urban-case-study-tunis/).

Appadurai, A. (1996): Modernity at Large. Cultural Dimensions of Globalization. Minneapolis: University of Minnesota Press.

Appadurai, A. (2004): The Capacity to Aspire: Culture and the Terms of Recognition. In: V. Rao, & M. Walton (eds.). Culture and Public Action. Palo Alto: Stanford University Press 59–84.

Appel, H. (2017): Toward an Ethnography of the National Economy. Cultural Anthropology 32, 2, 294–322. (https://doi.org/10.14506/ca32.2.09).

Appel, H. (2019): The Licit Life of Capitalism: US Oil in Equatorial Guinea. Durham London: Duke University Press.

ARD Mediathek (2024): Ausgesetzt in der Wüste. Europas tödliche Flüchtlingspolitik. (Film). (https://www.ardmediathek.de/film/ausgesetzt-in-der-wueste-europas-toedliche-fluechtlingspolitik/Y3JpZDovL2JyLmRlL2Jyb2FkY2FzdFNlcmllcy84YmUzMmM4NC1jMDQ5LTRjNDUtODAzYy00Mjc5ZGQyZGZmYWNfc2luZ2xlc2hvdw).

Arefin, M. (2019): Infrastructural Discontent in the Sanitary City: Waste, Revolt, and Repression in Cairo. Antipode 51, 4, 1057–78.

Arsan, A. (2018): Lebanon. A Country in Fragments. London: C. Hurst & Co.

Asima Tunis (2022): Strategic Planning and Multilevel Governance for a Resilient Metropolitan City. (https://medcities.org/project/asima-tunis-strategic-plan-of-tunis-7/).

Assaad, M. & Garas, N. (1993/94): Experiments in Community Development in a Zabbaleen Settlement. Cairo Papers in Social Sciences 16, 4. Cairo: American University of Cairo Press.

Assaad, R., Ghazouani, S. & Krafft, C. (2017): The Composition of Labour Supply and Unemployment in Tunisia (Working Paper 1150). Cairo: The Economic Research Forum.

Atwood, B. (2019): A City by the Sea: Uncovering Beirut's Media Waste. Communication Culture & Critique 12, 53–71.

Audano, E. (2023): Klassenzugehörigkeit in Tunesien. Die urbanen Mittelklassen nach 2011. (Class Affiliation in Tunisia. The Urban Middle-classes after 2011). PhD, Institute of Geography, Leipzig University. Leipzig.

Ayadi, W. (2021): Étudiants Subsahariens: Pourquoi sont-ils Moins Nombreux en Tunisie? Gnet news. (https://news.gnet.tn/les-etudiants-subsahariens-desertent-la-tunisie/).

Ayeb, H. (2011): Social and Political Geography of the Tunisian Revolution: The Alfa Grass Revolution. Review of African Political Economy 38, 129, 467–79. (https://doi.org/10.1080/03056244.2011.604250).

Ayeb, H. (2012): The Marginalization of Small Peasantry: Egypt and Tunisia. In: R. Bush & H. Ayeb (eds.): Marginality and Exclusion. Cairo: AUC Press 72–96.

Ayeb, H. & Bush, R. (2019): Food Insecurity and Revolution in the Middle East and North Africa: Agrarian Questions in Egypt and Tunisia. London and New York: Anthem Press.

Ayimpam, S. (2014): Économie de la Débrouille à Kinshasa. Informalité, Commerce et Réseaux Sociaux. Paris: Karthala.

Baccouche. I. (2018): L'Insertion Professionnelle des Diplômés de l'Enseignement Supérieur en Tunisie: Cas de Deux Écoles Supérieures de Sfax. International Journal of Management & Marketing Research 2, 165–173.

Bacha, H. B. O. & Legros, O. (2015): Introduction. Politiques Urbaines et Inégalités en Méditerranée. Les Cahiers d'EMAM – Études sur le Monde Arabes et la Méditerranée, 27. (https://journals.openedition.org/emam/1077).

Badalič, V. (2019): Tunisia's Role in the EU External Migration Policy: Immigration Law, Illegal Practices, and Their Impact on Human Rights. Journal of International Migration and Integration 20, 1, 85–100.

Bakari. S. (2015): The Issue of Unemployment of Young Graduates in Tunisia: Evolution, Limits, and Prospects (1990–2014). Munich Personal Archives.

Baker, L. M. (2022): The Sanitization of Garbage Politics: A Case for Studying Waste at the Local, State, and International Politics in the Mena. In: J. Sowers & M. Lynch (eds.): Environmental Politics in the Middle East and North Africa. 53–59. (https://pomeps.org/the-sanitization-of-garbage-politics-a-case-for-studying-waste-at-the-local-state-and-international-politics-in-the-mena).

Bamyeh, M. (2009): Anarchy as Order. The History and Future of Civic Humanity. Lanham: Rowman & Littlefield.

Bardawil, F. A. (ed.) (2020): Revolution and Disenchantment: Arab Marxism and the Binds of Emancipation. Durham: Duke University Press. (https://doi.org/10.1215/9781478007586).

Barthel, P.-A. (2008): Faire du «Grand Projet» au Maghreb. L'Exemple des Fronts d'Eau (Casablanca et Tunis). Géocarrefour – Revue de Géographie de Lyon 83, 1, 25–34.

Bauder, H. (2019): Urban Sanctuary and Solidarity in a Global Context: How Does Africa Contribute to the Debate? (MIASA Working Paper 1). Accra: University of Ghana.

Bayat, A. (2010): Life as Politics. How Ordinary People Change the Middle East. Stanford: Stanford University Press.

Bechir, R. (2018): The Tunisian Revolution and the Role of Regional Development Disparities in Its Outbreak. Contemporary Arab Affairs 11, 3, 69–84.

Behrends, A. (2024): Lifeworlds in Crisis. Making Refugees in the Chad-Sudan Borderlands. London: Hurst & Company.

Belhedi, A. (1999): Les Disparités Spatiales en Tunisie, État des Lieux et Enjeux Méditerranée. Persée-Portail des Revues Scientifiques 91, 1, 63–72.

Belmessous, F. & Roche, E. (2018): Accueillir, Insérer, Intégrer les Migrants à la Ville. Espaces et Sociétés 172–173, 1, 7–18.

Ben Achour, S. (2019): La Tunisie, une Terre d'Accueil pour les Réfugiés? In: S. Mazzella & D. Perrin (eds.): Frontières, Sociétés et Droit en Mouvement. Brussels: Éditions Bruyant, 221–244.

Ben Achour, S. & Ben Jemia, M. (2014): Plaidoyer pour une Réforme des Lois Relatives aux Migrants, aux Étrangers et à la Nationalité en Tunisie. (Euro-Mediterranean Human Rights Network, REMDH et Center of Tunisia for Migration and Asylum, CeTuMA). Sousse: Wink'ART 52.

Ben Amor. M. (2012): Le Chômage des Jeunes: Déterminants et Caractéristiques. Notes et Analyses de l'ITCEQ 5. Tunis: Institut Tunisien de la Compétitivité et des Études Quantitatives (ITCEQ). (www.itceq.tn).

Bendana, K. (2017): Parler en Historienne après 2011: Textes 2012–2016. (Série Recherches). Tunis: Publications Universitaires de la Manouba.

Bennholdt-Thomsen, V. (1984): Towards a Theory of the Sexual Division of Labor. In: J. Smith, I. Wallerstein and H.-D. Evers (eds.): Households and the World Economy, 252–271.

Ben Hadj Hassan, A. (2024): Travailleuses Subsahariennes en Tunisie après 2011. Tunis: Nirvana.

Ben Jelili, R. (2023): Is Tunisia's Democracy on its Deathbed? Social Capital, Economic Insecurity, Middle Class and Attitudes Toward Democracy. Cairo: Economic Research Forum. (https://hal.science/hal-04315628/document).

Ben Rouine, C. (2022): Economic Decolonisation and the Role of the Central Bank in Postcolonial Development in Tunisia. Africa Development XLVII, 1, 135–58.

Ben Sedrine S. (2018): Défis Relevés pour un Accueil Décent de la Migration Subsaharienne en Tunisie. La Marsa: Friedrich-Ebert-Stiftung.

Berg, J. & Ihlström, J. (2019): The Importance of Public Transport for Mobility and Everyday Activities among Rural Residents. Social Sciences 8, 2, 58.

Bhagat, A. (2020): Governing Refugee Disposability: Neoliberalism and Survival in Nairobi. New Political Economy 25, 3, 439–452.

Bhattacharya, T. (ed.). (2017): Social Reproduction Theory. Remapping Class, Recentring Oppression. London: Pluto Press.

Bisiaux, S. (2020a): La Tunisie, Terre d'Accueil... des Politiques Européennes, Plein Droit 2, 125, 27–30.

Bisiaux, S. (2020b): Politiques du Non-Accueil en Tunisie: Des acteurs Humanitaires au Service des Politiques Sécuritaires Européennes. Migreurop & FTDES. (https://ftdes.net/rapports/ftdes.migreu.pdf).

Bisiaux, S., Costa, M. & Zagaria, V. (2023): Familles des Disparus en Deuil et en Lutte: Aperçus des Deux Derniers Moments de Commémore-Action en Tunisie: Commémorer et Agir Contre Les Frontières Meurtrières. Afrique(s) En Mouvement 6, 2, 87–91. (https://doi.org/10.3917/aem.006.0087).

Blanton, R. & Blanton, S. L. (2016): Globalization and Collective Labor Rights. Sociological Forum 31, 1, 181–202. (https://doi.org/10.1111/socf.12239).

Blavier, P. (2016): Sociogenèse de la Révolution Tunisienne: Expansion Scolaire, Chômage et Inégalités Régionales. (Actes de la Recherche en Sciences Sociales 1). Cairn: Softwin, 55–71.

Blomley, N. (2003): Law, Property, and the Geography of Violence: The Frontier, the Survey, and the Grid. Annals of the Association of American Geographers 93, 1, 121–141.

Bolt, M. (2012): Waged Entrepreneurs, Policed Informality: Work, the Regulation of Space, and the Economy of the Zimbabwean–South Africa Border. Africa 82, 1, 111–130.

Bono, I, Hibou B., Meddeb, H & Tozy, M. (2015): L'Etat d'Injustice au Maghreb. Maroc et Tunisie. Paris: Karthala.

Boris, E. & Parreñas, R. S. (2010): Introduction. In: E. Boris & R. S. Parreñas (eds.): Intimate Labors – Cultures, Technologies, and the Politics of Care. Stanford: Stanford University Press, 1–17.

Boubakri, H. (2000): Échanges Transfrontaliers et Commerce Parallèle aux Frontières Tuniso-Libyennes. Monde Arabe Maghreb / Machrek 170, 39–51.

Boubakri, H. (2015): Migration et Asile en Tunisie depuis 2011: Vers de Nouvelles Figures Migratoires? Revue Européenne des Migrations Internationales 31, 3/4, 17–39.

Bouhlel, M. (2020): Les Problèmes de la Gestion des Déchets et Décentralisation dans les Pays Arabes. Arab Council for Social Sciences. (Working Paper No. 10).

Boukhayatia, R. (2022): Sub-Saharan Migrants in Tunisia: Marginalization of a Replacement Workforce. Nawaat, October 19.

Bouraoui, M. (2011): L'Équité Territoriale. Une Revendication de la Révolution Tunisienne. Archibat 12, 22, 18.

Bourdieu, P. (1983): Ökonomisches Kapital, kulturelles Kapital, soziales Kapital. In: R. Kreckel (Hrsg.): Soziale Ungleichheiten. Göttingen: Schwartz, 183–198.

Bourdieu, P. (1986): The Forms of Capital. In: J. Richardson (ed.): Handbook of Theory and Research for the Sociology of Education (Originally published in German; in: R. Kreckel, Hrsg., 1983). Westport CT: Greenwood 241–58.

Bourdieu, P. (1984): Distinction. A Social Critique of the Judgment of Taste. Cambridge: Harvard University Press.

Bouzid, S., (2020): L'Essor des Taxis Collectifs dans le Grand Tunis, une Réponse aux Besoins de Mobilité des Périurbains. Étude de Cas d'el Mornaguia. Riurba 9, 1–13. (https://www.riurba.review/article/09-objets/taxis/).

Braune, I. (2018): Gender. In: J. Gertel & R. Hexel (eds.): Coping with Uncertainty. Youth in the Middle East and North Africa. London: Saqi, 97–113.

Breda, G., Cassarini, C. & Giusa, C. (2023): Confluences Tunisiennes: Émigration(s) et Immigration(s) dans la Tunisie de l'Après-2011. Afrique(s) en Mouvement 6, 2, 16–19. (https://doi.org/10.3917/aem.006.0016).

Brésillon, T. (2019): Kais Saied nous a Rendu l'Espoir: En Tunisie, un Sursaut Citoyen Accompagne le Nouveau Président. Middle East Eye 23.10.2019. (https://www.middleeasteye.net/fr/opinion/kais-saied-nous-rendu-lespoir-en-tunisie-un-sursaut-citoyen-accompagne-le-nouveau-president).

Bryceson, D. F., Gough, K. V., Rigg, J. and Agergaard, J. (2009): Critical Commentary. The World Development Report 2009. Urban Studies 46, 4, 723–738. (https://www.jstor.org/stable/43197992).

Bureau International du Travail (BIT) (2015): L'Inventaire de l'Emploi des Jeunes en Tunisie: Trente ans de Politiques de l'Emploi (IEJ). Genève: Organisation Internationale du Travail.

Business News. (2021): Des Migrants de l'Afrique Subsaharienne Victimes de Violence et de Racisme à Sfax. (https://www.businessnews.com.tn/Des+migrants+de+l%92Afrique+subsaharienne+victimes+de+violence+et+de+racisme+%E0+Sfax,544,109233,3).

Cairns, K. and Johnston, J. (2015): Food and Femininity. London: Bloomsbury.

Callon, M. (2007): What Does it Mean to Say that Economics is Performative? In: D. MacKenzie, F. Muniesa & L. Siu (eds.): Do Economists Make Markets? On the Performativity of Economics. Princeton: Princeton University Press, 311–357.

Capasso, M. (2021): From Human Smuggling to State Capture: Furthering Neoliberal Governance in North Africa. Journal of Labor and Society 24, 3, 440–466. (https://doi.org/10.1163/24714607-bja10001).

Carling, J. (2001): Aspiration and Ability in International Migration: Cape Verdean Experiences of Mobility and Immobility. Oslo: University of Oslo, Centre for Development and the Environment. (https://www.files.ethz.ch/isn/136983/2001_09_Aspiration_Ability_International_Migration.pdf).

Carling, J. (2002): Migration in the Age of Involuntary Immobility: Theoretical Reflections and Cape Verdean Experiences. Journal of Ethnic and Migration Studies 28, 1, 5–42.

Carling, J. & Collins, F. L. (2018): Aspiration, Desire and Drivers of Migration. Journal of Ethnic and Migration Studies 44, 6, 909–926. (https://doi.org/10.1080/1369183X.2017.1384134).

Carling, J. & Schewel, K. (2018): Revisiting Aspiration and Ability in International Migration. Journal of Ethnic and Migration Studies 44, 6, 945–963. (https://doi.org/10.1080/1369183X.2017.1384146).(https://brill.com/view/journals/jlso/24/3/article-p440_440.xml).

Casas, M., Cobarrubias, S. and Pickles, J. (2011): Stretching Borders Beyond Sovereign Territories? Mapping EU and Spain's Border Externalization Policies. Geopolítica(s). Revista de Estudios Sobre Espacio y Poder 2, 1, 71–90.

Cassarini, C. (2020): L'Immigration Subsaharienne en Tunisie: de la Reconnaissance d'un Fait Social à la Création d'un Enjeu Gestionnaire. Migrations Société 179, 1, 43–57. (https://doi.org/10.3917/migra.179.0043).

Cassarini, C. & Geisser, V. (2023): Une Politisation en Devenir?: L'Immigration Subsaharienne dans les Tourments d'une Xénophobie Stratégique'. Afrique(s) en Mouvement 6, 2, 72–81. (https://doi.org/10.3917/aem.006.0072).

Castel, R. (1994): La Dynamique des Processus de Marginalisation: de la Vulnérabilité à la Désaffiliation. Cahiers de Recherche Sociologique 22, 11–27.

Chabbi, M. (1999): La Réhabilitation des Quartiers Populaires en Tunisie: De l'Intégration à la Régulation Sociale. (L'Urbain dans le Monde Arabe: Politiques, Instruments et Acteurs). 187–200.

Chabbi, M. (2006): L'Urbanisation en Tunisie, Transformation et Tendances d'Évolution. In: N. Boumaza (ed.) Villes Réelles, Villes Projetées: Fabrication de la Ville au Maghreb. Paris: Maisonneuve et Larose, 219–243.

Chabbi, M. (2012a): Fonctions et Usages des Études d'Urbanisme dans la Production de la Ville au Maghreb. In: M. Chabbi (ed.): L'Urbain en Tunisie: Processus et Projets. Tunis: Nirvana, 200–215.

Chabbi, M. (2012b): Une Nouvelle Forme d'Urbanisation à Tunis: L'Habitat Spontanée Péri-urbain. In: M. Chabbi (ed.): L'Urbain en Tunisie: Processus et Projets. Tunis: Nirvana, 86–103.

Chalcraft, J. (2008): The Invisible Cage: Syrian Migrant Workers in Lebanon. Stanford: Stanford University Press.

Chalfaouat, A. (2016): 'Morocco's Political Tensions Play Out in the Media'. Sada Blog: 22 September. (https://carnegieendowment.org/sada/64661).

Chemlali, A. (2023): Rings in the Water: Felt Externalisation in the Extended EU Borderlands. Geopolitics, April, 1–24. (https://doi.org/10.1080/14650045.2023.2198125).

Chemlali, A. & El Ghali, A. (2022): Ne rien Faire et ne rien Laisser Faire. Les Enjeux de la Non-Politique Migratoire Tunisienne. Revue Tunisienne de Science Politique 7, 1, 81–105.

Cirelli, C. & Florin, B. (2015): Sociétés Urbaines et Déchets, Éclairages Internationaux. Tours: Presses Universitaires François Rabelais.

Coleman, M. & Stuesse, A. (2014): Policing Borders, Policing Bodies: The Territorial and Biopolitical Roots of US Immigration Control. In: R. Jones & C. Johnson (eds.): Placing the Border in Everyday Life. Farnham: Ashgate, 33–63.

Commune de Tunis (CdT) (2022): Rapport. Cadre Stratégique de la SDV de Tunis Projet Asima Tunis 2022. Tunis. (https://medcities.org/wp-content/uploads/2021/04/cadre-strategique-conferenceVF.comprimido.pdf).

Concialdi, P. (2021): Un Budget de la Dignité pour la Tunisie. Tunis: Friedrich-Ebert-Stiftung et International Alert.

Crawley, H., Düvell, F., Jones, K., McMahon, S. & Sigona. N. (2017): Unravelling Europe's 'Migration Crisis'. Journeys Over Land and Sea. Bristol: Bristol University Press.

Crozier, M. & Friedberg, E. (1977): L'Acteur et le Système. Paris: Éditions du Seuil.

Cuttitta, P. (2020): Non-Governmental Civil Society Organisations and the European Union Externalisation of Migration Management in Tunisia and Egypt. Population, Space and Place 26, 7, 1–13.

Dahmani, F. (2023): Drame de la Migration: Sfax, en Tunisie, à Bout de Nerfs. Jeune Afrique, 4 July. (https://www.jeuneafrique.com/1460026/politique/drame-de-la-migration-sfax-en-tunisie-a-bout-de-nerfs/).

Dakhli, L. (2021): The Fair Value of Bread: Tunisia, 28 December 1983 – 6 January 1984. In: L. Dakhli & V. Bonnecase: When 'Adjusted' People Rebel: Economic Liberalization and Social Revolts in Africa and the Middle East (1980s to the Present Day). (International Review of Social History, 29). Cambridge: Cambridge University Press, 47–68.

Dakhli, L. & Bonnecase, V. (2021): Introduction: Interpreting the Local Economy through Local Anger. In: L. Dakhli & V. Bonnecase (eds.): When 'Adjusted' People Rebel: Economic Liberalization and Social Revolts in Africa and the Middle East (1980s to the

Present Day). (International Review of Social History, 29). Cambridge: Cambridge University Press, 1–21.

Dakhlia, J. (2023): Les Coudées Franches: Parcours d'Émancipations des Sciences Sociales du Maghreb. Mondes Arabes 3, 1, 5–21. (https://doi.org/10.3917/machr2.003.0005).

Daoud, A. (2011): La Révolution Tunisienne de Janvier 2011 une Lecture par les Déséquilibres du Territoire. EchoGéo 1–14.

Darling, J. (2017): Acts, Ambiguities, and the Labour of Contesting Citizenship. Citizenship Studies 21, 6, 727–736. (https://doi.org/10.1080/13621025.2017.1341658).

Darmangeat, Ch. (2016): La Division Sexuelle du Travail aux Origines de la Domination Masculine: Une Perspective Marxiste. (https://www.researchgate.net/publication/305324365_La_division_sexuelle_du_travail_aux_origines_de_la_domination_masculine_une_perspective_marxiste).

Darwish, S. (2020): Flowers in Uncertain Times: Waste, Islam, and the Scent of Revolution in Tunisia. Ethnos 1–22.

Darwish, S. (2018): Balad el-Ziblé (Country of Rubbish): Moral Geographies of Waste in Post-Revolutionary Tunisia. Anthropological Forum 28, 1, 61–73.

Das, R. (2017): David Harvey's Theory of Accumulation by Dispossession: A Marxist Critique. World Review of Political Economy 8, 4, 590–616. (https://doi.org/10.13169/worlrevipoliecon.8.4.0590).

De Certeau, M. (1990): L'Invention du Quotidien. Arts de Faire. Paris: Gallimard.

De Gaulejac, V. (1996): Les Sources de la Honte. Paris: Desclée de Brouwer.

De Genova, N. (2002): Migrant 'Illegality' and Deportability in Everyday Life. Annual Review of Anthropology 31, 1, 419–447. (https://doi.org/10.1146/annurev.anthro.31.040402.085432).

De Haas, H. (2021): A Theory of Migration: The Aspirations-Capabilities Framework. Comparative Migration Studies 9, 8. (https://doi.org/10.1186/s40878-020-00210-4).

Delpueh, A. (2021): Italian Waste: The Vast Corruption Network Behind the Environmental Scandal. Inkyfada. (https://inkyfada.com/en/2021/03/09/investigation-waste-corruption-italy-tunisia/).

Destremeau, B. (2009): La Protection Sociale en Tunisie. Nature et Cohérence de l'Intervention Publique. In: M. Catusse, B. Destremeau & E. Verdier (eds.): L'État Face aux Débordements du Social au Maghreb Formation, Travail et Protection Sociale. Paris: Karthala, 129–172.

Di Méo, G. (1998): Géographie Sociale et Territoires. Paris: Nathan.

Dini, S., & Giusi, C. (2020): Externalizing Migration Governance Through Civil Society: Tunisia as a Case Study. Cham: Springer International Publishing.

Djerbi, D. (2023): Foreign Debt versus Organised Labour: Reflections on the UGTT's Stance on IMF Loans in Post-Uprising Tunisia. Review of African Political Economy 50, 176, 251–260.

Djerbi, D. (2024): The Social Reproductive Roots of Agrarian Contention: Gendered Labour amid Peasant Struggles in Tunisia. Antipode 1–25. (https://doi.org/10.1111/anti.13081).

Dlala, H. (2013): Les Marges Périurbaines en Tunisie et au Maghreb. Tunis: Centre de Publication Universitaire Tunisienne.

Dobré, M. (2002): L'Écologie au Quotidien. Éléments pour une Théorie Sociologique de la Résistance Ordinaire. Paris: L'Harmattan.
Dörre, K. (2019): Precariousness in the Eurozone: Causes, Effects and Developments. In: S. Schmalz & B. Sommer (eds.). Confronting Crisis and Precariousness. Organized Labour and Social Unrest in the European Union. London: Rowman and Littlefield 15–32.
Doyel, S., Forin, R. & Frouws, B. (2023): A Damaging Deal: Abuses, Departures from Tunisia Continue Following EU Agreement. Mixed Migration Centre. (https://mixedmigration.org/eu-tunisia-damaging-deal/).
Draouil, N. & Jmel, N. (2022): Learning to 'Field': Experiments in Interviewing. Jadaliyya. (https://www.jadaliyya.com/Details/44514).
Düvell, F. (2012): Transit Migration: A Blurred and Politicised Concept. Population, Space and Place 18, 4, 415–427.
Dupuy, G. (1991): L'Urbanisme des Réseaux. Paris: Armand Colin.
El Ghali, A. (2022): The Protection of Sub-Saharan Migrants in Tunisia: Community Responses and Institutional Questioning. Journal of the British Academy 10, 3, 145–165. (https://doi.org/10.5871/jba/010s3.145).
Elloumi, M. (2013): Les Terres Domaniales en Tunisie. Histoire d'une Appropriation par les Pouvoirs Publics. Études Rurales 192, 43–60.
Escobar, A. (1995): Encountering Development. The Making and Unmaking of the Third World. New Jersey: Princeton University Press.
European Training Foundation (ETF). (2011): Women and Work in Tunisia. (https://www.etf.europa.eu/sites/default/files/m/300DDD6D021DB90FC125797C0040FD1C_Women%20&%20work_Tunisia_EN.pdf).
European Union (EU) (2023): Emergence Trust Fund for Africa. Mediterranean City-to-City Migration (MC2CM) – Phase II. (https://trust-fund-for-africa.europa.eu/our-programmes/mediterranean-city-city-migration-mc2cm-phase-ii_en).
Fassin, D. (2007): Humanitarianism as a Politics of Life. Public Culture 19, 3, 499–520.
Fautras, M. (2021) Paysans dans la Révolution. Un Défi Tunisien. Paris, Tunis: Éditions Karthala et IRMC.
Ferguson, J. (1994): The Anti-Politics Machine: "Development", Depoliticization and Bureaucratic Power in Lesotho. London: University of Minnesota Press.
Ferguson, J. & Li, T. M. (2018): Beyond the 'Proper Job:' Political-Economic Analysis after the Century of Labouring Man (Working Paper 51). Cape Town: PLAAS, UWC. (http://dx.doi.org/10.13140/RG.2.2.12894.54085).
Fiddian-Qasmiyeh, E. (2014): Gender and Forced Migration. In: E. Fiddian-Qasmiyeh, G. Loescher, K. Long & N. Sigona (eds.): The Oxford Handbook of Refugee and Forced Migration Studies. Oxford: Oxford University Press, 395–408.
Flonneau, M. & Ordeuil J.-P. (2016): Vive la Route! Vive la République! Essai Impertinent, L'Urgence de Comprendre. La Tour-d'Aigues: L'Aube.
Florin, B (2015a): Les Chiffonniers du Caire, Soutier de la Ville ou Businessman des Ordures. Ethnologie Française 45, 487–498.
Florin, B. (2015b): Les Récupérateurs de Déchets à Casablanca: l'Inclusion Perverse de Travailleurs à la Marge. Sociologie et Sociétés 47, 1, 73–96. (https://doi.org/10.7202/1034419ar).

Florin, B. (2016): De l'Indignité à l'Indignation: Petites Luttes, Résistances Quotidiennes et Tentatives de Mobilisation des Récupérateurs de Déchets à Istanbul. Cultures & Conflits 101, 99–119. (https://doi.org/10.4000/conflits.19184).

Foucault, M. ([1972] 1991): Die Ordnung des Diskurses (L'Ordre du Discours), Frankfurt Main: Fischer, 1991.

Foucault, M. (1991): Governmentality. In: G. Burchell, C. Gordon & P. Miller (eds.): The Foucault Effect Studies in Governmentality. Chicago: The University of Chicago Press.

Fredericks, R. (2014): Vital Infrastructures of Trash in Dakar. Comparative Studies of South Asia, Africa, and the Middle East 34, 3, 532–48.

Frische, J. (2022): Urbane Ungleichheit, Informalität und Prekarität in Tunesien: Zwischen Teilhabe und Ausgrenzung. Berlin: Frank & Timme.

Fröbel, F., Heinrichs, J. & Kreye, O. (1981): The New International Division of Labor. Cambridge/New York: Cambridge University Press.

Frontex. (2023): Risk Analysis for 2023/24. Warsaw 2023. (https://data.europa.eu/doi/10.2819/920282).

Fulco, C. & Giampaolo, M. (2023): The Neoliberal Cage. Alternative Analysis of the Rise of Populist Tunisia. *Middle East Critique* 32, 27–52.

Furniss, J. (2012): Metaphors of Waste: Several Ways of Seeing 'Development' and Cairo's Garbage Collectors. PhD Thesis, University of Oxford. Oxford. (https://ora.ox.ac.uk/objects/uuid:856c3220-f60b-4c36-829c-5585431312a0).

Furniss, J. (2017): What Type of Problem is Waste in Egypt. Social Anthropology / Anthropologie Sociale 25, 3, 301–17.

Furniss, J. (2022): Reading the Signs: Some Ways Waste is Framed in Tunisia. In: Z. Gille & J. Lepawsky (eds.): The Routledge Handbook of Waste Studies. London: Routledge.

Galerand. E. & Kergoat. D. (2014): Les Apports de la Sociologie du Genre à la Critique du Travail. La Nouvelle Revue du Travail 4. (https://isidore.science/document/10.4000/nrt.1533).

Galtier, M. (2020): Tunisie: Bhar Lazreg, ce Quartier Maudit «Dont il ne faut pas Prononcer le Nom». *Middle East Eye*. Décembre 4, édition française.

Galtung, J. (1971): Gewalt, Frieden und Friedensforschung. In: D. Senghass (ed.): *Kritische Friedensforschung*. Frankfurt am Main: Suhrkamp, 55–104.

Gana, A. (2012): The Rural and Agricultural Roots of the Tunisian Revolution: When Food Security Matters. *The International Journal of Sociology of Agriculture and Food* 19, 2, 201–213.

Gana, A. & Taleb, M. (2019): Mobilisations Foncières en Tunisie. Révélateur des Paradoxes de l'Après Révolution'. *Confluences Méditerranée* 1, 108, 31–46.

Garelli, G. & Tazzioli, M. (2017): Tunisia as a Revolutionized Space of Migration. London: Palgrave Macmillan.

Garnaoui, W. (2023): Externalisation des Frontières Européennes et Politiques Migratoires Tunisiennes: Une Psychologie des Impacts Socio-Politiques. Confluences Méditerranée 125, 2, 107–22. (https://doi.org/10.3917/come.125.0109).

Garnaoui, W. (2022): Harga et Désir d'Occident, Étude Psychanalytique des Migrants Clandestins Tunisiens. Tunis: Nirvana.

Garraoui, T. (2023): Graduate Unemployment in Tunisia: The Case of Greater Tunis. PhD, Institute of Geography, Leipzig University. Leipzig.

Geha, C. (2019): Politics of a Garbage Crisis: Social Networks, Narratives, and Frames of Lebanon's 2015 Protests and their Aftermath. Social Movement Studies 18, 1, 78–92.

Geisser. V. (2019): Tunisie, des Migrants Subsahariens Toujours Exclus du Rêve Démocratique. Migrations Société 3, 3–18.

Gertel, J. (2005): Inscribed Bodies within Commodity Chains. In: N. Fold & B. Pritchard (eds.): Cross-Continental Food Chains. London: Routledge, 109–23.

Gertel, J. (2007): Mobility and Insecurity: The Significance of Resources. In: J. Gertel & I. Breuer (eds.). Pastoral Morocco. Globalizing Scapes of Mobility and Insecurity. Wiesbaden: Reichert, 11–30.

Gertel, J. (2010): Globalisierte Nahrungskrisen: Bruchzone Kairo (Globalised Food Crises: Cairo as Zone of Ruptures). Bielefeld: transcript.

Gertel, J. (2017): Arab Youth – A Contained Youth? Middle East Topics and Arguments 9, 25–33. (https://archiv.ub.uni-marburg.de/ep/0003/article/view/7218).

Gertel, J. (2018a): Uncertainty. In: J. Gertel & R. Hexel (eds.): Coping with Uncertainty. Youth in the Middle East and North Africa. London: Saqi, 23–54. (https://library.fes.de/pdf-files/iez/18100.pdf).

Gertel, J. (2018b): Economy and Employment. In: J. Gertel & R. Hexel (eds.): Coping with Uncertainty. Youth in the Middle East and North Africa. London: Saqi, 135–161. (https://library.fes.de/pdf-files/iez/18100.pdf).

Gertel, J. (ed.) (2023): Globale Getreidemärkte. Technoliberalismus und gefährdete Existenzsicherung in Nordafrika (Global Grain Markets. Technoliberalism and Endangered Livelihoods in North Africa). Bielefeld: Transcript. (https://www.transcript-verlag.de/media/pdf/d6/96/71/oa9783839464182.pdf).

Gertel, J. (2024a): Hunger and Violence. In: J. Gertel, D. Kreuer & F. Stolleis (eds.): The Dispossessed Generation. Youth in the Middle East and North Africa. London: Saqi Books, 132–156.

Gertel, J. (2024b): Lifestyles. In: J. Gertel, D. Kreuer & F. Stolleis (eds.): The Dispossessed Generation. Youth in the Middle East and North Africa. London: Saqi Books, 205–229.

Gertel, J. & Breuer, I. (2011): Alltagsmobilitäten – Marokkos neue soziale Landschaften. In: J. Gertel & I. Breuer (eds.): Alltagsmobilitäten. Aufbruch marokkanischer Lebenswelten. Bielefeld: transcript, 11–31.

Gertel, J. & Hexel, R. (eds.): (2018): Coping with Uncertainty. Youth in the Middle East and North Africa. London: Saqi Books. (https://library.fes.de/pdf-files/iez/18100.pdf).

Gertel, J. & Kreuer, D. (2018): Values. In: J. Gertel & R. Hexel (eds.): Coping with Uncertainty. Youth in the Middle East and North Africa. London: Saqi Books, 57–79. (https://library.fes.de/pdf-files/iez/18100.pdf).

Gertel, J. & Ouaissa, R. (2018): Middle-Class. Precarity and Mobilisation. In: J. Gertel & R. Hexel (eds.): Coping with Uncertainty. Youth in the Middle East and North Africa. London: Saqi Books, 162–179. (https://library.fes.de/pdf-files/iez/18100.pdf).

Gertel, J. & Wagner, A.-C. (2018): Mobility, Migration, and Flight. In: J. Gertel & R. Hexel (eds.): Coping with Uncertainty. Youth in the Middle East and North Africa. London: Saqi Books, 198–219. (https://library.fes.de/pdf-files/iez/18100.pdf).

Gertel, J. & Kreuer, D. (2021): The Impact of the Pandemic on Young People: A Survey Among 'Young Leaders' in the Middle East and North Africa. La Marsa: Friedrich-Ebert-Stiftung 2021. (http://library.fes.de/pdf-files/bueros/tunesien/18326.pdf).

Gertel, J. & Grüneisl, K. (2024): Dispossession of Opportunities and Livelihoods. In: J. Gertel, D. Kreuer & F. Stolleis (eds.): The Dispossessed Generation. Youth in the Middle East and North Africa. London: Saqi Books, 40–72.

Gertel, J., Kreuer, D. & Stolleis, F. (eds.) (2024a): The Dispossessed Generation. Youth in the Middle East and North Africa. London: Saqi Books.

Gertel, J., Kreuer, D. & Stolleis, F. (eds.) (2024b): Youth in Middle East and North Africa. In: J. Gertel, D. Kreuer & F. Stolleis (eds.): The Dispossessed Generation. Youth in the Middle East and North Africa. London: Saqi Books, 3–35.

Gertel, J., Kreuer, D. & Stolleis, F. (eds.) (2024c): The Covid-19 Pandemic. In: J. Gertel, D. Kreuer & F. Stolleis (eds.): The Dispossessed Generation. Youth in the Middle East and North Africa. London: Saqi Books, 75–98.

Ghanem, D. (2020): Algeria's Borderlands: A Country Unto Themselves. Washington: Carnegie Endowment for International Peace. (https://carnegie-production-assets.s3.amazonaws.com/static/files/Ghanem-Algeria-Tunisia.pdf).

Gherib, B. (2012): Économie Politique de la Révolution Tunisienne. Les Groupes Sociaux Face au Capitalisme de Copinage. Revue Tiers Monde 212, 4, 19–36.

Gibson-Graham, J. K. (2006a): The End of Capitalism (As We Knew It): A Feminist Critique of Political Economy. Oxford: Blackwell Publishers 1996 (2. Edition Minneapolis: UMP).

Gibson-Graham, J. K. (2006b): A Postcapitalist Politics. Minneapolis: University of Minnesota Press.

Gibson-Graham, J. K. (2008): Diverse Economies. Performative Practices for Other Worlds. Progress in Human Geography 32, 5, 613–632.

Gibson-Graham, J. K. & Dombroski, K. (eds.) (2020): The Handbook of Diverse Economies. Northampton, MA, USA: Edward Elgar Publishing.

Giddens, A. ([1984] 1990a): The Constitution of Society. Outline of the Theory of Structuration. Cambridge & Oxford: Polity Press.

Giddens, A. (1990b): The Consequences of Modernity. Stanford: Stanford University Press.

Giguère. E., St-Arnaud, L., & Bilodeau, K. (2020): Travail Invisible et Rapports Sociaux de Sexe lors des Parcours d'Insertion Socioprofessionnelle des Femmes Cadres. L'Orientation Scolaire et Professionnelle 49, 2, 281–312.

Gilbert, L. (2009): Immigration as Local Politics: Re-Bordering Immigration and Multiculturalism through Deterrence and Incapacitation. International Journal of Urban and Regional Research 33, 1, 26–42. (https://doi.org/10.1111/j.1468-2427.2009.00838.x).

Gluchman, V. (2019): Human Dignity as the Essence of Nussbaum's Ethics of Human Development. Philosophia 47, 1127–1140. (https://doi.org/10.1007/s11406-018-0034-2).

Gonzales de la Rocha, M. (2007): The Construction of the Myth of Survival. Development and Change 38, 1, 45–66.
Goswami, M. (2004): Producing India: From Colonial Economy to National Space. Hyderabad: Orient Blackswan.
Grüneisl, K. (2021): The Fripe as Urban Economy: Market- and Space-Making in Tunis. PhD Thesis: Durham University. Durham. (http://etheses.dur.ac.uk/14116/).
Guardian (2024): The Brutal Truth Behind Italy's Migrant Reduction: Beatings and Rape by EU-funded Forces in Tunisia. Guardian 19 September. (https://www.theguardian.com/global-development/2024/sep/19/italy-migrant-reduction-investigation-rape-killing-tunisia-eu-money-keir-starmer-security-forces-smugglers).
Gubert, F. (2010): Pourquoi Migrer? Le Regard de la Théorie Économique. Regards Croisés sur l'Économie 2, 8, 96–105.
Guirao, B., Campa, J. L. & Casado-Sanz, N. (2018): Labour Mobility Between Cities and Metropolitan Integration: The Role of High-Speed Rail Commuting in Spain. Cities 78, 140–154.
Hannafi, S. (2017): Indicateurs des Droits de l'Homme des Migrants et de leurs Familles en Tunisie. Documents de Travail 24 de KNOMAD. Tunis. (http://www.migration.nat.tn/images/pdf/2021/indicateurs-droit-homme-migrants-familles-tunisie.pdf).
Hall, S. (1992): The Question of Cultural Identity. In: S. Hall, D. Held, & A. McGrew (eds.): *Modernity and its Futures*. London: The Open University Press. 273–326.
Haraway, D. (1988): Situated Knowledges: The Science Question in Feminism and the Privilege of Partial Perspective. Feminist Studies 14, 3, 575–599. (http://www.jstor.org/stable/3178066).
Harrington, B. (2024): Offshore. Stealth Wealth and the New Colonialism. New York: W. W. Norton & Company.
Harvey, D. (1989). The Condition of Postmodernity. An Enquiry into the Origins of Cultural Change. Oxford: Blackwell.
Harvey, D. (2003): The New Imperialism. Oxford: Oxford University Press.
Harvey, D. (2005): A Brief History of Neoliberalism. New York: Oxford University Press.
Hecking, B. E. (2021): Jugend und Widerstand in Algier. Alltagsräume im Kontext urbaner Transformation. Bielefeld: transcript.
Helfrich, S. & Bollier, D. (eds.) (2015): Patterns of Commoning. Bielefeld: transcript. (https://patternsofcommoning.org/contents/).
Helfrich, S. & Bollier, D. (2019): Fair, Frei und Lebendig. Die Macht der Commons. Bielefeld: transcript. (https://www.transcript-verlag.de/978-3-8376-4530-9/frei-fair-und-lebendig-die-macht-der-commons/?number=978-3-8394-4530-3).
Herbert, M. (2022): Losing Hope: Why Tunisians are Leading the Surge in Irregular Migration to Europe. Geneva: The Global Initiative Against Transnational Organized Crime. (https://globalinitiative.net/wp-content/uploads/2022/01/GI-TOC-Losing-Hope_Tunisia-Report-2021.pdf).
Hertel, S. (2009): Human Rights and the Global Economy: Bringing Labor Rights Back In. Maryland Journal of International Law, 24, 283. (https://www.semanticscholar.org/paper/Human-Rights-and-the-Global-Economy%3A-Bringing-Labor-Hertel/fa41b15ca271813a5f781a3104f0ca3ea3ec919a).

Hibou, B. (2009): Work Discipline, Discipline in Tunisia: Complex and Ambiguous Relations. African Identities 7, 3, 327–352. (https://doi.org/10.1080/14725840903069114).

Hibou, B. (2011a): Tunisie. Économie Politique et Morale d'un Mouvement Social. Politique Africaine 121, 1, 5–22.

Hibou, B. (2011b): The Force of Obedience: The Political Economy of Repression in Tunisia. (La force de l'obéissance, Paris 2006). Cambridge: Polity Press.

Hibou, B. (2015): La formation asymétrique de l'état en Tunisie: Les territoires de l'injustice. In: I. Bono, B. Hibou, H. Meddeb, & M. Tozy (eds.) L'État d'Injustice au Maghreb: Maroc et Tunisie. Paris: Éditions Karthala, 99–149.

Hibou, B., Meddeb, H. & Hamdi, M. (2011): Tunisia after 14 January and its Social and Political Economy: The Issues at Stake in a Reconfiguration of European Policy. Euro-Mediterranean Human Rights Network (EMHRN), June. (https://www.refworld.org/pdfid/515013412.pdf).

Hmed, C. (2016): Au-delà de l'Exception Tunisienne: Les Failles et les Risques du Processus Révolutionnaire. Pouvoirs 156, 1, 137–47. (https://revue-pouvoirs.fr/au-dela-de-l-exception-tunisienne/).

Hobson, K. (2016): Closing the Loop or Squaring the Circle? Locating Generative Spaces for the Circular Economy. Progress in Human Geography 40, 1, 88–104.

Hudson, R. (2018): The Illegal, the Illicit and New Geographies of Uneven Development. Territory, Politics, Governance 8, 2, 161–176. (https://doi.org/10.1080/21622671.2018.1535998).

ICMPD (International Centre for Migration Policy Development) (n.d.): MC2CM (Mediterranean City-to-City Migration) Project. (https://www.icmpd.org/our-work/projects/mc2cm).

ICMPD, UCLG & UN-HABITAT (n.d.): I-MIGR (Inclusion, Migration, Integration and Governance) in Raoued and La Marsa (MC2CM). (https://www.icmpd.org/content/download/53313/file/I%20MIGR%20in%20Raoued%20and%20La%20Marsa_EN.pdf).

INS (Institut National de la Statistique) (1994): Recensement Général de la Population et de l'Habitat. Les Premiers Résulants. Gouvernorat de Manouba.

INS (2012): Classification Nationale des Unités Administratives. Code Géographique Tunisie. INS: Tunis. (https://www.ins.tn/publication/classification-nationale-des-unites-administratives).

INS (2014): Recensement Général de la Population et de l'Habitat. INS: Tunis.

INS (2017): Enquête Nationale sur la Population et l'Emploi, 2017. (https://www.ins.tn/enquetes/enquete-nationale-sur-la-population-et-lemploi-2017).

INS (2019): Annuaire Statistique de la Tunisie. INS: Tunis.

INS, ONM (Observatoire National de la Migration) & ICMPD (International Centre For Migration Policy) (2021): L'Enquête Nationale sur la Migration Internationale. Tunis. (https://ins.tn/publication/rapport-de-lenquete-nationale-sur-la-migration-internationale-tunisia-hims#:~:text=Ce%20rapport%20publi%C3%A9%20par%20l%E2%80%99Institut%20National%20de%20la,enqu%C3%AAte%20sur%20la%20migration%20internationale%20entreprise%20en%20Tunisie.).

International Alert (2020): L'Unité de Recyclage des Barbechas à Ettadhamen en Tunisie: Un Projet Pilote basé sur les Principes de l'Économie Sociale et Soli-

daire. (https://www.international-alert.org/fr/publications/lunite-de-recyclage-des-barbechas-a-ettadhamen-en-tunisie/).
ILO (International Labour Office) (2011): Tunisia. A New Social Contract for Fair and Equitable Growth. Geneva.
ILO (2018): Women and Men in the Informal Economy: A Statistical Picture. Geneva.
ILO (2022): Tunisia COVID-19 Country Case Study. Geneva.
ILO (2024): Decent Work. Geneva: ILO (https://www. ilo.org/topics/decent-work).
Jouffe, Y., Caubel, D., Fol, S. & Motte-Baumvol, B. (2019): Dealing with Inequality in Mobility: Tactics, Strategies and Projects for Poor Households on the Outskirts of Paris. Cybergeo: European Journal of Geography, 708. (https://journals.openedition.org/cybergeo/33479).
Jouili, M. (2023): Imperialism and Neoliberal Redeployment in Post-Uprising Tunisia. Middle East Critique 32, 2, 195–215.
Kaboub, F. (2012): From Neoliberalism to Social Justice: The Feasibility of Full Employment in Tunisia. Review of Radical Political Economics 44, 3, 305–12. (https://doi.org/10.1177/0486613412446042).
Kaboub, F. (2014): The Making of the Tunisian Revolution. In: I. Diwan (ed.): Understanding the Political Economy of the Arab Uprisings. Hackensack, NJ: World Scientific.
Kahloun, H. (2008): Les Processus d'Urbanisation des Petites Villes à la Grande Périphérie de Tunis. (Urbanisation Processes in Small Towns on the Outskirts of Tunis). Tunis: École Nationale d'Architecture et d'Urbanisme. (PhD Thesis).
Kahloun, H. (2020): La Société Civile Tunisienne à l'Épreuve de la Participation: Mobilisation, Pression et Compromis autour des Projets de Développement Urbain. Insanyat 90, 99–120. (https://doi.org/10.4000/insaniyat.24419).
Karagiannis, E. (2015): When the Green Gets Greener: Political Islam's Newly-Found Environmentalism. Small Wars & Insurgencies 26, 1, 181–201.
Kaufmann, V. (2005): Mobilités et Réversibilités: vers des Sociétés plus Fluides? Cahiers Internationaux de Sociologie 1, 118, 119–135. (https://doi.org/10.3917/cis.118.0119).
Kaufmann, V. & Flamm M. (2002): Famille, Temps et Mobilité : Etat de l'Art et Tour d'Horizon des Innovations. Rapport de Recherche CNAF, LVM. Paris: CNAF et La Ville en Mouvement. (https://side.developpement-durable.gouv.fr/ACCIDR/doc/SYRACUSE/234141/famille-temps-et-mobilite-etat-de-l-art-et-tour-d-horizon-des-innovations-recherche-realisee-a-l-int?_lg=fr-FR).
Kaufmann, V. & Widmer Éric D. (2005): L'Acquisition de la Motilité au Sein des Familles, État de la Question et Hypothèses de Recherche. Espaces et sociétés 2, 120–121, 199–217. (https://doi.org/10.3917/esp.120.0199).
Keane, W. (2003): Semiotics and the Social Analysis of Material Things. Language & Communication 23, 3-4, 409–425.
Kerrou, M. (2021): Jemna. L'Oasis de la Révolution. Tunis: Cérès Editions.
Khalil, J. F. (2017): Lebanon's Waste Crisis: An Exercise of Participation Rights. New Media and Society 19, 5, 701–12.
Khiari, S. (2022): Démocratisme & Dictature Plébiscitaire. Tunis: Barr al Aman.
Kraidy, M. (2016): Trashing the Sectarian System? Lebanon's 'You Stink' Movement and the Making of Affective Publics. Communication and the Public 1, 19–26.

Kreuer, D. & Gertel, J. (2024): Values and the Formation of Groups. In: J. Gertel, D. Kreuer & F. Stolleis (eds.): The Dispossessed Generation. Youth in the Middle East and North Africa. London: Saqi Books, 263–282.

Krippner, G. R. (2011): Capitalizing on Crisis: The Political Origins of the Rise of Finance. Cambridge: Harvard University Press.

Kthiri, W. (2019): Inadéquation des Qualifications en Tunisie: Quels sont les Déterminants de Sous-Emploi? (Document de Travail). Tunis: Notes et Analyses de l'Institut Tunisien de la Compétitivité et des Études Quantitatives. (http://www.itceq.tn/files/emploi/inadequation-des-qualifications-en-tunisie.pdf).

Lamloum, O. & Ali Ben Zina, M. (eds.) (2015): Les Jeunes de Douar Hicher et d'Ettadhamen: Une Enquête Sociologique. Tunis: Arabesque.

Laroussi, H. (2009): Micro-Crédit et Lien Social en Tunisie: La Solidarité Instituée. Paris/Tunis: Karthala/IRMC.

Laroussi, H. (2018): Femmes et Développement Local en Tunisie. Acteurs et Enjeux. Paris: Harmattan.

Laroussi, H. (2021): La Tunisie en Pandémie: De la Corruption à la Solidarité. Paris: Harmattan.

Laroussi, H. (2024): Tunisia in Crises. Local Tensions and Conflicts in Post-Revolutionary Context. Paris: Harmattan.

Lazali, K. (2021): Colonial Trauma. A Study of the Psychic and Political Consequences of Colonial Oppression in Algeria (Le Trauma Colonial, 2018). Cambridge: Polity Press.

Le Blanc, G. (2009): L'Invisibilité Sociale. Paris: Presses Universitaires de France.

Le Breton, E. (2015): La Société Mobile et le Droit du Passant. Université Rennes 2 et Institut pour la Ville en Mouvement. Limoges.

Le Monde (2023): En Tunisie le Président Kais Saied s'en Prend aux-Migrants Sub-Sahariens. (https://www.lemonde.fr/afrique/article/2023/02/22/en-tunisie-le-president-kais-saied-s-en-prend-aux-migrants-subsahariens_6162908_3212.html.).

Les Observateurs France 24 (2016): Trois Jeunes Congolais Agressés au Couteau à Tunis: 'Ce n'est pas un Cas Isolé'. (https://observers.france24.com/fr/20161226-tunisie-agression-etudiants-congolais-africains-couteau-gorge-racisme-hopital).

Li, T. M. (2014): Land's End. Capitalist Relations on an Indigenous Frontier. Durham: Duke University Press.

Likic-Brboric, B. & Schierup, C.-U. (2012): *Asymmetric Governance, Labour Standards, and Migrants' Rights: A Transatlantic Perspective on Migration, 'Decent Work', and the Role of Civil Society in Fair Globalization* (Themes on Ethnic and Migration Studies No. 40). Norrköping: Remesco.

Loschi, C. (2016): Sweeping Too Much Dirt under a Small Carpet. How Local Rubbish Collection Reforms Uncover the Destabilizing Force of Authoritarian Persistence in Tunisia. PhD at the University of Turin.

Loschi, C. (2019): Local Mobilisations and the Formation of Environmental Networks in a Democratizing Tunisia. *Social Movement Studies* 18, 1, 93–112.

Loukil-Tlili, B. (2013): Parcs et Jardins de Tunis: Gestion et Usages des Espaces Paysagers. In: M. Bourgou & A. Hatzenberger (eds): *Des Paysages*. Tunis: Centre de Publication Universitaire Tunis. 115–124.

Lubkemann, S. C. (2008): Involuntary Immobility: On a Theoretical Invisibility in Forced Migration Studies. *Journal of Refugee Studies* 21, 4, 454–475.
MacKenzie, D. (2021): *Trading at the Speed of Light: How Ultrafast Algorithms are Transforming Financial Markets.* Princeton: Princeton University Press.
MacKenzie, D., Muniesa, F., & Siu, L. (eds.) (2007): *Do Economist Make Markets? On the Performativity of Economics.* Princeton: Princeton University Press.
Mackinnon. A.C. (1987): *Feminism Unmodified: Discourse on Life and Law.* Harvard: Harvard University Press.
Malik, A. & Gallien, M. (2020): Border Economies of the Middle East: Why Do They Matter for Political Economy? *Review of International Political Economy* 27, 3, 732–62.
Mancina, P. (2012): The Birth of a Sanctuary-City: A History of Governmental Sanctuary in San Francisco. In: R. Lippert & S. Rehaag (eds.): *Sanctuary Practices in International Perspectives.* London/New York: Routledge, 205–218.
Mansour, N. & Ben Salem, S. (2020): Socio-Economic Impacts of Covid-19 on the Tunisian Economy. Journal of the International Academy for Case Studies 26, 4, 1–13.
Mansouri, F. (2002): La Réhabilitation des Quartiers d'Habitation dans l'Agglomération de Tunis. Archibat 5, 66–69.
Marcus, G. E. (1995): Ethnography in/of the World System: The Emergence of Multi-Sited Ethnography. Annual Review of Anthropology 24, 95–117.
Martini, L. S. & Mergisi, T. (2023): Road to Nowhere: Why Europe's Border Externalisation is a Dead End. European Council on Foreign Relations. (https://ecfr.eu/publication/road-to-nowhere-why-europes-border-externalisation-is-a-dead-end/).
Maruani, M. (2005): Femmes, Genre et Sociétés, l'État des Savoirs. Paris: La Découverte.
Marzouki, M. (2022): Is Democracy Lost? Journal of Democracy 33, 1, 5–11. (https://doi.org/10.1353/jod.2022.0000).
Massey, D. (1993): Power-Geometry and a Progressive Sense of Place. In: J. Bird, B. Curtis, T. Putnam, G. Robertson, & L. Tickner (eds.): Mapping the Futures: Local Cultures, Global Change. London/New York: Routledge, 59–69.
Mattes, H. (2016): Entwicklung der tunesischen Binnenregionen: Hohe Erwartungen – schwierige Umsetzung. Hamburg: German Institute for Global and Area Studies (GIGA). (https://www.giga-hamburg.de/de/publikationen/giga-focus/entwicklung-der-tunesischen-binnenregionen-hohe-erwartungen-schwierige-umsetzung).
Matthies-Boon, V. (2023): *Breaking Intersubjectivity. A Critical Theory of Counter-Revolutionary Trauma in Egypt.* Lanham: Rowman & Littlefield.
Mayer-Ahuja, N. (2023): Power at Work. Approaching a Global Perspective. In: M. van der Linden & N. Mayer-Ahuja (eds.): *Power at Work: A Global Perspective on Control and Resistance.* Berlin/Boston: De Gruyter Oldenbourg, 289–317.
Mazzucotelli, F. (2017): Rebordering the Lebanese Shi'i Public Sphere. In: R. Di Peri & D. Meier (eds): *Lebanon Facing the Arab Uprisings: Constraints and Adaptation.* London: Palgrave Macmillan, 55–69.
McFarlane, C. & Waibel, M. (2012): Urban Informalities: Reflections on the Formal and Informal (Book Review). Economic Geography 89, 2, 201–202.
MC2CM (Mediterranean City-to-City Migration) (2023): Emergency Trust Fund for Africa. European Union. (https://trust-fund-for-africa.europa.eu/our-programmes/mediterranean-city-city-migration-mc2cm-phase-ii_en).

Meddeb, H. (2010): La Tunisie. Pays Émergent? (https://fasopo.org/node/78).

Meddeb, H. (2011): L'Ambivalence de la «Course à el Khobza» Obéir et se Révolter en Tunisie. Politique Africaine 121, 1, 35–51.

Meddeb, H. (2016): Smugglers, Tribes and Militias: The Rise of Local Forces in the Tunisian-Libyan Border Region. In: L. Narbone, A. Favier & V. Collombier (eds.): Inside Wars. Local Dynamics of Conflicts in Syria and Libya. Florence: European University, 38–43. (http://cadmus.eui.eu/bitstream/handle/1814/41644/Inside%20wars_2016.pdf).

Meddeb, H. (2017): Peripheral Vision: How Europe Can Help Preserve Tunisia's Fragile Democracy. European Council on Foreign Relations (ECFR). (https://www.ecfr.eu/page/-/ECFR202_PERIPHERAL_VISION2.pdf).

Meddeb, H. (2020): The Volatile Tunisia-Libya Border: Between Tunisia's Security Policy and Libya's Militia Factions. (Malcolm H. Kerr Carnegie Middle East Center) Washington. (https://carnegieendowment.org/research/2020/09/the-volatile-tunisia-libya-border-between-tunisias-security-policy-and-libyas-militia-factions?lang=en&center=middle-east).

Meddeb, H. (2021) The Hidden Face of Informal Cross Border Trade in Tunisia after 2011. (Malcolm H. Kerr Carnegie Middle East Center) Washington. (https://carnegieendowment.org/research/2021/05/the-hidden-face-of-informal-cross-border-trade-in-tunisia-after-2011?lang=en&center=middle-east).

Meddeb, H., & Louati., F. (2024): Tunisia's Transformation into a Transit Hub: Illegal Migration and Policy Dilemmas. (Malcolm H. Kerr Carnegie Middle East Centre). Washington. (https://carnegieendowment.org/research/2024/03/tunisias-transformation-into-a-transit-hub-illegal-migration-and-policy-dilemmas?lang=en).

Melliti, I. (2011): Les Jeunes et le Travail en Tunisie. In: M. Vultur & D. Mercure (eds.): Perspectives Internationales sur le Travail des Jeunes. Québec: Presses de l'Université Laval, 87–106.

Melliti, I. (2022): Économies Morales d'Injustice. Terrains Maghrébins et Français. Tunis/Paris: Karthala.

Melliti, I. (2023): Les Jeunes en Tunisie. Étude sur la Jeunesse au Moyen-Orient et en Afrique du Nord. La Marsa: Friedrich-Ebert-Stiftung. (https://library.fes.de/pdf-files/bueros/tunesien/20505.pdf).

Melliti, I., Moussa, H., & Observatoire National de la Jeunesse Tunisia (eds.) (2018): Quand Les Jeunes Parlent d'Injustice: Expériences, Registres et Mots en Tunisie. Paris: Harmattan.

Mernissi, F. (1975): Beyond the Veil: Male-Female Dynamics in Modern Muslim Society. Cambridge: Schenkman.

Mezzadra, S. & Neilson, B. (2013): Border as Method, or, the Multiplication of Labor. Durham: Duke University Press.

MEHI (Ministère de l'Équipement, de l'Habitat et de l'Infrastructure) (2020): Pour une Approche Opérationnelle d'Intervention et de Restructuration Urbaine, Cas des Cités de Bahr Lazreg et el Matar: Rapport de Synthése Final. Programme d'Appui à la Politique de la Ville.

Milanovic, B. (2016): Global Inequality. A New Approach to the Age of Globalization. Harvard: Harvard University Press.

Ministry of Interior, Tunisia (2019): Ras Gadir – Ben Gardane / Five Injured among Civil Defence Forces after the Explosion of a Vehicle Tank (in Arabic). (www.interieur.gov.tn/actualite/12776).

Miossec, J. (1985): Urbanisation des Campagnes et Ruralisation des Villes en Tunisie. Annales de Géographie 521, 38–62.

Mitchell, T. (1988): Colonising Egypt. Cambridge: Cambridge University Press.

Mitchell, T. (1991): The Limits of the State: Beyond Statist Approaches and their Critics. American Political Science Review 85, 77–96. (https://doi.org/10.2307/1962879).

Mitchell, T. (2002): *Rule of Experts: Egypt, Techno-Politics, Modernity.* Berkeley: University of California Press.

Mitchell, T. (2007): The Properties of Markets. In: D. MacKenzie, F. Muniesa & L. Siu (eds.): *Do Economist Make Markets? On the Performativity of Economics.* Princeton: Princeton University Press, 244–275.

Mitchell, T. (2008): Rethinking Economy. Geoforum 39, 3, 1116–21. (https://www.doi.org/10.1016/j.geoforum.2006.11.022).

MMC (Mixed Migration Centre) (2020): Urban Mixed Migration Tunis Case Study (MMC Briefing Paper 27). Tunis: MMC. (https://mixedmigration.org/resource/urban-case-study-tunis/).

MMC (2021): Les Épreuves Cachées d'une Main d'Œuvre Invisible. La Vie Économique des Réfugiés et des Migrants en Tunisie. Tunis: MMC. (https://mixedmigration.org/wp-content/uploads/2021/10/MMC-HBS-Leaflet-Hidden-hardship-FR-28Oct.pdf).

MMC & UNHCR (United Nations High Commissioner for Refugees) (2022): Going to Town: A Mapping of City-to-City and Urban Initiatives Focusing on the Protection of People on the Move Along the Central and Western Mediterranean Routes. Tunis: MMC. (http://www.mixedmigration.org/).

Mnasri, C. (2023): Tunisian harga: Facts, Theories, and Conclusions. The Journal of North African Studies 28, 1037–1045.

Monteith, W., Vicol, D.-O. & Williams, P. (eds.) (2021): Beyond the Wage: Ordinary Work in Diverse Economies. Bristol: Bristol University Press. (https://doi.org/10.2307/j.ctv1pwns8p).

Morabito, C., Negre, M. & Niño-Zarazúa, M. (2021): The Distributional Impacts of Development Cooperation Projects (AFD Research Papers, 208). 1–61. (https://shs.cairn.info/journal-afd-research-papers-2021-208-page-1?lang=en).

Moreno-Sainz, L. M. (2007): Les Récupérateurs des Déchets à Buenos Aeros, de l'Exclusion à l'Intégration Sociale? Autrepart 43, 3, 25–34.

Moulin, M. (2022): Du Terrorisme Écologique en Tunisie: les Tensions Socio-Politiques au Prisme des Déchets. Paris: Harmattan.

Mountz, A. & Hyndman, J. (2006): Feminist Approaches to the Global Intimate. Women's Studies Quarterly 34, 1–2, 446–463.

Msakni, F. (2020): From Sub-Saharan African States to Tunisia. A Quantitative Study on the Situation of Migrants in Tunisia: General Aspects, Pathways and Aspirations – FTDES. Tunis: FTDES (Tunisian Forum for Economic and Social Rights). (https://ftdes.net/en/from-sub-saharan-african-states-to-tunisia-a-quantitative-study-on-the-situation-of-migrants-in-tunisia-general-aspects-pathways-and-aspirations/).

Mullin, Corinna (2023): The 'War on Terror' as Primitive Accumulation in Tunisia: US-Led Imperialism and the Post-2010-2011 Revolt/Security Conjuncture. Middle East Critique 32, 2, 167–193.

Mzalouat, H. (2019): L'Accès à l'Eau, Une Injuste Répartition. Inkyfada: Clair Edition. (https://inkyfada.com/fr/2019/03/06/tunisie-eau-potable-chiffres/).

Nachi, M. (2006): Introduction à la Sociologie Pragmatique. Paris: Armand Colin.

Nachi, M. (2001): La Vertu du Compromis: Dimensions Éthique et Pragmatique de l'Accord. Revue Interdisciplinaire d'Études Juridiques 46, 81–110. (https://shs.cairn.info/revue-interdisciplinaire-d-etudes-juridiques-2001-1-page-81?lang=fr).

Nasraoui, M. (2017): Les Travailleurs Migrants Subsahariens en Tunisie face aux Restrictions Législatives sur l'Emploi des Étrangers. Revue Européenne des Migrations Internationales 33, 4, 159–178. (https://doi.org/10.4000/remi.9244).

Natter, K. (2022): Tunisia's Migration Politics Throughout the 2011 Revolution: Revisiting the Democratisation–Migrant Rights Nexus. Third World Quarterly 43, 7, 1551–1569.

Nikro, N. S. & Hegasy, S. (eds.) (2018): The Social Life of Memory. Violence, Trauma, and Testimony in Lebanon and Morocco. Cham: Palgrave Macmillan. (https://doi.org/10.1177/0268580919830920b).

Nubli, M. K. & Jefferey, J. B. (2023): *Tunisia's Economic Development. Why Better Than Most of the Middle East but not East Asia.* Milton Park: Routledge.

Nussbaum, M. C. (2001): *Women and Human Development.* Cambridge: Cambridge University Press.

Nussbaum, M. C. (2011): *Creating Capabilities: The Human Development Approach.* Cambridge: Harvard University Press.

Nussbaum, M. C. (2012): The New Religious Intolerance: Overcoming the Politics of Fear in an Anxious. Cambridge: HUP/Belknap Press.

Nussbaum, M. & Sen, A. (1993): The Quality of Life (UNO Wider Studies in Development Economics). Oxford: Clarendon Press.

ONEQ (Observatoire Nationale de l'Emploi et des Qualifications) (2013): Le Marché du Travail en Tunisie. Ministère de la Formation Professionnelle et de l'Emploi.

Offner, J.-M. (2020): Anachronismes Urbains. Paris: Presses des Sciences Po.

Panebianco, S. & Cannata, G. (2024): (Im-)Mobility Partnerships: Limits to EU Democracy Promotion Through Mobility in the Mediterranean. In: R. Zapata-Barrero & I. Awad (eds): Migrations in the Mediterranean (IMISCOE Regional Reader). Cham: Springer 2024, 71–88. (https://library.oapen.org/handle/20.500.12657/85074).

Papadopoulos, T. (2005). The Recommodification of European Labour: Theoretical and Empirical Explorations. European Research Institute, University of Bath. (https://researchportal.bath.ac.uk/en/publications/the-recommodification-of-european-labour-theoretical-and-empirica).

Papillon [@Papiillon] (2023): Racisme Décomplexé sur nos Médias. La Suite. On a ce Tocard (Ex Ministre) qui Prévient les Tunisiens 'si la Migration des Tunisiens Continue, les Africains vont Venir se Marier chez Nous et Nous Remplacer. Aucune Réaction de la 'Journaliste' bien Évidemment. (https://x.com/Papiillon/status/1609859657216200711?mx=2).

Parikh, S. (2021): The Limits of Confronting Racial Discrimination in Tunisia with Law 50. MERIP Middle East Report 299, n. p. (https://merip.org/2021/08/the-limits-of-confronting-racial-discrimination-in-tunisia-with-law-50/).

Parikh, S. (2023): Making Tunisia Non-African Again – Saied's Anti-Black Campaign. Review of African Political Economy March 1. (https://roape.net/2023/03/01/making-tunisia-non-african-again-saieds-anti-black-campaign/).

Passeron, JC. (2001): Acteur, Agent, Actant: Personnages Enquête d'un Scénario Introuvable. Revue Européenne des Sciences Sociales. (http://journals.openedition.org/ress/643).

Paugam, S. (2006): La Disqualification Sociale. Essay sur la Novelle Pauvreté. Paris: Presses Universitaires de France.

Pepicelli, R. (2021): 'People Want a Clean Environment': Historical Roots of the Environmental Crisis and the Emergence of Eco-Resistances in Tunisia. Studi Magrebini 19, 1, 37–62.

Pettit, H. (2024): The Labor of Hope. Meritocracy and Precarity in Egypt. Stanford: Stanford University Press.

Pettit, H. & Ruijtenberg, W. (2019): Migration as Hope and Depression. Existential Im/Mobilities in and Beyond Egypt. Mobilities 14, 730–744.

Pluta, A. (2020): Pas de Révolution pour la Police? Syndicats et Organisations Internationales autour de la « Réforme du Secteur de la Sécurité » en Tunisie après 2011. Lien Social et Politiques 84, 122–141.

Pratt, G. & Rosner, V. (eds.) (2012): The Global and the Intimate: Feminism in Our Time. New York: Columbia University Press.

Quijano, A. (1974): Marginaler Pol der Wirtschaft und marginalisierte Arbeitskraft. In: D. Senghaas (ed.): Peripherer Kapitalismus. Analysen über Abhängigkeit und Unterentwicklung. Frankfurt: Suhrkamp, 298–341.

Raach, F., Sha'ath, H., & Spijkerboer, T. (2022): Country Report: Tunisia (Country Reports: WP5 ASILE; Global Asylum Governance and the European Union's Role). Amsterdam: VU.

Rabo, A. (2008): 'Doing Family': Two Cases in Contemporary Syria. *Hawwa* 6, 2, 129–53.

Rajaram, P. (2018): Refugees as Surplus Population: Race, Migration and Capitalist Value Regimes. *New Political Economy* 23, 5, 627–639.

Ramsay, G. (2020): Humanitarian Exploits: Ordinary Displacement and the Political Economy of the Global Refugee Regime. *Critique of Anthropology* 40, 1, 3–27.

Rehbein, K. (2021): The Tunisian Debt Crisis in the Context of Covid-19 Pandemic. Debt Repayments over Human Rights. Tunis: Friedrich-Ebert-Stiftung. (https://library.fes.de/pdf-files/bueros/tunesien/18186-20210910.pdf).

Remy, J. (1996): La Transaction, une Méthode d'Analyse: Contribution à l'Émergence d'un Nouveau Paradigme. *Environnement et Société* 17, 9–31.

Rennick, S. A. (2023): Losing Support to Democracy. Political Socialization, Popular Conceptualizations, and the Formation of Political Grievances among Marginalized Youth in Tunisia. *Mediterranean Politics*, 1–25.

rlfmedia (2020): Tunisie – Immigration: Lancement des guichets d'informations et d'orientation pour migrant. RLF média. (https://www.facebook.com/RLFLibreFran

cophone/videos/reportage-lancement-du-guichet-dinformation-pour-migrant-en-tunisie/431569391567128/).

Robert, D. (2021): Contestations Croisées des Nuisances Environnementales des Industries et des Injustices Territoriales à Gabès et Kerkennah (Tunisie). Justice Spatiale / Spatial Justice, 1. (https://hal.science/hal-03457133).

Robeyns, I. & Fibieger Byskov, M. (2023): The Capability Approach. In: E. N. Zalta & U. Nodelman (eds.): The Stanford Encyclopaedia of Philosophy. (https://plato.stanford.edu/archives/sum2023/entries/capability-approach/).

Rosa, H. (2019): Resonance. A Sociology of our Relationship to the World. Cambridge: Polity Press.

Rosewarne, S. (2012): Temporary International Labor Migration and Development in South and Southeast Asia. Feminist Economics 18, 2, 63–90. (https://doi.org/10.1080/13545701.2012.696314).

Sadawi, N. (1969): Women and Sex. Cairo: El Shaab.

Safar Zitoun, M. (2021): Le Hirak ou la 'Révolution Propre' en Algérie: Renaissance de la Conscience Environnementale ou Expression Symbolique de Réappropriation des Espaces Publics Confisqués? (Présentation au Workshop 'La question Environnementale en Débat: Réinvestissement de l'Espace Public et Émergence de Nouvelles Valeurs', 10–11 Février 2021). IRMC Tunis/LPED Aix-Marseille Université.

Saib Musette, M. & Maamar, M. (2024): Capturing Irregular Migrations through a Macro-Sociological Lens: The Harga Process in Twelve Steps from North Africa to Europe. In: R. Zapata-Barrero & I. Awad (eds): Migrations in the Mediterranean. Cham: Springer. 251–266 (https://library.oapen.org/handle/20.500.12657/85074).

Saleh, E. (2017): A Tangled Web of Lies: Reflections on Ethnographic Fieldwork with Syrian Turkmen Women on the Side of a Road in Beirut. Contemporary Levant 2, 2, 55–60.

Salman, L. (2023): Revolutionary Debtscapes: Domestic Territories of Contestation in Tunisia. Gender, Place & Culture, 1–20. (https://colab.ws/articles/10.1080%2F0966369x.2023.2280747).

Santos, M. (1979): The Shared Space. The Two Circuits of the Urban Economy in Underdeveloped Countries. (L´Espace Partagé, 1975). London, New York: Methuen.

Scott, J.W. (1991): The Evidence of Experience. Critical Inquiry 17, 4, 773–797. (http://www.jstor.org/stable/1343743).

SDVT (Tunis City Development Strategy) (2023): A Strategic Development Framework for the City of Tunis. (https://south.euneighbours.eu/publication/a-strategic-development-framework-for-the-city-of-tunis/).

Sen, A. (1979): Equality of What? In: S. McMurrin (ed.): Tanner Lectures on Human Values. Cambridge: Cambridge University Press, 197–220

Sen, A. (1985): Commodities and Capabilities. Amsterdam: North-Holland.

Sen, A. (1989): Development as Capability Expansion. Journal of Development Planning 19, 41–58.

Sen, A. (1999): Development as Freedom. Oxford: Oxford University Press.

Sen, A. (2004): Human Development Report 2004: Cultural Liberty in Today's Diverse World. UNDP & UN Human Development Reports. 13–25. (https://hdr.undp.org/content/human-development-report-2004).

Searle, J. R. (1983): Intentionality. An Essay in the Philosophy of Mind. Cambridge: Cambridge University Press.

Shâfi'i, F. (2020): Dynamique de la Sphère Urbaine et Transformations Économiques et Sociales à Ben Gardane (The Dynamics of the Urban Sphere and Economic and Social Transformations in Ben Gardane). Ph.D. Thesis, Department of Geography, Faculty of Humanities and Social Science, University of Tunis, Tunis.

Smith, J., Wallerstein, I. & Evers, H.-D. (eds.) (1984): Households and the World-Economy. London: Sage Publications.

Som, J. D. & De Facci, D. (2017): La Démocratie au Concret: Les Enjeux Politiques et Territoriaux de la Mise en Place du Budget Participatif dans la Tunisie Post-Ben Ali (2011–2016). L'Année du Maghreb 16, 245–267.

Spivak, G. C. (1988): Can the Subaltern Speak? In: C. Nelson & L. Grossberg (eds.): Marxism and the Interpretation of Culture. Urbana: University of Illinois Press, 271–313.

Stamatopoulou-Robbins, S. (2019): Waste Siege. The Life of Infrastructure in Palestine. Stanford: Stanford University Press.

Stuesse, A., & Coleman, M. (2014): Automobility, Immobility, Altermobility: Surviving and Resisting the Intensification of Immigrant Policing. City & Society 26, 1, 51–72. (https://doi.org/10.1111/ciso.12034).

Sukarieh, M. & Tannock, S. (2019): Subcontracting Academia: Alienation, Exploitation and Disillusionment in the UK Overseas Syrian Refugee Research Industry. Antipode 51, 2, 664–80. (https://doi.org/10.1111/anti.12502).

Taleb, M. & Sallemi, R. (2015): Les Trajectoires Périurbaines de l'Industrie: L'Ouest du Grand Tunis, une Marge Convoitée? (Colloque Recomposition et Développement des Espaces Périurbaines dans le Bassin Méditerranéen). *El Jadida* 29–31 Octobre 2, 423–446.

Tanchum, M. (2021): The Fragile State of Food Security in the Maghreb: Implication of the 2021 Cereal Grains Crisis in Tunisia, Algeria and Morocco. MEI Policy Center. (https://www.mei.edu/sites/default/files/2021-11/The%20Fragile%20State%20of%20Food%20Security%20in%20the%20Maghreb-%20%20Implication%20of%20the%202021%20Cereal%20Grains%20Crisis%20in%20Tunisia%2C%20Algeria%2C%20and%20Morocco%20.pdf).

Tazzioli, M. (2021): 'Choking without Killing': Opacity and the Grey Area of Migration Governmentality. Political Geography 89, 1–9. (https://doi.org/10.1016/j.polgeo.2021.102412).

Tekce, B., Olham, L. & Shorter, F. C. (1994): A Place to Live. Families and Child Health in a Cairo Neighborhood. Cairo: American University Press.

Terradot, J. (2023): Externalisation des Visas: Les États Opèrent à l'Ombre du Privé. Inkyfada. (https://inkyfada.com/fr/2023/06/24/externalisation-visas-etats-tls-contact-tunisie/).

Thieme, T. A. (2018): The Hustle Economy: Informality. Uncertainty and the Geographies of Getting By. Progress in Human Geography 42, 4, 529–548. (https://doi.org/10.1177/0309132517690039).

Thomann, S. (2010): Stratifications Générationnelles au Sein d'Espaces Périurbains: Une Opportunité du 'Vivre Ensemble'? Journal of Urban Research 5. (https://journals.openedition.org/articulo/1403).

Thomann, S. (2009): Familles, Femmes et Générations Exposées à l'Étalement Urbain. Installation Résidentielles et Dépendance Automobile dans l'Aire Métropolitaine Marseillaise. PhD-Thesis, Aix-en-Provence: Institut d'Urbanisme et d'Aménagement Régional.

Thompson, E. P. (1971): The Moral Economy of the English Crowd in the Eighteenth Century. Past & Present 50, 76–136.

Ticktin, M. I. (2011): Casualties of Care: Immigration and the Politics of Humanitarianism in France. Berkeley: University of California Press.

Topak, Ö. E. (2019): Humanitarian and Human Rights Surveillance: The Challenge to Border Surveillance and Invisibility? Surveillance & Society 17, 3/4, 382–404. (https://doi.org/10.24908/ss.v17i3/4.10779).

Tsing, A. L. (2005): Friction. An Ethnography of Global Connection. Princeton: Princeton University Press.

Tsourapas, G. (2013): The Other Side of a Neoliberal Miracle: Economic Reform and Political De-Liberalization in Ben Ali's Tunisia. Mediterranean Politics 18, 1, 23–41.

Tunisian Observatory of the Economy (2021): FMI: Impact of Tunisia's Currency Devaluation. (https://www.economie-tunisie.org/en/observatory/fmi-impact-tunisia%E2%80%99s-currency-devaluation).

Turner, L. (2019): Syrian Refugee Men as Objects of Humanitarian Care. International Feminist Journal of Politics 21, 4, 595–616.

UNDESA (The United Nations Department of Economic and Social Affairs) (2019). International Migrant Stock 2019: Country Profile Tunisia.

UNDP (United Nations Development Program) (2020): Economic Impact of COVID-19 in Tunisia. (2020). UNDP. (https://www.undp.org/arab-states/publications/economic-impact-covid-19-tunisia).

UNHCR (United Nations High Commissioner for Refugees) (2014): Tunisia – Syrian Refugee and Asylum-Seekers in Tunisia. UNHCR Global Focus. (https://reporting.unhcr.org/node/8788).

UNHCR (2020): Tunisa Special Update #2 Mayors' Forum on Inclusive Cities in North Africa (Press Release, November). (https://data.unhcr.org/en/documents/details/83657).

UNHCR (2022): Refugees and Asylum-Seekers in Tunisia. UNHCR Operational Data Portal. (https://data.unhcr.org/en/country/tun/).

UNHCR (2024): Tunisia. UNHCR. (https://www.unhcr.org/uk/countries/tunisia).

UN-Habitat (n.d.): Launch of Call for Targeted City Actions. (https://unhabitat.org/launch-of-call-for-targeted-city-actions).

UN Women (2017): Women Working: Jordanian and Syrian Refugee Women's Labour Force Participation And Attitudes Towards Employment. Amman: UN Women and REACH. (https://jordan.unwomen.org/en/digital-library/publications/2017/3/jordanian-and-syrian-refugee-womens-labour-force-participation-and-attitudes-towards-employment).

Urry, J. (2007): Mobilities. Cambridge: Polity Press.

Van Schendel, W. & Abraham, I. (2005): Illicit Flows and Criminal Things: States, Borders, and the Other Side of Globalization. Bloomington: Indiana University Press.

Varsanyi, M. W. (2008): Immigration Policing Through the Backdoor: City Ordinances, the "Right to the City," and the Exclusion of Undocumented Day Laborers. Urban Geography 29, 1, 29–52. (https://doi.org/10.2747/0272-3638.29.1.29).

Votre Salaire (2022): Salaires Minimums – Tunisie. Votre Salaire. (https://votresalaire.org/tunisie/salaire/salaire-minimum-1).

Wachter, S. (2004): Trafics en Ville, l'Architecture et l'Urbanisme au Risque de la Mobilité. Paris: Éditions Recherche.

Wallace C. (2002): Household Strategies: Their Conceptual Relevance and Analytical Scope in Social Research. *Sociology* 36, 2, 275–292.

Weißenfels, A. (2024): *Development at Work. Postcolonial Imaginaries, Global Capitalism, and Everyday Life at a Factory in Tunisia.* Wiesbaden: Springer VS.

Weipert-Fenner, I. (2020): Unemployed Mobilisation in Times of Democratisation: The Union of Unemployed Graduates in Post-Ben Ali Tunisia. *The Journal of North African Studies* 25, 1, 53–75.

Wells, T. (2023): Sen's Capability Approach. Internet Encyclopaedia of Philosophy (IEP). (https://iep.utm.edu/sen-cap/).

Winegar, J. (2016): A Civilized Revolution: Aesthetics and Political Action in Egypt. American Ethnologist 43, 4, 609–22. (https://doi.org/10.1111/amet.12378).

Wong, D. (1984): The Limits of Using the Household as a Unit of Analysis. In: J. Smith et al. (eds.): Households and the World-Economy. London: Sage, 56–63.

World Bank (2014): The Unfinished Revolution: Bringing Opportunity Good Jobs and Greater Wealth to All Tunisians. (https://documents1.worldbank.org/curated/en/658461468312323813/pdf/861790DPR0P12800Box385314B00PUBLIC0.pdf).

World Bank (2022a): Labor Force Participation Rate, Female (Percent of Female Population Ages 15+) (Modeled ILO Estimate) – Middle East & North Africa. World Bank Data. (https://data.worldbank.org/indicator/SL.TLF.CACT.FE.ZS?locations=ZQ).

World Bank (2022b): Labor Force Participation Rate. Female (Percent of Female Population Ages 15–64) (modeled ILO estimate) – Tunisia. World Bank Data. (https://data.worldbank.org/indicator/SL.TLF.ACTI.FE.ZS?locations=TN).

Wyss, A., Zittoun, T., Pedersen, O. C., Dahinden, J. & Chamillot, E. (2023): Places and Mobilities. Studying Human Movements Using Place as an Entry Point. Mobilities 18, 567–581Wright, S. (2010): Cultivating Beyond-Capitalist Economies. Economic Geography 86, 3, 297–318.

Zagaria, V. (2019): The Morally Fraught Harga. The Cambridge Journal of Anthropology 37, 2, 57–73. (https://doi.org/10.3167/cja.2019.370205).

Zagaria, V. (2020): A Small Story with Great Symbolic Potential: Attempts at Fixing a Cemetery of Unknown Migrants in Tunisia. American Behavioral Scientist 64, 4, 540–63. (https://doi.org/10.1177/0002764219882994)

Zapata-Barrero, R. & Awad, I. (eds.) (2024): Migrations in the Mediterranean (IMISCOE Regional Reader). Cham: Springer. (https://www.imiscoe.org/publications/library/9-imiscoe-regional-readers/199-migrations-in-the-mediterranean).

Zardo, F. (2020): The EU Trust Fund for Africa: Geopolitical Space Making through Migration Policy Instruments. Geopolitics 27, 2, 584–603. (https://doi.org/10.1080/14650045.2020.1815712).

Zelizer, V. A. (2005): The Purchase of Intimacy. Princeton: Princeton University Press.

Zemni, S. (2015): The Roots of the Tunisian Revolution: Elements of a Political Sociology. In: L. Sadiki (ed.): Routledge Handbook of the Arab Spring Rethinking Democratization. New York, NY: Routledge.

Zemni, S. & Ayeb, H. (2015): Between Hegemony and Resistence. Moral Economy of the Tunisian Revolution. London School of Economic, LSE Middle East Centre: SoundCloud. (https://soundcloud.com/lsemiddleeastcentre/lse-zemni).

Zuntz, A.-C. (2024a): Migration and Displacement. In: J. Gertel, D. Kreuer & F. Stolleis (eds.): The Dispossessed Generation. Youth in the Middle East and North Africa. London: Saqi Books. 157–181.

Zuntz, A.-C. (2024b): City of Welcome and Transit. Migrants' and Refugees' Livelihoods and Migration Projects in Sousse, Tunisia. Tunis: Mixed Migration Centre, MMC. (http://www.mixedmigration.org/resource/urban-case-study-tunis/).

Zuntz, A., Ben Hadj Hassen, A., Bouneb, M. & Zuntz, J. (2022): Destination North Africa – Syrians' Displacement Trajectories to Tunisia. Tunis: MMC. (https://mixedmigration.org/wp-content/uploads/2022/08/Destination_North_Africa_Syrians_Tunisia.pdf).

Acknowledgements

This book has been a collective project from the outset, and emerged first and foremost from the wonderful collaboration among the Fellows of the Interdisciplinary Fellow Group (IFG) *Inequality and Mobility* from the Merian Centre of Advanced Studies in the Maghreb (MECAM), the academic coordinators from Leipzig University (LU), and the many Tunisian or Tunisia-based scholars who enabled and participated in the IFG's seminars, events and field trips.

Essential for this collaborative work has been the scientific cooperation with Tunisian universities and academics, among which the following partners were particularly central: the Laboratoire Gouvernance et Développement Territorial at the Université de Tunis, with the active support and participation of Mourad Ben Jalloul, Faouzi Zerai, Hend Ben Othman and others; the Laboratoire SYFACTE at the Université de Sfax with the active support and participation of Ali Bennasr, Hassan Boubakri, Maha Bouhlel and others; the Department of Anthropology at the Université de Sousse with collaborative efforts led by Ramzi Ben Amara; the Institute of Environmental Technologies, Urban Planning and Building at Carthage University (ISTEUB) with the invaluable support of Yassine Turki and others. Hoda Laroussi from the Université de Carthage/Tunis and Imed Melitti from the Université de Tunis El Manar were always ready to share with us their unique insights and perspectives on Tunisian society. The editors would like to thank these institutions and colleagues for their warm welcome and spirit of collaboration and academic enthusiasm!

The editors would also like to thank the independent researchers and civil society organisations, as well as art space institutions, who participated in co-organising public events, field trips or discussions in Tunisia with the MECAM fellow group, amongst whom we express particular thanks to: Arwa Labidi, the Observatoire Tunisien de l'Économie (OTE), Habib Ayeb and the L'Observatoire de la Souveraineté Alimentaire et de l'Environnement (OSAE), Olfa Lamloum and the team of International Alert, Central Tunis, Marouan Taleb and the Institut de Recherche sur le Maghreb Contemporain (IRMC), Leila Ben Gacem and the entire team of Dar Ben Gacem as well as the Dar El Harka coworking space, and the many other stakeholders and activists – from the municipality of Kesra, to environmental activists in Sfax – who shared their insights with and dedicated time to our Fellow Group. The meetings and discussions with Moroccan partners in Tunis, particularly with Fatma Ait Mous and Hind Ftouhi, in the summer of 2022, not only led to new collaborations with Tunisian institutions and social scientists, but also inspired new approaches to and research formats for the promotion of early-career researchers.

Without committed institutional support and precise administrative knowledge, such a multidimensional co-operation project is inconceivable. From the very beginning, Habib Sidhoum, president of Université de Tunis, together with Rachid Ouaissa from Marburg University, were the driving force in the joint development of the MECAM in Tunis. We thank the local management and administrative team of MECAM for their support to our Fellow Group. In an early phase of the project, Sihem Lamine, from the Centre of Middle East Studies, Harvard University, generously shared with us her expertise in the establishment of a research centre in Tunisia.

Our particular thanks go to the administrative staff of Leipzig University. They have been consistently committed to the meaningful realisation of our collaborative research project, even in challenging situations. Our very special thanks go to Sindy Schug, Application Counselling and Research Funding (LU), for sharing her administrative knowledge and facilitating access to different institutions within Leipzig University; to Kerstin Hirsch and Angelika Dunkel, management of third party funds (LU), for their professional and very labour-intensive inputting of receipts and certificates into electronic accounting systems and the clarification of queries by the project administrator, the German Aerospace Centre (DLR Projektträger); and to Birgit Dräger, former Chancellor of Leipzig University, for developing the LU Guidelines for the Award of Research Fellowships to Senior and Junior Fellows (including doctoral candidates) for MECAM. These fellowship guidelines tackled inequality in academia and allowed for equal payment of the fellows, independent of their origin.

Translating and editing this volume were also co-working processes: all contributors engaged in discussing and commenting on early drafts of the chapters in Arabic, French, and English, starting with the joint writing and peer review workshop in Nabeul in summer 2022. This was followed by in-depth-discussions and revisions of all papers. From the original final drafts, two chapters written in Arabic and French were translated into English by Leonie Nückell and Najla Achek. Subsequently, other non-English chapters have been translated into English and all received further feedback by the editors. Max Sivertsen did a great job in providing a first language review of the entire draft version in English. Jalda Simon de Martinez not only facilitated communication between the authors, she also helped to organise the workshop and meetings in Tunis and Nabeul, as well as reviewing the drafts, and checking citations and bibliography. Jessica Sommer has kindly taken over the formatting of the manuscript. Finally, Erena Le Heron very skilfully engaged in the scientific proofreading of the edited volume. She has significantly improved the readability of our texts, so our very special thanks go to her.

The team at transcript publisher, particularly Karin Werner, supported this book project from the very beginning and allowed it to develop. Thank you 'team transcript' for this outstanding collaboration!

Ultimately, our most heartfelt thanks go to the contributors, first and foremost for your stellar research and book chapters, but also for your trust and openness to new encounters and experiences, the eagerness to learn and listen, and the motivation to continuously engage in multiple translations (e.g. linguistic, cultural, methodological) that are the basis for critical research – all this, for us, has been great fun and a fantastic learning experience, and has made this book possible!

About the Authors

Myriam Amri, PhD, is an anthropologist and filmmaker. Her scholarship investigates the politics of capitalism in North Africa and the Middle East. She completed her PhD in Anthropology and Middle Eastern Studies at Harvard University. Her dissertation *Cash Country*, is an ethnography of Tunisia's national currency, the Dinar, in times of political upheavals. In addition, she has published on borderlands, the environment, visual culture, and colonial histories.

Enrica Audano, PhD, is a Postdoctoral Researcher at the Institute of Geography, Leipzig University. She completed her PhD in Human Geography with a thesis on class membership and the urban middle classes in Tunisia. Her research interests include social structure analysis, political and social forms of engagement and participation, as well as the relation between migration and urban space.

Olfa Ben Medien, PhD, is an architect. Olfa obtained a master degree in Town and Regional Planning and a doctorate in Town Planning. She is a Senior Lecturer at ISTEUB (Institute of Environmental Technologies, Urban Planning and Building), Director of Studies and Internships, and Vice-President of APERAU International (Association pour la Promotion de l'Enseignement et de la Recherche en Aménagement et Urbanisme). She took part in drafting Tunisia's national report for Habitat III (Quito, 2017) and works as a consultant.

Maha Bouhlel-Abid, PhD, holds a doctorate in Geography. She is a Lecturer at the University of Manouba and a researcher at the SYFACTE Laboratory (University of Sfax, Tunisia). She was awarded a short-term postdoctoral fellowship in the Humanities by the Arab Council for the Humanities and the Fondation Maison des Sciences Humaines de Paris (FMSH) at the CERI and Sciences-Po Paris on the subject of 'Waste Management and Decentralisation in the Arab World'. Her research areas include urban policies, public service management, and sustainable urban development.

Marwen Bouneb, PhD, is the Maghreb Action on Displacement and Rights (MADAR) coordinator for Tunisia. He graduated in Cultural Studies (Masters) at the University of Sousse. His dissertation focused on apartheid in South Africa addressing the recent student protests. He worked for the Tunisian Council for Refugees and participated in two research projects: 'Migrants in Countries in Crisis' and in 'Power2Youth'.

Souhir Bouzid, PhD, is Assistant Professor in Urban Planning at the Higher Institute of Environmental Technologies, Urban Planning and Building (ISTEUB) in Tunis and also member of the Governance and Territorial Development Research Laboratory. Souhir completed a PhD in urban planning at the National School of Architecture and Urban Planning (ENAU) in 2018. Her teaching and research in urban planning focuses on the relationship between daily mobility, residential choices, lifestyles and the evolution of territories.

Hanen Chebbi, holds a PhD in Sociology from the University of Sfax. She is a Postdoctoral Researcher at the ECUMUS research laboratory (State, culture and social change), Faculty of Letters and Human Sciences, at the University of Sfax, where she teaches in the Sociology Department. Her research focuses on the environment, the circular economy and urban waste management. Through ethnographic surveys, she examines the practices and socio-cultural realities of the various players involved in the circular economy and waste management.

Johannes Frische, PhD, is an independent researcher specialising in Human Geography of the MENA-region. Being part of the Graduate School Global and Area Studies, Johannes earned his PhD from Leipzig University in 2021. As a postdoctoral researcher, he joined the Interdisciplinary Fellow Group 'Inequality and Mobility'. Focusing on North Africa and the Middle East, his scientific interests include youth studies, urban studies, sociology, and migration.

Jamie Furniss, PhD, completed ethnographic fieldwork on Cairo's waste collectors and has been a postdoctoral fellow, lecturer, and visiting fellow with the Centre National de la Recherche Scientifique (CNRS), the University of Edinburgh, and the Centre for Near and Middle East Studies (CNMS) at the University of Marburg. From 2019–2023 he was employed at the Institut de Recherche sur le Maghreb Contemporain (IRMC) in Tunisia. His primary research interests are environment and climate change, international development, and anthropology of the Middle East and North Africa

Wael Garnaoui, PhD, is Associate Professor of Psychology and Psychoanalysis at the University of Sousse, and founder of the research group on border studies at the University of Sousse. He is the author of *Harga et Désir d'Occident, Étude Psychanalytique des Migrants Clandestins Tunisiens* (*Harga* and the Desire for the West, a Psychoanalytical Study of Tunisian Clandestine Migrants) published by Nirvana, 2022.

Thouraya Garraoui, PhD, is a Postdoctoral Researcher at the University of Leipzig. She completed her PhD in Geography titled 'Graduate Unemployment in Tunisia: The Case of

Greater Tunis' at the University of Leipzig in 2024. Her current research explores graduate unemployment in Tunisia, employability challenges across Africa and the MENA region, and broader structural issues related to labour market inequalities.

Jörg Gertel is Professor of Arabic Studies and Economic Geography at Leipzig University. His work and research have taken him to the Universities of Freiburg, Damascus, Cairo, Khartoum, Leipzig, Tunis, Seattle, and Auckland. His main research interests are the relations between insecurity and uncertainty in the context of technoliberalism.

Katharina Grüneisl, PhD, is a Postdoctoral Research Fellow in Social Anthropology at the University of Nottingham and the École des Hautes Études en Sciences Sociales (EHESS) in Paris. She is also an Associate Researcher at the Institut de Recherche sur le Maghreb Contemporain (IRMC) in Tunis. She completed a PhD in Human Geography at Durham University in 2021. Her research interests include processes of urban change in North Africa, the evolution of worlds of work, and the used clothing (*fripe*) and textile industry in Tunisia and Jordan.

Asma Ben Hadj Hassen is a PhD student in Anthropology at the International Graduate School of African Studies (BIGSAS) at the University of Bayreuth, Germany. She holds a Masters in African Studies from the University of Sousse in Tunisia. Her doctoral project focuses on the ethnography of the experiences and trajectories of Ivorian domestic workers in the Mediterranean.

Hatem Kahloun, PhD, is an Associate Professor of Urbanism and Urban Planning at the University of Carthage (ISTEUB). His research focuses on urban development, particularly on urban sprawl, upgrading schemes, small cities, and informal housing. His publications address the issues of pandemic and urban health crises; sustainable city design, and the role of civil society organisations in the participatory process of the urban project.

David Kreuer, PhD, is a Social Scientist at the Institute of Geography, Leipzig University. He wrote his PhD thesis on the significance of drought in eastern Morocco. His research interests include environmental policy, pastoralism, youth and social change in rural societies. He is co-editor of the *Dispossessed Generation. Youth in the Middle East and North Africa* (2024).

Khaoula Matri holds a PhD in Sociology from the University of Tunis and the University of Paris V Descartes. She is Senior Lecturer at the Anthropology Centre, Faculty of Letters and Human Sciences, Sousse (FLSHS) and Associate Researcher at the Institute for Research on the Contemporary Maghreb (IRMC). She is Fellow at the Académie Pilote Postdoctorale Africaine (PAPA) in Bamako, Mali. Since 2023, she is Scientific Manager of the IRMC/ MADAR research programme: 'Vulnerabilities, racism and political subjectivities in Tunisia: The ethnographic case of West African migrants'.

Shreya Parikh, PhD, is a Lecturer and affiliated researcher at Sciences Po Paris, where she also serves as a member of the Scientific Council of the MENA Programme. She received a Dual Ph.D. in Political Science from Sciences Po Paris and in Sociology from the University of North Carolina at Chapel Hill in 2024. Her dissertation, titled 'Mirages of Race: Blackness, racialization, and the Black Movement in Tunisia', examines the intersections of race, migration, and citizenship to propose the first grounded theory of Blackness in contemporary Tunisia.

Hiba Sha'ath is a PhD candidate in Critical Human Geography at York University in Canada and a Graduate Research Fellow at its Centre for Refugee Studies. Her dissertation examines the impact of multiscale borders on the everyday lives of Sub-Saharan migrants in Tunis. Prior to starting her PhD, she worked at International Organisation for Migration's Libya office and the organisation's Regional Office for West and Central Africa.

Fathi Shâfi'i, PhD, is from Ben Gardane in southern Tunisia. He obtained a doctorate in Geography in 2020 from the Faculty of Human and Social Sciences, University of Tunis. He is member of the Laboratoire de Recherche sur la Gouvernance et le Développement Territorial. His scientific research focuses on the study of borders.

André Weißenfels, PhD, is a political scientist. With a background in Near and Middle Eastern Studies (University of Marburg) and Sociology (Goldsmiths College, London), he worked as a scientific associate at the Otto-Suhr-Institute for Political Science at the Freie Universität Berlin. He is also a Fellow of the Berlin Graduate School for Muslim Cultures and Societies. His PhD is published under the title *Development at Work. Postcolonial Imaginaries, Global Capitalism and Everyday Life at a Factory in Tunisia* (2024). André's research interests are political economy, anarchist theory and practice, and ethnographic methodology.

Ann-Christin Zuntz, PhD, is currently a British Academy Postdoctoral Fellow at the University of Edinburgh, where she will take up a position as Lecturer in Anthropology of Development starting in 2026. Her research looks at the nexus between displacement, labour migration and global supply chains in the Middle East and North Africa. She collaborates with Syrian researchers as part of the interdisciplinary OneHealth FIELD Network, which involves fieldwork with Syrian farmers in Turkey. In 2023, she and her fellow Syrian researchers co-produced the documentary film *With the Sickle and Songs*.